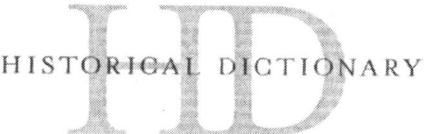

HISTORICAL DICTIONARY

The historical dictionaries present essential information on a broad range of subjects, including American and world history, art, business, cities, countries, cultures, customs, film, global conflicts, international relations, literature, music, philosophy, religion, sports, and theater. Written by experts, all contain highly informative introductory essays of the topic and detailed chronologies that, in some cases, cover vast historical time periods but still manage to heavily feature more recent events.

Brief A–Z entries describe the main people, events, politics, social issues, institutions, and policies that make the topic unique, and entries are cross-referenced for ease of browsing. Extensive bibliographies are divided into several general subject areas, providing excellent access points for students, researchers, and anyone wanting to know more. Additionally, maps, photographs, and appendixes of supplemental information aid high school and college students doing term papers or introductory research projects. In short, the historical dictionaries are the perfect starting point for anyone looking to research in these fields.

HISTORICAL DICTIONARIES OF DIPLOMACY AND FOREIGN RELATIONS

Jon Woronoff, Series Editor

Historical Dictionary
of British Foreign Policy

Peter Neville

The Scarecrow Press, Inc.
Lanham • Toronto • Plymouth, UK
2013

Published by Scarecrow Press, Inc.
A wholly owned subsidary of The Rowman & Littlefield Publishing Group, Inc.
4501 Forbes Boulevard, Suite 200, Lanham, Maryland 20706
www.rowman.com

10 Thornbury Road, Plymouth PL6 7PP, United Kingdom

British Library Cataloguing in Publication Information Available

Library of Congress Cataloging-in-Publication Data

Neville, Peter, 1944-
 Historical dictionary of British foreign policy / Peter Neville.
    pages cm. — (Historical dictionaries of diplomacy and foreign relations)
 Includes bibliographical references.
 ISBN 978-0-8108-7173-1 (cloth : alk. paper) — ISBN 978-0-8108-7371-1 (ebook)
 1. Great Britain—Foreign relations—Dictionaries. I. Title.
 DA45.N48 2013
 327.41003--dc23

                                                                    2012042459

♾™ The paper used in this publication meets the minimum requirements of American National Standard for Information Sciences—Permanence of Paper for Printed Library Materials, ANSI/NISO Z39.48-1992. Printed in the United States of America.

To Phuong Anh

Contents

Editor's Foreword

British diplomacy reaches far back in time in various ways, but, for the purpose of this book, the starting point of modern foreign policy is the creation of the Foreign Office in 1782. This is hardly a negligible time span, and, indeed, few other countries have been significant players for such a long period of time. As a matter of fact, there are many that were not even in existence then or were, as it happens, colonies or dependencies of Great Britain. Admittedly, it was not all onward and upward; if anything, it was the contrary. Britain was once the strongest great power, but it has gradually been pushed out of that circle by such upstarts as the United States, China, and the Soviet Union, which was earlier and later Russia. This puts the state in a second circle of important, but not quite great, powers, although it certainly has seniority over the others, which does not count for much in international affairs. Nonetheless, the United Kingdom of Great Britain and Northern Ireland, more commonly known as Great Britain, is a power with a difference. There is still some remnant of the special relationship between Britain and the United States; the state does hold significance in the European Union (EU), when it bothers to get involved in EU matters; and it is still the head of the British Commonwealth of Nations. Britain has ambassadors in an amazing number of countries, with embassies in London, and it does get mixed up, in one way or another, in virtually any serious crisis.

Given the number of countries with which Britain has relations and the plethora of international organizations it is a member of, to say nothing of the assorted crises and issues in which it gets involved, there is plenty to say about British diplomacy, and the real problem faced by *Historical Dictionary of British Diplomacy* is keeping things straight. That is a primary task of this volume, and it does so most evidently and, in some ways, most helpfully, through the extensive chronology, which traces the movements of the state during this long period. The list of acronyms and abbreviations will come in handy in tracing the players who do not always appear under their full name. But it is the impressive dictionary section that forms the core of the book. The dictionary takes a closer look at important people, places, and events in several hundred succinct, but informative, entries. There are, of course, those on British prime ministers and foreign secretaries (as well as U.S. presidents and secretaries of state), and an assortment of ambassadors and a few other significant officials, as well as those on the various crises and issues, to say nothing of those on the countries with which it has interacted, sometimes as friend, sometimes as foe, but, fortunately, most of the time as just another player. For a state with such a long history, it is obvious that only so much can be said in this book, thus the bibliography directs readers to additional sources of information.

Peter Neville has been teaching history at British universities since 1992, including at Queen Mary, University of London; the University of East Anglia; and Kingston University. His focus is clearly on British foreign policy, and his specialization is appeasement and policy toward Vietnam. This has resulted in an impressive number of articles and several books, among them, and in historical order of the topics, are *Appeasing Hitler: The Diplomacy of Sir Nevile Henderson, 1937–1939* (2000), *Hitler and Appeasement: The British Attempt to Prevent the Second World War* (2005), *Mussolini* (2004), and *Britain in Vietnam: Prelude to Disaster, 1945–1946* (2007). A fellow of the Royal Historical Society, he has also made contributions to the *Oxford New Dictionary of National Biography*. The author clearly has a grasp of modern British diplomacy that covers all nooks and crannies of this sometimes obscure panorama, and his insight, especially his ability to sum up complex situations in succinct entries, makes him an excellent guide for beginners and a fine companion for the more advanced.

Jon Woronoff
Series Editor

Acknowledgments

There are a number of people to thank for their help in writing this book. First, special thanks go to my editor, Jon Woronoff, for allowing me extra time to complete the manuscript. Second, I extend many thanks to Professor Tony Lentin and Dr. Zara Steiner for reading and commenting on the material. Pauline Scatterty's help has also been invaluable throughout the process. My greatest debt, as ever, has been to my wife, Phuong Anh, for her forbearance during my numerous disappearances into my study while this project was being completed.

Reader's Note

To facilitate the rapid and efficient location of information and make this book as useful a reference tool as possible, extensive cross-references have been provided in the dictionary section. Within individual entries, terms that have their own entries appear in **boldface type** the first time they appear. Related terms that do not appear in the text are indicated in the *See also*. *See* refers to other entries that deal with this topic.

Acronyms and Abbreviations

ANC	African National Congress
ANF	Atlantic Nuclear Force
ANO	Abu Nidal Organization
ANZAC	Australian and New Zealand Army Corps
ARA	Armada de la República Argentina
AV	alternative vote
BBC	British Broadcasting Corporation
BEF	British Expeditionary Force
BENELUX	Belgium, Netherlands, Luxemburg Customs Union
BRIAM	British Advisory Mission
CAP	Common Agricultural Policy
CDU	Christian Democratic Union
CENTO	Central Treaty Organization
CET	common external tariff
CFSP	Common Foreign and Security Policy
CIA	Central Intelligence Agency
CND	Campaign for Nuclear Disarmament
COS	chiefs of staff
CSS	Confederate States' Ship
DEA	Department of Economic Affairs
DRC	Defense Requirements Committee
DRV	Democratic Republic of Vietnam
DTI	Department of Trade and Industry
EAM	National Liberation Front
EC	European Community
ECB	European Central Bank
ECSC	European Coal and Steel Community
EDC	European Defense Community
EEC	European Economic Community
EFTA	European Free Trade Association
EIJ	Egyptian Islamic Jihad
ELDR	European Liberal Democrat and Reform Group
EMS	European Monetary System

EMU	European Monetary Union
EOKA	National Organization of Cypriot Fighters
EPP-ED	European People's Party
ERM	Exchange Rate Mechanism
ERP	European Recovery Program
EU	European Union
EURO	European Common Currency
FAO	Food and Agricultural Organization
FCO	Foreign and Commonwealth Office
FO	Foreign Office
FRG	Federal Republic of Germany
GATT	General Agreement on Tariffs and Trade
GDP	gross domestic product
GDR	German Democratic Republic
GNP	gross national product
HM	His Majesty/Her Majesty
HMG	His Majesty's Government/Her Majesty's Government
HMS	His Majesty's Ship/Her Majesty's Ship
ICC	International Criminal Court
ICJ	International Court of Justice
ICTY	International Criminal Tribunal for the Former Yugoslavia
IFOR	Implementation Force
IMF	International Monetary Fund
IRA	Irish Republican Army
ISAF	International Security Assistance Force
ISI	Interservices Intelligence
JIC	Joint Intelligence Committee
JNA	Yugoslav National Army
KFOR	Kosovo Force
KGB	Komitet Gosudarstvennoy Bezopasnosti (Committee for State Security)
LDP	Liberal Democratic Party
LEGCO	Legislative Council
MAD	mutually assured destruction
MBA	master of business administration
MEP	Member of the European Parliament
MLF	Multilateral Force
MOD	Ministry of Defense
MP	Member of Parliament
NAFTA	North American Free Trade Association
NATO	North Atlantic Treaty Organization
NHS	National Health Service

NUM	National Union of Mineworkers
OBR	Office of Budget Responsibility
OEEC	Organization for European Economic Cooperation
OGPU	Obyedinyonnoye gosudarstvennoye politicheskoye upravleniye (Joint State Political Directorate under the Council of People's Commissars of the USSR)
PASOK	Panhellenic Socialist Movement
PCO	passport control officer
PFLP	Popular Front for the Liberation of Palestine
PIRA	Provisional Irish Republican Army
PLF	Palestine Liberation Front
PLO	Palestine Liberation Organization
PPP	Pakistan People's Party
PRC	People's Republic of China
PUS	permanent undersecretary
RAF	Royal Air Froce
RMS	Royal Mail Ship
RUC	Royal Ulster Constabulary
SALT 1	Strategic Arms Limitation Talks 1
SAS	Special Air Service
SDI	Strategic Defense Initiative
SDP	Social Democratic Party
SEA	Single European Act
SEAC	South-East Asia Command
SEATO	Southeast Asia Treaty Organization
SIS	Secret Intelligence Service
SOE	Special Operations Executive
SPD	Social Democratic Party
SSIA	Sudanese People's Liberation Army
START	Strategic Arms Limitation Talks
TGWU	Transport and General Workers Union
TNA	The National Archives
UDI	Unilateral Declaration of Independence
UK	United Kingdom
UN	United Nations
UNCTAD	United Nations Conference on Trade and Development
UNESCO	United Nations Educational, Scientific, and Cultural Organization
UNPROFOR	United Nations Protection Force
U.S.	United States
USSR	Union of Soviet Socialist Republics (Soviet Union)
VE-DAY	Victory in Europe Day

VJ-DAY	Victory in Japan Day
WEU	Western European Union
WHO	World Health Organization
WMD	weapons of mass destruction
WTO	World Trade Organization
ZANU	Zimbabwe African National Union

Chronology

1702 The War of the Spanish Succession begins.

1713 The Treaty of Utrecht is signed. Great Britain obtains Gibraltar from Spain.

1740 The War of the Austrian Succession begins. Britain becomes involved in the war in India and Canada.

1748 The Treaty of Aix-la-Chapelle is signed.

1756 The Seven Years' War begins.

1759 Quebec falls to the British.

1763 **10 February:** The Treaty of Paris is signed.

1765 **22 March:** The Stamp Act is passed.

1768 **1 October:** British troops arrive in Boston.

1773 **2 December:** The Boston Tea Party takes place.

1776 **2 May:** France authorizes secret aid to the Americans. **4 July:** The American colonies declare their independence from Great Britain.

1778 **6 February:** The Franco–American alliance is signed.

1781 **19 October:** The British surrender at Yorktown.

1782 The Foreign Office is created as a separate department of the state.

1783 **3 September:** The Treaty of Versailles is signed. Britain cedes independence to the United States.

1789 **July:** The French Revolution breaks out.

1793 **23 January:** News of the execution of Louis XVI reaches Britain. **February:** Britain declares war on France. The Duke of York lands with the British army in Holland. **6 September:** The British attack on Dunkirk fails. **18 December:** The Royal Navy evacuates Toulon.

1795 **January:** The British army evacuates from Holland.

1798 **2 August:** Horatio Nelson destroys the French fleet at the Battle of the Nile. **September:** The French invade County Mayo. Irish revolt crushed by British.

1799 Napoleon Bonaparte becomes first consul of France.

1802 **27 March:** The Treaty of Amiens brings temporary pause to war with France.

1803 **18 May:** The Anglo–French War resumes.

1805 **21 October:** Horatio Nelson defeats the combined Franco–Spanish fleet at Trafalgar. **2 December:** Napoleon routs the Allied army at Austerlitz.

1806 **23 January:** William Pitt the Younger dies.

1807 **25 March:** George Canning becomes foreign secretary.

1808 **July:** British troops land in Portugal.

1812 **18 February:** Lord Castlereagh becomes foreign secretary. **23 June:** Napoleon invades Russia. **22 July:** The Duke of Wellington routs the French at Salamanca.

1813 **21 June:** Wellington gets his final victory in Spain at Vitoria. **16 October:** British units take part in the "Battle of the Nations" in Leipzig.

1814 **30 May:** The First Treaty of Paris is signed.

1815 **June 18:** The British and Prussians defeat Napoleon at Waterloo. **November:** The Second Treaty of Paris keeps occupying British troops in France. The Quadruple Alliance provides for Great Powers meetings.

1818 **29 September:** Castlereagh represents Britain at the Congress of Aix-la-Chapelle. Occupation troops withdraw from France.

1820 **5 May:** Castlereagh produces his state paper on the conduct of British foreign policy.

1821 **March:** The Greeks revolt against Ottoman Turkey.

1822 **12 August:** Castlereagh commits suicide.

1823 **December:** The Monroe Doctrine gains the supported of British prime minister George Canning.

1827 **8 August:** George Canning dies. **20 October:** The Royal Navy takes part in the victory over the Ottoman Turks at Navarino Bay.

1829   The Treaty of Adrianople gives Greece its independence.

1839   Great Britain signs the Treaty of London to guarantee Belgian independence.

1841   Lord Henry John Palmerston secures the Straits Convention to control navigation of the Dardanelles.

1842   The British column is trapped and massacred during its retreat from Kabul, Afghanistan.

1847–1850   Great Britain becomes involved in the Don Pacifico Affair.

1850   **25–26 June:** Palmerston gives his classic exposition of foreign policy in the House of Commons.

1854   **27 February:** Russia is handed the Anglo–French ultimatum. **28 March:** Britain and France declare war and invade Crimea.

1855   **4 February:** Palmerston becomes prime minister. **December:** Austria threatens to join war against Russia.

1856   **25 February:** The Congress of Paris opens. **30 March:** The Treaty of Paris curbs the Russian naval threat to Ottoman Turkey.

1857   **May:** The Indian Mutiny breaks out to endanger British rule.

1858   **8 July:** The Indian Mutiny ends. The British Crown takes over the authority of East India Company.

1861   **13 May:** Britain declares its neutrality in the American Civil War (1861–1865).

1870   Britain opts for neutrality in the Franco–Prussian War of 1870–1871.

1872   British prime minister William Gladstone agrees to pay the United States $15.5 million for damage done by the CSS *Alabama*.

1875   **November:** British prime minister Benjamin Disraeli (Lord Beaconsfield) buys a majority shareholding in the Suez Canal Company for £4 million.

1876   Disraeli declares Queen Victoria the empress of India.

1878   **13 June:** The Congress of Berlin opens. Bulgaria becomes fragmented. Britain obtains Cyprus. The Second Afghan War commences (1878–1880).

1879   **22 January:** The British colonial force is destroyed by Zulus at Isandhlwana in South Africa. **July:** The British envoy is murdered in Kabul.

1880 Disraeli dies.

1881 The First Boer War commences. The British are defeated at Majuba.

1882 **July:** The British fleet bombards the Egyptian port of Alexandria.

1884 **January:** General Charles Gordon is sent to evacuate a garrison from Khartoum.

1885 Gordon is killed by Sudanese rebels.

1895 Lord Salisbury rejects U.S. interference in the Venezuelan Question. **December:** The Jameson Raid into the Transvaal fails.

1897 Queen Victoria's Diamond Jubilee is held.

1898 **January:** The Fashoda Crisis between Britain and France commences. **September:** Khalifa Abdullahi's army is destroyed at Omdurman in Sudan.

1899 **October:** The Second Boer War breaks out.

1900 **24 May:** Britain annexes the Orange Free State.

1901 **1 January:** The Federal Constitution of Australia goes into force.

1902 **30 January:** The Anglo–Japanese alliance is signed. **31 May:** The Peace of Vereeniging ends the Boer War.

1903 **January:** King Edward VII is proclaimed emperor of India in New Delhi.

1904 **8 April:** The Anglo–French Entente Cordiale is signed, ending imperial disputes.

1906 **6 December:** Transvaal is granted self-government by Britain.

1907 **August:** The Anglo–Russian Entente divides Persia into British and Russian zones of influence.

1908 **7 October:** Austria-Hungary annexes Bosnia-Herzegovina from Turkey without British opposition.

1909 **August:** The South Africa Act is passed, approving the union of Cape Colony, Natal, and the Orange Free State.

1911 **July–November:** The Agadir Crisis takes place. Britain warns Germany about consequences of interference in Morocco.

1912 **October:** The First Balkan War breaks out.

1913 **30 May:** The First Balkan War is brought to an end by the Treaty of London. **August:** The Second Balkan War is halted by the Treaty of Bucharest.

1914 **28 June:** Archduke Franz Ferdinand is assassinated in Sarajevo. **4 August:** Britain and its Commonwealth declare war on Germany. President Woodrow Wilson declares U.S. neutrality. **5–10 September:** The First Battle of the Marne is waged. The British Expeditionary Force halts the German advance on Paris. **12 October–12 November:** The First Battle of Ypres is fought in Belgium. **8 December:** The Battle of the Falklands is waged. The British fleet defeats the German Pacific Squadron.

1915 **22 April:** The Second Battle of Ypres begins. **24 April:** The Anglo–French land campaign against the Turks on the Gallipoli peninsula starts. **October:** The McMahon Pledge is authorized to create an independent Arab kingdom.

1916 **April:** The Sykes–Picot Agreement, also known as the Asia Minor Agreement, on postwar partition of the Ottoman Empire is signed by Britain and France. **24–29 April:** The Easter Rising against Britain by Irish republicans takes place in Dublin. **31 May:** The Battle of Jutland is fought. Despite greater naval losses, Britain maintains the blockade of Germany. **1 July:** The British lose 20,000 men on the first day of the Battle of the Somme. **7 November:** Woodrow Wilson is reelected president of the United States. **6 December:** David Lloyd George becomes prime minister of Great Britain.

1917 **16 March:** Tsar Nicholas II abdicates. **6 April:** The United States enters World War I. **31 July:** The Third Battle of Ypres is waged. The British stage an unsuccessful attack in Flanders. **2 November:** British foreign secretary Arthur Balfour concedes to the principle of the Jewish home. **7 November:** The Bolsheviks seize power in Russia.

1918 **8 January:** U.S. president Woodrow Wilson puts forward his Fourteen Points. **May:** British and Allied forces intervene in the Russian Civil War. **18 July–10 November:** The Allied offensive on the Western Front forces the German army to retreat. **4 October:** British and Arab forces capture Damascus. **11 November:** Britain and the Allied Powers sign an armistice with Germany at 11 a.m.

1919 **18 January:** The Paris Peace Conference starts. **14 March:** Lloyd George and Woodrow Wilson offer a guarantee of assistance to France. **25 March:** George publishes the Fontainebleau Memorandum. **21 June:** The Germans scuttle the High Seas Fleet at Scapa Flow. **28 June:** Treaty of Versailles signed.

1920   19 March: The U.S. rejection of Versailles causes the Anglo–American guarantee to France to lapse. **23 December:** The Government of Ireland Act is signed.

1921   23 August: The British establish the kingdom of Iraq. **12 November:** The Washington Naval Conference begins. **6 December:** The Anglo–Irish Treaty is signed.

1922   6 February: The Anglo–Japanese Treaty lapses. **19 October:** George resigns as prime minister following the Chanak Crisis.

1923   24 July: The Treaty of Lausanne is signed between Turkey and the Allies.

1924   22 January: Ramsey MacDonald becomes prime minister of Britain's first Labour government.

1925   October: The Treaty of Locarno is signed in London.

1926   September: Germany joins the League of Nations. **November:** The Balfour Declaration at the Empire Conference accepts effective independence of the Dominions.

1928   August: Britain signs the Kellogg–Briand Pact, also known as the Pact of Paris, to renounce war as an instrument of policy.

1929   October: The Wall Street Crash occurs.

1930   November: The first Round Table Conference on India begins.

1931   January: The Statute of Westminster recognizes de facto Dominion independence. **September:** Japanese troops invade Manchuria. Britain sends a diplomatic protest.

1932   June–July: The Lausanne Conference ends reparations.

1933   30 January: Adolf Hitler becomes German chancellor. **26 April:** British ambassador Sir Horace Rumbold warns Foreign Office about Nazism in final dispatch.

1935   April: Britain, France, and Italy form Stresa Front. **18 June:** The Anglo–German Naval Treaty is signed. **3 October:** Italy invades Ethiopia.

1936   7 March: Germany occupies the demilitarized zone of Rhineland despite Anglo–French protests. **December:** King Edward VIII abdicated from the throne.

1937   28 May: Neville Chamberlain becomes Britain's premier.

1938 **20 February:** Anthony Eden resigns as Britain's foreign secretary because of Italian policy. **20–21 May:** Britain warns Germany about the apparent threat to Czechoslovakia. **15 September:** Chamberlain meets Hitler at Berchtesgaden. **22 September:** Chamberlain meets with Hitler at Godesberg. **29–30 September:** The Munich Conference is held.

1939 **16 January:** The Irish Republican Army (IRA) begins its bombing campaign in Britain. **15 March:** Hitler occupies rump Czechoslovakia. **31 March:** Chamberlain gives a guarantee of assistance to Poland. **23 August:** The Nazi–Soviet Pact is signed. **25 August:** Britain signs a military agreement with Poland. **1 September:** Germany invades Poland. **3 September:** Britain declares war on Germany at 11 a.m. **December:** The Royal Navy squadron forces the pocket battleship *Graf Spee* to scuttle itself.

1940 **10 May:** Winston Churchill replaces Neville Chamberlain as prime minister. Germany invades France and the Low Countries. **July–September:** The Battle of Britain is waged. **17 September:** Hitler postpones the invasion of Britain. **9 November:** Chamberlain dies.

1941 **10 May:** The London Blitz ends. **22 June:** Germany invades the Soviet Union. **9–12 August:** Winston Churchill meets President Franklin D. Roosevelt in Placentia Bay, Newfoundland. **7 December:** The Japanese attack Pearl Harbor.

1942 **February:** Singapore falls to the Japanese. **20 June:** The British base of Tobruk, in Libya, is captured by the Germans. **19 August:** British commandos launch a costly raid on the French port of Dieppe.

1943 **November:** Winston Churchill, Joseph Stalin, and Franklin D. Roosevelt meet in Tehran.

1944 **6 June:** British and U.S. troops land in Normandy. **October:** The "Percentages" Agreement is signed between Churchill and Stalin in Moscow. **December:** Churchill mediates in the Greek Civil War.

1945 **February:** Churchill, Stalin, and Roosevelt meet in Yalta. **April:** President Roosevelt dies. **8 May:** The Germans surrender in Europe. **26 July:** Churchill is defeated in the general election. He is replaced by Clement R. Attlee at the Potsdam Conference. **2 September:** Japan surrenders.

1946 **March:** Churchill gives his "Iron Curtain" speech in Fulton, Missouri. **September:** Churchill gives his "United States of Europe" speech in Zurich.

1947 **5 June:** The Marshall Plan is announced. **15 August:** Britain grants independence to India and Pakistan.

1948   26 June: The Russians impose a blockade on British, U.S., and French zones in West Berlin.

1949   4 April: The North Atlantic Treaty Organization (NATO) is established. **6 October:** The blockade of Berlin ends.

1950   6 January: Attlee's government recognizes the "People's Republic of China" (PRC). **25 June:** The Korean War starts, with British participation.

1951   7 June: Guy Burgess and Donald Maclean defect to the Soviet Union. **October:** Churchill returns to power for the last time.

1952   1 January: The European Coal and Steel Community commences operation without Britain. **October:** Britain explodes its first atomic bomb. The Mau Mau Uprising takes place in Kenya.

1953   March: Stalin dies. **June:** Elizabeth II becomes queen and head of the Commonwealth.

1954   7 March–7 May: Dien Bien Phu is seized. Britain refuses to become involved in the operation to save the French garrison. **20 July:** The Geneva Agreement is signed. **17 November:** Colonel Jamal Abd al Nasser replaces General Mohammed Neguib as president of Egypt. **December:** The Southeast Asia Treaty Organization is established.

1955   6 April: Anthony Eden becomes prime minister. **18 April:** Nikita Khrushchev and Nikolai Bulganin arrive for a visit to Britain. **June:** The Messina Meeting on the foundation of the European Economic Community (EEC) is held.

1956   March: King Hussein of Jordan dismisses Sir John Glubb. **26 July:** Colonel Nasser nationalizes the Suez Canal. **29 October:** Israeli troops attack Egypt. **5–6 November:** British and French troops invade Egypt. **29 November:** British forces withdraw from Egypt.

1957   March: The Treaty of Rome is signed without British involvement. **April:** Duncan Sandys produces the Defence White Paper. **May:** Britain explodes a hydrogen bomb.

1958   1 January: The EEC Treaty enters into force. Chancellor Peter Thornycroft resigns over economic policy.

1959   February: Harold Macmillan visits Moscow. **31 August:** Macmillan and U.S. president Dwight D. Eisenhower make first live television broadcast from 10 Downing Street. **October:** Macmillan wins the election.

1960   February: Macmillan gives his "Winds of Change" speech in Cape Town, South Africa. **21 March:** The Sharpeville Massacre takes place in

South Africa. **1 May:** The U-2 spy plane crisis occurs. **September:** The Labour Party's Hugh Gaitskell denounces unilateral nuclear disarmament.

1961   31 July: Macmillan announces that Britain will apply to join the EEC. **September:** The British negotiating team arrives in Brussels.

1962   27 October: The United States and Union of Soviet Socialist Republics (USSR) go on full nuclear alert over Cuba. **28 October:** Soviet ships are ordered back. **20 November:** The United States lifts the naval blockade of Cuba.

1963   14 January: General Charles de Gaulle vetoes Britain's first EEC application. **5 August:** The Nuclear Test Ban Treaty is signed by Britain, the United States, and the USSR. **October:** Macmillan resigns. **22 November:** U.S. president John F. Kennedy is assassinated in Dallas.

1964   October: Harold Wilson becomes prime minister. Nikita Khrushchev falls from power in the USSR.

1965   11 November: The Unilateral Declaration of Independence of Southern Rhodesia is signed.

1966   February: The Defence White Paper on Britain's withdrawal from a global role is produced. Harold Wilson visits Moscow. **22 April:** Cabinet approval is secured for a second British EEC application.

1967   24 January: A meeting between Harold Wilson and Charles de Gaulle is held in Paris. **June:** The Six-Day War breaks out in the Middle East. **27 November:** De Gaulle vetoes Britain's second EEC application.

1968   16 January: The Wilson government announces its decision to withdraw all forces east of Suez by 31 March 1971. **29 January–25 February:** The Tet Offensive takes place in Vietnam. **15 March:** George Brown resigns as British foreign secretary. **August:** Warsaw Pact forces invade Czechoslovakia.

1969   28 April: De Gaulle resigns as French president. **14–15 August:** British troops are sent in after riots in Belfast and Derry.

1970   30 June: Britain renews entry talks with the EEC.

1971   20–21 May: Edward Heath and Georges Pompidou hold a summit in Paris. **28 October:** The House of Commons votes 356 to 244 in favor of an EEC entry.

1972   January: Prime Minister Edward Heath signs the Treaty of Accession with the EEC. The "Bloody Sunday" incident occurs in Derry. **2 February:** The British embassy is burned in Dublin.

1973 **1 January:** Britain becomes a member of the EEC. **6 October:** The Yom Kippur War starts in the Middle East. **24 October:** A cease-fire is ordered in the Middle East.

1974 **20 July:** Turkey invades Northern Cyprus. **9 August:** Richard Nixon resigns as president of the United States.

1975 **11 February:** Margaret Thatcher is elected leader of the Conservative Party. **October:** Australian prime minister Gough Whitlam is dismissed by the British governor general.

1976 Britain applies for funding from the International Monetary Fund (IMF). Wilson stands down as premier.

1979 **4 May:** Thatcher is elected Britain's first female prime minister. **21 December:** The Lancaster House Conference agrees to black majority rule in Southern Rhodesia (Zimbabwe).

1980 **30 May:** An agreement is reached between Britain and the EEC about a contribution rebate. **14 July:** U.S. president Jimmy Carter agrees to sell Britain the U.S. Trident nuclear missile.

1982 **2 April:** Argentina invades the Falklands. **5 April:** The British task force sails. **2 May:** A British nuclear submarine sinks the ARA *General Belgrano.* **14 May:** British forces land in the Falklands. **14 June:** The British recapture Port Stanley.

1983 **25 October:** The United States invades the Commonwealth island of Grenada without prior consultation with Britain.

1984 **11 October:** Thatcher survives an assassination attempt by the Provisional IRA in Brighton.

1985 Mikhail Gorbachev becomes general secretary of the Soviet Communist Party.

1986 **14 April:** Britain allows U.S. president Ronald Reagan to use Royal Air Force bases for the Libya bombing. **13 December:** Defense secretary Michael Heseltine resigns from the Thatcher government over the Westland Affair.

1988 **December:** Pan Am Flight 103 is blown up over Lockerbie, Scotland.

1989 **July:** Thatcher removes Sir Geoffrey Howe as foreign secretary. **9 November:** The Berlin Wall comes down.

1990 **2 August:** Iraq invades Kuwait. **22 November:** Thatcher resigns as prime minister. **28 November:** John Major becomes prime minister.

1991 **17 January:** The First Gulf War begins under the code name "Operation Desert Storm." **25 June:** Slovenia declares its independence from Yugoslavia. **7 October:** Croatia declares its independence. **21 October:** Bosnia declares itself independent. **December:** The Treaty of Maastricht is signed.

1992 **20 December:** Prime Minister John Major meets U.S. president George H. W. Bush at Camp David to discuss the Yugoslav problem.

1993 **January:** The Vance–Owen Plan for the division of Bosnia is presented.

1995 **30 November:** U.S. president Bill Clinton visits Belfast as part of the peace process. **14 December:** The Dayton Agreement is signed in Paris to end the Bosnian War.

1997 **2 May:** Tony Blair becomes prime minister of Great Britain. **30 June:** Power is transferred from Britain to the PRC in Hong Kong. **11 December:** The Kyoto Protocol on climate change is adopted.

1998 **10 April:** The Good Friday Agreement restores devolved government in Northern Ireland.

1999 **24 March:** NATO states, including Britain, bomb Serbia to enforce its withdrawal from Kosovo. **22 April:** Blair lays down the concept of "principled intervention" in a speech in Chicago. **10 June:** Serbian president Slobodan Milošević agrees to withdraw forces from Kosovo. NATO ends its bombing of Serbia.

2001 **11 September:** Jihadist terror attacks are carried out on the World Trade Center in New York and the Pentagon in Arlington, Virginia. **7 October:** Britain and the United States launch air strikes against Afghanistan.

2002 **24 September:** The British government releases the "September Dossier" on Iraq. **October:** David Trimble resigns as Northern Ireland's first minister due to the slow pace of the IRA weapons decommissioning. **8 November:** The United Nations Security Council adopts Resolution 1441 on Iraq.

2003 **17 March:** Robin Cook resigns as leader of the House of Commons over Iraq War. **20 March:** Operation Iraqi Freedom begins, with British involvement. **18–21 November:** George W. Bush makes the first state visit to Britain by an incumbent U.S. president. **20 November:** The Northern Ireland Assembly elections are held.

2004 **29 March:** Bulgaria, Estonia, Latvia, Lithuania, Romania, Slovakia, and Slovenia join NATO. Great Britain allows unrestricted access to migrants in new European Union states, including the Czech Republic, Estonia, Hungary, Latvia, Lithuania, Malta, Poland, Slovakia, and Slovenia.

2005   16 February: The Kyoto Treaty (ratified by Britain) comes into force. **7 July:** A terrorist bombing kills more than 50 civilians on the London transport system.

2006   July: Britain's new foreign secretary, Margaret Beckett, is criticized for failing to condemn Israeli action in Lebanon. **October:** Beckett calls for closure of the U.S. detention camp at Guantanamo Bay, Cuba. **30 December:** Saddam Hussein is executed by the Iraqi government. **31 December:** Britain makes its final payment on a U.S. loan given to finance World War II debts.

2007   May: The final press conference between Prime Minister Tony Blair and President George W. Bush underwrites their "special relationship." Nicolas Sarkozy becomes the new French president. **27 June:** Blair stands down as British prime minister, to be replaced by Gordon Brown. David Miliband is appointed foreign secretary. **19 July:** The credit crunch begins, with a statement by the U.S. Federal Reserve chairman that the U.S. subprime lending market could cost up to $8,100 billion. **29–30 July:** Prime Minister Gordon Brown meets President George W. Bush at Camp David. **14 September:** Financial panic spreads to Britain as Northern Rock depositors queue to withdraw savings. **17 September:** Chancellor Alistair Darling states that the government will guarantee all Northern Rock deposits. **19 September:** The Bank of England announces injection of £10 billion into British money markets. **9 October:** The treasury announces the extension of the Northern Rock guarantee to all deposits. **6 December:** President Bush outlines his plans to freeze rates on subprime mortgages for five years.

2008   21 January: Global stock indexes, including the FTSE 100, record their biggest falls since the 9/11 terrorist attacks. **17 February:** Northern Rock is nationalized. **17 April:** Prime Minister Brown meets with President Bush in Washington, D.C. **26 June:** Barack Obama meets with Prime Minister Brown in London. **31 July:** Housing prices in the United Kingdom show their biggest decline since 1991. **10 September:** The European Commission warns that Britain, Germany, and Spain will go into recession by the end of 2008. **15 September:** Lehman Brothers files for bankruptcy in the United States. **13 October:** Chancellor Darling makes a statement to the House of Commons about the recapitalization of Halifax Bank of Scotland, Lloyds TSB, and the Royal Bank of Scotland. **4 November:** Barack Obama is elected president of the United States. **19 November:** The IMF approves a £1.4 billion loan for Iceland. The British, Dutch, and German governments confirm loans to Iceland of $6.3 billion. **31 December:** The FTSE 100 has its worst year on record, closing down at 31.3 percent.

2009 **15 January:** The Irish government nationalizes the Anglo–Irish Bank. **5 March:** The Bank of England announces the start of "quantitative easing." The bank decides to purchase £75 billion worth of assets using created funds. **2 April:** Prime Minister Brown meets leaders of the world's largest economies at the G20 Summit in London. **July:** Foreign Secretary Miliband meets with the Spanish foreign minister in Gibraltar.

2010 **24 March:** Chancellor Darling reports a 50-percent increase in the price of oil in his budget statement. **6 May:** The general election results in a hung Parliament as no one party wins the outright majority. **11 May:** Brown resigns as prime minister. David Cameron forms a coalition government. **23 June:** Julia Gillard becomes Australia's first female prime minister.

2011 **March–May:** Great Britain and France launch air strikes against Libya to help bring down the regime. **8–9 December:** Great Britain refuses to sign a fiscal rescue package at the EU summit in Brussels. **11 December:** Prime Minister David Cameron is criticized by coalition partner and Deputy Prime Minister Nick Clegg over his EU policy.

2012 **February:** Prime Minister Cameron visits Washington, D.C., where he receives a cordial reception by President Barack Obama. **19 April:** Libyan jihadist Abdel Hakim Belhaj takes out libel actions against former British foreign secretary Jack Straw. **May:** François Hollande is elected French president. **29 May:** The Foreign and Commonwealth Office expels Syrian diplomats following a massacre.

Introduction

British foreign policy has always been based on distinctive principles since the establishment of the Foreign Office in 1782 as one of the two original offices of state, the other being the Home Office. As a small island nation, Britain was historically fearful of mighty continental powers that might seek to menace its trade routes, and naval primacy was essential. Britain felt that it was necessary to dominate at sea, while avoiding involvement in major continental wars.

Until the end of the 19th century, Britain was successful at doing so, defeating threats to its domination of the seas by Holland and France. The rise of German naval power by the start of the 20th century meant that the nation could not rely entirely on its own naval resources, nor could it ignore the fact that the United States was beginning to challenge in the Pacific by 1900. This challenge was masked during the period between World War I and World War II by U.S. isolationism. World War II and the Cold War after 1945 made it abundantly clear that the United States was now the global naval super power.

The United Kingdom of Great Britain and Northern Ireland, to give it the full official name, had to adapt to a secondary, supportive role. This was to be based on its membership of regional defense and economic organizations in Europe. This reflected the fact that Britain was now a second-rank power dependent on U.S. or European assistance to achieve its foreign policy objectives. Attempts to ignore this reality, as at Suez in 1956, tended to lead to disaster. By then, Britain lacked the military and economic power to play its old role. The use of the name "Great Britain" now seemed faintly anomalous. More often, it was just called "Britain" or the "United Kingdom." The independence of the Irish Free State, now the Irish Republic, in 1922, reduced the United Kingdom to England, Scotland, Wales, and Northern Ireland (26 southern counties formed the Irish Republic, leaving only six northern ones under British jurisdiction).

THE ACHIEVEMENT OF GLOBAL POWER

The main aim of the British Foreign Office became maintaining a balance of power that would prevent any one European power, be it France, Germany,

1

or Russia, from dominating Europe and, in particular, those areas historically known as the Low Countries (Holland and Belgium), bordering the English Channel and the North Sea. The transition of Britain from being a European power to a global one in the 18th century depended on this geographical security. The first great war of that century, however, the War of the Spanish Succession (1702–1713), showed that, on occasion, when it deemed its interests sufficiently threatened, Britain would fight large-scale continental campaigns, in this instance to break French domination. Two further wars in mid-century, the War of the Austrian Succession (1740–1748) and the Seven Years' War (1756–1763), were won with a blue water strategy, whereby Britain acted as a paymaster for continental allies like Austria and Prussia, and used mercenary troops in its limited involvement in European campaigns. This meant that small British land forces, combined with total naval dominance, could be used to achieve victory over France in India and North America and create Britain's first global empire. This was a reality by 1763.

Military and naval muscle was not the only component of British power. Britain had been an early user of paper currency, had a central bank in the Bank of England as early as 1694, and made decisive use of its credit facilities to finance its wars. The nation's main rival, France, lacked this capacity in the 18th century, which made the subsidy a key weapon in avoiding the need for larger, more expensive land armies. It was far better to let Prussian grenadiers do the fighting in Europe rather than British ones.

Cheap credit, overwhelming naval power, and astute manipulation of continental allies thus characterized British policy up to the French Revolutionary and Napoleonic wars (1793–1815). It was a successful formula, but one that required that all these components remain in place. When they were not maintained, the potential for disaster still existed, most notably when, as a result of the American War of Independence (1775–1783), Britain lost its 13 colonies in North America, which came to constitute the new United States of America. In this case, insensitive taxation policy, coupled with the brief loss of naval domination to France, brought about the decisive British defeat at Yorktown in 1781. During this period, Britain had allowed itself to become isolated from potential continental allies. Its army, thousands of miles away and partly mercenary, was also unable to crush the American rebels.

THE 19TH CENTURY PAX BRITANNICA

The lesson was well learned. Napoleon Bonaparte was never able to utilize his superior military power against Britain after the devastating naval defeat he suffered at Trafalgar in October 1805. Britain had to endure setbacks from

1805–1807, as paymaster of the anti-French coalition, but its naval and financial resources ultimately procured victory. There were different features behind this victory. When Napoleon tried to blockade the British Isles with his Continental System from 1807–1812, the Royal Navy counterblockaded him. And, for the first time since the War of the Spanish Succession, a large British army fought on the continent and drove Napoleon's armies out of Spain.

British diplomats were active in creating coalitions against Napoleon, and it was the fourth of these alliances that brought him down in 1814. But they were of much more ancient vintage than the Foreign Office itself. King Henry VIII (1509–1547) was the first British monarch to send envoys abroad during the 16th century, in both instances to Paris, but in those early days they were denoted as agents rather than ambassadors. By the end of the 18th century, resident ambassadors were given the title ambassador extraordinary and the additional title of plenipotentiary. This merely meant that their government gave them the right to negotiate with their host government. There were still relatively few British ambassadors when the Napoleonic Wars finally ended in 1815.

In the half-century that followed, more than half of Britain's diplomats were still aristocrats at a time when a rising business and mercantile class had broken into the corridors of power in Whitehall (the center of British government in London). Nevertheless, the conduct of diplomacy was still in the hands of the products of public schools, often one such school, Eton. Even those boys, however, were increasingly middle class, as wealthy industrialists sought to enhance their status by sending their sons to Eton, Harrow, or Westminster. Between 1815–1860, more than one-quarter of British diplomats were educated at Eton and a further one-fifth at other leading public schools.

The presumption behind British foreign policy in the 18th century, when the Foreign Office became a distinctive department of State, was that France was the enduring threat to British interests around the globe. This assumption continued in the 18th century, but with a subtext. There was an increasing perception that Russia, with its ambition to dismantle the Ottoman Turkish Empire, was a growing threat to British interests. In particular, successive British governments became fixated by the idea that Tsarist Russia had designs on the jewel in the imperial crown, British India, as Russia was beginning a massive expansion eastward into Central Asia.

In the first instance, however, the British wished to protect the increasingly weak Ottoman Empire and prevent any Russian penetration into the Mediterranean Sea. Their distinguished foreign secretary, Lord Castlereagh (1812–1822), feared Russian ambition in Europe after Napoleon's defeat. A few months after that final defeat at Waterloo, in 1815, Castlereagh wrote what came to be seen as a classic dispatch to his diplomats, in which he declared Britain to be a satisfied power whose objective should be to preserve the Peace Settlement and the balance of power in Europe. Future colonial expansion was to remain subordinate to those essential principles.

Castlereagh was associated with the Congress System (1815–1823), which attempted to settle issues between the major European powers through periodic meetings, but disillusionment set in even before his death in 1822. Britain ultimately could not support the rigid enforcement of the status quo by force in Spain or its Latin American colonies, which were in the process of rejecting Spanish rule. The more enlightened British attitude toward the revolt of the Spanish American colonies helped secure British commercial influence in Latin America for generations, and the power of the Royal Navy effectively underwrote the Monroe Doctrine (1823), which Castlereagh's colleague George Canning supported so that good relations between the United States and Britain could be established.

The mid-19th century was the era of the so-called Pax Britannica (British Peace), preserved by dominant naval power, which could intervene anywhere around the globe from Greece to China in the British interest. The "Great" in "Great Britain" was indisputable. British naval power was underwritten by an industrial revolution, which made mid-Victorian Britain the workshop of the world.

But Great Britain kept a wary eye on its continental neighbors. The Crimean War (1853–1856) was fought to prevent Russian attempts to fragment the Ottoman Empire, and, in this case, British interests coincided with those of France. Russia had to dismantle naval fortifications after its defeat, and its Black Sea fleet could not access the Mediterranean through the Straits. In fact, British fears about Russia were exaggerated, but the Crimean War, for all its notoriously bungled military operations, saw a coincidence of imperial concerns with classic balance of power ones. British paranoia about France, which was still strong in the 1850s, even when the two powers were brief allies, remained potent.

The zenith of Russophobia in Britain came with the second premiership of Benjamin Disraeli (1874–1880), when he played a leading role in defusing the crisis created by Russian sponsorship of a large, independent Bulgaria freed from Ottoman domination. Disraeli followed the examples created by Castlereagh at the end of the Napoleonic Wars by attending a great power conference in Berlin in 1878, which greatly reduced the size of Bulgaria and neutralized the Russian threat. Disraeli gained much public applause at the time, although the passage of time would prove that Bulgaria was capable of looking after its own independence.

By the time of the Bulgarian Crisis (1876–1878), the key position of secretary of state was also changing its nature. Disraeli's foreign secretary, Lord Salisbury, began to travel abroad more frequently, adding personal experience through face-to-face diplomatic meetings to his already considerable knowledge of French and German language and culture. Like many in the British élite, Salisbury felt that the newly united Germany, as the process was completed in 1871, was a natural friend and ally for Britain, which had had a German royal family (the Hanoverians) since the 18th century. Otherwise, like most members of the establishment, Salisbury treated foreigners with suspicion. This was not surprising. By the 1870s, Britain was a satiated power desiring both to preserve a peaceful European balance and its massive empire, now almost out of its earlier expansionist phase.

The fact that Britain ruled over such an empire, covering one-fifth of the earth's surface, did not mean that successive British governments coveted what came to be called "splendid isolation." British statesmen were aware of the limits of the British military, apart from naval power. In 1871, Lord Salisbury pointed out that where the Austrians and Germans could put more than 1,000,000 men into the field, and the Russians a further 500,000, Britain had only 100,000 men at its disposal. It was circumstances, caused in large part by the exhaustion of the great powers after the Napoleonic Wars, that favored Great Britain in the years before 1870, and allowed it to concentrate on industrial and imperial expansion.

British policy was pragmatic. Mediterranean agreements were made with the two weaker great powers, Austria-Hungary and Italy, which had completed its unification in 1870, during Salisbury's first period as prime minister (1886–1892), while arbitration was increasingly used by the Foreign Office as a means of heading off conflict. An example of this is the 1891 Newfoundland Fisheries dispute with France (most famously, William Gladstone, prime minister from 1868–1874, had paid $15.5 million in compensation to the United States in 1872, for damage done by British-built confederate raiders during the American Civil War [1861–1865]).

British policy was also in transition. During his second premiership (1895–1900), Salisbury told the new Russian tsar Nicholas II (1894–1917) that Britain would no longer oppose Russian acquisition of the Straits and Constantinople. This was in 1896, two years before the Fashoda Incident, when France challenged British predominance in the Sudan. This was to be Britain's last serious clash with its ancient rival because of the diplomatic revolution in Europe that was about to occur.

BRITAIN AND WORLD WAR I

The Second Boer War (1899–1902) marked a real watershed in the evolution of British foreign policy before World War I. Although it was a colonial war to crush a rebellion by a few hundred thousand Dutch-speaking Boer settlers in South Africa, it had severe ramifications for Britain's role as a great power and its relationship with continental Europe. First, the war's catastrophic opening phase sparked a national debate about Britain's military status and potential. Second, the British government was shaken by the degree of hostility that its war against the Boers aroused among the other European great powers. This brought home, as nothing else had done in the 19th century, the constraints on British power. There had been some awareness of the growing commercial and industrial threat to British predominance from the United States and Germany, but, during the Boer War, the British began to feel distinctly isolated, whereas its continental neighbors, Germany, Austria-Hungary, and Italy on the one side, and France and Russia on the other, were bound together by alliance systems.

This feeling of isolation was combined with the knowledge that the Royal Navy's age-old domination of the seas could no longer be taken for granted. Since 1889, it had been official British policy that the Royal Navy should equal the combined strengths of the next two largest fleets, the so-called two-power standard, but, by 1900, Britain no longer ruled the waves. Germany had embarked on a massive naval expansion program in the 1890s, and, recognizing the futility of challenging growing U.S. power, Britain withdrew nearly all its naval units from North America and the Caribbean in the early years of the 20th century. By 1908, the United States was second only to Britain in its number of battleships. France and Russia also had considerable fleets.

These factors helped precipitate a diplomatic revolution whose beginning could be seen in 1900 and 1901, when two treaties acknowledged the U.S. right to build and fortify the Panama Canal, which had initially been a joint Anglo–American project. Then, more significantly, Britain signed a defensive alliance with Japan, the rising power in the Far East, that countered the threat from larger Russian and French naval units in that region. The treaty was only to be in force for five years in the first instance, but it ended the diplomatic and military insecurity of Britain.

A more spectacular development followed in 1904, which was a direct consequence of the Anglo–Japanese Treaty. In 1898, Britain and France had come close to war over the Sudan, but the French government feared that its alliance with Russia, dating from 1893, might bring it into conflict with Britain, now an ally of Japan, which was in dispute with Russia about the control of Korea. The result, which was aided by a successful visit to Paris by King Edward VII (1901–1910), was the Entente Cordiale of 1904. This agreement was about a recognition of spheres of colonial influence, thus it was accepted that the Sudan lay within the British sphere and did not involve a military alliance.

There was still a potential for problems with France's ally, Russia, especially when it went to war with Japan in 1904. In the spring of 1905, the new British premier, Arthur Balfour (1902–1905), decided to extend the Anglo–Japanese alliance two years before its expiration date. Britain recognized Japan's claims to Korea in exchange for a Japanese undertaking to defend British India if it was attacked by Russia, an unlikely scenario.

Russian blundering had almost sparked a war with Britain in October 1904, when their Baltic fleet, on its way to the Far East, grotesquely opened fire on British trawlers in the North Sea, which it supposedly mistook for Japanese torpedo boats. French good offices were important here in preventing hostilities, and Russian naval power was destroyed by Japan in the Tsushima Straits after the belated arrival of the Baltic fleet in the Far East. Britain had helped by closing the Suez Canal and forcing the Russians to sail all the way around the Cape. The overwhelming Japanese triumph, speedily followed by a peace treaty that recognized the victory, allowed Britain to reduce its naval forces in the Pacific. By a further historical paradox, Russia's defeat in 1905 opened the way for a colonial accommodation with it in 1907. The Anglo–Russian convention of 31 August 1907 neutralized Tibet, where both states had interests; accepted that Afghanistan lay within the British sphere of influence; and divided Persia, with a neutral central zone separating a Russian sphere in the north and a British one in the south.

A remarkable change had taken place in Britain's global position, and it was now in a more secure position than it had been at the turn of the century. In one sense, however, the traditional norms of British diplomacy had been observed, for neither the agreement with France, nor that with Russia, involved a commitment by Great Britain to send armed forces to the continent. The Triple Entente of Britain, France, and Russia was thus quite different in character from the Triple Alliance of Germany, Austria-Hungary, and Italy. Yet, inevitably, the very existence of the Triple Entente meant that in any foreign policy disputes, Britain was likely to side with France and Russia, thus creating an expectation in Paris and Saint Petersburg that this might be translated into military assistance, a presumption that the Foreign Office did not wish to encourage.

The need for agreement with France and Russia became more urgent as relations with Germany worsened, largely as a result of its decision in 1897 to implement an ambitious program of naval building. As Germany had a small colonial empire, certainly in comparison with Great Britain, it was difficult for policy makers in Whitehall to see the need for a fleet, which, in European waters, was second only to the Royal Navy.

A revolution in technology took place in 1905–1906, whereby all previous capital ships were made obsolete by the appearance of the Dreadnought battle cruiser, which was faster and more heavily armored than anything seen before. An Anglo–German naval race followed in the remaining years before 1914. The then Liberal government of H. H. Asquith (1908–1916) was forced into heavy expenditures on naval building, which caused bitter rows about cost between the Admiralty and other ministries.

The naval race did not make war between Britain and Germany inevitable, but it was combined with a series of crises when Britain felt bound to support France against Germany. They were focused on Morocco in 1905 and 1911; in each instance, Britain made it clear to the Germans that it supported French authority over Morocco.

The absence of a specific commitment with regard to British land forces was a source of confusion in 1914; however, the assassination of the heir to the Austro-Hungarian throne precipitated a war between Russia and Austria-Hungary and its ally Germany. France could hardly stand by and allow its Russian ally to be crushed, but Britain's only commitment to France was a rather vague naval agreement in 1912. This pact specified that if France concentrated its fleet in the Mediterranean, Great Britain would concentrate its navy in the North Sea and the English Channel. The inference in French eyes was that the Royal Navy would defend their Channel coastline.

It is possible that if the British commitment had remained so limited, Britain would have stayed out of the war. As it was, the Cabinet was bitterly divided about what to do, and the decisive factor was the German decision to invade France via neutral Belgium, avoiding the defenses on the Franco–German frontier. In so doing, Germany broke the 1839 Treaty of London safeguarding Belgian neutrality, to which Britain was a cosignatory. The British government could thus go to war on 4 August 1914, as the defender of a small nation's integrity, although it is possible to argue that, in any case, Britain could not, in the longer run, allow France to be overrun by Germany, which would then be in a position to threaten its trade routes. The logic of classic British foreign policy points in this direction.

THE IMPACT OF WORLD WAR I ON BRITAIN

Involvement in World War I meant abandoning the traditional principle of noninvolvement in continental struggles, although Britain's small army of 100,000 men was dwarfed by those of both its allies. The additional nature of the conflict, which went on to last far longer than any of the belligerent powers expected, meant that Britain had to enlist a large volunteer army and then, from 1916 onward, introduce conscription. Losses were devastating, as 20,000 men died on the first day of the Battle of the Somme, on 1 July 1916, alone.

Diplomacy was a second arm of military strategy for Britain. Russian designs on Constantinople were accepted by the Foreign Office in 1914, to keep Britain's cumbersome eastern ally in the conflict. Extensive concessions were made by the Anglo–French in 1915, to bring Italy into the war against its supposed allies, and the aspirations of the subject races of Austria-Hungary, such as the Czechs and Poles, were encouraged to undermine the war effort of the dual monarchy and its German ally.

Diplomatic horse-trading was most evident in the Middle East. The Ottoman Empire was a real threat to the Suez Canal and British interests in Egypt. It had joined the rival Austro–German alliance in 1914. This enabled Britain to overthrow its traditional policy of supporting the declining Ottoman state. Every diplomatic means was now used to undermine it. In 1915–1916, the British made the McMahon Pledge about Arab independence designed to encourage an Arab uprising against the Ottomans. In 1916, the Sykes–Picot Agreement divided Palestine, Lebanon, Jordan, and Iraq with Britain's ally France. Then, fatefully, in 1917, the then-British foreign secretary, Arthur Balfour, made his famous declaration stating that the Jews could have a national home, but not a state, in Palestine. This was aimed at securing the help of wealthy Zionists for the Allied war effort. The fact that such promises proved to be contradictory did not seem to trouble the British government or the Foreign Office.

World War I was devastating with regard to loss of life, with more than 1 million British and imperial fatalities. The Royal Navy maintained its predominance in the naval struggle against Germany, but Britain's status as a world power was severely undermined. This was a matter of finance, for although Britain borrowed less money than other belligerent powers to pay for its war effort, its national debt in 1919 was 10 times what it had been in 1914. The astronomical cost of World War I meant that even this level of borrowing was not enough to fully finance the war. After 1916, Britain was financially dependent on the United States because the war was costing the state £5 million a day. Two fifths of this amount had to be raised in the United States, a situation only partly assisted by American entry into the war in April 1917. Britain's gold reserves for supporting the pound sterling had fallen so low by this time that an arrangement had to be set for monthly U.S. advances to be made available. Such financial weakness was to have obvious consequences for the conduct of postwar British foreign policy.

BRITISH DIPLOMACY BETWEEN THE WARS

As a victor power over Germany, Austria-Hungary, and Turkey in 1918, Britain had particular aims in the treaty settlement that followed. German naval power had to be broken so that it could no longer threaten Britain. Reparations were to be paid by Germany to Britain and its allies for the cost of the war and the damage done by the Germans to occupied France and Belgium. The British government was insistent that the Germans pay the cost of British war pensions. Last, Germany was to be deprived of its colonies.

These aims were achieved by the efforts of British prime minister David Lloyd George (1916–1922), who sidelined the Foreign Office. Although the German High Seas Fleet scuttled itself at Britain's major naval base, a high level of reparations was fixed, and former German East Africa and South West Africa became mandated territories under the overall control of the League of Nations. This organization was designed to preserve international peace and was the brainchild of President Woodrow Wilson (1913–1921). There were pro-League enthusiasts in Britain, but successive governments approached its inception with a degree of pragmatism, the new Labour Party being more enthusiastic than the Conservatives. The French accepted the concept of the League of Nations with ill grace. Their price was an Anglo–American guarantee of assistance to France if it were attacked by Germany. In the event, both powers reneged on this commitment when the United States refused to either ratify the Treaty of Versailles, which dealt with defeated Germany, or join the League of Nations.

Anglo–American views largely coincided, and, when France and Belgium occupied the industrial area of the Ruhr in 1923, because Germany had defaulted on its reparations payments (the final figure fixed was £6,600,000,000), Britain and the United States opposed such action. The American-sponsored Dawes Plan (1924) and Young Plan (1929) rescheduled German payments and made extensive U.S. loans available to a Germany devastated by hyperinflation in 1923. The U.S. generosity did not extend to loans given to Britain to fund its war effort.

In regards to the global power balance, a new situation faced Britain in the 1930s. Japan was an aggressive expansionist power in the Far East, and, although Britain deplored its annexation of Manchuria in 1931, it, like France and the United States, was not disposed to use military force against the aggressor. The threat to Britain's Far Eastern colonies, including Malaya, Singapore, and Burma, remained obvious, while the League of Nations was discredited by its inability to prevent Japanese aggression.

Italy, too, was a revisionist, expansionist power under the leadership of Benito Mussolini (1922–1935), jealous of Britain's power and influence in the Mediterranean and Africa. Imperialism and fascism went hand in hand, and, in 1935, fascist Italy attacked Ethiopia which was one of only two independent African states. Anglo–French attempts to secure a compromise failed and merely sharpened Mussolini's contempt for what he regarded as a decadent British empire.

This growing atmosphere of international instability caused the British government to set up the Defense Requirements Committee (DRC) in 1933, which had Foreign Office and British Armed Services representatives, as well as representatives from the treasury, as members. The DRC identified Germany as the main threat to the British Empire, followed by Japan, in recognition of the dangerous potency of Adolf Hitler's xenophobic, racist regime (1933–1945), which, in 1933, had already left the League of Nations and the Disarmament Conference in Geneva. If Hitler's early foreign policy demonstrated a degree of subtlety by, for example, making a nonaggression pact with Poland in 1934, his desire to overthrow the postwar peace settlement was clear enough. Led by Stanley Baldwin (premier, 1935–1937), the British government was particularly alarmed by Germany's announcement of its illegal peacetime air force in 1935, as well as the gathering pace of German aerial rearmament. The pace of international German illegality also increased. In March 1936, Hitler reoccupied the demilitarized Rhineland in breach of international treaties, and he went on to annex Austria in 1938, action clearly forbidden by the Treaty of Versailles.

The British response to this German aggression under prime ministers Stanley Baldwin and Neville Chamberlain (1937–1940) was one of appeasement—the term appeasement has become one of the most pejorative in modern British history—but on one level it was a pragmatic response to the threat from three great powers—Germany, Italy, and Japan—simultaneously. Britain suffered from imperial overstretch in the eyes of the Whitehall establishment, with its great empire vulnerable to a three-pronged attack, which, if coordinated, would be catastrophic. The appeasers believed that the answer was to secure an accommodation with at least one of its potential enemies. They knew that the United States would not assist Britain, distrusted Communist Russia, and doubted the reliability of Britain's sole great-power ally, France.

The zenith of appeasement came in September 1938, when Hitler demanded the cession of the German-speaking areas of Czechoslovakia, and war briefly seemed inevitable. Instead, the Munich Conference set up by Chamberlain ceded the Czech Sudetenland to Germany, and so avoided a war, which Chamberlain and his colleagues believed Britain was in no position to fight. It lacked aerial defenses, and its tiny army was in no position to assist the Czechs, even if its French ally were inclined to do so (and it was not). Munich has remained highly controversial since 1938, because, whatever Chamberlain's intention, which was honorable, it did not ultimately prevent war. Within the Foreign Office itself, there was some skepticism about Chamberlain's policy, but the British Armed Services chiefs broadly agreed with it, providing that the rearmament program was accelerated. The treasury had anxieties that Britain's recovery from the economic slump of the early 1930s would be put at risk by excessive rearmament, and these worries were shared by Chamberlain, a former chancellor of the exchequer. But, in 1939, Britain was spending more than 21 percent of its gross national product (GNP) on defense, only slightly less than Germany.

Hitler destroyed the assumptions behind appeasement. Concessions achieved nothing, and, six months later, in March 1939, independent Czechoslovakia ceased to exist. This brought about a major change in British foreign policy, with the Chamberlain government offering a guarantee of assistance to Poland, and, subsequently, to Rumania, Greece, and Turkey, if those states were attacked by Germany. More important, however, Britain guaranteed only the continued existence of Poland, not its existing frontiers.

Since Britain had refused to give such a guarantee to Czechoslovakia a year before, this diplomatic revolution had one obvious flaw. Assistance to Poland could not be effectively rendered without Soviet assistance, and Poland would not allow the Red Army on its territory. Britain abandoned its policy of treating the Union of Soviet Socialist Republics (USSR) as a pariah and joined France in sending a mission to Moscow. In August 1939, it failed to secure an agreement whereby the two sides would become allies, and, shortly afterward, Germany and the Soviet Union signed the infamous nonaggression pact, which divided Poland between the two great powers.

The Nazi–Soviet Pact removed the Soviet Union from the equation as far as Hitler was concerned, and, on 1 September 1939, he attacked the Poles ostensibly to reclaim lost territory, but, in reality, with a much more sinister agenda. After a two-day delay, Chamberlain was obliged to honor his guarantee to the Poles on 3 September, as were the French. Britain found itself in a world war for the second time in 25 years. Japanese behavior beginning in 1937, when they launched a full-blown invasion of China, suggested that Britain's resources in the Far East would also soon be tested.

BRITAIN AND WORLD WAR II

Great Britain entered World War II with the assumption that an economic blockade based on superior Anglo–French naval power would bring down the Nazi regime within two years. The premise was that lack of foreign currency and essential raw materials would so weaken Germany that this would be inevitable. An additional hope was that internal opposition might remove Hitler, and the dictator did, in fact, only narrowly avoid assassination in November 1939. But it proved to be a false hope, and the period between late September, when Poland was defeated, and April 1940, was notable for this lack of activity, which became known as the "phoney war."

This phase ended in April 1940, when Hitler invaded both Denmark and Norway. Anglo–French aid failed to save Norway, and it was an irony that it was the bungled Norway campaign, which Winston Churchill had organized as first lord of the Admiralty, that brought down the Chamberlain government. Churchill became prime minister on 10 May, and he became the man who ran the British war effort.

On that very day, Hitler invaded France and the Low Countries, and, within six weeks, his forces had defeated France and driven the British Expeditionary Force off the continent. By June 1940, Great Britain was facing the most desperate crisis in its entire history. Contrary to contemporary propaganda, Churchill did consider a possible negotiated settlement with Germany, but he reasoned, unlike some of his colleagues, that Hitler was not to be trusted and it made more sense to continue to fight.

His ultimate hope was that the United States could be persuaded to aid Britain, and, half American himself, he cultivated his relationship with President Franklin D. Roosevelt. American isolationism precluded any U.S. military involvement, and Britain fought off the aerial assault by the German air force.

On 17 September 1940, Hitler called off his planned invasion of the British Isles, choosing instead to step up the blitz on British cities in the winter of 1940–1941. The period between September 1940 and May 1941 was the darkest in modern British history, as Britain's cities were pounded, its ships were sunk in large numbers by German submarines, and it was defeated on land by the Axis powers in North Africa and Crete.

In June 1941, Churchill seized the opportunity presented by Germany's attack on the USSR to offer all the assistance he could to Joseph Stalin. Many brave seamen died taking supplies on the Arctic route to Murmansk, eliciting little gratitude from Stalin and his government. As always, however, Churchill looked westward, and he had as reward the Atlantic Charter, which emerged from his meeting with Roosevelt at Placentia Bay, Newfoundland. This was in August 1941, and, months later, on 7 December, Japan's attack on Pearl Harbor brought the United States into the World War II. This was just as well as far as Britain was concerned, as it was in no position to defend the Far East from Japanese aggression. Japan had already taken advantage of France's collapse in 1940, to dominate the colonial administration in Indochina, and it intensified the war in China, too. After Pearl Harbor, there was a run of Japanese victories in Malaya, Burma, the Philippines, and the Dutch East Indies. The fall of Singapore, in February 1942, was an especially devastating blow to British prestige and power.

Britain now had powerful allies indeed, and Churchill reluctantly recognized that they were more powerful than it was itself. Thus, the remainder of the war saw Britain having to adjust its wartime objectives to accommodate Stalin and Roosevelt. Stalin criticized the Anglo–Americans for not immediately opening a second front in France and taking the pressure off the hardpressed Red Army. The American generals were prepared to launch an invasion as early as 1942 or 1943, whereas the British preferred to target North Africa and Italy, the soft underbelly in theory of the Axis alliance.

In 1942, the British were the senior partners, and their argument won the day, although for many Americans defeating Japan was a greater priority. Financially, Britain was overwhelmingly dependent on the Americans, and the Lend–Lease Bill in 1941 allowed it to purchase much-needed war materials in the United States (Britain ultimately borrowed $27 billion from its ally). This financial dependence was speedily followed by military dependence as the Americans also poured men, aircraft, and ships into the war. Both allies pounded Germany with their bombers from 1942 onward, the Royal Air Force by night, and the Americans by day. In the Pacific, the Americans were the kingpins, devastating Japan's naval power at Midway in 1942. Roosevelt was unsympathetic to the idea of restoring Britain's imperial power, since, for him, Churchill was a hopelessly old-fashioned Edwardian imperialist. He was largely correct, as Churchill continued to obstruct the creation of Indian independence to the disgust of his coalition partners in the Labour Party, who had, through their wartime leaders Clement Attlee and Aneurin Bevan, organized the working class for victory.

The Anglo–American invasion of France ultimately came on 6 June 1944, at a time when the Red Army was already pressing in on Germany's eastern borders. Although there was doughty German resistance in the west, Hitler's last counteroffensive in the Ardennes, in December 1944, merely used up his last reserves. The Allies pressed in on Germany from all sides, and the end of the European war came on 8 May 1945. In the Far East, relentless U.S. pressure destroyed Japan's cities and captured the territory so rapidly lost in 1941–1942. Britain regained Burma after tough fighting, but it took the dropping of two atomic bombs on Hiroshima and Nagasaki in August to end the world war. The decision to use the terrible weapon was made by President Harry S. Truman, who had replaced Roosevelt as president in April. Churchill himself did not survive the conflict either. In July 1945, his Conservative Party was heavily defeated at the polls by the Labour Party, which fancied that it might deal more easily with Britain's devious eastern ally, Stalin.

BRITAIN AND THE COLD WAR

Churchill had worried about the long-term ambitions of the Soviet Union, even if he could not avoid a certain sneaking admiration for its dictator, Stalin. His anxieties were justified. Britain had gone to war in 1939, for Poland's integrity, whereas Stalin had treacherously divided it up with Germany. Stalin had no intention of allowing an independent, free postwar Poland to reemerge in 1945, and, in October 1944, he had been inadvertently encouraged by the British prime minister, who appeared to accept Soviet claims to predominance in Eastern Europe. Poland nevertheless remained a sore point at the February 1945 Yalta Conference, even if the great powers agreed upon such matters as the establishment of a new United Nations Organization (UN), with its headquarters in New York.

The future of Germany was more easily settled. In July 1945, the Potsdam Agreement arranged its partition by the four great powers (France was also included). This meant that a Britain already crippled by vast war debts was obliged to provide a large occupation force for its sector of Germany. Britain, which had cooperated to the evolution of the atomic bomb through the Manhattan Project during World War II, also invested large sums in the development of its own atomic bomb.

This task was deemed essential because Labour Party hopes of a cordial relationship with Stalin proved illusionary. The Labour government did not need Churchill's famous "iron curtain" speech of 1946 to highlight the Soviet threat, and the government's tough new foreign secretary, Ernest Bevin, a strongly anti-Communist former trade union leader, tolerated no nonsense from Stalin's henchman Vyacheslav Molotov at international conferences. In fact, events spoke for themselves, as a "Cold War" developed between the East and West. The states of Central Europe and Eastern Europe, ending with Czechoslovakia in February 1948, turned Communist, with governments dominated by Moscow. Bevin saw it as his task to construct anti-Communist bulwarks in Western Europe, starting with the Anglo–French Treaty of 1947. He and Prime Minister Attlee reacted favorably to the 1947 Marshall Plan, whereby generous U.S. aid helped shore up a stricken British economy. Yet, they had been profoundly disappointed by America's abrupt decision to end Lend–Lease in 1945, although Britain's great economist John Maynard Keynes had been able to negotiate a low-interest loan of $3.75 billion.

The German settlement had made Berlin a four-power city perched precariously inside the Soviet Sector, and, in 1948, Stalin tried to force the Western allies out by severing road and rail links. Britain played its full part in feeding the West Berliners for 11 months, and Bevin reacted to the further Soviet threat by sponsoring the North Atlantic Treaty Organization (NATO) in 1949. Stalin called off his siege of West Berlin the same year.

Another alarming development in 1949 was the coming to power of the Chinese Communist Party under Mao Zedong, with its potential threat to the crown colony of Hong Kong. The British reaction was pragmatic rather than ideological, as the United States tended to be. Thus, the United States would not extend diplomatic recognition to the Communist People's Republic of China (PRC), whereas Britain did so.

In fact, the next Cold War crisis, which affected Britain, involved a surrogate of the Soviet Union and the new regime in Beijing. In June 1950, the forces of Communist North Korea invaded the South. A UN force under U.S. leadership was immediately sent to Korea. Britain sent troops as part of this contingent, which remained in Korea until stalemate ended the war in 1953. It was alarmed by saber rattling by the U.S. commander in chief, Douglas MacArthur, who seemed to be prepared to use nuclear weapons against the USSR and PRC.

Nevertheless, Britain's Cold War relationship with the United States grew ever closer. During the 1948–1949 Berlin Crisis, Bevin had, in fact, invited the United States to send B-29 bombers to Britain. This was an extraordinary derogation from British sovereignty, as critics pointed out. Never before in peacetime had a foreign power been allowed bases on British territory without parliamentary consent. The dependence increased in September 1954, when U.S. nuclear weapons began to be stationed in Britain. By 1957, Britain had its own hydrogen bomb (following a successful atom bomb test in 1952), but the state conspicuously failed to evolve a reliable delivery system, and an American one, Polaris, had to be purchased.

Churchill, who returned to power in 1951, believed that he would be able to talk to the new Soviet leadership after Stalin died in March 1953; however, he was persistently prevented from engaging in summit diplomacy with Moscow by the Americans. Only well away from the heartland of the Cold War in Europe was Britain able to assert a degree of independence, namely over Indochina. There, the French were defeated by the Viet Minh in 1954, and the Geneva Conference partitioned the country along the 17th parallel. This was a triumph in the teeth of U.S. opposition for Bevin's successor, Anthony Eden (1951–1955), who was prepared to accept the likelihood of a victory for the Ho Chi Minh's Communists in the All-Vietnam elections. The Americans set themselves against such a solution by invoking the domino theory, which predicted a Communist takeover in Southeast Asia if Indochina was allowed to go Communist.

By now the Cold War was truly global. In the Middle East, inept British policy allowed Egyptian president Jamal Abd al Nasser to claim a victory when, in November 1956, an ill-advised Anglo–French invasion had to be aborted after U.S. financial pressure and a refusal by President Dwight D. Eisenhower to support his primary ally, even at the UN. As a result of the Suez fiasco, the USSR obtained influence in Egypt and Syria, but, despite dire predictions, British influence remained significant in Jordan and the Persian Gulf. Suez had undoubtedly shown that Britain was now a second-class power unable to mount military operations without American approval. The 1957 Defence White Paper recognized Britain's weakness and the untenable spending of 10 percent of Britain's GNP on defense. Dependence on the United States was even more evident to Eden's half-American successor, Prime Minister Harold Macmillan (1957–1963). It was Macmillan who persuaded President John F. Kennedy to sell Polaris submarines to Britain in 1962.

Macmillan also presided over an agonizing reappraisal of Britain's global position. Decolonization was well underway by the late 1950s, with Ghana being the first of a wave of African colonies to secure independence in 1957. The Commonwealth of British former colonies was clearly not going to be a meaningful substitute for the Empire, and the "special relationship" with the United States had Britain very much as the junior partner. Macmillan recognized that the old imperial phase was dead in a celebrated speech in Cape Town, South Africa, in February 1960.

Macmillan's successor, Sir Alec Douglas-Home (1963–1964), followed Macmillan's Cold War policy. The new Labour prime minister, Harold Wilson (1964–1970), found himself in a new scenario. The Cold War situation in Europe did little to prevent the Soviet Union's intervention in Czechoslovakia (1968) aimed at crushing reform. This was strongly condemned by the Wilson government. In the Far East, however, a deepening U.S. involvement in Vietnam put Wilson under pressure to make a British military commitment there, which he steadfastly refused to do, as did his Labour successor, James Callaghan (1976–1979).

Margaret Thatcher (1979–1990), who followed Callaghan, took a tough line in relations with the Soviet Union, heavily criticizing the Soviet invasion of Afghanistan in 1979, which proved to be a long-term disaster for Moscow. She was quick, however, to recognize that Mikhail Gorbachev, the new general secretary of the Soviet Communist Party in 1985, was someone it would be possible to work with. Thatcher later claimed that the ultimate collapse of the USSR was a result of the tough line that she and President Ronald Reagan (1981–1989) had taken toward the Soviet Union during the period from 1979–1985. She was essentially traditional, nonetheless. When the Communist satellite states collapsed in 1989, her negative reaction to the prospect of German reunification was exemplified by the convening of a conference of right-wing historians and journalists to confirm her anti-German prejudices, a product of growing up in wartime Britain.

Thatcher's great hero was Winston Churchill, but she led a Britain with much greater constraints on its power than she sometimes seemed to appreciate. She had seen the nuclear alliance with the Americans as crucial. In October 1983, American cruise missiles were allowed into British bases, and, in 1986, Thatcher secured a promise from President Reagan that Britain's Trident submarine fleet would be modernized. Thatcher was alarmed when Reagan appeared to be trying to eliminate nuclear weapons in summit talks with Gorbachev that same year. Throughout this period, the Campaign for Nuclear Disarmament strongly demonstrated against the U.S. nuclear presence in Britain, and unilateral nuclear disarmament was official Labour policy in the 1983 general election, in which it was heavily defeated by the Conservative Party because a right-wing faction of the party under Roy Jenkins had broken away and set up the Social Democratic Party.

BRITAIN AND EUROPEAN INTEGRATION

The solution adopted by Macmillan in the 1960s to achieve a new British international role was to apply for membership to the European Economic Community (EEC) in July 1961. Britain's relationship with postwar Europe already had a checkered history. Churchill appeared to encourage a united Europe in 1946, but he never envisaged British membership in it. The Labour Party, in power at the time, was not willing to join the European Coal and Steel Community (ECSC), which evolved into the EEC, when asked to do so in 1951. Indeed, in 1958, Britain founded the rival European Free Trade Association, in a clear attempt to sabotage the EEC, but half of its citizens were British, and it lacked the economic clout of the EEC, with its six members and larger industrial and demographic resources.

President Kennedy encouraged the British application to the EEC, reasoning that European unity would dovetail with the existing defense structure provided by NATO. He and Macmillan reckoned without France's formidable president, Charles de Gaulle, who had never forgiven the Anglo–Americans for allegedly ignoring French interests in World War II. In January 1963, de Gaulle vetoed Britain's application to join the EEC, wrecking Macmillan's European strategy with a stroke, although Commonwealth countries were relieved at not being faced by a common European tariff wall, with Great Britain inside it.

It wasn't until 1972 that Prime Minister Edward Heath (1970–1974) secured British membership. He, the most pro-European and least enthusiastic Atlanticist among Britain's postwar premiers, was fortunate that de Gaulle had resigned in 1969. When Harold Wilson became prime minister again in February 1974, internal Labour Party feuding about Europe obliged him to call a referendum about Britain's EEC membership. The Foreign Office and pro-EEC big business sponsored a campaign that produced a decisive "yes" vote in June 1975.

Storms lay ahead, especially when Margaret Thatcher became prime minister in May 1979. Thatcher was a robust, many thought chauvinistic, leader who placed British interests first, especially where British contributions to EEC funding were concerned. In 1968, her strong pro-American stance produced a cabinet crisis regarding the Westland Helicopter Affair, and she antagonized other European leaders. Other Conservative leaders enforced her resignation in 1990, and British–European relations appeared to be set for a more peaceful phase under Prime Minister John Major (1990–1997).

This proved to be an illusion. Britain's membership in the European Exchange Rate Mechanism (ERM), whereby the value of the pound was linked to that of the German mark, was a disaster, and it resulted in financial meltdown in 1992, with Britain being forced to withdraw from the ERM. Thereafter, Major was beset by internal Conservative feuding over European issues.

The Labour Party returned to power in May 1997, and its leader, Tony Blair, had the reputation of being pro-European; however, he was unable, or unwilling, to secure British membership of the common European currency, arguably as a result of the notoriously anti-euro posture of the then-chancellor of the exchequer, Gordon Brown. Successive Conservative leaders after Major were strongly anti-euro.

Blair also made a tactical error in allowing unrestricted immigration from the new Eastern European members of the EEC, Britain being one of only three existing EEC members to do so. When he stood down as prime minister in 2007, immigration had become a controversial issue, and the cause of the euro was hopelessly lost, as his successor, Brown, who was defeated at the polls in May 2010, was a persistent critic of the common currency. Throughout the entire period of British membership in what was now known as the European Union (EU), Britain's membership in the organization remained highly controversial, with prime ministers and their parties changing opinions and policies with baffling rapidity. British policy toward Europe appeared to be confused, first by the countervailing importance of the "special relationship," and, second, by a perception that Great Britain—unlike other European powers—had a distinctive global role.

POST–COLD WAR BRITAIN

The Heath government of 1970–1974 was notable for its pro-Europeanism, but its most serious problem was the Oil Price Crisis, sparked by the October 1973 Yom Kippur War, when Arab oil producers began to use the price of oil as an economic weapon. Even with the oil available from the North Sea, by 1976, Britain found itself in a serious economic crisis that required intervention by the International Monetary Fund and the imposition of serious austerity measures. A persistent problem in Northern Ireland, with a bloody campaign of bombings and shootings by the Irish Republican Army, plagued the Labour governments of Harold Wilson and James Callaghan. Culturally, Britain might have seemed to be a swinging society in the 1960s and 1970s, but, in other ways, it was deemed to be the sick man of Europe, with poor industrial relations and inflationary pressures on the economy.

The election of Margaret Thatcher marked something of a watershed, both because it brought an end to the Keynesian consensus in economic policy, and because her conduct of foreign policy was both robust and nationalistic. It sometimes appeared maladroit. In retrospect, Thatcher's relatively permissive attitude to the apartheid regime in South Africa in the 1980s, for example, had a negative impact in the Third World. Yet, she received considerable kudos for her handling of the Falklands Crisis in 1982, when British forces recovered control of the remote islands in the South Atlantic from Argentina.

U.S. satellite intelligence was important here and emphasized the strength of Thatcher's relationship with President Ronald Reagan, which demonstrated the importance the "special relationship" still had for Downing Street. In October 1983, however, the vulnerability of Britain was highlighted when Reagan decided to invade the Commonwealth island of Grenada, ostensibly to remove a leftist regime, and did not bother to consult Thatcher first. Even at the time of the Falklands War, elements in the Reagan administration favored supporting Argentina in its long-standing territorial dispute with Great Britain. British leaders seemingly did not realize that the "special relationship" was never as important for Washington as it was for London.

The Middle East had always been an area of key interest for Britain, which consistently supported conservative monarchies in the Gulf region against more radical regimes in Syria, Iran, and Iraq. When the Iraqi dictator Saddam Hussein invaded Kuwait in 1991, Britain thus figured prominently in the 33-nation force led by the United States and authorized by the UN, which drove the Iraqis out after just four days.

The Anglo–Americans may have subsequently regretted that they did not complete the job by driving on to Baghdad and bringing down Hussein's regime. There was no UN mandate to do so, and Prime Minister John Major put forth the idea of "safe havens" for the Iraqi Kurds, who had been encouraged by President George H. W. Bush to revolt against Hussein.

Interventionism was popular in the 1990s, especially with Prime Minister Tony Blair (1997–2007), who secured NATO intervention against the Serbian dictator Slobodan Milosevic when ethnic cleansing threatened the largely Muslim province of Kosovo. Blair's critics later claimed that the 1999 war against Serbia went to his head, especially as a second intervention by Britain to end civil war in Sierra Leone also proved successful. Like Thatcher, Blair was a strong supporter of the American alliance, and he was quick to offer support when jihadist terrorists attacked the Twin Towers in New York City, and the Pentagon in Arlington, Virginia, with airliners in 2001, killing 3,000 people. The 9/11 terrorist attacks dominated British foreign policy for the next decade. Britain supported and took part in the 2001 invasion of Afghanistan and still had 10,000 troops stationed there in 2010. Blair also supported the far more controversial attack on Iraq ordered by President George H. W. Bush in March 2003. Blair's former foreign secretary, Robin Cook (1997–2001), resigned from his position as leader of the House of Commons. Accusations about the illegality of the war pursued Blair long after he resigned in 2007.

Blair was a smooth publicist for his government, a skill that his successor, Gordon Brown, lacked. He could, however, claim credit for uniting the international community to deal with the devastating financial crisis provided by the U.S. subprime mortgage scandal in 2007. Brown's action was arguably the most important contribution by a British premier in decades, as he courageously took failing banks into partial state ownership. Yet, it did not save Brown from electoral defeat in May 2010, when he was replaced as prime minister by David Cameron of the Conservative Party as head of the first official coalition since 1945, in this instance with the Liberal Democrats.

Cameron came into office pledging to avoid the "liberal interventionism" of Tony Blair evident in Kosovo and Iraq. He promised to pull British troops out of Afghanistan and was resolutely Eurosceptic, refusing to give British cash to the troubled economies of such European partners as Greece. An exception was made for Ireland, so closely linked to Britain, which was granted a £4 billion loan.

Cameron seemed to be shifting his ground again when the North African and Middle Eastern crisis of January to March 2011 resulted in the fall of the Tunisian and Egyptian dictatorships. The draconian repression of his own people by the Libyan dictator Muammar al-Gaddafi persuaded Cameron that a "no-fly zone," used with some success in Kurdish Iraq in the 1990s, would stop bombing in Libya. The only one of Britain's EU partners to agree was France. The United States was also initially unenthusiastic, and Cameron was accused of being inconsistent. Coordinating foreign policy with his Liberal Democrat coalition partners, who had long been enthusiastic Europeans, also posed problems.

On 20 March 2011, Cameron succeeded in securing a UN resolution that sanctioned a no-fly zone in Libya. It was cosponsored by France and Lebanon, although China and Russia abstained on the UN Security Council. American and Canadian backing was forthcoming and crucially the agreement of the Arab League. On 21 March, Cameron's interventionist policy in Libya was overwhelmingly endorsed in the House of Commons by a vote of 557 to 13.

In the latter stages of 2011, British foreign policy was focused on the sovereign debt crisis, which afflicted the EU, especially the Eurozone. Ireland and Portugal received "bailouts" from the European Central Bank, but Great Britain, not a member of the Eurozone, did not contribute. A crisis point was reached on 8–9 December 2011, when, at a meeting in Brussels regarding a fiscal treaty, Cameron declined to sign the agreement. There was a good deal of acrimony between Cameron; the French president, Nicolas Sarkozy; and the German chancellor, Angela Merkel. Britain believed that the fiscal package might adversely affect its financial services industry. Relations with the Eurozone remained frosty into 2012. Greece was the center of the financial crisis, and the British government was impatient with Eurozone attempts to deal with the Greeks. In May 2012, a general election in Greece favored parties that opposed the EU austerity program. At the same time, the newly elected French president, François Hollande, differed with Cameron about the need for growth within the EU and a financial transaction tax, which Britain bitterly opposed. When the Greeks fixed a second election for 17 June, Cameron urged voters to treat it as a referendum about whether Greece should stay in the Euro, advice that was not welcomed in Greece. The overall impact of the crisis in Britain was to sharpen anti-EU sentiment. This was especially true in the Conservative Party. Polls showed that almost to 70 percent of party members wanting to leave the EU altogether. Resentment against a (perceived) loss of sovereignty to the EU had been growing since the fierce internal Conservative debates of the 1990s. This reflected a general anti-European hostility in Great Britain.

The other great issue in 2012 was Syria. Britain had taken part in the successful removal of Colonel Muammar al-Gaddafi in 2011. The operation had seemed to be an example of what Tony Blair had called "principled interventionism" in 1999. Syria, where the government of Bashar al-Assad had been massacring its people since March 2011, proved to be a different matter. Britain favored using the UN Security Council against Assad, but it was hamstrung by the use of the veto by Russia and China. Following an especially bloody massacre of women and children in Houla, Britain (and its NATO allies) ordered Syrian diplomats to leave on 29 May. Foreign secretary William Hague expressed his government's outrage, but also its impotence, unless force could be used. Syria demonstrated the frailty of what had been called the Blair Doctrine.

A

ABERDEEN LORD (1784–1860). Lord Aberdeen was Britain's prime minister in the early part of the Crimean War from 1854–1855, when Britain went to war to defend the Ottoman Turkish Empire from Russian aggression. He disliked war and was criticized for his unenthusiastic leadership in contrast to that of his successor, Lord **Henry John Palmerston**, a much more robust leader who brought Britain to victory in 1856. Aberdeen was more successful as **foreign secretary** during the Tory administration of 1844–1846, when he tried to avoid the saber-rattling of predecessors in the past, especially by improving relations between the French and the British.

ACHESON, DEAN (1893–1971). Dean Acheson is best remembered for his remark in 1962 that, "Great Britain had lost an empire and has not yet found a role." This suggested skepticism about Great Britain, which did not really represent what Acheson stood for. When, on 21 February 1947, Britain's **foreign secretary, Ernest Bevin**, told the **United States** that it could no longer provide aid to **Greece** and **Turkey**, it was Acheson, as undersecretary of state in the **Harry S. Truman** administration, who persuaded Congress to support what became known as the **Truman Doctrine**, whereby $8,400 million was pumped into those states.

Acheson, who went on to become secretary of state from 1949–1953, also worked with Bevin to set up the **North Atlantic Treaty Organization**, and at the onset of the **Korean War** in 1950. By the time of his celebrated remarks in 1962, Acheson was acting in an advisory capacity in the **John F. Kennedy** administration (1961–1963), but by then it could be argued that Great Britain had indeed found a role, for, in 1961, Prime Minister **Harold Macmillan** applied to join the **European Economic Community** to mitigate Britain's declining imperial role and provide a counterweight to the "**special relationship**" with the United States. By that time, it was realized that the **Commonwealth** could not be a real substitute for the **British Empire** in trading or political terms.

ADMIRALTY. The Admiralty is the senior department in the administration of the British armed forces responsible for the Royal Navy, dating back to the time of King Charles II in the 17th century. It is now subsumed under the overall umbrella of the **Ministry of Defense**. During the 18th century, notably at the time of the American War of Independence, corruption was at risk of jeopardizing the Admiralty's effectiveness and British naval power, but, for much of Britain's modern history, the so-called "Senior Service" was an awesome instrument of power. Failures of perception by the Admiralty, which included a curious unwillingness to introduce convoy systems during both **World War I** and **World War II**, could prove to be extremely dangerous for an island nation so dependent on its trade routes. Responsibility for the Admiralty was traditionally shared between the first lord of the Admiralty, a civilian, and the first sea lord, a professional sailor. The Royal Marines, a famously tough and professional element in the Royal Navy, provides the Admiralty with a potent land force to back up the surface fleet.

AFGHANISTAN. Great Britain's concern about **India** in the 19th century meant that British foreign policy also focused on its northern neighbor, Afghanistan, at a time when imperial **Russia** was expanding across Central Asia. In the 1830s and 1840s, Britain's long-standing **foreign secretary**, Lord **Henry John Palmerston** (1835–1841), indulged in what became known as the "Great Game," whereby Britain and Russia struggled to assert their influence. Palmerston was involved in replacing the native Afghan ruler with a more pliable ally from the Indian Punjab, but, as always, foreign interference provoked Afghan resentment. When Palmerston left the **Foreign Office** in 1841, the British were forced to withdraw their army from the Afghan capital of Kabul. In the retreat, the British were massacred by Afghan tribesmen. Just one man out of 15,000 survived. In the years that followed, the British focus on Afghanistan weakened, but the coming to political power of the great Conservative prime minister **Benjamin Disraeli**, in 1874, sharpened British interest, because his government suspected the Russians of intriguing at the court of the Afghan ruler or Emir. The previous British policy of leaving the Afghans well alone was abandoned, and, in September 1878, the new viceroy of India, Lord Lytton, tried to invade Afghanistan. The British were repulsed, and, although Disraeli believed that Lytton had exceeded his brief, he thought British honor was at stake and ordered a full-scale invasion of Afghanistan in November 1878. Britain maintained control, but, in September 1879, its envoy in Kabul was murdered. British reprisals followed, and Lytton wanted to break Afghanistan into a series of smaller states. Others wished to annex the country outright. Disraeli's defeat in the general election of April 1880 prevented either policy from being adopted. The new Liberal prime minister, **William Gladstone**, appointed a new viceroy, Lord Ripon, who guaranteed Afghanistan against foreign invasion, but only at the price of British control of its foreign policy. Afghanistan effectively became a British protectorate, but affairs there continued to be turbulent in the 1880s and 1890s. As far as the British were concerned, there was the looming concern that the Afghans might support a Russian invasion of India.

This threat only disappeared in 1907, when Russia joined Britain and **France** in the so-called Triple Entente, although British anxieties reappeared between **World War I** and **World War II**, when the new Soviet Union encouraged revolution in Asia and Japan's aggressive foreign policy threatened India in the 1930s. An actual Japanese attempt to invade India was beaten off in 1944, and Afghanistan was not involved in World War II. Its native rulers remained in power until 1978, when a Soviet-backed Communist coup overthrew President Daud Khan. By 1979, the Communist government itself was under threat from tribal opposition, and Soviet military help had to be sought. This intervention was strongly condemned by British prime minister **Margaret Thatcher**, but Britain did not follow the U.S. example of boycotting the Moscow Olympic Games in 1980. A crucial development in Afghanistan in the 1980s was the appearance of the Mujahidin (holy warriors), who waged guerrilla-style warfare against the Russians and their Communist surrogates. Foreign Islamists flowed into the country, including the soon-to-be-notorious Saudi Osama bin Laden, who benefited from U.S. military aid.

The end of the **Cold War** in 1989 brought about the withdrawal of Soviet troops, although the Communist puppet regime in Afghanistan struggled onward until 1992. Tribal rivalries sparked a civil war in which the victors were the Islamic fundamentalists known as the Taliban (literally "students"), who captured Kabul in 1996, and overthrew the Communist government. Some estimates suggest that approximately 1 million people died in the Afghan civil war. Even then, Taliban authority was not absolute, but the involvement allowed bin Laden and his new al-Qaeda organization to maintain bases in Afghanistan.

Following the jihadist attacks on the **United States** on 11 September 2001, the Americans and British launched an invasion of Afghanistan. The first phase of the operation was a concentrated bombing campaign, before a land invasion was launched under the code name "Operation Enduring Freedom." The object of the operation was to drive out and destroy the **terrorist** network of Osama bin Laden and al-Qaeda who had launched the surprise attacks in New York and Virginia. A large coalition of states, including **Australia**, **Canada**, France, **Germany**, **Italy**, and **Japan**, was assembled to support the U.S. action. British' prime minister **Tony Blair** was forthright in his support of the Afghanistan campaign and President **George W. Bush**.

The campaign proved to be difficult, and, in December 2001, the **United Nations (UN)** authorized the creation of an International Security Assistance

Force (ISAF) led by the **North Atlantic Treaty Organization (NATO)** to help the government of Afghanistan, which had been set up to replace the Taliban. By 2010, Britain had 10,000 troops in Afghanistan, which Prime Minister **David Cameron** pledged to keep there until 2014. Britain had been largely responsible for military operations in the province of Helmand, where its forces suffered major losses.

Considerable efforts were made by Great Britain, the United States, and UN to improve Afghan living standards and secure the position of Western-style democracy, supported by their NATO allies. In 2006, NATO was fighting a large guerrilla-style force, with the British being held responsible for the Helmand province, but, by 2010–2011, this had changed, and the Taliban had lost their safe havens around Kandahar. They had evolved into a solely terrorist organization. The British field commander, General James Bucknall, thought that Kabul was a safer capital than its **Pakistan** equivalent, Islamabad, although in December 2011, he conceded that Afghan security was still fragile. Britain is still committed to remain in Afghanistan until 2014, and it and its NATO allies remain concerned about the level of corruption associated with the incumbent Afghan president, Hamid Karzai. An ominous development was the appearance of Sunni-Shi'ite sectarianism in 2011.

ALEXANDER, DOUGLAS (1967–). The current shadow foreign secretary, Douglas Alexander is the Labour member of Parliament for Paisley and Renfrewshire South. He was educated at Edinburgh University and the University of Pennsylvania, before briefly practicing law in Scotland. Elected to Parliament in 1997, Alexander was then involved in organizing his party's campaign for the general election of 2001. After Labour's victory, **Tony Blair** appointed him minister of state, with responsibility for commerce and competitiveness at the Department of Trade and Industry (DTI), between June 2001–May 2002. He then moved to the Cabinet Office (May 2002–June 2003), before making a further transition as minister of state for trade at DTI. This post carried a parallel responsibility at the **Foreign and Common-wealth Office (FCO)**. The FCO link continued after Labour's third victory in the 2005 election, when Alexander was made minister of state for Europe at the FCO. As someone with close links to chancellor of the exchequer, **Gordon Brown**, he was not an enthusiast for the euro. Further promotions followed. Alexander was secretary of state for transport, while also acting as secretary of state for Scotland (both in 2006). When Brown became prime minister on 27 June 2007, he made Alexander secretary of state for international development, giving Alexander the experience that makes him an excellent foreign-secretary-in-waiting.

Unfortunately for Alexander, Labour's electoral loss in May 2010 put a stop to his advancement. His sister, Wendy, briefly served as Labour chief minister in Scotland's devolved assembly until 2008. On 20 January 2011, Alexander was made shadow secretary of state for foreign and commonwealth affairs by Labour leader **Ed Miliband**.

ALL SOULS COLLEGE, OXFORD. All Souls College, Oxford, is a constituent college of Oxford University, but one without undergraduates. It became an intellectual home for politicians, senior academics, and other members of the British establishment. In the 1930s, the institution was wrongly credited with influencing the adoption of British appeasement policy, partly because such leading members of the government as Edward Wood, Viscount Halifax (foreign secretary, 1938–1940), were fellows of the college. *See also* HALIFAX, LORD.

ALSACE-LORRAINE. These two easterly French provinces were annexed from **France** by **Germany** in 1871, and only returned after Germany's defeat in **World War I**. In 1940, they were again incorporated directly into the German state, before returning permanently to French administration in 1945.

AMERICAN BASES IN BRITAIN. Since 1948, the **United States** has maintained a number of air bases in Great Britain, an unprecedented situation in peacetime. There had, of course, been a large number of U.S. servicemen stationed in Britain during **World War II**. The explanation for this situation lay with the onset of the **Cold War** between the Soviet Union and the West, and, in particular, the **Berlin Blockade** in 1948. British **foreign secretary Ernest Bevin** asked President **Harry S. Truman's** administration to send B-29 bombers to Britain. The actual decision to allow the American bombers to land at bases in Britain was made at a secret Cabinet session on 28 June 1948, when ministers, led by Prime Minister **Clement Attlee**, rubber-stamped Bevin's request. This decision, made without reference to Parliament, was, at least in theory, unconstitutional and highly controversial. The first American Strategic Air Command on British soil was subsequently established at RAF Lakenheath, in Suffolk, yet the British had no control over the use of U.S. nuclear bombers flying from its soil. There were estimated to be more than 100 American bases in Britain by the 1980s. The rationale behind Britain's policy was put forward in a **Foreign Office** memorandum in 1950, which maintained that the role as an advanced air base must be accepted as the price of a continual U.S. commitment to the defense of Western Europe.

The American presence became an issue in British domestic politics. The Campaign for Nuclear Disarmament demonstrated strongly against the American bases, and protests outside the Greenham Common base were a feature of the 1980s. The paradox was that the British still wanted their own highly expensive nuclear deterrent.

AMERY, LEO (1873–1955). Born in India, Leo Amery went on to become a Conservative secretary of state for the colonies and dominion affairs from 1924–1929. Out of office in the 1930s, Amery was critical of the **appeasement** policy toward **Germany**. In May 1940, he famously turned on party leader **Neville Chamberlain** in the House of Commons. Quoting Oliver Cromwell, he shouted, "In the name of God, go!" Amery's son Julian was a Conservative Cabinet minister in the 1950s and 1960s.

ANGELL, SIR NORMAN (1874–1967). Sir Norman Angell was a publicist and author. His *Great Illusion* (1910), which attacked international armaments and alliance systems, is his best-known book. This book and his other writings had considerable influence on Labour thinking during the interwar period. He was a Labour member of Parliament from 1929–1931, and a winner of the **Nobel Peace Prize** in 1933.

ANGLO–AMERICAN LOAN AGREEMENT (1945). At the end of **World War II**, Britain's economy was in a parlous state as a result of the vast expenditure needed to sustain a six-year war effort. The desired solution depended upon a large loan from the **United States**. The chief British negotiator, **John Maynard Keynes**, hoped to secure $8 billion, but this proved to be hopelessly unrealistic, as did his assumption that it would be interest free. Hard bargaining produced an American offer to write off Britain's wartime **Lend–Lease** debts, amounting to $27 billion for a flat payment of $650 million. This would be paralleled by an American loan of $3.75 billion at 2 percent interest. The United States also demanded that the British implement the 1944 **Bretton Woods Agreement** and make the pound sterling convertible into dollars. Keynes was exhausted by the talks with the Americans.

ANGLO–BOER WAR (1899–1902). At a time when Great Britain's empire appeared to be at its zenith in the closing years of the Victorian era, the empire faced its greatest internal challenge since the American War of Independence. This was the Second Anglo–Boer War, during which the British suffered a number of embarrassing military defeats. In 1881, the First Boer War had resulted in a British defeat at Majuba Hill, after the Dutch-speaking Boer settlers, who had arrived in South Africa long before the British, resisted encroachment on the two Boer republics, the Transvaal and the Orange Free State. The subsequent discovery of gold in the Transvaal in 1886 created tensions as British and other foreign prospectors poured into the area. The Boers resisted the idea of giving the incomers voting rights and tried to tax the gold speculators. British imperialists like Cecil Rhodes were attracted by the mineral wealth of the Boer republics, and, in 1895, one of Rhodes's supporters, Leander Jameson, invaded the republics in an attempt to overthrow Boer rule. The **Jameson Raid** was a disaster and merely increased Anglo–Boer tensions. Joseph Chamberlain, the British colonial secretary at the time, was suspected of encouraging an aggressive forward policy in **South Africa**.

Failure to resolve the issue of voting rights for non-Boers ultimately led to war in October 1899. The highly mobile Boers initially held the advantage, and their knowledge of the high grasslands allowed them to ambush British columns. Draconian tactics were required by the British commander in chief, Herbert Kitchener, to defeat the Boers. These included the use of "concentration camps," in which many of the family members of Boer fighters died of neglect. Peace only came in 1902. The war began an important debate in Britain about the fitness of working-class youths, whom the war had shown to be physically unfit. It also brought about the abandonment of highly visible red tunics in favor of the less-visible khaki for troops.

ANSCHLUSS. The word *anschluss* is a German word meaning "union," generally used in the case of Austria and **Germany**, after Adolf Hitler's annexation of his homeland in March 1938. Although Germany had clearly broken Article 80 of the **Treaty of Versailles**, which forbade union between the two states, Britain and **France** merely protested about German action.

APPEASEMENT. Appeasement is the name commonly given to the British policy in the 1930s designed to bring about accommodation with such totalitarian powers as Nazi **Germany**, Fascist **Italy**, and Imperial **Japan**. This pejorative use of the word is inaccurate, as appeasement, an attempt to reach understanding with foreign states, has always been part of British foreign policy. The 1930s variant of appeasement was a product of particular circumstances under the premierships of **Stanley Baldwin** and **Neville Chamberlain**. Great Britain was a victim of imperial overstretch, whereby its vast empire was potentially at risk from the three Great Powers, Germany, Italy, and Japan, simultaneously. It had only one main ally, **France**, as the **United States** was in isolation from Europe, save where financial matters were concerned, and the Soviet Union was deemed to be beyond the ideological pale. Successive British governments thus believed that appeasement of at least two of its three hostile adversaries was required in the short run.

Contrary to myth, appeasement did not mean rejecting rearmament. The debate with such critics as **Winston Churchill** was about the pace of rearmament, not the principle. It was while the appeasers were in office that crucial technology like radar and the Spitfire Fighter evolved. The ultimate criticism of appeasement in the 1930s was that it failed to achieve its primary objective, which was the preservation of international peace. Mainstream appeasement, designed to improve international understanding, remains an essential component in foreign policymaking. *See also* AMERY, LEO; BUTLER, RICHARD AUSTEN; VANSITTART, SIR ROBERT.

ARGENTINA. As part of Spain's huge Latin American empire, Argentina was a target for Great Britain's industrial exports before its attained independence. British prime minister **William Pitt the Younger** (1783–1806) and his first lord of the **Admiralty,** Lord Melville (1802–1806), were keenly interested in Latin America. They did not approve of a unilateral venture headed by General Sir William Beresford and Commodore Sir Hope Popham in 1806. On 27 June, Beresford's force of 1,600 men, which had sailed from Cape Town across the Atlantic, landed outside the Argentine capital Buenos Aires, all without permission from the Crown. Beresford deposed the Spanish viceroy and declared himself governor of Buenos Aires under the authority of King George III. Just one British soldier was killed in the capture of Buenos Aires. The escapade did not last long. Local aristocrats united to defeat the British in August 1806, and, rather generously, the British force was allowed to sail back to London. The spark of freedom had been planted in Latin America. British pride had also been affronted, but a second expedition against Buenos Aires in 1808, led by Lieutenant General John Whitlocke, was even more catastrophic. The British lost 2,200 men in the fighting.

The Argentines overthrew the new Spanish viceroy in 1810. Their subsequent history was to be interlinked with Britain, especially in the trade and commercial sector. An Anglo–Argentinian commercial treaty in 1825 opened the country to British exports. British foreign policy underwrote the **Monroe Doctrine** (1823), which prevented a Spanish reconquest of Argentina and its sister Latin American republics. As the 19th century wore on, Argentina provided the perfect satellite economy for Britain. While it was not part of the **British Empire**, it was dependent on Britain in commercial and financial terms. Britain built the railways, not just in Argentina, but throughout Latin America. It was the primary foreign investor throughout the subcontinent. Britain singularly failed to pass on its democratic tradition to Argentina. One dictator followed another, as the Buenos Aires elite was unable to control agrarian, rancher overlords in the interior. One warlord, Juan Manuel de Rosas, held power until 1852, when he was succeeded by another, Justo José Urguiza. It was a historical irony that Rosas retired to England to become a friend of Lord **Henry John Palmerston**. In 1853, Argentina became a federated republic. Only when Bartholomé Mitre came to power in 1862 was Argentina able to utilize its great resources of beef and grain, assisted by the coming of refrigeration. In 1914, Argentina was one of the world's wealthiest states. It did not participate in **World War I**.

Argentinian politics during much of the interwar period was dominated by Hipólito Yrigoyen (president, 1916–1922, 1928–1930), a radical politician. In 1930, he was overthrown in yet another of the endless Argentinian military coups. Like other countries, Argentina suffered in the global depression of the early 1930s. By then, it had a large number of Scots and Welsh immigrants, but also a large number of Italian migrants. The British ambassador to Buenos Aires, **Sir Nevile Henderson** (1935–1937), reported on how the Italian papers in the city ran a violent anti-British campaign because of the dictator Benito Mussolini's Ethiopian adventure. Henderson noted the Argentinians were already exercised about the issue of the Falkland Islands. In 1936, much time was devoted to the negotiation of the level of import duty levied by Britain on chilled Argentinian beef. Fray Bentos corned beef was one of the best-known foreign brand names in Britain at the time.

Argentina, like the rest of Latin America, also did not take part in **World War II**. It came close to involvement in the Battle of the River Plate in December 1939, when a German pocket battleship was interned in Uruguay's Montevideo harbor and looked as if it might make a run for Buenos Aires. The Royal Navy ensured that the warship was forced to scuttle itself.

The difference between the Argentinian experience in World War II and Britain's became clear-cut after 1945. Fascism was an utterly discredited creed in Britain, but, in Argentina, power was held by the neofascist Juan Perón (president, 1946–1955, 1973–1974). Perón had been a military attaché in Mussolini's **Italy**. His power relied on army support and his courting of the industrial working class, the so-called "shirtless ones." In this, he was much aided by his charismatic wife, Eva Duarte Perón, or Evita, as she was known. Perónism remains a potent force in Argentinian politics. Perón himself briefly returned to power in 1973–1974, and he always emphasized the justice of Argentina's claim to the British-occupied Falkland Islands. Argentina alternated between military rule and Perónism. The military coup of 1976 resulted in repression and state-sponsored murders, which undermined the regime's popularity. The catastrophic 1982 Argentinian invasion of the Falklands was a desperate attempt by the military to restore its popularity, which failed after the brief, bitter **Falklands War**. Perónism gained from this failure. Democracy was restored in 1983. The Perónist president, Carlos Menem, then held power for a decade (1989–1999). During this time, Menem avoided provoking the British about the Falklands, and economic and political stability were restored.

Serious economic problems then brought Argentina to the verge of bankruptcy. In December 2001, no less than five men held the post of president of Argentina. The Perónist Eduardo Dualde clung to power as president (2001–2003), before giving way to Nestor Kirchner (2003–2007). This more moderate form of Perónism still saw the advantages of populism. In 2007, Kirchner was succeeded as president by his wife, Cristina, and she won an even more decisive electoral mandate in October 2011. This new Evita, as she was commonly known, reactivated the controversial issue of the Falklands. In 2012, Kirchner seized on the 30th anniversary of the Falklands War to describe Britain as a "coarse and decadent colonial power." She also tried to get fellow Latin American states on board. In December 2011, Brazil and Chile agreed to begin blocking ships flying Falkland flags from entering their ports. There was also a threat to suspend the flights between Falkland's capital, Port Stanley, and the South American mainland. Kirchner also described a visit by Prince William to the islands as provocative. Argentinian accusations were rejected by British **foreign secretary William Hague** in the House of Commons in 2012. Britain's commitment to the Falkland islanders remains absolute.

ASQUITH, HERBERT HENRY (1852–1928). Herbert Asquith was Britain's prime minister at the onset of **World War I**. He was replaced by **David Lloyd George** in 1916. Asquith was deserted by members of his own Liberal Party because his direction of the war was deemed to be too lethargic. He never held political office again. Asquith was created Earl of Oxford.

ASTOR, NANCY, VISCOUNTESS ASTOR (1879–1964). Nancy Astor was born in Virginia, in the **United States**. A Conservative Unionist member of Parliament (1919–1945), she was the first woman to take her seat in the House of Commons. She mixed socially with such Conservative leaders as **Stanley Baldwin** and **Neville Chamberlain**, who came to stay for weekends at her country house, Cliveden, in Berkshire. Contrary to myth, however, she did not have any real influence on the evolution of the **appeasement** policy. Astor was a parliamentary critic of **Winston Churchill**, with whom she frequently clashed in the chamber on foreign policy.

ASTOR, WALDORF, VISCOUNT ASTOR (1879–1952). Waldorf Astor was educated at **Eton College** and Oxford. He was less celebrated than his wife, **Nancy Astor**. A Conservative member of Parliament (1910–1919), his wife took over his seat in Plymouth. Astor was a delegate to the **League of Nations** in 1931, and chairman of directors at the *Observer* newspaper. He was also chairman of the Royal Institute of International Affairs (Chatham House), a noted foreign policy think tank (1935–1949).

ASWAN DAM. When **Jamal Abd al Nasser** became prime minister of **Egypt** in 1954, and subsequently president in 1956, modernization of his country was a priority. Nasser negotiated Britain's withdrawal from the Suez Canal Zone with **Anthony Eden** and facilitated the creation of a great dam over the Nile at Aswan, the linchpin of his development plans. His hope was that Britain and the **United States** would fund the construction of the dam via the World Bank, but, suspicious of Nasser's socialist leanings and purchase of arms from Communist **Czechoslovakia**, they refused to do so. This directly contributed to Nasser's decision to nationalize the Suez Canal in July 1956. The Aswan Dam was ultimately built with aid from the Soviet Union, and it opened in 1968. *See also* SUEZ CRISIS.

ATLANTIC CHARTER (1941). Issued on 14 August 1941, the Atlantic Charter was signed by Prime Minister **Winston Churchill** and President **Franklin D. Roosevelt** and announced to the world after their meeting at Placentia Bay, Newfoundland. Churchill, who was always keenly aware of the need to maintain strong links with the **United States**, wanted to demonstrate the community of interest between the two countries. Principles were laid down in the charter, which involved Anglo–American commitments to freedom of the seas, self-determination, free government, and liberal economic and trade policies. Churchill tried to avoid the application of the principle of self-determination to the **British Empire**; he had long been an opponent of independence for **India**. This was unacceptable to the Americans. Also anxious to placate his new ally, the Soviet Union, Churchill argued that it should be allowed to keep its June 1941 frontiers with annexed Polish territory. Roosevelt insisted that article three of the Atlantic Charter on self-determination must still be applied. Nevertheless, the charter was to be a blueprint for the **United Nations** declaration of 1 January 1942.

ATLANTIC CONFERENCE (1941). When he became prime minister of Great Britain in May 1940, **Winston Churchill** (whose mother, **Jennie Jerome**, was American) was acutely aware of the need to strengthen ties with the **United States**. He emphasized the personal aspect of having known President **Franklin D. Roosevelt** since the days when Churchill had been first lord of the **Admiralty** and Roosevelt had been navy secretary. He signed letters to the president, "former naval person."

Churchill's courtship of Roosevelt had its reward, when, from 9–12 August 1941, they met with their staffs onboard the USS *Augusta* at Ship Harbour, Placentia Bay, off the Canadian province of Newfoundland. It was, in fact, the first time the two leaders had met since the 1920s, and the first of nine wartime meetings between the two men.

In August 1941, the United States was still neutral, so the secret Placentia Bay meeting was designed to discuss strategy for war against the Axis powers in the event that the United States would become a belligerent. The war had already been extended with Adolf Hitler's decision to attack the Soviet Union on 22 June. Churchill and Roosevelt announced the **Atlantic Charter** and agreed to hold regular meetings, and the American president agreed to further assist Britain through the **Lend–Lease** program.

ATTLEE, CLEMENT R. (1883–1967). Clement R. Attlee was Britain's first Labour prime minister, from 1945–1951. He never held political office thereafter. Educated at public school and an Oxford graduate, Attlee became leader of the Labour Party in 1935. During **World War II**, he was **Winston Churchill's** deputy from 1940–1945, and an important unifying figure. When Labour won the general election of 26 July 1945, Attlee replaced Churchill at the **Potsdam Conference**, which was deciding the fate of postwar Europe. He led a massive program of domestic reform that nationalized 20 percent of British industry, created the National Health Service, and also put transport infrastructure under state ownership. At the same time, Attlee and **Ernest Bevin,** his chief Cabinet supporter and **foreign secretary**, were determined that Britain must cling on to its great power status, this despite the financial burden that winning World War II had placed on the country's economy.

While a loyal ally of the **United States**, Attlee was critical on occasion of what he deemed to be an American tendency to see things in oversimplistic terms. He was not as naïve as some of his more left-wing colleagues, who thought that Labour's left-wing credentials would give it an advantage in dealing with the postwar Soviet Union.

Attlee's difficulties were primarily economic. He was obliged to send the great economist **John Maynard Keynes** to America to negotiate a loan when the United States abruptly ended **Lend–Lease**. As had been the case after **World War I**, the Americans drove a hard bargain, obliging the British to repay $650 million in exchange for a $3.75 billion loan at 2 percent interest. This caused resentment in London, but it was far from being the only source of Anglo–American tension. Britain had contributed to the wartime Manhattan Project, which produced the first atomic bomb, but, in 1946, President **Harry S. Truman** approved the **McMahon Act**, which ended all nuclear cooperation between the two powers, allegedly because of successful Soviet espionage in the British scientific community. Neither did the Americans consult Britain about the composition of governments in such soon to be Communist states as Poland and Bulgaria. As Churchill had begun to recognize during the war, Britain was now very much the junior partner in the **"special relationship."**

Attlee was more pragmatic than Bevin, to a degree, although he was no less committed to the survival of Britain as a global power. In 1945, he argued in a memorandum that Britain should rein itself in somewhat in the Eastern Mediterranean and East of Suez, but he could not convince Bevin. He did, however, preside over the liquidation of Britain's old **League of Nations** mandate in **Palestine**, when Bevin's judgment became clouded by an Arab bias, and 100,000 British troops were withdrawn in 1948.

The problem was the vastness of British commitments elsewhere. Impoverished by austerity, Britain was paying 70 percent of the food costs of the German population in its occupation zone in northwest **Germany**. **India, Pakistan,** Burma, and Ceylon had to be abandoned in 1947–1948, because Britain lacked the resources to maintain these colonies, although it was true that Labour had long supported independence for India. There were also the enormous costs of transforming British society, but Attlee and his colleagues insisted on the equally costly development of a British atomic bomb. The military argued that Britain, a small island well within range of Soviet bombers, and with more than 40 percent of its people living in large cities, needed its own deterrent. This claim was debatable, but Attlee was certainly open to criticism for agreeing on the 1951 budget, which put struggling Britain's defense expenditure at 14 percent of the gross national product, even higher than that of the United States.

The American **Marshall Plan** of 1947 improved Anglo–American relations and pumped dollars and much-needed material into the British economy. The **Truman Doctrine** of the same year also followed Britain's insistence on a withdrawal from **Greece**, and Attlee played a key role, along with Bevin, in setting up the **North Atlantic Treaty Organization** in 1949. The Labour government followed the United States into Korea in June 1950, although Attlee showed some independence by expressing concern about U.S. attitudes toward Communist **China**. Britain had, in fact, recognized Mao Zedong's government in 1949, something Washington refused to do.

Attlee lost power in October 1951, even though Labour was ahead in the popular vote. He gave up the leadership of the Labour Party in 1955, and was created Earl Attlee.

AUSTRALIA. In its early years of linkage with Great Britain, Australia was a remote colony best known for its role as a penal colony, the most celebrated of which was the 18th-century foundation of Botany Bay. Initially entirely dependent on the British Crown, the Australian colonies had a degree of autonomy by 1860. The exception was Western Australia. This was in line with the British policy of diarchy, whereby in the white dominions in the 19th century, foreign policy and defense were a Crown preserve, while local administrations dealt with other matters. An Australian federation was created in 1901, and, in 1931, all remaining British powers were abrogated under the Statute of Westminster, thus making Australia effectively independent, although the British monarch remained head of state. Long before this, Australia had taken on impartial responsibilities in the Pacific. In 1887, the administration of New Guinea was taken over by the state of Queensland. During **World War I**, Australia and **New Zealand** together liquidated the German colonial empire in the Pacific. Australia's commitment to the motherland was demonstrated by the fact that 59,000 Australians died in the war. Australians fought heroically at Gallipoli in 1915–1916. The severe losses were blamed on the ineptitude of British commanders, creating an enduring nationalist mythology.

Ethnic ties with Britain were extremely close. In the 1930s, 80 percent of Australians were still of British descent. Australia invariably followed British policy, although there were some early signs of an independent streak. In the Chanak Crisis of 1922, between Britain and **Turkey**, Australia wavered in its support for British policy. Thereafter, the most distinctive difference between the two countries concerned the most English of sports, cricket. So great was Australian resentment of English tactics during the 1932–1933 English tour of Australia that diplomatic relations were nearly broken off. Sport was always a major Australian interest, which allowed it to worst English or British teams. Dependence remained a reality in defense. In 1937–1938, Australia spent only 1 percent of its budget on defense, compared to Britain's 5.7 percent. Yet, Australians complained about the absence of a peacetime Royal Navy from the Pacific. Their governments were strong supporters of British **appeasement** of **Japan**, **Germany**, and **Italy** in the 1930s. When this policy failed, Australia backed the British effort in **World War II**, in the Middle East, the Pacific, and Italy. Australia was part of the **British Commonwealth**, a term then only used in regards to the white dominions of Australia, New Zealand, **Canada**, and **South Africa**. It provided two million men for Britain's war effort.

A knee-jerk Australian loyalty to Britain survived well into the postwar era. This was very much associated with the premiership of Robert Menzies (prime minister, 1949–1966). Strongly anti-Communist, in 1950, Menzies failed in an attempt to make the Communist Party illegal in Australia. Abroad, he was a **Cold War** ally of the **United States**, on whom Australia had become increasingly dependent. Australia was the first state to send troops to Korea in 1950 under U.S. command. In 1951, it signed the defense agreement with the United States and New Zealand known as the ANZUS Treaty. This became the **Southeast Asia Treaty Organization** in 1954. Menzies allowed Britain to test atomic bombs in Australia in 1950, and he sent

Australian soldiers to assist Britain in its Communist emergency in Malaya in 1955. When everyone else deserted Britain at the time of the 1956 **Suez Crisis**, Australia was one of only two **Commonwealth** states to support it at the **United Nations (UN)**.

Menzies's pro-British stance was shown most clearly in his reverence for the British Crown. In 1954, he sponsored the visit by the young **Queen Elizabeth II** to Australia, the first by a British monarch. By the 1960s, Menzies belonged to an older generation of Australians (he was born in 1894). Australian leaders increasingly backed away from Britain to the Pacific region. Even Menzies recognized the greater importance of the United States by sending troops to Vietnam in 1965, unlike Britain. The British themselves sought and gained entry to the **European Economic Community**, which made it harder for Australian goods to access British markets beginning in 1973. Some Australians thought Britain's constitutional position in Australia to be anomalous. Crown interests were represented by the governor general, although Australian prime ministers appointed him. When a more radical Labor prime minister, Gough Whitlam (1972–1975), came to lead Australia in 1972, this complex link created a full-blown crisis in Anglo–Australian relations, indeed the worst since Australia secured independence. The crisis arose because Whitlam had no majority in the Senate, the upper house of the Australian parliament. His Liberal opponent, Malcolm Fraser, operated ruthlessly by refusing to pass the budget in October 1975. Instead, Fraser demanded new elections, a request rejected by Whitlam. This was party politics, but no one foresaw how the crisis would end. It did so because Sir John Kerr, governor general at the time, intervened using obscure constitutional powers to sack Whitlam and call a general election. Labor supports called Fraser "Kerr's Cur," but he duly won the 1975 election. This unprecedented behavior by the governor general accelerated a debate about whether Australia should become a republic. Whitlam had ended Australian involvement in Vietnam, and, rather surprisingly, his right-wing opponent Fraser (prime minister, 1975–1983) allowed 100,000 Vietnamese refugees to settle in Australia. Fraser also cultivated better relations with the People's Republic of China, a very different approach from that of his party colleague Menzies. As a convinced antiracist who conceded more rights to native Aborigines, Fraser strongly condemned the apartheid regime in South Africa, which Britain, under **Margaret Thatcher**, seemed prepared to condone. Fraser played a key role in the 1979 meeting of Commonwealth heads of government. This led to independence for Zimbabwe in 1980.

Fraser's successor, Bob Hawke (prime minister, 1983–1991), was an Oxford graduate like his predecessor, which demonstrated the strength of residual British links. During Hawke's term, international economic problems hit Australia, which was badly affected by the October 1987 world stock market crash. Growth had been stimulated between 1983–1986, but Australia's foreign debt mushroomed. Hawke's Labor successor, Paul Keating (prime minister, 1991–1996), who came from the large Irish Australian community, had been his finance minister. Under Keating, the foreign debt problem ($150 billion in 1993) worsened. Keating's response was to try to convince Australians that the future lay with Asia. Part of his modernization policy involved making Australia a republic and ending the ancient link with the British Crown. In other respects, Keating pursued an orthodox Australian foreign policy. Australia, like Britain and the United States, supported UN action against Iraqi dictator Saddam Hussein in 1991.

A long period of rule by the conservative Liberal and Country parties started in 1996. Under John Howard (prime minister, 1996–2007), the Australian economy boomed, but, surprisingly, for an anti-Republican, Howard put the issue of the British monarchy to a referendum in 1999. The vote narrowly went in favor of keeping the link with the British Crown. Howard supported the British and American involvement in **Afghanistan** and **Iraq** in 2002 and 2003. He even stepped up Australian troop levels in 2005–2006, despite public criticism. Howard's tough immigration policy was more popular. He lost power in December 2007, to the Labor Party, after becoming the longest-serving Liberal prime minister since Menzies. Howard's successor was the former diplomat Kevin Rudd (2007–2010), a fluent Chinese speaker who advocated Australian withdrawal from Iraq and support for the Kyoto Protocol on climate change. This last position was shared by the British. Internal Labor Party feuding resulted in Rudd's removal as prime minister on 24 June 2010. He was succeeded by Julia Gillard (prime minister, 2010–present), who confessed to a lack of interest in foreign affairs. Gillard visited Australian troops in Afghanistan on 2 October 2010, and she backed the Australian presence there. She believed that Australia's constitutional position should remain the same in the lifetime of Queen Elizabeth II. Afterward, Australia should be prepared for a transition to a republic.

AUSTRIAN STATE TREATY (1955). In 1945, Austria, like **Germany**, was divided into four occupation zones held by Great Britain, the **United States,** the Soviet Union, and **France.** Joseph Stalin, the Soviet leader, refused to countenance any change in Austria's status. This only came with the relative thaw in the **Cold War** that followed Stalin's death in March 1953. As a result of the May 1955 Austrian State Treaty, Allied troops were withdrawn from Austria, which was to remain permanently neutral, renounce nuclear weapons, and promise never to enter into the sort of union with Germany that had taken place in 1938.

AUSTRO-HUNGARIAN EMPIRE. Austria had been a traditional ally of Britain until the latter half of the 19th century, as the two powers had worked together to contain the Russian threat in the Balkans and preserve the Ottoman Turkish Empire. The alliance between Austria, or Austria-Hungary as it became known after 1867, and **Germany** destroyed the old Anglo–Austrian axis, even though there were no obvious areas of dispute between the two Great Powers. In 1919, the Treaty of Saint-Germain broke up the Austro-Hungarian Empire with approval of British prime minister **David Lloyd George**. Only the rump state of Austria remained. *See also* TURKEY.

B

BALDWIN, STANLEY (1867–1945). Stanley Baldwin was the most quint-essentially English of prime ministers. He deliberately cultivated a pipe-smoking, country-loving image, although he was, in fact, a fourth generation ironmaster. His family was wealthy enough to send him to Harrow School and Cambridge University, but for years he was content working for the family firm in Bewdley, Worcestershire.

Baldwin's political ascent, after he entered the House of Commons in 1908, was comparatively rapid. This owed much to the split in the Conservative Party between the leadership, which wanted to preserve the coalition with Liberal prime minister **David Lloyd George** and the rank and file, which revolted against the coalition in 1922. As a result, Baldwin, who had been a lowly financial secretary in the treasury, found himself chancellor of the exchequer, and, as early as 1923, prime minister.

In December 1923, he unwisely chose to call an election over the issue of free trade and protection, which he lost to the Labour Party before returning in 1924 to head a second administration that lasted for five years. As a prime minister, Baldwin was frequently accused of taking little interest in foreign policy. This was an exaggeration. It was true that he had greater touch in domestic policy, but he fully supported **Austen Chamberlain's** attempts as **foreign secretary** to reintegrate **Germany** into the European state system in the **Treaty of Locarno** (1925). He also supported his chancellor of the exchequer **Winston Churchill**'s dubious decision to return Great Britain to the gold standard.

A second Labour administration came into power in 1929, and it failed to deal with the economic crisis facing the country by 1931. The interim period was a difficult one for Baldwin, whose position as leader of the Conservative Party was undermined by the press barons **Lord Beaverbrook** and Lord Rothermere. Baldwin would not stand down, and, in 1931, he was offered a senior position in the Conservative-dominated National Government under **Ramsay MacDonald**, the former Labour prime minister. Baldwin replaced the aging MacDonald in 1935, still acting as leader of a coalition government of Conservatives, Liberals, and a rump of National Labour members.

Baldwin's last administration saw him being associated with the **appeasement** of Nazi Germany and Fascist **Italy**. He was puzzled on a personal level by the political extremes represented by fascism and communism and was subsequently criticized for neglecting rearmament. This was unfair, as Baldwin was a great patriot who took a more emollient line with the trade unions and working class Labour members of Parliament than other senior Conservatives. He was also a strong supporter of the **British Empire** and **Commonwealth**, seen at his best in handling the delicate crisis leading to the abdication of King **Edward VIII** in 1936. Baldwin resigned in May 1937, to endure years of abuse for his role in the appeasement policy, notably in the famous polemic *Guilty Men*, published in 1940.

BALFOUR, ARTHUR J. (1848–1930). Arthur Balfour was British prime minister from 1902–1905, and the nephew of Lord Salisbury. He had a famously relaxed bachelor lifestyle and presided over one of the greatest electoral defeats ever sustained by the Conservative Party in 1906, over the vexed issued of protectionism. Unusually, Balfour is best remembered for his role as Britain's foreign secretary from 1916–1922, in particular, for the Balfour Declaration of 2 November 1917, in which Great Britain declared itself in support of the concept of a national home, but not a state, for the Jews in **Palestine**. This was done in spite of the fact that the British had made equivalent pledges to the Arabs. Balfour also represented Britain at the **Paris Peace Conference** in 1919.

BANGLADESH. This **Commonwealth** state achieved its independence in December 1971, after a bloody conflict with **Pakistan**, with assistance from **India**. This put an end to a completely unsatisfactory British imperial creation in 1947, which left Pakistan in two sections, East Pakistan and West Pakistan, with many miles of Indian Territory between them, because both had Muslim majorities.

After more than two decades of independence, East Pakistan, as Bangladesh was then known, was economically underdeveloped, even though its supplies of jute provided Pakistan with most of its foreign currency earnings. A revolt against the central government in Karachi resulted in the flight of millions of refugees to India and the Third Indo-Pakistan War. The Pakistani forces in East Pakistan surrendered on 15 December 1971, allowing the founding of an independent Bangladesh under Sheikh Mujibur Rahman. He had previously been imprisoned by the Pakistan authorities.

BEAVERBROOK, LORD (1879–1964). One of Great Britain's greatest press barons, Max Aitken 1st Lord Beaverbrook was of Canadian extraction, but he became an important figure on the British political scene. He owned the Express group of Fleet Street newspapers, which included the *Daily Express* and the *Sunday Express*. They took distinctive lines on foreign policy and domestic issues. Like **Winston Churchill**, Beaverbrook was a strong supporter of **King Edward VIII** in 1936, before the doomed monarch was forced to abdicate. In 1940, his friendship with Churchill brought him the post of minister of aircraft production. Beaverbrook characteristically invented such elaborate propaganda stunts as collecting iron railings in London and elsewhere. These were supposed to help build Spitfire fighters. They could not, of course, but it made citizens feel better. In the postwar period, Beaverbrook was not involved in government. His papers concentrated their fire on Britain's decision to apply for membership in the **European Economic Community**. Membership was granted in 1961, despite Beaverbrook's fierce opposition, which owed much to his Canadian background. *See also* BALDWIN, STANLEY; COMMONWEALTH, BRITISH

BECKETT, MARGARET (1943–). Margaret Beckett became Great Britain's first female **foreign secretary** when she was appointed to that post in 2006, by Prime Minister **Tony Blair**. A long-standing stalwart of the Labour Party left and member of Parliament for Lincoln, she came under criticism from colleagues for not calling for an immediate ceasefire during the July 2006 fighting between Israeli and Hezbollah forces in the Lebanon. Beckett did make protests to her U.S. counterpart, **Condoleezza Rice**, about the American use of Prestwick Airport in Scotland for carrying American bombs to Israel. She also called for the closure of the U.S. detention camp at Guantanamo Bay, Cuba, stating the British view that continued imprisonment of alleged **terrorists** without trial was an abuse of human rights and could increase global Muslim opposition to Anglo–American involvement in **Iraq**. Beckett's short period at the **Foreign Office** ended in June 2007, when **Gordon Brown** replaced Blair as prime minister. He appointed **David Miliband** as her successor.

BELGIUM. The crucial geographical position of Belgium (formerly part of the Spanish and Austrian Netherlands) made it a key interest of successive governments of Great Britain. It remained an objective of British foreign policy from the end of the 18th century to prevent Belgium falling under the control of an overly mighty **France**. Britain thus supported the decision of the 1815 **Vienna Congress** to place what is now Belgium in union with the Netherlands, an arrangement that resulted in a revolt against Dutch rule in 1830. The independence of Belgium was subsequently guaranteed by an 1839 treaty signed by Britain. It was the infringement of Belgium's neutral status by **Germany** that brought Britain into **World War I** on 4 August 1914.

British troops suffered badly in the bloody battles around Ypres, part of the tiny strip of Belgium not occupied by Germany from 1914–1918. Belgium's territorial integrity was restored by the 1919 **Treaty of Versailles,** which also confiscated Eupen and Malmedy from Germany and gave them to Belgium. Belgium was closely allied to France throughout much of the interwar period, and, in 1923, its troops joined France in a punitive occupation of the industrial Ruhr when Germany defaulted on the reparations payments due under the Treaty of Versailles. Britain opposed Franco–Belgian action, a rare instance of Anglo–Belgian discord. When, in 1936, Belgium abandoned its pro-French stance and opted for neutrality, Britain supported its new position. It was a reflection of internal tensions. The Flemish Protestant part of Belgium had long disliked the French alliance. Neutrality did not, however, save Belgium from German invasion on 10 May 1940, and, as in 1914, Britain came to its aid. The subsequent Belgian capitulation later in the month put the Belgian king Leopold II in a dilemma. Rather than join a government in exile in Britain, Leopold opted to remain in Belgium, a decision that provoked much adverse comment in Britain, where he was widely regarded as a collaborator with the Nazis.

Belgium had to wait until the summer of 1944 before it was liberated by Anglo–American forces. The Belgians had learned important lessons during **World War II,** one being the need for European unity and cooperation after hostilities ceased. In 1944, together with the Netherlands and Luxemburg, Belgium set up the Belgium, Netherlands, Luxemburg Customs Union (BENELUX), which created an external tariff against non-BENELUX states. Britain was encouraging, but only from the sidelines, as it saw no need to involve itself directly in any form of **European Union (EU).** It was a disappointment to Paul Henri Spaak, the distinguished Belgian statesman and founding father of the **European Economic Community (EEC),** that Britain disassociated itself from the process. Belgium was one of the six signatories of the **Treaty of Rome,** which set up the EEC in 1957. It was also as one of the smaller EEC states consistently in favor of British membership in the years between 1961–1969, when Britain vainly tried to change tack and join the EEC. Belgium was also a loyal member of the **North Atlantic Treaty** Organization (NATO) when it was formed in 1949. Brussels became the headquarters of the EEC and also, in 1966, the headquarters of NATO when France ejected the organization from Paris. These developments coincided with the end of Belgium's colonial role in the Congo in Africa amid much controversy and bloodshed in 1960. Like other Western states, Britain was highly critical of Belgian rule, which had done little for native Africans.

Belgium was at the core of the European integration process, although its size made it nervous about perceived Franco–German domination of what had become the EU by 1992, under the terms of the **Treaty of Maastricht**. This came into force in November 1993, and created a single market for European goods. Unlike Britain, Belgium then joined the European common currency (euro) in 2000. As a member of the **Eurozone**, the financial crisis of 2008–2011 put Belgium under some pressure, although it also struggled with internal problems. Tension between Flemish and French speakers remained acute, and, in 2010–2011, Belgium spent a lengthy period without a government because of the problems involved in forming a coalition.

BERLIN BLOCKADE (1948–1949). Berlin was the capital city of united **Germany** from 1871–1945, and, before that, the capital of Prussia, the largest German state. It lost its status as a united city and capital in 1945, when the collapse of the defeated Nazi regime resulted in the division of the city into four zones of occupation. These were occupied by the **United States**, the Soviet Union, Great Britain, and **France**, but the western zones were cut off from their major zones of occupation by territory, which was part of the Soviet zone. Communication with the French, British, and U.S. zones could only be achieved along prescribed road and rail links, all under Soviet control.

The crisis, which led to the blockade of Berlin, arose from the decision by the Western powers in June 1948 to introduce a new deutschmark to achieve economic stability in their zones. The Soviet Union objected to this move, claiming that the 1945 Potsdam Agreement required the unanimous approval of the Allied Powers for such action. When the Western powers went ahead and introduced the deutschmark into their zones of occupation in Berlin, the Soviet Union closed all access routes to the rest of Germany, by road, rail, and canal, a distance of 120 miles (192 kilometers). Electricity supplies, upon which the western zones depended, were also cut off.

The 2.4 million inhabitants of West Berlin were thus totally cut off from the outside world, other than via limited air corridors also under Soviet control. As the leader of the Western Alliance, the U.S. decided not to confront the Soviet Union along the land communications routes, but to rely instead on an airlift, a decision fully supported by Great Britain and France. The blockade lasted from 24 June 1948 to 12 May 1949.

During this period, there was an aircraft coming into Tempelhof Airport every 30 seconds bringing the essential fuel and food supplies needed for the survival of the West Berliners. Joseph Stalin's bluff was called, and he was unable to force the Western powers out of Berlin or ultimately prevent the creation of West Germany as a free democratic state. West Berlin maintained its unique status deep inside what became the German Democratic Republic until the reunification of Germany took place in 1990.

BERLIN CRISIS (1961). In the years after the division of **Germany**, Berlin remained a focus for tensions between the Western powers and the Soviet Union. The unusual status of West Berlin many miles inside the German Democratic Republic (GDR) and separated from the Federal Republic of Germany heightened the strain, especially since, by 1960–1961, the drift of East Berliners to the West had become an embarrassment both for the GDR regime of Walter Ulbricht and the Soviet Union. Soviet prime minister Nikita Khrushchev had also stepped up the pressure in 1958 by demanding that the Berlin problem be solved within six months. In 1959, attempts to resolve the problem of Berlin failed, although British premier **Harold Macmillan** was able to persuade Khrushchev that a four-power meeting between the **United States**, Great Britain, **France**, and the Soviet Union should be held to discuss the issue. The summit meeting between Khrushchev and President **Dwight D. Eisenhower** in Paris, in May 1960, turned into a fiasco in the wake of the U-2 spy incident, when a U.S. spy plane was shot down over the USSR. Macmillan remained loyal to his American ally, but the USSR was able to assume the moral high ground.

Khrushchev then met President **John F. Kennedy** in Vienna, in June 1961, but he remained obstructive about the Berlin issue. His impression that Kennedy was a young, inexperienced leader may have contributed to the USSR government's sanctioning of the building of a wall between East Berlin and West Berlin in August 1961. This ended all movement between the eastern and western sections of the city. There was a brief period of confrontation as U.S. and Soviet tanks faced one another across "Checkpoint Charlie," the best-known cross-Berlin security checkpoint; however, the status quo was rapidly accepted. The wall became a feature of Berlin life until 1989. In the shorter run, West Berliners were assured of U.S. support in President Kennedy's "I am a Berliner" speech of 26 June 1963. He also spoke for Britain and the rest of the **North Atlantic Treaty Organization** alliance. *See also* BERLIN BLOCKADE.

BEVAN, ANEURIN (1897–1960). The best parliamentary orator ever produced by the British Labour Party and the founder of the National Health Service, Aneurin Bevan, "Nye" as he was popularly known, came from a Welsh mining background. In addition to poverty, he also had to overcome a boyhood stutter. Bevan was a Labour member of Parliament from 1929–1960 who frequently clashed with the party leadership. He was also a critic of **Winston Churchill's** wartime coalition government. Prime Minister **Clement R. Attlee** gave him the important post of health minister in 1945, which he held until 1951. Bevan resigned in dramatic circumstances. He opposed the £13 million cut in health service expenditure imposed by the chancellor of the exchequer, **Hugh Gaitskell,** intended, in part, to fund an enormous increase in defense expenditure at the time of the **Korean War.** In Bevan's mind, it was a matter of principle. The 1948 health service reform was supposed to make health provision free at the point of delivery. Gaitskell wanted to put charges on false teeth and spectacles.

After Labour's electoral defeat in 1951, Bevan stood unsuccessfully against Gaitskell for the Labour leadership in 1955. He then became the party spokesman on foreign affairs, when it had a strong unilateralist left-wing opposed to British possession of the hydrogen bomb. At the party conference in 1957, Bevan shocked his left-wing colleagues by refusing to support a resolution calling for **unilateral disarmament** in Britain. Bevan had always been on the left-wing of the Labour Party, and leftists now regarded him as a traitor. In 1959, following Labour's third successive election defeat, Bevan became deputy leader of his party before his premature death the following year. His widow, Jennie Lee, later became a Labour minister.

BEVIN, ERNEST (1881–1951). The most effective **foreign secretary** produced by the Labour Party, Ernest Bevin came up through the trade union movement from humble origins in Bristol. As general secretary of the Transport and General Workers Union, he became the most important British trade union leader by the 1930s. He made a devastating speech at the party conference in 1934 attacking the Labour Party's pacifist leader, George Lansbury. This effectively ended Lansbury's career and pressed home Bevin's view that fascism could only be defeated by the rearmament program. In 1940, **Winston Churchill** invited Bevin to join his coalition government as minister of labour. Bevin rapidly became the second most important member of the coalition, easily outshining Labour leader **Clement R. Attlee.** Churchill relied on Bevin's prestige as a trade unionist to secure working-class support for the war effort.

To the surprise of many, Attlee made Bevin foreign secretary after Labour's overwhelming election victory in July 1945. Yet, Bevin proved to be an outstanding success, rapidly winning over public school Oxbridge-educated officials in the **Foreign Office.** He was the architect of the **North Atlantic Treaty Organization** in 1949, and, using his trade union experience, he took no nonsense from the notoriously difficult Soviet foreign minister, Vyacheslav Molotov. His one major failure was over **Palestine,** where the closing years of the old **League of Nations** mandate saw the British trapped between Jewish **terrorism** and Arab hostility. The criticism that Bevin was unduly influenced by the pro-Arabism of the Foreign Office seems just in retrospect, but he was in a difficult position dictated by the 1939 decision to restrict Jewish migration to Palestine at the very time that desperate survivors from Nazi death camps sought to reach the Holy Land. Bevin's attempt to stick to the prewar policy made him unpopular in the **United States**, which he always saw as the linchpin of the Western Alliance system. He was a reluctant decolonizer but recognized the need to concede independence to **India**, **Pakistan**, Burma, and Ceylon in 1947–1948.

Like many Labour colleagues, Bevin was not an enthusiast for postwar European unity, although he agreed to sign the 1948 **Brussels Treaty**, which strengthened Anglo–French ties. He rejected Franco–German overtures to get Great Britain to join the **European Coal and Steel Community** in 1950–1951. This was reiteration of the persistent British belief until the 1960s that the **British Empire** and **Commonwealth** and the "**special relationship**" with the United States took priority over any links with Europe.

Bevin is best remembered for the decision to abandon Great Britain's role in the eastern Mediterranean in 1947, which ensured that the Americans would have to replace Great Britain as the dominant power. The **Truman Doctrine** of 1947, followed by **Marshall Plan** aid, flowed directly from Bevin's recognition that Britain lacked the resources to combat the Soviet threat in the area. He and Attlee also made the decision that Britain must have an independent nuclear weapon. Bevin held his position as foreign secretary until 1951, when persistent heart trouble forced him to step down. He had been the most dominant figure in the postwar Labour government but always remained scrupulously loyal to the much more introverted Attlee. He always referred to the prime minister as "my little man." Bevin died five weeks after his resignation from the Foreign Office. His favorable reputation as foreign secretary continues on.

BISMARCK, OTTO VON (1809–1898). The man who unified **Germany** in 1871, Otto von Bismarck was nicknamed the "Iron Chancellor" because of his ruthless pursuit of the Prussian and German national interest. His attempt to create a European balance largely ignored Great Britain, which had remained neutral at the time of Prussia's decisive victory over **France** in 1870–1871. Many people in Britain, which had a royal family of German descent, saw Germany as a natural ally. It was under Bismarck, however reluctantly he may have sanctioned it, that Germany became a colonial power in the 1880s and began to build a large navy. This was ultimately seen to be a threat to British interests. His alliance system, which balanced Germany and Austria-Hungary against France and **Russia**, needed his hand on the tiller. When he was dismissed by Emperor William II in 1890, his successors proved to be less adept. William proved to be especially tactless in his interventions in Anglo–Germans relations. *See also* WORLD WAR I.

BLAIR, TONY (1953–). Labour's most successful prime minister in electoral terms, Tony Blair won the general elections of 1997, 2001, and 2005,
while also remaining the party's most controversial postwar prime minister.
He resigned on 27 June 2007, four years after his decision to support the U.S.
invasion of **Iraq**. This choice reflected Blair's belief that the Anglo–U.S.
axis was the most important element in British foreign policy. He forged
close relationships with President **Bill Clinton** and President **George W.
Bush**. The latter development was a surprise, but it should not have been.
Blair, who carried little ideological baggage, had no difficulty in relating to
a right-wing republican like Bush. Critics complained about his wooliness in
domestic policy, but Blair's foreign policy position was dictated by his belief
in interventionism. Successful interventions in Sierra Leone and in **Kosovo**
in 1999, when a reluctant Clinton was persuaded to bomb **Serbia**, seemed to
convince Blair that Britain and the West had a mission to impose democracy
on dictatorial regimes. This led to Britain's leading role in **Afghanistan** in
2001, following the jihadist attack on New York City and Arlington, Virginia. The limitations of this approach were demonstrated in Iraq in 2003.
Blair ignored the doubts of his attorney general and international law advisors
in the **Foreign Office** in wholeheartedly endorsing the U.S. decision to attack
Iraq without a second **United Nations** resolution. Although the campaign in
Iraq brought down dictator Saddam Hussein, there was no trace of any weapons of mass destruction (WMD), which provided the supposed cover for the
invasion. This refocused attention on the so-called "dodgy dossier," a docu-
ment supposedly providing intelligence on the WMDs. In 2011, the *Guardian*
newspaper reported a confession by the main intelligence source "Curveball"
that he had lied about the WMDs. Blair himself was obliged to testify twice
to the Chilcot inquiry in 2010–2011 about the events surrounding the decision
to go to war in 2003.

Blair remained consistent in his allegiance to the American alliance, reasoning that this, rather than through the European link, was the way to exercise
meaningful British influence. On Europe, he was indecisive. He appeared to
support the European common currency (euro) but was unable to persuade his
long-standing chancellor of the exchequer, **Gordon Brown**, of the virtues of
membership. Blair deserved credit for solving the enduring Northern **Ireland**
problem via the 1998 Good Friday Agreement, through patient negotiation
and effective use of his friendship with President Clinton. The devolution
of power to Scotland and Wales was another of his achievements. Yet, the
shadow of Iraq lay over the whole of Blair's last administration. His resignation in 2007 was precipitated, in part, by his announcement after the previous
election that he would go after two years. By then, his popular support had
declined markedly. *See also* IRISH REPUBLICAN ARMY.

BLUE STREAK. Although Great Britain successfully exploded atomic and hydrogen bombs in the 1950s, it had difficulty evolving its own delivery system. The Blue Streak system was one of several attempts to resolve this problem. It aimed to provide a medium-range nuclear missile capable of reaching the Soviet Union. Problems soon arose. It became clear that Britain would have to rely on American technology and that a liquid-fueled missile would not be able to be launched against the Soviet Union quickly enough. A preemptive strike by the USSR would thus render the British deterrent effectively useless. The government of Prime Minister **Harold Macmillan** decided to cancel the Blue Steak project in February 1960. Britain has subsequently relied on U.S. systems. *See also* POLARIS MISSILE; THOR MISSILE.

BONAPARTE, NAPOLEON (1769–1821). Great Britain's greatest foe in the 19th century was undoubtedly Napoleon Bonaparte, a Frenchman by only one year. It was only in 1768 that Bonaparte's home island of Corsica became French. He dominated European affairs from 1799–1815, with much of his time being consumed by his desire to defeat and subjugate what he called "the nation of shopkeepers," Britain. Bonaparte won many victories over Austria, Prussia, and **Russia**, but he could not defeat the British at sea. In the meantime, Britain followed its classic blue water strategy of avoiding land warfare, except in **Spain** and Portugal, and blockading Napoleon's empire with the Royal Navy. Bonaparte's attempt to break the blockade through his Continental System (1811) antagonized the other European powers, although closing ports to British goods did damage Britain's economy.

The final irony of Bonaparte's career followed his defeat at Waterloo in June 1815. He petitioned the Prince Regent, soon to be George IV, to be able to live out his days in exile in Britain. Unsurprisingly, his request was denied. Bonaparte died on the British-owned island of Saint Helena in the South Atlantic in 1821, a punishment for the countless wars he had initiated. *See also* FRANCE.

BOSNIA-HERZEGOVINA. The former Ottoman and Yugoslav province of Bosnia-Herzegovina was a polyglot one. When civil war broke out there in 1992, 44 percent of the population was Muslim, 34 percent Serb, and 17 percent Croat. Bosnia declared its independence from the rump Yugoslav state in February 1992. Soon thereafter, the leader of the large Serbian minority, Radovan Karadžić, announced the establishment of a separate Serb state in Bosnia. The Muslim element in the population was severely disadvantaged in the struggle that followed. This was because an international arms embargo, to which Britain subscribed, left them disarmed. In contrast, the Serbs and the Yugoslav National Army, which aided them, were heavily armed. In a short time, the Serbs had overrun 70 percent of Bosnia. The impotence of the United Nations Protection Force, which was sent to Bosnia in February 1992, soon also became clear. It had no armor, no artillery, and no air support. The Bosnian Serbs had the support of Serbian leader Slobodan Milošević. Aid from the **United Nations (UN)** meant to be sent to Bosnian areas like Sarajevo was, in fact, seized by Bosnian Serb general Ratko Mladić. Mediation also failed when offered by the UN/**European Community** negotiators Lord **David Owen** and **Cyrus Vance**. Owen, a former British **foreign secretary** (1977–1979), was distrusted by the Bosnian Muslims, who called him the "Serbian doctor" (Owen was also a qualified doctor).

In January 1993, Owen and Vance produced a plan to divide up Bosnia into 10 provinces, largely on ethnic grounds. The plan was rejected by the Bosnian Serbs, who refused to give up any of the territory seized in 1992. In April 1993, so-called "safe areas" were set up by the UN, including Sarajevo, the Bosnian capital, and Srebrenica. The reaction of the international community, including Britain, was confused. Where the **United States** wished to end the arms embargo, which disadvantaged the Muslims, and be tougher with the Serbs, who laid siege to Sarajevo, British foreign secretary **Douglas Hurd** would not support any further action. As a result, a large part of the Muslim Bosnian population was driven out or massacred. The creation of the Contact Group, which included **Russia**, the United States, Britain, **France**, and **Germany**, in July 1994, did little to improve the situation. It proposed that the Serbs get 49 percent of Bosnia, and the Muslims and Croats 51 percent. Again, the Bosnian Serbs rejected the deal. Belatedly, Britain now agreed, with France to supply a 10,000-man rapid reaction force. This was to have armor and artillery. It was unable to prevent the seizure of Srebrenica in July 1995, when Mladić executed thousands of Muslim men and boys in cold blood.

During that same month, the situation changed radically. The Croats, who had been rearming for three years, launched an offensive. They overran Serb enclaves and reduced the amount of land held by the Serbs in Bosnia from 70 percent to 55 percent. The **North Atlantic Treaty Organization (NATO)** also decisively intervened. Air strikes led by the United States destroyed Bosnian Serb infrastructure. The Royal Air Force took part in these strikes. In parallel with NATO action, UN involvement ceased. Instead, the United States persuaded all the ethnic parties in Bosnia to attend talks. On 21 November 1995, the Dayton Agreement created a technically united Bosnian state with a Bosnian–Croat federation and a centralized Serb republic. NATO left 60,000 troops, including a British contingent, in Bosnia under overall UN auspices. This force was reduced to 20,000 in 2002.

Bosnia struggled. Three quarters of the population was out of work, and it proved difficult to create integrated police and armed forces. Bosnia joined the NATO Partnership for Peace program in 2006; however, the Serbs continued to obstruct integration and even tried to achieve independence. They spent years obstructing NATO forces in their efforts to bring Karadžić and Mladić to justice. The Serbian Orthodox Church was suspected of involvement. Both men were eventually arrested and sent to face the International Criminal Tribunal for the Former Yugoslavia at the Hague, accused of war crimes. Mladić's trial began in May 2012. British members of the NATO intervention force saw firsthand evidence of Bosnian Serb atrocities carried out during the civil war.

BRETTON WOODS AGREEMENT (1944). The economic crisis of the 1930s had been worsened by protectionist and ultimately nationalistic policies designed to protect individual economies, like those of the United States and Britain, against foreign competition. The Bretton Woods Agreement of July 1944 was an attempt to learn the lessons of this experience. It flowed from the meeting of 44 Allied delegates at the **United Nations** Monetary and Financial Conference in the town of Bretton Woods, New Hampshire. The agreement was preceded by two years of collaborative work between the U.S. and British treasuries. Key figures were the well-known British economist **John Maynard Keynes** and Harry Dexter White of the U.S. Treasury. Keynes, in particular, had learned the lesson of the 1930s, and the conference established the International Monetary Fund and the International Bank for Reconstruction and Development. These bodies began to operate in 1946. They involved an application of the supranational principle to global economic problems, rather than narrow nationalism. The Bretton Woods Agreement established an exchange rate for currencies, which was pegged to the value of gold. It survived until August 1971.

BRITISH COMMONWEALTH. *See* COMMONWEALTH, BRITISH.

BRITISH EMPIRE. Britain's imperial adventure really began with the acquisition of its North American colonies in the 17th century. These were lost in the American War of Independence, although **Canada** had been annexed from **France** in 1763. The loss of the Thirteen Colonies was compensated for by the conquest of **India**, although the British used a method of indirect imperial rule until 1858, when the East India Company role was replaced by that of the Crown. Even then, Great Britain was adept at using native princes to administer the "jewel in the crown." Thereafter, Britain was fully engaged in the scramble for Africa in the latter half of the 19th century. **South Africa,**

Northern Rhodesia, **Southern Rhodesia,** and Nigeria fell under Britain's control during this period. The revolt of the white Dutch-speaking Afrikaners in South Africa was crushed in the Second Boer War, fought from 1899–1902.

An important distinction arose in Britain's imperial possessions during this period. The so-called "white dominions" of **Australia,** Canada, **New Zealand,** and South Africa were granted a considerable degree of autonomy, while the African and Asian colonies were not. This changed in the 20th century, when the more enlightened elements in the British establishment realized that some form of self-government for India would be necessary. This principle was accepted in the 1935 **India Act.** The great catalyst for decolonization was **World War II.** The catastrophic British defeats at the hands of the Japanese in 1941–1942 undermined imperial authority and the myth of white invincibility. India already had a strong nationalist movement, and, despite ferocious opposition from Premier **Winston Churchill,** it was recognized that independence after 1945 was only a matter of time. It duly came via Britain's Labour government in 1947, although the country was partitioned, with the Muslim majority areas forming **Pakistan.** Burma and Ceylon obtained their independence in 1948.

Yet, the imperial focus in British foreign policy remained its potency, evident in the existence of a separate Colonial Office. Decolonization in British Africa was also far slower in coming, perhaps accelerated by the **Suez Crisis** in 1956, but it was certainly recognized as inevitable in Prime Minister **Harold Macmillan's** "Winds of Change" speech in Cape Town in 1960. Macmillan recognized that economic ties with Western Europe were likely to be more significant in the long run. Even so, Britain would still have to fight a full-scale war with **Argentina** in 1982, over the Falkland Islands, a small far-flung imperial possession. Another, **Gibraltar,** obtained as long ago as 1713, is a persistent cause of tension with Britain's **European Union** partner, **Spain.** *See also* COMMONWEALTH, BRITISH.

BROWN, GEORGE (1914–1985). British **foreign secretary** from 1966–1968, George Brown was also deputy leader of the Labour Party. A fiery character, he came up through the trade union movement before unsuccessfully challenging **Harold Wilson** for the Labour Party leadership in 1963. When Labour won power in 1964, Brown was given responsibility for the Department of Economic Affairs, which was supposed to revamp the ailing British economy alongside the treasury. This experiment was not a success, and Brown was delighted to be appointed foreign secretary. He was a fervent pro-European, strongly supportive of Great Britain's second abortive attempt to enter the **European Economic Community (EEC)** in 1966–1967.

Brown's relationship with Wilson was always tense, and he resigned on 15 March 1968, after complaining about Wilson's "dictatorial" methods of running the government. He continued to be a leading supporter of British entry into the EEC and was created a life peer.

BROWN, GORDON (1951–). The longest-serving Labour chancellor of the exchequer, from 1997–2007, and then prime minister until his electoral defeat in May 2010, Gordon Brown's political base was in Scotland, where he attended university in Glasgow. Entering Parliament in May 1983, after Labour's worst electoral defeat, Brown soon became a key advisor to the new Labour leader, Neil Kinnock. By the time of Labour's landslide electoral victory in May 1997, Brown was the acknowledged economic expert in **Tony Blair's** first administration. His first key decision was to make the Bank of England, rather than himself, chancellor of the exchequer, responsible for setting bank interest rates. Brown's aim was to show that London had nothing to fear from a Labour government.

Brown became prime minister on 27 June 2007, when Tony Blair resigned. He was notably pro-American in outlook but skeptical about Europe. It was an open secret in Whitehall that he had obstructed British entry into the European common currency, the euro. Brown's premiership was dominated by the impact of the global financial crash in 2007–2008. If, like many, he had been credulous about the financial boom of the previous decade, Brown showed some courage and leadership in partly nationalizing major banks. This was recognized abroad, where British action was copied. Brown's relationship with President **George W. Bush** was not as close as that of his predecessor, Blair, but there is no real evidence that he offered serious opposition to the controversial war in **Iraq**. His notoriously tense relationship with Blair, whom he allegedly believed had overstayed his time in **No. 10 Downing Street**, was a byword in Whitehall.

BRUSSELS TREATY (1948). On 17 March 1948, Great Britain, **France**, **Belgium**, the Netherlands, and Luxembourg signed a collective defense agreement designed to protect Western Europe from the Soviet Union, but also from future German aggression. The Brussels Treaty evolved into the Western European Defense Organization in September 1948, and the **North Atlantic Treaty Organization** in 1949. In May 1955, the treaty was modified into the Western European Union and the membership extended to include the Federal Republic of Germany (West Germany) and **Italy**. Enthusiasts for European unity on the continent tended to be misled by arrangements like the Brussels Treaty about Britain's attitude toward the future of Europe. **Winston Churchill** may have spoken in 1946 about a "kind of United States of Europe," but neither he nor his Labour counterpart, **Clement R. Attlee**, wanted full-scale integration beyond the defense sphere. *See also* COLD WAR.

BULGARIA. This Balkan kingdom was formed out of the crisis of 1877–1878, when it seemed that it would become a Russian satellite state. This brought about the intervention of British prime minister **Benjamin Disraeli**, who ensured at the Congress of Berlin, in 1878, that the so-called "Big Bulgaria" was reduced in size. As it turned out, the Bulgars were never the pliant tools of Tsarist **Russia** that Great Britain had feared. During **World War I**, Bulgaria was on the opposite side of Russia as part of the losing Austro–German coalition. Only after 1945 were Disraeli's fears realized when Bulgaria did indeed become part of the Soviet satellite system in Eastern Europe.

Bulgaria was already a full-fledged Communist state by 1945 (**Winston Churchill**, the British prime minister, had already recognized Russia's dominant influence in October 1944) and the most pliable of the states in the Soviet Bloc. The most serious crisis in Anglo–Bulgarian relations took place under the dictatorship of Todor Zhivkov (1954–1989) in 1978. A Bulgarian defector, Georgi Markov, who worked for the BBC's World Service, was murdered by the Bulgarian secret service on London's Waterloo Bridge with a poisoned-tipped umbrella. Markov had angered Zhivkov with his persistent attacks on the Bulgarian language service. **David Owen** (1977–1979), the British **foreign secretary** at the time, strongly protested about this outrage, which the Bulgarians denied was their responsibility.

Zhivkov's regime was generally regarded as a Soviet surrogate. In 1981, his secret service was suspected of involvement in the failed attempt on the life of Pope John Paul II. Zhivkov fell from power in 1989, when Soviet leader Mikhail Gorbachev made it clear that the bayonets of the Red Army would not be used to prop up the Communist regime. After the **Cold War**, Bulgaria remained economically backward. The country did not become a member of the **European Union** until 2007, and it remained pro-Russian in orientation. Relations with **Turkey**, its historic enemy, remain poor.

BUSH, GEORGE HERBERT WALKER (1924–). A former head of the Central Intelligence Agency and U.S. ambassador to the **United Nations (UN)**, George H. W. Bush was a Republican politician with a privileged East Coast background. He went on to become vice president under President **Ronald Reagan** from 1981–1989, and then president of the **United States** from 1989–1993. Bush seemed less enthused by the Anglo–American "**special relationship**," placing more emphasis on relations with a newly united **Germany** as the powerhouse of the **European Union**. The **Gulf War** of 1991, which followed Iraq's invasion of Kuwait in August 1990, restored the relationship to its previous cordiality. Prime Minister **Margaret Thatcher** fully backed the U.S.-led UN coalition against **Iraq,** as did her successor, **John Major.** He became prime minister just before Operation Desert Storm was put into action. The Iraqis were duly routed. Controversy remained about Bush's decision not to advance on Baghdad, while encouraging abortive risings by Kurds and Shia in Iraq.

Bush kept up the **détente** policy with the Soviet Union until its collapse in 1991. He disagreed with Major about the desirability of sending U.S. troops into **Bosnia-Herzegovina** when **Yugoslavia** began to fracture in 1991–1992, even though their role was to be purely humanitarian. In contrast, Britain sent in 2,000 troops. Like previous American presidents, Bush was influenced by the national nightmare of Vietnam and thought that the European powers should deal with the Yugoslav problem. *See also* BUSH, GEORGE WALKER.

BUSH, GEORGE WALKER (1946–). Son of President **George H. W. Bush,** the former governor of Texas was fortunate to be declared the winner of the bitterly contested presidential election of November 2000. Early indications were that George W. Bush would have little interest in foreign policy. All this changed on 11 September 2001, when the World Trade Center was attacked in New York City, and the Pentagon, in Arlington, Virginia. Bush, who allowed himself to be influenced by so-called "neo-cons" in his administration, secured considerable international support for the air strikes against **Afghanistan** and the subsequent invasion in 2002. This was designed to deprive the anti-Western **terrorists** of al-Qaeda of the hideouts provided by the ultrafundamentalist Taliban regime.

It quickly became clear that Bush had established a favorable rapport with British prime minister **Tony Blair,** as **Bill Clinton** had done as president of the **United States,** despite the apparent ideological differences between a Labour prime minister and a republican president. The Christian beliefs of both men, which Blair was publicly coy about, seemed to provide a common ground. Both men allowed themselves to be convinced that **Iraq,** which was not actually involved in the 2001 terrorist attacks, had weapons of mass destruction. Bush had a rather simplified view of foreign policy that divided the world into good and evil. Blair's was more sophisticated in that he hoped that unwavering British support for the U.S. invasion of Iraq in 2003 could be used to arouse Bush's interest in the problem of **Israel** and occupied **Palestine.** But it did not, as Bush was unwilling to take any real initiative on the Middle East or listen to the career diplomats in the U.S. Department of State. He did, however, offer Blair the option of withdrawing from the Iraq operation because of the unpopularity of the invasion project in Britain. Conversely, it was Blair who persuaded Bush about the need to obtain a **United Nations (UN)** sanction for the intervention. Bush believed that UN Resolution 1441 was sufficient authority for the invasion, while Blair unsuccessfully sought a second resolution. Britain ultimately supported Bush.

The close Bush–Blair axis was fractured only by environmental matters, where Bush seemed to have a blind spot. Unlike his defeated presidential opponent Al Gore, Bush appeared to reject climate change theory. This meant that unlike Britain and other developed nations, the United States refused to ratify the Kyoto Protocol. The British also criticized American detention of alleged terrorists who had not been brought to trial at the U.S. base in Guantanamo Bay, Cuba. Bush was reelected for a second term in November 2004, but, like Blair, his reputation was tarnished by the loss of life in Iraq.

BUTLER, RICHARD AUSTEN (1902–1982). As undersecretary of state in the **Foreign Office** from 1938–1941, Richard Austen Butler, or "RAB," as he was known to political contemporaries, was a strong supporter of British **appeasement** policy. His links with **Neville Chamberlain's** policy made it slightly surprising that **Winston Churchill** retained him in the Foreign Office in 1940. He was involved in a controversial incident that summer, when he seemed to be advocating a negotiated peace with Nazi **Germany** to a Swedish diplomat. Butler went on to become minister of education, and he sponsored the important 1944 Education Act. Prominent in the reform of the Conservative Party after its catastrophic defeat in the July 1945 general election, Butler went on to hold most of the great offices of state. He was variously chancellor of the exchequer from 1951–1955, home secretary in 1957, and deputy prime minister in 1962.

Widely expected to succeed **Anthony Eden** as premier after the **Suez Crisis** of 1956, Butler was outmaneuvered by **Harold Macmillan**. Upon Macmillan's retirement in 1963, Butler failed yet again to obtain the post of prime minister, albeit through an arcane Conservative election procedure that was undemocratic. His reputation as an appeaser in the 1930s may have counted against him in a party where Winston Churchill still had much influence, as did a tendency to make cryptic, mysterious remarks that confused friend and foe alike.

C

CADOGAN, SIR ALEXANDER (1884–1968). Alexander Cadogan succeeded **Sir Robert Vansittart** as permanent undersecretary at the **Foreign Office** in 1938, a post he retained until 1946. A product of **Eton College** and Balliol College, Oxford, Cadogan was the epitome of the hardworking, levelheaded Whitehall mandarin who was always based in London, apart from a brief period as British ambassador to Peking from 1933–1936. Knighted for his services to the Foreign Office in 1934, Cadogan was more in tune with the thinking behind the **appeasement** policy toward **Germany**, **Italy**, and **Japan** pursued by the **Stanley Baldwin** and **Neville Chamberlain** governments than was his predecessor.

There was one serious short-term revolt by Cadogan against British policy over the Godesberg peace terms in September 1938, when Cadogan was credited with stiffening the views of the Foreign Secretary, **Lord Halifax**, but he ultimately went along with the partition of Czechoslovakia agreed upon at the **Munich Agreement** on 29 September.

During World War II, Cadogan accompanied **Winston Churchill** to all the big wartime conferences at Casablanca, **Teheran**, **Yalta**, and **Potsdam**, a quiet but invaluable aide to his much more extroverted political master. In 1946, Cadogan became Britain's permanent representative to the **United Nations**. Published in 1971, three years after his death, his diaries shocked his contemporaries because of the caustic critical remarks he made about politicians and diplomats alike.

CALLAGHAN, JAMES (1912–2005). Leaving school at the age of 14, James Callaghan rose to the top of the Labour Party through the trade union movement. He then served as chancellor of the exchequer (1964–1967), home secretary (1967–1970), and **foreign secretary** (1974–1976) in the first and second **Harold Wilson** Cabinets. Although he had a cordial relationship with the West German chancellor, Helmut Schmidt, Callaghan's premiership from 1976–1979 saw a return to the friendly relations established by British prime ministers with U.S. presidents, which had not been a feature of the **Edward Heath** government (1970–1974).

Callaghan was beset by economic difficulties during his premiership, and, in 1976, Great Britain had to approach the International Monetary Fund for a substantial loan, which was tied to a package of internal cuts. Avuncular by character but sometimes abrasive, Callaghan was nicknamed "Sunny Jim" by the media. He made a serious tactical error in not calling an election in the autumn of 1978, waiting instead until May 1979, after Labour had suffered a so-called "winter of discontent" of trade union strikes. He duly lost the general election to **Margaret Thatcher**. Callaghan's appointment as foreign secretary by Wilson in 1974 was a surprise, as others were better qualified. Nevertheless, he proved adept at forging good personal relationships with foreign leaders. His friendship with President Jimmy Carter secured American support for sanctions against the illegal white majority government of Ian Smith in **Southern Rhodesia**. He was made a life peer.

CAMERON, DAVID (1966–). Appointed prime minister of Great Britain on 11 May 2010, David Cameron had never previously held a government post; however, he had the classic profile of a Conservative leader, being educated at **Eton College** and Christchurch College, Oxford. Cameron acquired some later notoriety because of his membership to the Oxford University Bullingdon Club, which was associated with excessive drinking and boorish behavior. Upon graduation, he worked for the Conservative Research Department from September 1988–1993. In 1991, Cameron was briefly seconded to **No. 10 Downing Street** to work under **John Major**. In the 1992 British general election, he was given the task of briefing Major on his daily press conferences. Prime Minister Major won an election that most expected him to lose. The Conservative victory brought Cameron the post of special advisor to the chancellor of the exchequer, Norman Lamont. Cameron was working for Lamont at the time of the so-called "Black Wednesday" in 1992, when Britain was forced out of the Exchange Rate Mechanism. He could be seen in the shadows as Lamont told the media about the catastrophic escalation in British interest rates. Cameron moved on to become an advisor to the home secretary Michael Howard, before leaving politics in 1994, to work in television, where he spent seven years before resigning in February 2001, to fight for the Conservative seat of Whitney in Oxfordshire in the general election. He was duly elected, but the Conservatives were heavily defeated by **Tony Blair's** Labour Party.

In the 2001–2005 Parliament, Cameron served as a member of the House of Commons Select Committee on Home Affairs, and, when his mentor, Howard, replaced **William Hague** as Conservative leader in November 2003, Cameron became shadow spokesperson on local government. Howard lost the 2005 general election to Labour and decided to stand down as Conservative leader. Cameron, still only 39 years of age, decided to stand in the election contest. He was relatively unknown in the party ranks but impressed in the contest with his ability to speak off the cuff without notes. In the final ballot on 20 October 2005, Cameron won with 90 votes from Conservative members of Parliament.

As leader, Cameron tried to distance the Conservatives from the abrasive legacy of **Margaret Thatcher**, and he was known to be an admirer of the nonideological, media-driven approach to politics of Tony Blair. Critics attacked him for alleged superficiality, as they had done with Blair. Traditional Conservatives found his approach glib and outside mainstream party tradition. As a modernizer, Cameron wanted more women and members of ethnic minorities inside his party. He found himself leader of the opposition during the Credit Crisis of 2008–2009, when the new Labour prime minister, **Gordon Brown** (who replaced Blair in June 2007), had to partly nationalize British banks. He performed better against Brown in the House of Commons than the more politically astute Blair.

At a time of recession, the worst in many years, Cameron would have expected a decisive election victory in the May 2010 contest. This was not forthcoming. His Conservative Party, with 306 seats, had to rely on Liberal Democrat support to take office. At just 43 years of age, Cameron became the youngest British prime minister since 1812.

In foreign policy, Cameron wanted to be distinctive. He rejected the interventionism of Blair, inappropriate at a time of national austerity, and was the most Eurosceptic leader since Thatcher. He demonstrated this by aligning the Conservatives with the sharply right-wing parties in the **European Union (EU)** parliament, rather than the center-right parties of **Germany** and **France**. In economics, he and his friend and chancellor **George Osborne** preached massive deficit reduction, thus implementing a cuts program in 2010–2011. Cameron was soon forced into a foreign policy revision in 2011, when events in **Libya** involved Britain in military intervention, albeit one that did not (unlike **Iraq**) involve ground troops. This intervention, alongside France and the **United States**, cost the British Exchequer £212 million.

Cameron faced the greatest crisis of his short premiership in December 2011. The sovereign debt crisis in the **Eurozone**, which involved substantial EU bailouts to **Ireland**, Portugal, and **Greece**, had helped to create a severe decrease in confidence. The Italian economy was also under threat, but, Britain, which had refused to join the euro in 2000, was not prepared to assist any state other than Ireland, with which it had especially close ties. Cameron was under severe pressure from Conservative Eurosceptics to hold a referendum on the EU, and they demanded repatriation of some powers from the union. Cameron did not want to leave the EU, but he also appeared anxious to appease his anti-EU right wing. His problem was that his Liberal Democrat allies, led by **Nick Clegg**, were the most pro-European of British parties.

A crucial EU summit was held in Brussels on the night of 8–9 December, when Cameron used the British veto against a new EU treaty that would have forced Eurozone states to be more provident in their spending or risk severe penalties. Cameron asked for a special protocol to protect Britain's financial services sector as the price of a British signature. This was rejected outright by the dominant EU leaders, including Angela Merkel, chancellor of Germany, and Nicolas Sarkozy, president of France. Ostensibly, Britain was left in a minority of one against 26. Cameron's strategy seemed to be to try to detach states like Sweden, the Czech Republic, and Hungary, which were noneuro states known to have reservations about the intergovernmental accord from the main body. On 17 December, it was agreed that Britain could send representatives to Eurozone discussions on fiscal discipline and other matters. The long-term impact of Cameron's European policy remained to be seen. Elsewhere, there was a degree of consistency. British troops were to be out of Iraq in 2014. Cameron was careful to regularly praise the efforts of Britain's armed forces. In a speech in July 2010, he was critical, as his Labour predecessors had been, of **Israeli** behavior in the Gaza Strip. This was in line with previous British policy, and Britain had always been more critical of Israeli behavior than the United States. Cameron was supportive of Arab efforts to overthrow decades of dictatorship in **Egypt**, Tunisia, Yemen, and Syria.

CANADA. Great Britain's links with Canada date back to the 18th century, and the conflicts known as the War of Austrian Succession (1740–1748) and the Seven Years' War (1756–1763). Originally a French settlement, Canada became of crucial strategic importance since Britain had Thirteen Colonies to the south. The Seven Years' War was decisive in securing British control and defeating the much smaller French settler population with its Indian allies. British victory meant the French-speaking population centered in Quebec would have to endure Anglo–Saxon domination for centuries. Subsequent U.S. invasions of Canada after independence from Britain in 1776 failed, as did invasion by Irish republicans from the **United States** in the 1860s. British Canada emerged as a self-governing dominion through the British North American Act on 1 July 1867. It was a federation made up of Ontario, Quebec, Nova Scotia, and New Brunswick. The fissure between French and English-speakers remained and affected relations with the mother country. Canada made a notable contribution to the British war effort in **World War I** (as part of the **British Empire**, its involvement was automatic). More than 56,000 Canadians died in the war. French Canadians objected to the imposition of compulsory military service. Britain still had control of Canada's foreign and defense policies. A move away from such dependence started to become evident at the 1919 **Paris Peace Conference**. Canada, under Prime Minister Mackenzie King, was allowed to represent itself. King was the dominant figure in Canadian politics from 1921–1948.

Awareness of Canada's growing reliance on its giant neighbor, the **United States**, also began to emerge. In 1921, there was strong Canadian backing for the abrogation of the 1902 Anglo–Japanese Treaty of Alliance, which the Americans objected to. An unwilling Britain wilted under U.S. and Canadian pressure; however, in 1925, Canada came under the auspices of the Dominions Office, which replaced the Colonial Office. Like **Australia** and **South Africa,** Canada strongly supported British **appeasement** policy in the 1930s. Like them, it secured control of its own foreign policy under the 1931 Statute of Westminster. King reiterated Canadian independence in an important 1936 statement. He reminded the British that only the Canadian parliament could make decisions about participating in wars involving other **Commonwealth** countries. Therefore, it was parliament that decided that Canada would support Britain when **World War II** broke out in September 1939.

During World War II, Canada again made a crucial contribution. The Royal Canadian Navy provided invaluable assistance in the Battle of the Atlantic. Canada suffered severely in casualties in the poorly planned British operation at Dieppe in 1942, and its soldiers were to the fore in Normandy in 1944. While the British link was maintained, the relationship with the United States became increasingly paramount. As early as 1940, the Ogdensburg Agreement recognized the strategic interdependence of Canada and the United States. When Britain's new Labour prime minister, **Clement R. Attlee,** raised the issue of a centralized Commonwealth defense policy at the Dominions Prime Ministers' Meeting in 1946, King was unreceptive. Canada joined the **North Atlantic Treaty Organization (NATO)** in 1949, and, in 1950, it contributed to the Commonwealth division sent to fight in Korea. It reserved the right to disagree with the former colonial power. At the time of the 1956 **Suez Crisis,** Canada opposed the policy of **Anthony Eden.** Louis St. Laurent, minister for external affairs at the time, was instrumental in keeping **India** and **Pakistan** in the Commonwealth over the issue.

Canada was adopting its own distinctive foreign policy. Its leader, **John Diefenbaker** (prime minister, 1957–1963), was an Anglophile, but, at the 1959 Commonwealth Conference, he took the lead in condemning apartheid before British policy became more assertive on the issue. This was the period when **Harold Macmillan** applied for membership in the **European Economic Community** (1961). Diefenbaker had to seek new markets for Canada's grain exports in China and Eastern Europe ahead of British membership. Pierre Trudeau (prime minister, 1968–1979 and 1980–1984) was of French Canadian origin, but he did not support the separatism favored by many of his fellow French-speakers. French and English received equal language status in 1969, and, in 1982, Trudeau obliged the House of Commons to give up residual British rights to legislate for Canada. This got rid of a clause in the Statute of Westminster inserted at the insistence of Quebec and Ontario allowing Britain to amend the Canadian constitution. **Margaret Thatcher** antagonized Canadians in 1988, when she lectured the Canadian parliament about the need for a free trade agreement with the United States. This ignored protocol about not interfering as a foreign head of government in the pending Canadian election, in which free trade was a controversial issue. In fact, Thatcher's lobbying proved to be prophetic. In 1989, Canada and the United States signed a free trade agreement, and, in 1993, the North American Free Trade Association was created.

One issue that remained outstanding was the status of Quebec. In 1980, its population rejected separate sovereignty, while in 1995 a referendum rejected it by only 1 percent. In 2006, the Canadian parliament recognized Quebec as a distinct nation within the Canadian federation. In its external policy, Canada was prepared to differ with both the British and Americans over the **Iraq War** (2003). No Canadian troops were sent, and Prime Minister Stephen Harper (2006–present) differed with Britain over the **Kyoto Protocol** (1997). Harper queried Canada's commitment to a 6-percent reduction of greenhouse gases after its emissions had risen by 25 percent between 1990–2005. The NATO intervention in **Afghanistan** in 2001–2002 found British troops alongside Canadian ones. In 2006, Canada renewed its commitment there, but, in 2011, it announced the start of a withdrawal process.

CHAMBERLAIN, AUSTEN (1863–1937). The older half brother of the better-known **Neville Chamberlain,** Austen Chamberlain was the member of the family expected to achieve the premiership of Great Britain. He was the son of Joseph Chamberlain, a well-known 19th-century Liberal politician who defected to the Conservatives. An unremarkable chancellor of the exchequer, Chamberlain found his niche as **foreign secretary** in **Stanley Baldwin's** second administration between 1924–1929. He was regarded as pro-French but could not get his colleagues to make a firm Anglo–French alliance. Chamberlain shared their suspicion of any binding commitment to **Poland** and Eastern Europe, remarking that it was not worth the "bones of a British grenadier." He died in the same year that his younger brother attained the premiership. He was a winner of the **Nobel Peace Prize** in 1926. *See also* LOCARNO, TREATY OF.

CHAMBERLAIN, NEVILLE (1869–1940). As Great Britain's prime minister from 1937–1940, Neville Chamberlain's success was remarkable. As a young man, he spent unrewarding years trying to grow sisal in the Bahamas under his father's direction. He was also deemed only capable of studying metallurgy at an obscure Birmingham college, rather than at Oxford, like his half brother, **Austen Chamberlain**. Always an efficient administrator, Chamberlain went on to be lord mayor of Birmingham, but he was nearly 40 years old before he became a Conservative member of Parliament in 1918. Circumstances then favored him when senior Conservative ministers went out of office with the **David Lloyd George** coalition government in 1922. He held the posts of postmaster general, paymaster general, minister of housing, and chancellor of the exchequer between 1922–1924. An effective health secretary, Chamberlain returned as chancellor of the exchequer from 1931–1937.

Chamberlain's considerable achievements as a domestic reformer, for example, he demolished many urban slums, have been overshadowed by the **appeasement** controversy. When he became prime minister in May 1937, Chamberlain believed that reaching an accommodation with the dictatorships in **Germany**, **Italy**, and **Japan** was essential because of Britain's economic situation. He did not oppose rearmament as such, but he thought that priority should be given to the fighter component of the Royal Air Force rather than to the army. Chamberlain did not believe that it was worth fighting a war for the Czech Sudetenland in September 1938, against Nazi Germany, an opinion shared by most of his fellow countrymen and countrywomen.

Appeasement of Germany ultimately failed, and Chamberlain's reputation never recovered. Some argue that it would have been in his best interest to resign as prime minister when **World War II** started in September 1939. Yet, Chamberlain was a loyal ally of **Winston Churchill** when he became prime minister in 1940. Chamberlain died of bowel cancer in November 1940.

CHEQUERS. This country residence, located some 40 miles from London, has been the official alternative home for British prime ministers since **David Lloyd George** acquired it in 1921. It is used during weekends and during holidays, while **No. 10 Downing Street** is the prime minister's weekday residence. Many foreign heads of state have stayed there, most notably U.S. presidents.

CHINA. Contacts between Great Britain and China date back to at least the 17th century. These agreements were mostly based on trade, but the relationship changed in the 1840s, when Britain forced a reluctant China to accept the Opium trade and annexed **Hong Kong**. Trading rights were also conceded to the British in Shanghai and other Chinese cities. This was part of the Open Door Policy toward China, whereby Great Britain, the **United States**, and **Japan** forced the Manchu dynasty to accept foreign trading primacy. The Chinese fiercely resented the intervention of the "foreign devils" but were too weak in military terms to do anything about it. In 1922, Britain and the United States, along with **France**, **Italy**, and Japan, were supposed to safeguard Chinese rights under the terms of the Washington Treaty. This was in exchange for trading and commercial rights.

In reality, the Anglo–Americans did nothing to protect China against the invasion by imperial Japan in the 1930s. The process started with the invasion of Manchuria and was extended to the Chinese eastern seaboard in 1937. The **Foreign Office** was always strongly pro-Chinese during the interwar period partly because of Britain's strong commercial interests there. By contrast, the British ambassador in Tokyo, Sir Robert Craigie, advocated the **appeasement** of Japan lest Britain be sucked into a costly Far Eastern war. Prime Minister **Neville Chamberlain** agreed with him. Such divisions created tensions in British foreign policy toward China. The domestic situation in China was complicated by a civil war between the Nationalist government, led by Chiang Kai-Shek, and the Chinese Communist Party, led by Mao Zedong. The Americans aided Chiang's regime after Japan's attack on **Pearl Harbor** in December 1941, being suspicious of the Communists. This continued to be U.S. policy in 1946, when the civil war in China resumed. The policy failed when the endemic corruption and incompetence of the Nationalist government resulted in its total defeat in 1949. The British Foreign Office immediately recognized the new People's Republic of China (PRC), while the administration of **Harry S. Truman** refused to do so. This remained U.S. policy until 1971.

British policy toward China remained more pragmatic. There was, however, tension about the remaining British colony in Hong Kong, and the Chinese invasion of North Korea in 1950 brought the Anglo–Americans together. Britain still believed that the PRC should be admitted to the **United Nations (UN)**, while the Americans used their veto on the UN Security Council to give the Chinese seat to Chiang, who had fled to the island of Taiwan in 1949, with the remnants of his regime. Britain also relaxed trade controls with China as early as 1957. The British were even prepared to work with China to improve international relations. In 1954, the foreign ministers of Britain and China, **Anthony Eden** and Chou En-Lai, respectively, were cochairmen of the **Geneva Conference**, which ended the war between France and Vietnamese nationalists in **Indochina**. The Americans took observer status only in the proceedings. They removed their veto on PRC membership of the UN in 1971, as a result of the diplomatic initiative by President **Richard Nixon**.

Anglo–Chinese relations remained generally tense. Britain could hardly be expected to approve of the PRC's attack on **India**, a member of the **British Commonwealth**, over a long-standing frontier dispute in 1962. It, like all the Western powers, was a victim of Chinese antiimperialist propaganda during the period of the Cultural Revolution (1966–1976).

The Crown colony of Hong Kong remained a sore spot in Anglo–Chinese relations. In the early 1980s, the PRC stated that it would aim to recover the whole of Hong Kong, and lengthy talks with the British followed. These resulted in the Sino–British Joint Declaration of 1984, when **Margaret Thatcher** was Britain's prime minister. Britain agreed to return Hong Kong (obtained on a 99-year lease in 1898) in 1997. Thereafter, for 50 years, Hong Kong would be a "special administrative region" with a capitalist system. This would allow Hong Kong to retain its status as a world financial center, and English was to remain the official language for 50 years.

The appointment of Christopher Patten as Hong Kong's last British governor (1992–1997) proved to be controversial. He announced that the British would allow the people of Hong Kong to vote for the majority of the members of the Legislative Council (LEGCO), which had been set up in 1991. There had been no consultation with the PRC beforehand, and Patten's action brought about a crisis in Anglo–Chinese relations. When the transfer of power came in 1997, the Chinese authorities abolished LEGCO. Hong Kong residents were not accorded nationality and thus could not immigrate to Britain if they wished to avoid Communist rule. Other countries, like **Canada**, became a target for those Chinese who left Hong Kong, and, from 1984–1997, more than 500,000 people left the former British colony.

Other issues remained between the two states. There was persistent criticism from the Foreign Office of Chinese policy in Tibet, which the PRC had annexed in 1949. Britain and China were invariably on opposite sides at the UN regarding such questions as **Bosnia** and **Kosovo** (1991), **Afghanistan** (2001), **Iraq** (2003), and **Libya** (2011). The Chinese fixation with "harmony" at home, in effect outlawing any kind of dissent, also applied to foreign policy. The PRC opposed any action that impinged on national sovereignty and might challenge the existing political system, be it in Europe, Africa, or Asia. British desire to access the huge Chinese market had to be balanced against human rights concerns. Visits to the PRC by **David Cameron**, with a huge delegation in 2011, and chancellor of the exchequer, **George Osborne**, in January 2012, reflected Britain's need to increase trade with the growing superpower. Yet, the desire for greater trade between Britain and China did not prevent sharp differences in 2012 regarding **Iran**. China claimed to oppose the Iranian nuclear program, but it opposed any attempt to impose sanctions on the Iranian regime, which were implemented by the **European Union**. Britain, the United States, and France were prepared to use force to keep the Straits of Hormuz open, while China was not. Other differences emerged regarding the Syrian revolt in 2012.

CHURCHILL, SIR WINSTON SPENCER (1874–1965). Winston Spencer Churchill was a relative of the Duke of Marlborough and the son of a former chancellor of the exchequer, Sir Randolph Churchill. His father married **Jennie Jerome**, a New Yorker, and Churchill used his American link effectively as prime minister from 1940–1945. His maternal grandfather owned the *New York Times.*

Churchill went to Harrow School, where he failed to shine and was deemed too unintelligent to be sent to university. An army career was speedily dropped in favor of one in journalism (a useful source of income for the rest of his life) and politics. He entered Parliament as a Conservative member of Parliament in 1900, but had deserted to the Liberal Party by the time it achieved office in 1906. As a young man, he was successively president of the Board of Trade, home secretary from 1911–1915, and first lord of the **Admiralty**. This was a natural home for Churchill, who throughout his life maintained a great interest in naval and military matters.

A misconceived plan to shorten **World War I** by landings at Gallipoli, in 1915, cost Churchill dearly, and he was forced to resign. He was then the only British government minister to actually serve in the trenches in **France**. He returned to government under his old ally **David Lloyd George** (prime minister, 1916–1922), before returning to the Tory Party, changing parties yet again. From 1924–1929, like his father, he served as chancellor of the exchequer in **Stanley Baldwin's** second administration.

Differences with the Conservative leadership over the **appeasement** policy toward **Germany** kept Churchill out of office, although he also discredited himself because of his attitude regarding Indian independence and the abdication of King **Edward VIII** in December 1936. Only the coming of war in September 1939 brought Churchill back into office in his old post as first lord of the Admiralty.

Churchill was by far the most belligerent member of the wartime government under **Neville Chamberlain**, but his rather rash plan to intervene in Norway brought down the government. On 10 May 1940, Churchill himself was appointed prime minister, presiding over a Conservative coalition with Labour and the Liberal Party. He offered Britain only "blood, toil, tears, and sweat." He found Great Britain in desperate straits. Its army was evacuated from France in a perilous operation at the end of May and early June, and, on 22 June, its main ally, France, was forced to surrender to the Germans. Always with an eye across the Atlantic and careful to build up a friendly personal relationship with President **Franklin D. Roosevelt**, Churchill was tough and ruthless enough to order the sinking of a large part of the French fleet on 4 July, lest it fall into German hands. This action was designed to impress U.S. opinion with British resolution in a crisis. Churchill's vivid rhetoric in Parliament and on the radio raised his people's own spirits during the Battle of Britain (July–September 1940), when the Royal Air Force fought off a German air assault designed to precede invasion.

Throughout the dismal winter and spring of 1940–1941, Churchill needed all his courage and resolution in providing leadership for a country suffering severe defeats in North Africa, the Mediterranean, and the Atlantic. He and Britain were saved, first by Adolf Hitler's invasion of the Soviet Union in June 1941, and then by the Japanese attack on **Pearl Harbor** on 7 December 1941. Cooperation with the **United States** was relatively easy, although Roosevelt still regarded Churchill as an Edwardian imperialist that with the Soviet Union was not. Churchill withdrew none of his criticism of Communism as a creed, but he loyally tried to assist Joseph Stalin with the limited resources at Britain's disposal.

The finite nature of those resources came back to haunt him as he tried to deal with two huge, powerful allies. He fought off U.S. demands for an early invasion of France in favor of a Mediterranean-based strategy. All he could offer Stalin, always suspicious of the West, was Royal Air Force participation in the bombing of Germany.

Eventually, U.S. pressures pushed aside Churchill's reservations about an amphibious landing on the French coast, and the invasion duly took place in June 1944. Churchill had increasing fears about long-term Soviet intentions despite his **"Percentages Agreement"** with Stalin in October 1944, whereby British interest in **Greece** was acknowledged. He fought a rearguard action against Roosevelt, who favored a dismantling of the **British Empire**, and Stalin, who wanted a Communist **Poland**, the antithesis of the free Poland Britain had been fighting for. These issues were not resolved by the **Yalta Conference** in February 1945, a summit in the **Crimea** attended by the "Big Three."

Victory over Germany came on 8 May 1945, but Churchill had been ejected from office on 26 July, before complete victory was gained. Midway through the **Potsdam Conference**, he learned that he had lost the general election to Labour. He was a bitterly disappointed man, but, in opposition, he famously warned about the **"Iron Curtain"** in 1946, and also encouraged European unity in another speech.

Foreign policy dominated Churchill's second administration (1951–1955). At 79 years of age, he wanted a summit with the Soviet leadership after Stalin's death in March 1953, alarmed as he was by the nuclear threat. As he put it, "jaw, jaw is better than war, war." He was unable to achieve this ambition, however, because of the opposition of U.S. president **Dwight D. Eisenhower**, despite the good relationship they had established in wartime, when Eisenhower was supreme allied commander. The two men did agree to cooperate to bring down the **Iranian** nationalist regime of Mohammed Mossadeq in August 1953. In 1954, Churchill's government negotiated the withdrawal of the large British occupation force from the Canal Zone in **Egypt**. He reluctantly stood down as prime minister in April 1955.

Churchill's last years were somewhat anticlimactic, featuring long trips abroad indulging his talent for painting. He was critical of his successor **Anthony Eden's** handling of the 1956 **Suez Crisis** and stood down as member of Parliament in 1959, after a half-century in the House of Commons. Churchill died on 23 January 1965, and, unusually for a commoner, was given a state funeral.

CLARK KERR, ARCHIBALD (1882–1951). Archibald Clark Kerr was of Scots origin, and he joined the Diplomatic Service in 1906. He served variously in **Germany**, **Egypt**, and **Iraq**, before being appointed British ambassador to **China** (1938–1942), the Soviet Union (1942–1946), and the **United States** (1946–1948). As ambassador in Moscow, he was required to accompany **Winston Churchill** to the crucial wartime **Yalta Conference** in the **Crimea** in February 1945. It was unfortunate for Clark Kerr that a distinguished career in the Diplomatic Service was to be blighted by the presence of the spy **Donald Maclean** in his Washington embassy. He was created 1st Baron Inverchapel in 1948.

CLEGG, NICK (1967–). As Great Britain's deputy prime minister after the general election of May 2010 created a coalition with the Conservatives, Nick Clegg became the most important Liberal politician since 1922. Since that date, his party has become known as the Liberal Democrats. Clegg became the leader of the Liberal Democrats in 2007. He had been member of Parliament for Sheffield Hallam since 2005, having previously been a member of the European Parliament from 1999–2004. Clegg was educated at Westminster School in London and Cambridge University, but also at the University of Minnesota and the College of Europe in **Belgium**. He is an unusual British politician. His mother is half Dutch, and his paternal grandmother was the daughter of a Russian baron who fled from his native land at the time of the Bolshevik Revolution in October 1917. Clegg, who speaks Dutch, French, German, and Spanish (he is married to Miriam González, the daughter of a Spanish politician who also worked in Brussels), is thus not the typical member of the British elite he seems. No British politician of recent years has been better qualified to deal with the **European Union (EU)**.

In 1994, Clegg took up a post at the European Commission working with an aid program to the former Soviet Union. Until 1996, he was in charge of developing direct aid programs to Central Asia and the Caucasus. He then worked for the vice president of the EU and trade commissioner Leon Brittan, a former Cabinet minister under **Margaret Thatcher**. In 1999, Clegg further demonstrated his European credentials by being elected as a Liberal Democrat candidate for the European Parliament in the East Midlands. In Brussels once again, Clegg was made spokesman for the European Liberal Democrat and Reform Group. He left the European Parliament in 2004 and, after a brief period as a political lobbyist, was selected as Liberal Democrat candidate for Sheffield Hallam in November 2004. Some part-time university teaching followed before Clegg was elected member of Parliament in the 2005 general election. He became Liberal Democrat spokesman on Europe and home affairs before winning the election for party leader when Sir Menzies Campbell stood down on 15 October 2007. Clegg took over as leader on 18 October.

As leader, Clegg rejected an appeal to work together with the Conservatives, claiming that his own party was the most progressive force in British politics. It had been the most pro-European party since the 1950s. The Liberal Democrats had also opposed the 2003 **Iraq War**. This meant that Labour, rather than the Conservatives, were more likely allies, as left-wing opinion had generally opposed the war, even if the then-government of **Tony Blair** had supported the **United States**. The result of the May 2010 general election meant that Clegg and his party held the balance of power, with 57 parliamentary seats and 23 percent of the vote. The prospect of power loomed for the Liberal Democrats. Clegg claimed that as the largest party with the biggest popular vote, the Conservatives were entitled to Liberal Democrat support. This was actually a historic fallacy. In the 1920s, Labour had formed two governments with a minority of seats and votes and relied on Liberal support to keep them in office. Some senior Liberal Democrats would have much preferred a coalition with Labour, but Clegg chose the Conservative leader **David Cameron** as a partner, rather than the outgoing Labour prime minister, **Gordon Brown**. Thus he assumed office as deputy prime minister on 12 May 2010.

Clegg was also appointed minister for constitutional reform so he could manage the attempt to bring in the alternative vote (AV) system, which was much closer to the proportional vote system commonly used in Continental Europe. The Liberal Democrats had long wanted an end to Britain's existing post system, and, on 5 July 2010, Clegg announced plans for a referendum on 5 May 2011. This was a disaster. In the AV referendum, the "yes" vote was just 32 percent, while the Conservative-backed "no" vote was more than 67 percent. A potentially worse disaster for Clegg lay in wait. He had supported the government's fierce austerity program but reiterated his party's commitment to membership of the EU. Clegg had accepted that Britain should not be a member of the **Eurozone**, but the December 2011 crisis occasioned by

Cameron's veto of a new EU treaty at the Brussels EU summit placed him in a deeply embarrassing situation. He was reportedly consulted beforehand on Britain's negotiation stance but then telephoned by Cameron early on the morning of 9 December to be told about the veto. Initially supportive, Clegg then strongly criticized what Cameron had done. After party consultations, he even absented himself from Prime Minister Cameron's statement about his Europe policy on 12 December. Clegg was adamant that his party would not support any demand to return powers from the EU to the Westminster Parliament. He saw it as his task to repair bridges to the EU and the Eurozone. This would not be easy, when many of his Conservative coalition partners were so strongly hostile toward Europe.

CLINTON, WILLIAM JEFFERSON "BILL" (1946–). Bill Clinton, who was president of the **United States** from 1993–2001, had long-standing links with Great Britain. He was a **Rhodes Scholar** at Oxford University in the late 1960s, and his daughter Chelsea also attended the university. Clinton was a Democrat, and during his first presidential campaign in 1992 there was some tension with the Conservative government of **John Major**, which was felt to be overtly assisting the Republicans. Documents were released relating to Clinton's anti–**Vietnam War** activities as a student at Oxford, and the Democrats took a dim view of this. Like **George W. Bush**, Clinton had avoided the draft.

Clinton was not an especially Anglophile president, but he did play a key role in the Northern **Ireland** peace process. Irish republicans had considerable support in the United States and in the Democratic Party, but only if they abandoned the use of violence. Clinton worked with Major and his successor, **Tony Blair** (prime minister, 1997–2007), to persuade republican leaders, and especially the **Irish Republican Army,** to use the ballot box and not the bullet. The result was the Good Friday Agreement of 1998, which set Northern Ireland on the road to peace.

Clinton and Blair forged a close relationship, and the latter was able to persuade the U.S. president to intervene in **Kosovo** in 1999, when Muslims were threatened with ethnic genocide. When he left the White House in January 2001, Clinton received an honorary doctorate from Oxford University, something it had refused to grant **Margaret Thatcher**.

COLD WAR. The term *Cold War* was first used by financier Bernard Baruch and made popular by journalist Walter Lippmann. It describes the confrontation between the superpowers, the **United States**, the Soviet Union, and their allies, which did not evolve into an open confrontation. Signs of tension were already present during **World War II** over such issues as **Poland**, which

Winston Churchill felt especially strongly about. He warned about Soviet ambitions in his famous "**Iron Curtain**" speech in 1946, by which time it was clear that Stalin intended to create a series of subservient satellite states in Central Europe and Eastern Europe. This process was complete by February 1948, with the Communist takeover in **Czechoslovakia.**

The American response came with the **Marshall Plan** in 1947, and the promise in the **Truman Doctrine** that free people in Europe would receive assistance. Stalin's attempt to blockade Berlin in 1948–1949 led to the founding of the **North Atlantic Treaty Organization**, in which British foreign secretary **Ernest Bevin** was heavily involved. British foreign policy was generally strongly supportive of the Americans in their confrontation with Moscow. Thus, British troops were sent to Korea in June 1950, to support the U.S.-led coalition against Communist aggression there. But there were blips. Prime Minister **Clement Attlee** was alarmed by the aggressive posturing of General Douglas MacArthur in Korea, and, unlike the United States, Great Britain had recognized the People's Republic of China when Mao Zedong seized power in 1949. Thereafter, there were disagreements when Churchill was frustrated during his second administration (1951–1955) by U.S. opposition to summits with the post-Stalin Soviet leadership. The British were also prepared to accept the possibility of a Communist government in Vietnam when the French were defeated in 1954. The Americans were not.

Nevertheless, the Cold War drove the two Anglo–Saxon democracies closer together. For example, in an unprecedented move, U.S. nuclear bombers were allowed to be stationed in Britain during peacetime, and Britain became increasingly dependent on American delivery systems like **Polaris**. Disagreements about the **Vietnam War** continued into the 1960s, when Prime Minister **Harold Wilson** refused to send any British combat troops to Vietnam when the Cold War continued in its Far Eastern dimension, despite considerable pressure from President **Lyndon B. Johnson**. The Cold War also meant that both U.S. and British troops had to be stationed in large numbers in the Federal Republic of Germany, well after the creation of the new state in 1955. Britain also tested its own nuclear devices as part of its Cold War profile. Ernest Bevin memorably remarked that the British must have an atomic bomb with the "Union Jack flying on top of it." The first British atomic bomb was duly exploded in October 1952, followed by a hydrogen bomb detonation in May 1957. Some maintained that the British nuclear deterrent was a waste of resources, but, after 1945, the government argued that the proximity of the Soviet Union—it was much closer to Great Britain than to the United States—made British possession of nuclear weapons essential. This was more important than the argument that Britain needed a bomb to assert its great power status, as Bevin's famous remarks implied.

In the 1950s and 1960s, the British government strongly condemned Soviet tyranny in Central Europe and Eastern Europe. This was most sharply evident in November 1956, when Hungary revolted and was crushed by the Red Army (even hard-line British Communists deserted the party in outrage). Equally outrageous in British eyes was the brutal invasion of Czechoslovakia, experimenting with a more liberal Communism by Warsaw Pact forces in August 1968.

Looming over these events was the nuclear threat, which brought the world to the brink of disaster because of Cuba in October 1962. Britain's prime minister, **Harold Macmillan,** was steadfast in supporting the United States, and his government adhered to the 1963 **Nuclear Test Ban Treaty** that followed the crisis.

British foreign policy followed traditional pro-American lines in the 1970s, with an emphasis on **détente** with the Soviet Bloc. There was a short-term crisis in 1971, when the British foreign secretary **Sir Alec Douglas-Home** expelled a large number of Soviet diplomats for espionage activities. Otherwise, the administrations of **Edward Heath** (1970–1974) and Harold Wilson (1974–1976) supported the West German attempt in 1974 to regularize diplomatic relations with East **Germany** and Poland, the Soviet Union's most important satellites during the Cold War. A colder diplomatic wind blew in 1979, when Prime Minister **Margaret Thatcher** followed U.S. president Jimmy Carter's condemnation of the Soviet invasion of **Afghanistan** by adding her own criticism of Soviet policy. She did not, however, follow Carter in boycotting the 1980 Olympic Games in Moscow.

Carter's successor, **Ronald Reagan,** continued the anti-Soviet tone in U.S. policy, and it was Thatcher who spotted the potential for change when the new Soviet leader, Mikhail Gorbachev, became general secretary of the Soviet Communist Party in 1985. She effectively acted as a bridge between Washington and Moscow in the lead up to the groundbreaking U.S.–Soviet summit at Reykjavik in 1986. Like everyone else, Thatcher was surprised by the sheer speed with which the Soviet empire in Eastern Europe collapsed in 1989. One concern was the reunification of Germany in 1990, which Thatcher, who had grown up during World War II, had some fears about. The Cold War effectively ended with the disappearance of the Soviet Union at the end of 1991. Reagan and Thatcher believed that they had won the war by standing up to the Soviet Union and forcing Gorbachev to seek the winding down of the arms race because the Soviet Union could no longer afford it. Other analysts thought that Gorbachev's internal concessions had hastened the end of the conflict. *See also* MASSIVE RETALIATION.

COMMONWEALTH, BRITISH. As far back as 1884, a future prime minister of Great Britain, Lord Roseberry, had referred to the Commonwealth as a more enlightened, informal version of the **British Empire**. When this empire began to disappear in the 20th century, former colonies and dominions (self-governing white countries like **Australia** and **Canada**) were invited to join this looser form of link with Britain while retaining, if they wished, the British monarch as head of state. Not all former colonies chose to do so. Burma, for example, opted to become a republic outside the Commonwealth in 1948. The Irish Republic also decided to end the link with the British Crown in 1949, although as the Irish Free State, it had been a member of the Commonwealth since 1922. The Commonwealth was deemed to be especially important by the **Foreign Office** during the immediate period after **World War II** because there were fears that **India**, newly independent in 1947, might come under the orbit of the Soviet Union. The Commonwealth was seen as a means of influencing India's future development without any obvious infringement of its sovereignty by Britain, the former colonial power. The Commonwealth Conference of 1949 allowed republican India to become a Commonwealth member because it accepted the King George VI as head of the Commonwealth, but not as India's head of state (it had its own president).

The Commonwealth prides itself on being a global, multiethnic organization. It was also a vehicle for retaining a degree of British influence, however symbolic, in member states. In fact, race has been a major issue in the history of the Commonwealth. In 1960, **South Africa** left the Commonwealth because its apartheid ethos, based on the concept of separate racial development, was regarded as being unacceptable. Only in the 1990s did South Africa return to the Commonwealth. Likewise, in 1965, **Southern Rhodesia's** Unilateral Declaration of Independence created a similar situation with a minority white government. It was the Commonwealth Conference of 1979 that forced British prime minister **Margaret Thatcher** to convene the Lancaster House Conference, which brought about the end of the minority racist regime and set up free elections in what became Zimbabwe. An ongoing problem with the Commonwealth has been that despite the British link, member states, unlike those of the **European Union (EU)**, are not always democratic. **Pakistan**, for instance, has spent much of the period since achieving independence in 1947 under military dictators. This is something of an anomaly (and Pakistan is not the only example) given that the Commonwealth was supposed to be based on British democratic precepts. Conversely, the existence of the Commonwealth was a complication for successive British governments during the period when they were attempting to become members of the then **European Economic Community**, now the EU (1961–1972). British interests did not always coincide with those of Commonwealth states. Nevertheless, the organization has been a forum for vigorous debate and dissent. One notable example was in 1956, when the Indian government bitterly opposed Britain's Suez operation.

The Commonwealth has created its own distinctive structure. Conferences of member states have been held since 1887, and the 1926 Balfour Declaration stated that all Commonwealth states were equal in status. This applied only to the white, self-governing dominions, a relationship with the British Crown that was formalized by the 1931 Statute of Westminster. Britain's colonies in Africa and Asia did not acquire such a status until after World War II. There are currently just 14 British overseas territories, and the accelerating decline of British imperialism was marked by the London Declaration of April 1949, when the actual word *British* was omitted from the title. The London Declaration is regarded as the beginning of the modern Commonwealth, as it allowed member states to become republics (as in the case of India) or retain their own constitutional monarchs. A differentiation was also made between the *Old Commonwealth*, a term used about the pre–1945 Commonwealth, and the *New Commonwealth*. The latter term has been used to describe states that were decolonized in the 1950s and 1960s. It has also been used in the context of the intense internal British debate about Commonwealth immigration since the 1950s.

The Commonwealth has frequently been criticized for not living up to its principles. Initially outlined in the 1971 Singapore Declaration, these were meant to commit the Commonwealth to world peace, representative democracy, opposition to racism, individual liberty, a campaign against poverty, and free trade. These principles were restated by the Harare Declaration in 1991, yet the very state where this declaration was made, Zimbabwe, has been the subject of the draconian dictatorship of **Robert Mugabe** for more than a decade. He was knighted by **Queen Elizabeth II** and then had the honor withdrawn. Indeed, Zimbabwe left the Commonwealth in 2003, after the Commonwealth heads of government suspended its membership owing to human rights abuses.

Most Commonwealth members had a constitutional link with Britain by virtue of being former colonies, but there are exceptions. Mozambique, a former Portuguese colony, was admitted in 1995, and, Rwanda, a former Belgian trust territory, in 2009. In 2012, the membership of the Commonwealth constituted 2.1 billion of the global population, nearly one-third of the total. Britain ranked fourth in population, behind India, Pakistan (shorn of **Bangladesh** since 1971), and Nigeria. Sixteen of the 54 Commonwealth members accepted Elizabeth II as their head of state. The **Foreign and Commonwealth Office** continues to have responsibility for the 14 dependent overseas territories.

Queen Elizabeth II has been the head of the Commonwealth since 6 February 1952. It has had its own secretary general, currently Kamalesh Sharma (since 1 April 2008), and secretariat since 1965. There is also a chairperson in office, now the Australian premier Julia Gillard.

COOK, ROBIN (1946–2005). As Great Britain's **foreign secretary** (1997–2001), Robin Cook saw himself as something of a reformer, trying to modernize its practices and, most importantly, its ethos. Cook wanted Britain to have an ethical foreign policy. This could be said to have been a motivation behind the **Tony Blair** government's intervention in **Kosovo** and Sierra Leone. Cook was disappointed to be removed from the **Foreign Office** in 2001, and he was appointed leader of the House of Commons instead (2001–2003). He demonstrated a great deal of courage in resigning his post on 17 March 2003, in opposition to British involvement in the war in **Iraq**. In his resignation speech, Cook made clear his doubts about the existence of weapons of mass destruction, the ostensible justification for the war. His personal distress at having to vote against his own Labour government was clear.

COWPER-COLES, SIR SHERARD (1955–). Sherard Cowper-Coles played a key role in **Afghanistan** in 2009–2010, as the special representative of Great Britain's **foreign secretary**. He joined the Diplomatic Service in 1977, serving in Cairo from 1980–1983, before becoming first secretary in the planning staff of the **Foreign and Commonwealth Office (FCO)** (1985–1987). Cowper-Coles then served in Washington (1987–1991), before returning to London as an assistant in the Security Policy Department of the FCO, where he served from 1991–1993. After a brief period at the International Institute for Strategic Studies in 1993–1994, Cowper-Coles became head of the Hong Kong Department at the FCO in 1994, where Britain was preparing for the surrender of British sovereignty to the People's Republic of China. His posting ended when the British left the Crown colony in 1997. A period in Paris as political counselor (1997–1999) led to his appointment as principal private secretary to the Labour foreign secretary, **Robin Cook** (1999–2001), at a time when Cook was advocating a new morality in British foreign policy.

CRIMEA. The Crimea is a peninsula running into the Black Sea, notable for the war between **Russia**, Great Britain, and **France** (1853–1856). The intervention by the Anglo–French was designed to prevent Russia from partitioning the weak Ottoman Turkish Empire and seizing control of Constantinople and the Straits between the Black and Mediterranean seas. The war that followed was one of the most inept, bungled campaigns in modern European history. Eventually, in 1855, the conflict was effectively decided by the capture of the great Russian naval base at Sevastopol. It dragged on until 1856, before being ended by the Treaty of Paris, which forced Russia to dismantle fortifications around the Black Sea. The diplomacy before the outbreak of the war saw one of the last examples of a British ambassador, Stratford Canning (later 1st Viscount de Redcliffe), playing a dominant role, albeit not as significant as contemporaries thought. British ambassadors were increasingly reflecting on rather than formulating policy. *See also* ABERDEEN, LORD.

CROATIA. Great Britain established diplomatic relations with Croatia on 25 June 1992. This took place just after Croatia had declared itself independent of the Federal Republic of Yugoslavia on 7 October 1991. Largely Catholic, Croatia had formed the second largest part of the former republic. The bitter civil war that followed owed much to the folk memory of the Serb minority in Croatia about their persecution by the fascist regime in **World War II**. In the early stages of the civil war in Croatia (1992–1995), the Serbs seized territory, but it was regained by the Croats in 1995. During this period, Croatia was led by the extreme nationalist Franjo Tudjman (1992–1999), who was responsible for the ethnic cleansing of Muslims in neighboring **Bosnia**, where Croats made up 17 percent of the population. Britain was a strong supporter of the International Criminal Tribunal at The Hague, but Tudjman tried to shield those who had committed war crimes in both Croatia and Bosnia.

Croatia eventually adopted a more cooperative policy. It signed the Dayton Agreement (1995) to formalize the end of the Yugoslav civil war. Croatia tried to end its international isolation by joining the World Trade Organization in 2000, and signing an association agreement with the **European Union (EU)**. It has indicated that it wishes to become a full member of the EU, a project that has full British support. Entry talks began in 2005. In this context, the issue of atrocities committed during the civil war has been important to Britain. In December 2005, General Ante Gotovina was moved to the International Criminal Tribunal by the Croatian government, an act that brought about an improvement in Anglo–Croatian relations. Croatia demonstrated its commitment to regional cooperation on 21 October 2011. The Croatian parliament adopted the Declaration on Promoting European Values in South East Europe. This agreement states that bilateral issues between states, for example, border disputes, are not allowed to obstruct the accession of candidate states to the EU from the start of the accession process.

CUBAN MISSILE CRISIS (1962). The nearest that the rival superpowers the **United States** and the Soviet Union came to a nuclear conflict was in October 1962. A 13-day crisis regarding the island of Cuba ended with war being narrowly averted. The origins of the crisis lay with the coming to power of the Cuban leader Fidel Castro, who overthrew the corrupt dictatorship of Fulgencio Batista in 1959. Although he had achieved power with the aid of other opposition parties, Castro soon concentrated power in his own hands. Despite not initially claiming to be a Communist, Castro nationalized foreign holdings and aligned himself with the Soviet Union. The **John F. Kennedy**

administration (1961–1963) inherited a misconceived Central Intelligence Agency (CIA) plan to overthrow Castro, whose popular support was seriously underestimated. This resulted in the disaster at the Bay of Pigs in April 1961. CIA-funded anti-Castro forces were routed and the Kennedy administration gravely embarrassed. The Americans imposed a total trade embargo on Cuba in February 1962, but Great Britain refused to apply economic sanctions against the island country. Britain believed them to be of dubious value, basing this judgment on the previous use of sanctions against Benito Mussolini before **World War II**, and Iranian leader Mohammed Mossadeq in the 1950s. The issue of Anglo–Cuban trade remained a controversial one.

In 1962, Soviet leader Nikita Khrushchev decided to place nuclear missiles in Cuba to protect his ally, Castro, from invasion. Photographic intelligence made President Kennedy aware of this, and, on 16 October, he authorized passing this information on to the British. Prime Minister **Harold Macmillan** was informed of the breaking crisis and became somewhat concerned about the likely effect of such a crisis on Europe. Britain was faced with a possible Soviet nuclear attack on the British Isles because of an issue that threatened its national security as a result of the presence of U.S. nuclear forces on its territory. Thus, Macmillan argued in favor of a diplomatic settlement. He even suggested a trade-off of American **Thor missiles** in Britain for the Soviet ones in Cuba. This suggestion was rejected. President Kennedy ultimately set aside more hawkish suggestions that Cuba be invaded in favor of a quarantine zone of 500 miles, which would allow approaching Soviet vessels with supplies the opportunity to veer off and avoid confrontation with the U.S. Navy. The Soviet leadership backed down and agreed to remove the missiles from Cuba (which could easily reach the coast of Florida, some 90 miles away, and other U.S. cities). A secret deal between Kennedy and Khrushchev took up Macmillan's earlier suggestion about a trading of missiles. In this instance, the United States agreed to remove Jupiter missiles from **Turkey**, which were stationed there under **North Atlantic Treaty Organization** arrangements. The United States and Britain worked closely together during the crisis, and the two countries signed the **Nuclear Test Ban Treaty** in 1963, somewhat reducing the threat of nuclear war. The importance of the role played by the British ambassador in Washington, D.C., David Ormsby Gore, was subsequently recognized by historians.

CURZON, GEORGE NATHANIEL (1859–1925). A British **foreign secretary** (1919–1923) and substantial political figure, George Curzon had been a young, ambitious viceroy of **India** but proved too sensitive as foreign secretary to work effectively under the premiership of **David Lloyd George** (1916–1922) or deal with such ruthless foreign statesmen as **Raymond**

Poincaré of **France**, whose behavior reduced him to tears. Curzon did succeed in restoring some order to the administrative shambles created in the **Foreign Office** by his predecessor, **Arthur Balfour** (1916–1919). He assumed that he would succeed Bonar Law as Conservative Party leader and prime minister, but the fact that he was a member of the House of Lords counted against him, as did his reputation for pomposity. He was created Marquess Curzon of Kedleston.

CYPRUS. The island country of Cyprus was a British colony since 1878, when it was obtained by British prime minister **Benjamin Disraeli** at the Congress of Berlin. It won its independence on 16 August 1960. This followed a long and bloody struggle with British Crown forces. Great Britain prevented the island from uniting with **Greece**, as its majority Greek Cypriot community wished. A lengthy Greek Cypriot **terrorist** campaign had preceded the cession of independence by Britain, in which the minority Turkish Cypriot community had generally sided with the British. After independence, relations between the two Cypriot communities were so fraught that in 1964, a **United Nations** peacekeeping force had to be sent to the island and has remained there ever since. Matters were not helped by the seizure of power by the Greek Colonels regime in 1967, with its known objective of union with Cyprus. In 1974, encouraged by the Greek government, the Greek Cypriot military overthrew the government of Archbishop Makarios, a revered figure on the island who had spent many years in British prisons.

The British Labour government, under **Harold Wilson**, hoped that the **United States** would use its influence with **Turkey**, a fellow member of the **North Atlantic Treaty Organization**, to prevent its intervention; however, it was unwilling to do so, mired as the administration of **Richard Nixon** was in the Watergate crisis. On 30 July 1974, a tripartite agreement between Great Britain, Greece, and Turkey provided for the partition of the island after Turkish forces invaded northern Cyprus. A "green line" then divided the Greek and Turkish areas. A Turkish puppet regime was set up in northern Cyprus, which only Turkey recognized. This covered 40 percent of the island.

CZECHOSLOVAKIA. The Czechoslovak state emerged from the wreckage of the old **Austro-Hungarian Empire** in 1918. During the interwar period, it was closely aligned with **France**, but it remained vulnerable because of its large non-Czechoslovak minorities, specifically the 3 million German-speaking people who lived in the frontier areas known as the Sudetenland. This became a particular problem after 1933, when Adolf Hitler proclaimed his desire to create a Greater **Germany**. It encouraged Sudeten German opposition to the Czech government in Prague. British policy encouraged the Czechs to try to settle the problem by conceding more autonomy to the Sudeten Germans. Yet, there was little real sympathy for the Czechs in Whitehall. Successive British ministers in Prague, Joseph Addison and Basil Newton, also did not disguise their view that the Czechoslovak state was unviable. The Czech government, under President Eduard Beneš, hoped for Anglo–French support, but, for most British people, Czechoslovakia was a "faraway country."

The crisis duly broke in 1938, when Hitler began to apply pressure about the Sudetenland and war threatened. A supposed German attack in May proved to be a false alarm, but the crisis brought about the intervention of British prime minister **Neville Chamberlain**, who dictated Anglo–French policy. Two fruitless meetings were held in Germany between Hitler and Chamberlain. War seemed inevitable when a last-minute conference at Munich, known as the **Munich Agreement**, on 29 September 1938, prevented it. The Sudetenland was ceded to Germany by the Agreement with Anglo–French acceptance. The Czechs were not allowed to take part in the conference, which deprived them of their sophisticated frontier fortifications. President Beneš resigned, his country disappearing as an independent entity from the map of Europe in March 1939. Munich was deplored in subsequent years as an extreme example of **appeasement**, while the unfortunate Czechs became part of Greater Germany; the Slovaks were allowed an illusion of independence as a German puppet state. Six years of German occupation followed for the ethnic Czech provinces of Bohemia and Moravia. Beneš took refuge in England, where exiled Czech military forces were organized. Czech parachutists, sent by the British, assassinated the notorious Nazi Reich protector for Bohemia and Moravia, Reinhard Heydrich, in Prague, in May 1942. A dreadful German atrocity followed at Lidice, where hundreds of Czechs were murdered. Despite this, **Foreign Office** policy could be myopic, taking far too long to fully recognize the Czech government in exile. The free Czechoslovak forces in Britain performed valuable service for the Allied cause from 1941–1945. Headed by President Beneš, the exiled government moved back to Czechoslovak territory in April 1945. There was already a rival Communist partisan organization in Slovakia.

In the Czechoslovak general election of 1946, after the return of President Beneš to Prague, the Communist Party obtained an impressive 38 percent of the vote. Under their leader, Klement Gottwald, they were already part of a coalition government and had obtained key posts, including the Ministry of the Interior. This brought control of the police. The Communists actually wanted to accept **Marshall Plan** aid from the **United States** in 1947, but they were prevented from doing so by Joseph Stalin, who controlled the actions of the Eastern European Communist parties. Following this interference, Communist support dropped to 25 percent. Gottwald armed the workers in a People's Militia in February 1948, effectively giving the Communists a 15,000-strong private army. As a result, 12 non-Communist government ministers resigned, leaving Gottwald and his supporters in charge of the government. Thousands of armed workers paraded through Prague, and, on 25 February, President Beneš, fearing civil war, accepted the creation of a Communist government. In the background loomed the power of the Soviet Union, and, in June, Gottwald secured Beneš's resignation. Gottwald himself became president. The well-known non-Communist foreign minister Jan Masaryk, a former popular Czech minister in London and the son of the Czech Republic's founding father, Tomaš Masaryk, was found dead outside his flat in the Foreign Ministry. Foul play was suspected.

These events strengthened the conviction of British **foreign secretary Ernest Bevin** that an anti-Soviet Western Alliance was required, with U.S. participation. This duly happened in 1949, making the Czech coup a key event in the history of the **Cold War**. A grim Stalinist regime governed Czechoslovakia in the 1950s and 1960s, under Antonin Novotný. It managed to undermine the relative prosperity of the interwar period with the achievement of minus growth. No armed revolt took place as in East Germany (1953) and Hungary (1956), but successive British governments deplored the soulless regimentation by the satellite Czechoslovak government. As prime minister in 1968, **Harold Wilson** protested alongside the **Foreign and Commonwealth Office** against the Warsaw Pact invasion of Czechoslovakia. A feature of the ill-fated government of Alexander Dubcek was that it allowed Czechoslovaks to travel freely for the first time in decades. Many were in Britain at the time of the invasion in August 1968 and did not return. After Dubcek's fall, matters reverted to the Stalinist norm. There were even accusations in Britain that the former Labour postmaster general, John Stonehouse, had been an agent of the Czech secret service, an effective surrogate for its KGB cousin. The charges were unproven, although Stonehouse went to prison for fraud in 1977. There was much sympathy in Britain for Charter 77, in which the playwright Václav Havel sponsored demands for human rights changes in Czechoslovakia. Havel, like other dissidents, was imprisoned. A dismal decade followed under the hard-liner Gustav Husak, before the collapse of Communism in the "Velvet Revolution" of November 1989. Havel became the first president of the new republic.

It was an irony of Czechoslovak history that the return of democracy in 1989 brought with it the eventual fracture of the unitary state. Slovaks had long complained about unequal treatment. On 1 January 1993, the Czechoslovak union was dissolved, and the new Czech and Slovak republics created. Havel continued in his role as president of the Czech Republic. He was one of the few Czechs prepared to face up to the moral issue remaining from the expulsion of nearly 3 million Sudeten Germans to Austria and Germany in 1945–1946. Havel regarded it as a stain on Czech history, just as some Britons regarded the failure to support Czechoslovakia in 1938 as one on theirs. Britain fully supported the Czech Republic's admission to the **North Atlantic Treaty Organization** on 12 March 1999, and the **European Union** on 1 May 2004. The European common currency (euro) was a problem for the Czech Republic, as it was for Britain. An original intention to adopt the euro in 2010 was set aside by the current center-right government in 2007. The Czech Republic remains outside the **Eurozone**. Its current president, Václav Klaus, is a Eurosceptic, and, like Britain's prime minister, **David Cameron**, he declined to sign the intergovernmental treaty formulated at the Brussels summit on December 2011. The Czech Republic is part of the Schengen Area (unlike Britain). On 21 December 2007, it completely opened its borders with Germany, Austria, **Poland**, and Slovakia.

D

D-DAY LANDINGS (1944). Once the **United States** had entered **World War II** in December 1941, there was an ongoing debate with Great Britain about when and where an invasion of Western Europe should take place. The Americans favored an early invasion of **France** in 1942 or 1943, but the British were much more cautious. Prime Minister **Winston Churchill**, in particular, was fearful about the human cost of an amphibious landing. He remembered only too well the failure of the Gallipoli landings in 1915–1916, which cost him his post as first lord of the **Admiralty**. Churchill's preference was for a Mediterranean-based strategy centered on the assumption that Fascist **Italy** was the "soft underbelly" of the Axis powers, but this did not prove to be the case, the Italian campaign from 1943–1945 being a hard slog for the Anglo–American armies.

It was ultimately agreed upon that Operation Overlord, the invasion of Northern France, would take place on 6 June 1944. An elaborate Anglo–American deception campaign was mounted to make the German High Command think that the invasion would take place in the Calais area, when, in fact, it took place in Normandy. The Allied commander in chief was General **Dwight D. Eisenhower**, which reflected the greater U.S. commitment in terms of troops, ships, and aircraft. British forces were landed on the eastern beaches of Gold and Sword, while the Canadians cooperated with the British on the beach code-named Juno. The Americans were landed on the western beaches. The absence of powerful German tank divisions, kept in a futile wait for a landing farther north, which never happened, assisted the success of the Anglo–American landings, as did Allied control of the air. Despite this, weeks of tough fighting were needed before the Anglo–Americans broke out of their Normandy bridgeheads. Churchill believed that the British commander, Bernard Law Montgomery, was too cautious, and the Americans agreed with him.

DALTON, HUGH (1887–1962). Starting out as a spokesman on foreign affairs for the Labour Party in the House of Commons in the 1930s, Hugh Dalton was a member of **Winston Churchill's** wartime coalition government from 1940–1945. As he had also been undersecretary of state at the **Foreign**

Office in Ramsey MacDonald's second Labour government (1929–1931), it was widely assumed that he, rather than **Ernest Bevin**, would be appointed **foreign secretary** after Labour's election victory in July 1945. Instead, **Clement R. Attlee** appointed him chancellor of the exchequer. Dalton had the onerous task of managing Britain's struggling postwar economy. He, like **John Maynard Keynes**, who negotiated the **Anglo–American Loan Agreement**, was disillusioned by its troublesome terms in December 1946. Dalton, a former academic at the London School of Economics, lost his post in highly unusual circumstances in 1947. He stopped to speak to a journalist before making his budget speech and inadvertently disclosed details of the budget. This information later appeared in an early edition of the *Evening Standard* newspaper. Dalton felt obliged to resign, although he remained in the Labour government. He was a mentor for a new generation of Labour leaders, one of whom, Anthony Crosland, went on to become foreign secretary in 1976–1977.

DALTON, SIR RICHARD (1948–). Richard Dalton is a Middle Eastern specialist at the **Foreign and Commonwealth Office (FCO)** who served as British ambassador to **Libya** (1999–2003) and **Iran** (2003–2006). He had joined the Diplomatic Service of the FCO in 1970, and served in Amman, **Jordan**, as second secretary, and consul general in Jerusalem. In 1998–1999, Dalton was head of personnel at the FCO. There was an aborted change of course in Dalton's career after he had contemplated leaving the FCO in 1983, to stand as the Conservative candidate for the constituency of Richmond in Yorkshire. He felt obliged to withdraw when his sister in law, Sarah Keays, made public her affair with the Conservative Cabinet minister Cecil Parkinson and he was forced to resign from **Margaret Thatcher's** Conservative government. Parkinson was the father of Keays's daughter.

DAWES PLAN (1924). The peace settlement in 1919 penalized **Germany** for starting **World War I** in a number of ways. One was the imposition of reparations, whereby Germany had to pay for the damage its forces caused in **France** and **Belgium**. Great Britain also received substantial reparations. A crisis arose in January 1923, when Germany defaulted on its reparations payments (which included payments in kind, as well as money), and Franco–Belgian troops occupied the Ruhr, Germany's largest industrial area. Great Britain, under Prime Minister **Stanley Baldwin**, refused to support Franco–Belgian action, claiming that it was illegal. For its part, Germany refused to cooperate with the occupying powers and started a campaign of passive resistance. This meant that German industry ground to a halt, and ruinous hyperinflation set in. By 1 November 1923, there were 133,000 million German marks to the dollar.

The **United States** shared Britain's objections to the hawkish French policy in the Ruhr, and American general Charles Dawes became the chairman of a committee established in 1924 to stabilize the German mark and balance the budget. Even the French saw the necessity of such an action.

But reparations could not be claimed from a bankrupt nation. The result was the Dawes Plan. This produced a new schedule for reparations payments, conditional on the evacuation of the Ruhr by Franco–Belgian troops. Dawes's assessment asked for 2.5 billion gold marks, 500 million less than the amount fixed by the Allied Reparations Commission in 1921. The evolution of the Dawes Plan demonstrated that Britain and the United States could still work effectively in the economic sphere, while British suspicions of an overly mighty France remained. The relationship between France's prime minister, **Raymond Poincaré**, and British foreign secretary **George Curzon** was notoriously bad, the latter being reduced to tears on occasion by the French statesman's behavior.

The work done by Dawes and his colleagues led to the granting of a massive loan to Germany, half funded by the United States, and a quarter funded by Britain. This gave crucial support to the German banking system; reestablished a viable German currency; and sparked a remarkable German economic recovery, which was tragically curtailed by the aftermath of the 1929 Wall Street Crash. *See also* VERSAILLES, TREATY OF.

DEFENSE, MINISTRY OF (MOD). Situated in Whitehall, the Ministry of Defense (MOD) is the umbrella organization for the British armed forces, having authority over the Royal Navy, the Royal Army, and the Royal Air Force. Political control is exercised by the secretary of state for defense and a number of junior ministers. The MOD has a large number of military, naval, and air attachés attached to British embassies abroad. They liaise closely with British diplomats, but also with officials in foreign defense establishments.

DEFENCE REQUIREMENTS COMMITTEE (DRC) (1933). Faced with an increasingly perilous international situation in 1933, Britain's National Government, a coalition government of Labour, Conservatives, and Liberals established in 1931, created the Defence Requirements Committee (DRC). This identified Nazi **Germany** as Britain's primary enemy, followed by **Japan** and then **Italy**. The DRC included representatives of the armed services, the **Foreign Office**, and the treasury who met periodically to discuss defense priorities and expenditure.

DÉTENTE. Détente is a policy of reducing tension and the chance of war between two or more parties, notably the **United States**, its allies, and the

Communist Bloc, led by the **Soviet Union**, during the **Cold War**. The term, whose origins are French (the language of international diplomacy until 1856), is used with special application to the relationship between the United States and the USSR, and the United States and **China**, during the 1970s. Its operation can nonetheless be traced back to the period immediately after the death of Soviet dictator Joseph Stalin in March 1953. **Winston Churchill,** the British prime minister from 1951–1955, was especially keen to engage in summit diplomacy with the new Soviet leadership led by Georgei Malenkov, fearing as he did the potency of nuclear weapons. The Americans were less keen and effectively vetoed Churchill's hoped for visit to Moscow. It would have had little purpose unless the new American president, **Dwight D. Eisenhower,** also agreed to go.

Great Britain could only play a subsidiary role during the golden age of détente diplomacy in the 1970s. This was associated with President **Richard Nixon**; his Soviet counterpart, General Secretary Leonid Brezhnev; and the U.S. secretary of state, **Henry Kissinger.** Détente was welcomed not least because its arms limitation agreements, like the one signed in 1972 (generally known as Strategic Arms Limitation Talks I [SALT I]), reduced the amount spent on armaments by both superpowers. There was a sharp change in British attitudes under Prime Minister **Margaret Thatcher,** when détente was out of favor until the appearance of the new Soviet leader Mikhail Gorbachev in 1985. The same was true in the United States, where President **Ronald Reagan** had categorized the Soviet Union as the "evil empire."

DIEFENBAKER, JOHN GEORGE (1895–1979). Prime minister of **Canada** (1957–1963) and leader of the Progressive Conservative Party, John Diefenbaker ended 22 years of Liberal Party rule in 1957. Diefenbaker was an Anglophile and strong supporter of the **Commonwealth.** He played a major role in securing a condemnation of apartheid or separate development in **South Africa** at the 1959 Commonwealth Conference. This resulted in the expulsion of South Africa from the Commonwealth in 1961. In the aftermath of the British application to join the **European Economic Community** in 1961, Diefenbaker secured markets for Canadian wheat in **China** and Eastern Europe. He remained leader of the Conservative Party until 1967.

DIEGO GARCIA. This British colony's future was discussed by the Labour government of Prime Minister **Harold Wilson** in 1965. Diego Garcia is one of the Chagos Islands formerly attached to Mauritius, which gained its independence in 1968, but without the islands. These were to be under the control of Great Britain, and the Wilson government made a deal with the **United States,** whereby Diego Garcia was to be leased as an air and naval base. It has remained as a U.S. base since the 1960s and been in regular use by American bombers flying to **Iraq** and **Afghanistan**.

This arrangement turned out to be highly controversial, because, in 1970, the British government agreed to the American request to relocate the native population to Mauritius. They received no compensation or choice in this matter, a shameful episode in British diplomacy. Numerous attempts have been made in British law courts by the islanders to secure a return to their homeland, but all have failed, and as many as 2,000 islanders have been deprived of their heritage.

DIEN BIEN PHU (1954). The decisive defeat of the French expeditionary force on 7 May 1954, at Dien Bien Phu, in northern Vietnam, marked the effective end of French colonialism in **Indochina**. It is often forgotten, however, that Great Britain played a significant role in the events leading up to the French defeat after eight years of war between them and the Viet Minh Communists. In 1945, the French colonialists were too thin on the ground following **Japan's** defeat to retake control of their colony. As agreed at the **Potsdam Conference** in July 1945, southern Vietnam below the 16th parallel, together with Laos and Cambodia, was under British control pending the return of the French. North of this line of latitude, Nationalist China was the occupying power.

British occupying troops belonged to the 20th Indian Division under General Douglas Gracey. Like his men, Gracey was a veteran of the Burma campaign. His division remained in Vietnam from September 1945–March 1946, when the French military and civil administration took control in Saigon and Hanoi. French resistance to the concept of Vietnamese independence meant that from December 1946–April 1954, a bitter colonial war was fought between **France** and the Viet Minh. The **Geneva Conference** in 1954 allowed the defeated French until 1956 to withdraw all their forces from Vietnam and the rest of Indochina. British **foreign secretary Anthony Eden** refused U.S. requests for bombardment of the Viet Minh positions around Dien Bien Phu, which he rightly saw could lead to World War III. The Geneva Conference opened formally on 26 April, some two weeks before Dien Bien Phu surrendered, and its remit included the postwar settlement in Korea. Significant policy divisions emerged between the **United States**, which played a passive and essentially negative role at Geneva, and Britain, which accepted the need for All-Vietnam elections, even though the Communists were likely to emerge victorious. *See also* DOMINO THEORY.

DISRAELI, BENJAMIN (1809–1881). Prime minister of Great Britain from 1867–1868 and 1874–1880, Benjamin Disraeli was a seminal figure in the history of British foreign policy, especially in its imperial aspects. Convinced that Russian ambitions in the Balkans and Near East (including the Ottoman Turkish Empire) endangered British interests, Disraeli succeeded in curbing Russian power at the Congress of Berlin (1878). Britain obtained **Cyprus** at the Congress and prevented the creation of an overly large pro-Russian **Bulgaria**. He had already bought a controlling interest in the Suez Canal Company in 1876, and made **Queen Victoria** (1837–1901), who doted on him, empress of **India**. Disraeli associated the Conservative Party with a flag-waving, expansionist foreign policy, whereas his great rival, **William Gladstone**, the Liberal leader, put more emphasis on morality in foreign policy. Disraeli was created Earl of Beaconsfield.

DOMINO THEORY. British foreign policy in the Far East followed a principle of pragmatism. Communist **China** was recognized in 1949, and the likelihood of a Communist victory in Vietnamese elections after France's defeat in 1954 accepted. This was not the American position, with its distinctive "domino theory." This doctrine, which was first enunciated by President **Harry S. Truman** in 1946, stated that action must be taken to prevent Communist subversion in **Greece** and **Turkey**, otherwise other states would fall like a row of dominoes. Truman then applied the **Truman Doctrine** in southeast to the effect that if Korea fell, then so would the rest of the region. His successor, **Dwight D. Eisenhower**, applied the domino analogy to **Indochina**, saying that if it became Communist, so too would Burma, Thailand, Malaya (**Malaysia**), and Indonesia. The domino theory was central in the U.S. determination to win the **Vietnam War** between 1961–1975. In fact, the domino theory was shown to be misconceived. Despite the Communist victory in Vietnam in 1975, Burma, Thailand, Malaysia, and Indonesia did not become Communist. Vietnam itself fought wars against two of its Communist neighbors, Cambodia (Kampuchea) and China, in 1978–1979. British prime minister **Harold Wilson** had resisted the pleas from President **Lyndon B. Johnson** to send troops to Vietnam from 1964–1970, although his Labour government broadly supported American policy there. The history of the domino theory demonstrated British preference for pragmatism over ideology, although U.S. foreign policy went on to adopt a new realism in the 1970s.

DOUGLAS-HOME, SIR ALEC (1903–1995). The premiership of Alec Douglas-Home (1963–1964) began when **Harold Macmillan** was forced to retire on medical grounds. He was probably the most poorly qualified of modern British Conservative prime ministers, with only a fourth-class degree from Oxford, but his aristocratic background enabled him to enter

Conservative politics in 1931. Douglas-Home was **Neville Chamberlain's** parliamentary private secretary at the time of the **Munich Agreement** and Chamberlain's triumphant return to Britain in September 1938. He became 14th Earl of Home when his father died in 1950. Although he had held a variety of smaller posts in Conservative governments, Douglas-Home's appointment as **foreign secretary** by Macmillan was a surprise in 1960. He remained in the background as Macmillan took the lead in pushing Britain's unsuccessful campaign to enter the **European Economic Community (EEC)** (1961–1963). He then emerged as a surprise compromise candidate for the premiership who defeated favored candidate **Richard Austen Butler**.

Douglas-Home was an unremarkable prime minister with a poor grasp of economics, and he also had the disadvantage of being a peer in the House of Lords. This was deemed inappropriate for a modern British prime minister, but the 1963 Peerage Act allowed him to renounce his peerage and return to the House of Commons as Sir Alec Douglas-Home. His term as prime minister in 1963–1964 was one of the shortest on record, and he achieved little of note. Yet, he lost the 1964 general election by only four seats to Labour. Douglas-Home stood down as prime minister in 1965, having at least introduced a more democratic leadership election system for the Conservative Party. A lifelong link with the **Foreign Office** resumed in 1970, when **Edward Heath** made him foreign secretary once again. Heath gave him a freer hand as foreign secretary than Macmillan had done, the exception being the third and successful British application to join the EEC, which Heath handled. In 1971, Douglas-Home created a stir in Anglo–Soviet relations by expelling a large number of Soviet diplomats for espionage. **Henry Kissinger** caused him some annoyance by failing to inform the Foreign Office of his 1973 plan for a new "**Atlantic Charter**." Following Heath's defeat in the February 1974 general election, Douglas-Home retired to the House of Lords, this time as a life peer rather than a hereditary one. He took the title Baron Home of the Hirsel.

DOWNING STREET, NO. 10. Since 1730, when Sir Robert Walpole was Great Britain's first recognizable prime minister, No. 10 Downing Street has been the home of British prime ministers. It has also housed a secretariat to support the prime minister in his work and is conveniently situated for easy access to the **Foreign Office**, the Cabinet Office, and the treasury. The residence is frequently used to entertain foreign heads of state and other dignitaries. Until the post–1939 period, security around Downing Street was somewhat casual, but it was bombed by the Germans during **World War II**. In 1991, the **Irish Republican Army** fired mortars into the back garden while **John Major's** Cabinet was in session, but no one was injured. The center of British government is surprisingly cramped with a very small flat for the prime minister. **Tony Blair,** who had a son Leo while living in No. 10 Downing Street, had to requisition the larger flat of his chancellor of the exchequer **Gordon Brown** for his expanding family at No. 11 Downing Street. **David Cameron** followed Blair in having a child born in Downing Street in 2010, a rare event in modern British politics.

DUFF COOPER, ALFRED (1890–1954). Educated at **Eton College** and Oxford University, Alfred Duff Cooper was a Conservative member of Parliament and a significant figure during the **appeasement** era in Great Britain, holding the posts of secretary of state for war (1935–1937) and first lord of the **Admiralty** (1937–1938). He was the only leading political figure of the day to resign in protest at the **Munich Agreement** in September 1938. When **World War II** broke out, he was made minister of information by **Winston Churchill.** He held the post from 1940–1941, but was not deemed a success. Duff Cooper, who was a Francophile, was a much more effective ambassador to **France** (1944–1947), and he helped bring about the **Dunkirk** Treaty between Britain and France in 1947. He was the author of a number of biographies, including two on the French statesmen Talleyrand and Haig, Britain's leading **World War I** general. Duff Cooper was created Viscount Norwich in 1954.

DULLES, JOHN FOSTER (1888–1959). John Foster Dulles represented the rather dour face of U.S. foreign policy as secretary of state from 1953–1959, under President **Dwight D. Eisenhower.** He had some pedigree in foreign policymaking as a man who was part of the U.S. delegation at the Versailles Conference in 1919. By then, he was already a well-known international lawyer. Dulles became a Republican spokesman on foreign affairs during the presidencies of **Franklin D. Roosevelt** and **Harry S. Truman.** He was an advisor to the U.S. government when the **United Nations** was created, and he negotiated the end of the San Francisco Treaty (1951) and the occupation of **Japan** by the **United States.** Eisenhower made him secretary of state in 1953, as the **Korean War** (1950–1953) was nearing an end.

Dulles loathed Communism and acquired a reputation as a classic "Cold War warrior" because of his sometimes-fiery rhetoric. He disapproved of British **foreign secretary Anthony Eden's** painstaking policy of compromise in relation to **Indochina** at the **Geneva Conference** (1954), and the two men had a difficult relationship. Eden found Dulles's tendency to indulge in lengthy monologues tedious, while Dulles was not seduced by Eden's old-world charm. There was a suggestion that Dulles was jealous of Eden's success at Geneva. This was unfortunate, as the two men had to work together during the **Suez Crisis** of 1956. Rather unwisely, Eden tended to take U.S. support against the **Egyptian** dictator **Jamal Abd al Nasser** (1954–1970) for granted, although there were ambiguities about American policy. On the one hand, Dulles withdrew financial support for the **Aswan Dam**, Nasser's pet project, in the summer of 1956 (when he discovered that Egypt had accepted weapons from the Soviet Bloc), thus precipitating Nasser's decision to nationalize the Suez Canal to fund the Aswan project. On the other hand, Dulles and Eisenhower declined to support the Anglo–French attack on Nasser in November 1956, effectively forcing their withdrawal from Egypt. Afterward, Dulles baffled many by drawing up the Eisenhower Doctrine (1957) to keep Communism out of the Middle East when he had opposed British policy over Suez, which was designed to bring down the (allegedly) pro-Soviet Nasser. Dulles remained fixated by Communism, but the main regional threat came from Nasser, who was a Pan-Arabist who wanted to unite Egypt and Syria and secure a dominant position in Yemen. By the time of his death in 1959, Dulles's extreme brand of anti-Communism seemed out of date in a world threatened by a nuclear holocaust. That same year, Soviet leader Nikita Khrushchev made a trailblazing visit to the United States.

DUMBARTON OAKS CONFERENCE (1944). The tragic failure of the old **League of Nations** made it clear to the victorious Allied Powers during **World War II** that an effective replacement was required. American, British, and Soviet representatives met at Dumbarton Oaks, near Washington, D.C., between August and October 1944, to map out the format that the new **United Nations** organization would take. It was established by the **San Francisco Conference** on 26 June 1945.

DUNKIRK (1940). By the end of May 1940, the British Expeditionary Force (BEF) found itself in a parlous position in northern **France**. It was in danger of encirclement, along with its French ally, and was unable to escape back across the English Channel. The so-called "Miracle of Dunkirk" (24 May–4 June 1940) was, against all expectation, able to save most of the British army. "Operation Dynamo," as the Dunkirk operation was called, took 337,000 men, of whom 110,000 were French, off the beaches around the port of Dunkirk. Several factors contributed to the success of the evacuation. Adolf Hitler, apparently concerned that his tanks would become bogged down in the marshy ground around Dunkirk, ordered a crucial three-day halt starting on 24 May. This enabled the Anglo–French to establish a defensive perimeter around Dunkirk. The task of destroying the BEF on the beaches was left to the German air force, whose commander, Field Marshal Hermann Göring, had boasted that his pilots could do the job; however, they proved remarkably ineffective. In the meantime, the British sent numerous ships across the English Channel to assist in the evacuation. The legend of the "little ships" however, should be regarded with caution. While small pleasure steamers and launches were sent to Dunkirk, they were largely used to ferry soldiers (standing in long lines in the water) to larger Royal Navy vessels waiting offshore. And the heroic resistance of the French 1st Army in Lille and the British rearguard in Calais slowed up the German advance on Dunkirk.

Dunkirk may have been a miracle, but it was not a victory. Wars are not won by evacuations, as Prime Minister **Winston Churchill** pointed out in the House of Commons. Great Britain had saved its army, although most of its heavy equipment had to be left behind. France was forced to sue for peace on 22 June, and its perspective on Dunkirk was very different. Churchill had tried to placate the French by insisting that British and French troops should be evacuated "arm in arm" from the beaches, but the French government suspected the British of leaving France to its fate. Churchill's offer of an indissoluble union between Britain and France, on 16 June, was rejected by the French Cabinet, although it had the support of the young French general Charles de Gaulle, who wished to continue resistance and rallied support in London.

E

EAST OF SUEZ DECISION (1968). The Labour government of Prime Minister **Harold Wilson** was beset by financial problems (he had been obliged to devalue the pound sterling in 1967) that affected the defense budget. On 16 January 1968, Wilson announced Great Britain's intention to withdraw its forces from the Far East to save money (the sole exception being **Hong Kong**). This was to be done by 31 January 1971, and all British forces in the Persian Gulf were to be withdrawn at the same time. The decision was not popular in the **United States,** where President **Lyndon B. Johnson** had been trying to get Britain to make a military contribution to the **Vietnam War.** Wilson was obdurate in his refusal, wisely as it turned out. He recognized, as did his defense secretary, **Denis Healey** (1964–1970), that Britain lacked the resources to sustain a global military posture any longer.

EDEN, SIR ANTHONY (1897–1977). Anthony Eden succeeded **Winston Churchill** as Britain's prime minister on 6 April 1955, but his term in office was brief because of the catastrophic **Suez Crisis** of November 1956. He was the son of a minor baronet in County Durham who followed the classic education path of his class through **Eton College** and Christchurch College, Oxford. His service in **World War I** was distinguished and, in 1918, left him as the youngest brigadier major in the British army. Unlike the other politicians with whom he later worked, Eden, therefore, knew about the realities of war.

His ascent after entering the House of Commons as a Conservative member of Parliament in 1923 was rapid and seemingly effortless. The **Foreign Office** seemed a natural home for a man with a first-class degree in Oriental languages. He was made parliamentary private secretary to **Foreign Secretary Austen Chamberlain** in 1926, on the recommendation of Prime Minister **Stanley Baldwin.** And so began Eden's 30-year association with the Foreign Office. He was a natural negotiator who soon won golden opinions. In 1931, he became undersecretary of state at the Foreign Office under Lord Reading and then Sir John Simon. The fall of **Sir Samuel Hoare** in 1935, as a result of the Ethiopian Crisis, gave Eden, at just 38 years of age, the chance to become foreign secretary.

His relationship with Stanley Baldwin as prime minister was cordial, but that with Baldwin's successor, **Neville Chamberlain,** less so. This was partly a result of Chamberlain's tendency to run his own foreign policy, and partly a consequence of Eden's own temperamental frailty. He resigned in February 1938, ostensibly over the **appeasement** of Benito Mussolini's **Italy,** but there is little in the record to show that he fundamentally disagreed with Chamberlain's attempt to appease Nazi **Germany.** Eden was subsequently a tenacious defender of his none too convincing role on appeasement put forth in his memoir *Facing the Dictators* (1962). Historians who cast doubt on Eden's role in the 1960s were threatened with litigation.

Eden was out of office until war broke out in September 1939, when Chamberlain made him secretary of state for the Dominions Office. Then, in 1940, when Churchill became dissatisfied with the existing foreign secretary, **Lord Halifax,** Eden was a natural replacement, and he retained the post until the general election of July 1945.

The two men had not always been close, and Churchill had been disappointed by Eden's rather passive role in 1938–1939, when he seemed overly concerned about the need to return to government. Nevertheless, Eden was a loyal lieutenant during the war and was seen by many as Churchill's natural successor as Conservative leader. Eden was at Churchill's side at the important wartime conferences at **Teheran, Yalta,** and **Potsdam.** He also presided over the important amalgamation of the Diplomatic Service with the Foreign Office in 1943, which ended the artificial separation of the two branches of the British foreign policymaking machine.

Eden was thrown out of office by the surprise Labour Party victory in the middle of the Potsdam Conference in July 1945; however, he recognized the good qualities of his successor, **Ernest Bevin,** and supported his policy. Eden's period out of government from 1945–1951 was marked by increasing frustration about Churchill's unwillingness to retire. When Churchill formed his second administration in October 1951, Eden was again the obvious choice as foreign secretary, although he grew increasingly impatient about his move into **Downing Street.**

The period from 1951–1955 marked the golden sunset of Eden's relationship with the Foreign Office. His skill and patience in negotiation secured notable successes, including the withdrawal of British troops from the Canal Zone in **Egypt** in 1954, and the end of French rule in **Indochina,** secured the same year at the **Geneva Conference,** at which Britain was co-chairman. Unlike his U.S. equivalent, **John Foster Dulles,** Eden was prepared to accept the likelihood of a victory for Ho Chi Minh's Communist Party in the All-Vietnam elections, which, in fact, were never held. Eden's personal relationship with Dulles was poor, a reality that had fateful consequences in 1956.

Eden also presided over British membership in the **Southeast Asia Treaty Organization**, set up in 1954 to combat the Communist threat. In 1955, he also played a role in formulating the Baghdad Pact, which was designed to play a similar role in the Middle East. The central irony of his career was that one of his greatest successes, the Egyptian Settlement, eventually brought him down. Eden's point of reference in the postwar period was the 1930s, and his experience of dealing with the European dictators. He persisted in seeing Egyptian leader **Jamal Abd al Nasser** (prime minister, 1954–1956; president, 1956–1970) as a reincarnation of Mussolini.

Nasser flirted with the Soviet Bloc in his attempts to secure his major objective of building the **Aswan Dam** over the River Nile. Eden and the Americans saw Nasser as an ally of Communism and intrigued against him. Nasser retaliated by nationalizing the Anglo–French Suez Canal Company in July 1956, and seizing control of the Suez Canal itself. Eden regarded this move as a personal affront and was determined to remove Nasser, by force, if necessary. His crucial error, not helped by his poor relationship with Secretary of State Dulles, was the assumption that U.S. president **Dwight D. Eisenhower** (1953–1961) shared his willingness to use force. Eisenhower's priority in 1956 was to secure reelection, and he preferred diplomacy to armed action. Eden compounded his error by involving Britain in a Byzantine plot with the French and Israelis, formalized in a secret meeting at Sèvres, whereby Nasser would be provoked into a war by collusion between these powers. Eden subsequently lied about his collusion with **France** and **Israel** in the House of Commons. The result was a disaster. An Anglo–French landing at Port Said was successful, but the **United States** voted against Anglo–French action at the **United Nations**, as did the Soviet Union. The pound sterling also came under pressure, and, Eisenhower, infuriated by his main ally's action, made it clear that no U.S. support would be forthcoming unless the British and French withdrew from Egypt immediately.

Eden was warned by the chancellor of the exchequer, **Harold Macmillan**, that Britain would be unable to resist U.S. financial pressure. The fury of President Eisenhower was heightened by the fact that the day the Anglo–French task force arrived coincided with Soviet action against the revolution in Hungary. The West lost the moral high ground because of Eden's action. Indeed, the Soviet Union felt able to threaten the West in support of Nasser. Britain, and an even more reluctant France, withdrew from Egypt, and, on 9 January 1957, Eden, his prestige terminally damaged by Suez, resigned as prime minister, to be succeeded by Macmillan, who had been just as enthusiastic about the Suez adventure.

A factor in the Suez crisis had been Eden's poor health, the result of a botched gall bladder operation, which meant that he was on medication, which might have affected his judgment. He was created 1st Earl of Avon in 1961.

EDWARD VIII, HM, KING (1894–1972). Only one British monarch has abdicated from the throne, and that was King Edward VIII, in December 1936, the result of Edward's strange failure to recognize that no British government would agree to his marriage to a twice-divorced American woman, Wallace Simpson. Mrs. Simpson seemed to be equally confused about Edward's constitutional position, which did not allow him to override the view of the government and, indeed, the opposition of such **Commonwealth** states as **Australia, New Zealand, Canada**, and **South Africa**, to such a marriage. The crisis was astutely handled by **Stanley Baldwin** (prime minister, 1935–1937), who wasted much time on it, time that might have been profitably spent on other matters. Edward was downgraded to Duke of Windsor, and his wife, when they did marry in **France**, refused a royal title. Edward caused both the British government and **Foreign Office** some irritation by his flirtation with Nazi **Germany** (he visited the country in 1937), so that during **World War II**, he was made governor general of the Bahamas to get him as far away from Britain and Europe as possible. It is unlikely that Edward would have become the Nazi stooge Adolf Hitler hoped for, but his behavior demonstrated the Duke of Windsor's naivety. His brother, George VI (1936–1952), proved to be a much more suitable monarch in peace and war.

EGYPT. Great Britain had a long historic link with Egypt, which had been part of the Ottoman Turkish Empire for centuries. Its imperial rival for control was **France**, and, in 1798, Admiral Horatio Nelson destroyed **Napoleon Bonaparte's** invasion fleet in the Battle of the Nile. The weakness of the Ottoman regime in Constantinople brought the Egyptian question to the fore. In the 1830s and 1840s, an overly mighty vassal of the Turkish Sultan, Mehemet Ali, who was supported by France, threatened British interests. The **Foreign Office** wanted to preserve **Turkey** as a bulwark against **Russia**; therefore, it opposed any fragmentation of the Turkish Empire. The strongest proponent of this as **foreign secretary** was Lord **Palmerston**, who used the Royal Navy against him in 1841, and ended Ali's attempt to make himself independent of the Sultan. The disappearance of Ali did not stop Egyptian rulers, nominally vassals of the Sultan, from seeking to increase their power. Khedive Ismail Pasha (1863–1879) wanted to create a European-style state in Egypt, but, in doing so, he ran up vast debts. This gave European creditors, notably the British and the French, the chance to interfere in Egypt. The French had built the Suez Canal, but it was British prime minister **Benjamin Disraeli** who bought Pasha's 44-percent holding in the Suez Canal Company in December 1875, for 4 million pounds. This act, more so than anything else, marked the start of Britain's official involvement in Egypt.

Pasha was ejected from Egypt by his Anglo–French creditors in 1879, but this provoked a full-scale nationalist uprising in the years that followed, and, in July 1882, the Royal Navy was sent to bombard the key Egyptian port of Alexandria. In December, the British defeated the Egyptian army, and the new British prime minister, **William Gladstone,** was left with the primary responsibility for Egypt, an important source of cotton imports. Britain was not in total control of Egypt, because Egypt's other creditors still had some say in its finances. In theory, once Egypt's debts were paid off, the country was supposed to have its "independence" under the Ottoman umbrella restored. The role of the non-British creditors ceased in practice in 1904 (as a consequence of the entente with France). Egypt effectively became a British protectorate; it was given this official status in December 1914. This was necessary because Ottoman Turkey had become an ally of **Germany** in **World War I.** A key British aim was to defend the Suez Canal, vital to communication with British **India.** To secure itself against revolt, Britain promised to consider self-government for Egypt following the war, although its officials thought the Egyptians were not ready for it.

Partial independence was conceded in 1922, in the Anglo–Egyptian Treaty. This was because Britain's victorious general over Turkey, Lord Allenby, the high commissioner, insisted on it. The treaty still gave Britain control over defense and foreign relations, and a British garrison guarded the Suez Canal. Egyptian nationalists still resented the British presence in the country. A second Anglo–Egyptian Treaty in 1936 removed most of the constraints on Egyptian freedom, but a large British force remained in the Canal Zone. During **World War II,** Britain was acutely aware of the Suez Canal's vulnerability to attack from both Fascist **Italy** and Nazi Germany. The war also offered an opportunity for nationalist army officers like Anwar Sadat, a future Egyptian president, to conspire with the Nazis against Britain. The Axis defeat in 1943 ended any threat to the canal.

After World War II, Egypt was ruled by a corrupt, playboy king, Farouk, and the old nationalist opposition (Wafd) was seen to be ineffective. It failed to end British occupation of Egypt, and this created an opportunity for the Free Officers group, which overthrew the monarchy in 1952 and set up a republic. Its leading figure was **Jamal Abd al Nasser** (president, 1954–1970), who negotiated the British evacuation of the Canal Zone in 1954. This apparently positive move in Anglo–Egyptian relations was negated by the **Suez Crisis** of November 1956, which followed Nasser's decision to nationalize the canal in July 1956. Nasser was a modernizer who wanted funds to build the **Aswan Dam,** a prestige project for his government.

British influence in the Middle East seemed permanently damaged, but this did not prove to be the case. It kept its influence in **Jordan**, Saudi Arabia, and the Persian Gulf monarchies, although the pro-British monarchy was overthrown in **Iraq** in 1958. Instead, it was the Pan-Arab Nasser who collapsed his dreams. The United Arab Republic, a union with Syria (1958–1961), failed, as did Egyptian intervention in Yemen. Nasser clung to an alliance with the Soviet Union, which supplied him with modern weapons, but this made relations with Britain and the **United States** difficult, especially given Nasser's unrelenting hostility toward **Israel**. In 1956, Israel had been an ally of Britain, but the situation changed with the 1967 Six-Day War, in which Egypt and its Arab allies were heavily defeated. Nasser briefly resigned (before being brought back by popular demand), and Egypt lost the Sinai Desert to Israel. This brought the new Egyptian–Israeli border to the Suez Canal. **United Nations (UN)** Resolution 242 subsequently demanded that Sinai and all the other Occupied Territories be evacuated by Israel. Successive British governments under premiers **Harold Wilson** and **Edward Heath** supported the UN demand. The **Foreign Office**, which has often been accused of being pro-Arab, did likewise. Israel ignored international opinion, and Nasser, its most bitter enemy, died suddenly of a heart attack in 1970.

Nasser was succeeded by his old Free Officers comrade Anwar Sadat, who continued the policy of refusing to recognize the state of Israel. In October 1973, Sadat, with his Syrian allies, attacked Israel in what became known as the Yom Kippur War. The Egyptian and Syrian armies won initial successes, and the Suez Canal was even crossed, but Israel, with much U.S. assistance, eventually prevailed. The Egyptian military's performance was much better than in 1967, and Sadat eased things for himself in an important respect. In 1971, he had abandoned Nasser's pro-Soviet stance and expelled hundreds of Russian advisors. This improved relations with the United States (diplomatic relations were restored after seven years) and enabled its secretary of state, **Henry Kissinger**, to act as a mediator. Kissinger's diplomacy in 1973–1974 secured the return of the Sinai Desert. In Britain, there was approval for Kissinger's policy, but a serious result of the 1973 war was a quadrupling of British oil prices. The Arab oil states fell in behind the anti-Israeli policy and, for the first time, used the price of oil as a political weapon. Egypt, lacking oil itself, needed this support.

Sadat's foreign policy underwent an even more dramatic transformation in 1977. On 20 November, Sadat flew to Israel to address the Israeli parliament (the Knesset) about the need for peace between the two states. The Arab states regarded this as a betrayal. Hatred of Israel had been an axiom of Egyptian and Arab politics since 1948. The gesture to Israel, widely applauded in Britain and the United States, led to the 1978 Camp David Agreement, which was sponsored by U.S. president Jimmy Carter. This was formalized into an Egyptian–Israeli peace treaty in Washington, D.C., in 1982. Sadat paid for his radical foreign policy with his life. He was assassinated by Islamic extremists at a military parade in 1981. He was succeeded as president by the former air force chief Hosni Mubarak (1981–2011). During Mubarak's time in office, the key relationship was not with the Soviet Union, and still less Britain, but with the United States. He cracked down on Islamists and moved into alliance with conservative Saudi Arabia and Jordan. In 1989, Egypt, forgiven for making peace with Israel, was readmitted to the Arab League. In 1991, Egypt contributed 35,000 men to the coalition against Iraq in the **Gulf War**.

In the West, Mubarak was seen as a reliable conservative ally, anti-Iranian and against all forms of Islamic extremism. Nonetheless, he was a dictator who rigged elections and abused human rights. Mubarak's main political opponent was the Muslim Brotherhood. In 1995, just one member of the brotherhood was elected to parliament. There would eventually be a price to pay for this undemocratic behavior, but many years passed before this became a reality. In 2003, Mubarak, like his Arab neighbors, did not join the Anglo–American attack on Iraq, although he posed as an enemy of international **terrorism**. The formation of the 2003 Egyptian Movement for Change should have been a warning to the regime, but Mubarak, with his control of the military and a feared secret police, ignored portents. Already 81 years of age in 2011, he seemed incapable of change. When demonstrations broke out against Mubarak's government in January 2011, organized gangs were used to kill demonstrators, while the army remained idle, supposedly neutral.

The United States, Britain, and other European states were confused. They knew about Mubarak's repression, but his position as a linchpin in the Middle East made the Anglo–Americans initially reluctant to condemn him. British foreign secretary **William Hague** called for dialogue, but the political opposition was determined that Mubarak must step down. He eventually did so on 11 February. The army, which still had great prestige as the bringer of revolution in 1952, held the ring, and Mubarak's vice president took his place. He was arrested and charged with complicity in the murders of demonstrators in Cairo's Tahrir Square. Parliamentary elections were supposed to be staged under army supervision, but, by 2012, the process, which was staged and very slow, was causing disillusion in Egypt's major cities. Rural areas where Muslim Brotherhood support was especially strong were more interested in stability than democracy. There was speculation about how relations with Britain, the United States, and the West would be affected if the brotherhood won the elections. One of the issues affecting Anglo–Egyptian relations was the appearance in 2011–2012 of discrimination against the Coptic Christian minority. This surfaced in attacks on Christian churches and property.

EISENHOWER, DWIGHT DAVID (1890–1969). In a tradition of soldier presidents, Dwight D. Eisenhower was the presidential nominee of the Republican Party in 1952. He served two terms (1953–1961) and would have been unbeatable had the U.S. constitution permitted him to stand again. Although a better president than he is sometimes given credit for being, Eisenhower is best remembered for being supreme Allied commander at the time of the **D-Day Landings** on 6 June 1944. Great Britain's senior general, Bernard Montgomery, spoke despairingly of Eisenhower's lack of combat experience and leadership, but he had a daunting task in dealing with generals with big egos, the likes of Montgomery and George Patton. Neither were political leaders, like **Winston Churchill** and Charles de Gaulle, and easy to deal with. "Ike" as he was commonly known, was a popular commander with most of his allies and a hero in the **United States**. This made him, rather than the more glamorous but volatile Douglas MacArthur, the choice of the Republicans to run as president. He was a sensible, pragmatic man who warned his fellow countrymen and countrywomen of the dangers of the "military-industrial complex" before leaving office in 1961. He had helped to extricate the United States from the **Korean War** (1950–1953) but differed with his British ally about how to deal with the Communist threat in Southeast Asia. Eisenhower wanted to intervene against the Vietnamese Communists at **Dien Bien Phu** in 1954, and the British did not. **China** was another bone of contention, with the Eisenhower administration refusing to recognize the Communist country or allow it a seat on the **United Nations** Security Council in New York. There was Anglo–American cooperation in **Iran** to bring down the government of Mohammed Mossadeq in 1953, but the two Western allies then fell out spectacularly over the Anglo–French invasion of **Egypt** in November 1956.

Eisenhower found himself at odds with trusted wartime colleagues, and it was fortunate that he was able to work so well with Prime Minister **Harold Macmillan** to restore the **"special relationship"** (the two men had worked closely together in North Africa during **World War II)**. At the Bermuda Conference in 1957, Eisenhower agreed to provide Britain with 60 **Thor missiles**. After a marked improvement in relations with the Soviet Union after the death of Joseph Stalin in March 1953, tensions reemerged over the U-2 spy plane affair, which wrecked the Paris summit with Soviet leader Nikita Khrushchev. Two further poisoned chalices were left by the Eisenhower administration, one over Vietnam, and the other over Cuba, where the Central Intelligence Agency made a disastrous appraisal of Fidel Castro's military strength and popularity. *See also* COLD WAR; SUEZ CRISIS.

ELIZABETH II, HM, QUEEN (1926–). As Great Britain's head of state since 1952, Queen Elizabeth II is one of the longest-serving of British monarchs. Although under the terms of the unwritten British constitution, her role is largely symbolic. It is Queen Elizabeth who accepts the credentials of foreign ambassadors and diplomats to what is known as the Court of St. James. It is also she who receives foreign presidents on state visits and entertains them formally at Buckingham Palace or Windsor Castle. The queen also visits foreign countries on behalf of the British government. In 2007, for example, Queen Elizabeth visited Jamestown, Virginia, at the time of its 400th anniversary. On occasion, the symbolism of a visit can have an important political aspect, as in 2011, when she visited Dublin in the Irish Republic. This was the first visit by a British monarch to the republic since Irish independence in 1921, and it marked a new and friendlier relationship.

Elizabeth II is the head of the **British Commonwealth** of Nations, and she presides over Commonwealth Conferences. She remains the head of state of **Australia, Canada**, and **New Zealand,** and she is known to attach great importance to the continued existence of the Commonwealth as an international organization. The year 2012 marked the 60th anniversary of Elizabeth II's accession to the British throne.

ETHIOPIA. The Ethiopian crisis of 1935–1936 found Britain deeply involved in the fate of this independent African kingdom, one of only two at the time. The circumstances were created by the attack made on the kingdom by the **Italian** dictator Benito Mussolini in October 1935, in an effort to enlarge Italy's colonial empire. In response, British **foreign secretary Samuel Hoare,** together with his French counterpart, Pierre Laval, put forth a plan that would have ceded most of Ethiopia. This so-called Hoare–Laval Pact was prematurely leaked by the French Foreign Office, causing outrage in Britain and forcing Hoare's resignation.

Anglo–French divisions about plans to deal with Mussolini, which included **League of Nations** sanctions, subsequently allowed the Italian leader to complete the conquest of the country; however, this did not last long, as Italy was driven out by the British in 1941. Ethiopian emperor Haile Selassie, whose bravery had impressed the world in 1935, returned to his throne. Hoare was replaced as foreign secretary by a youthful **Anthony Eden.**

ETON COLLEGE. The best-known of English public schools, Eton College has a strong historical link with the **Foreign Office.** It resisted the introduction of open competition for the administrative class of the home civil service in 1870. The claim was that the nature and requirements of diplomatic work were different. This allowed Eton and other public schools to dominate the entry. From 1900–1914, 67 percent of foreign and diplomatic service entrants were Etonians, and, as late as 1929, four out of 10 diplomatic appointments came from Eton. Thereafter, the Etonian, rather than public school, backgrounds of entrants lessened. During the postwar period, Etonians **Sir Anthony Eden** and **Sir Alec Douglas-Home** both held the posts of **foreign secretary** and prime minister. The current British prime minister, **David Cameron**, is also an Old Etonian. Critics regarded this as a regression after the British establishment had moved away from public school domination since the 1960s. It has to be conceded, however, that the current British foreign secretary, **William Hague**, was not a public schoolboy, although he did go to Oxford University.

EUROPEAN COAL AND STEEL COMMUNITY (ECSC). The European Coal and Steel Community (ECSC) came into existence on 1 January 1952. It placed the coal and steel industries of **France**, the Federal Republic of Germany, **Italy**, **Belgium**, the Netherlands, and Luxemburg under one common supranational authority. The idea was formulated by Jean Monnet, who had played a central role in the planning of the postwar French economy, although its foundation plan took the name of the French foreign minister Robert Schuman. Its primary aim was to prevent a new Franco–German war by putting the industries essential to war under supranational control. The Schuman Plan was then extended to bring in four new members, but not Great Britain. The British Labour government, under **Clement R. Attlee**, was invited to join but declined to do so. Britain still saw the "**special relationship**" with the **United States** and imperial commonwealth links as more important, a fact not always understood on the continent. **Winston Churchill's** "United States of Europe" speech at Zurich in 1946 had been misinterpreted by European unity enthusiasts. Britain would encourage from the sidelines, but it would not take part in the process of integration. Attlee and Foreign Secretary **Ernest Bevin** would not cede any aspect of British sovereignty to a supranational authority abroad. There were other factors as well. The National Union of Mineworkers, one of Britain's most powerful trade unions, had only secured nationalization of the coal industry in 1948. It did not wish control of the industry to be ceded to foreigners. *See also* EUROPEAN ECONOMIC COMMUNITY/EUROPEAN COMMUNITY.

EUROPEAN DEFENSE COMMUNITY (EDC). Faced with the threat of a resurgent **Germany**, European federalists evolved the idea of a supranational army that would incorporate Germany. The idea was formally introduced by French prime minister René Pleven in October 1950, and a treaty was signed to establish a six-member European Defense Community (EDC) on 27 May 1952. **France** was especially keen that Great Britain should join the new organization, but Britain's new Conservative government declined to do so. The reason was the same as the one prohibiting membership to the

European Coal and Steel Community: The British government would not agree to a derogation of sovereignty to a foreign supranational body. British refusal to join effectively doomed the EDC, even though the Americans were supportive of it as an anti-Soviet defense instrument. In August 1954, the French National Assembly refused to ratify the EDC treaty, and the concept perished. The French were acutely nervous about being left inside a defense community with West Germany, **Italy**, and the BENELUX states (**Belgium, the Netherlands, and Luxemburg**), without Britain. As it was, the Federal Republic of Germany joined the **North Atlantic Treaty Organization** in 1955.

EUROPEAN ECONOMIC COMMUNITY (EEC)/EUROPEAN COMMUNITY (EC). Great Britain always saw its relationship with the **United States** and the **British Commonwealth** as paramount, until the 1960s. It thus rejected invitations to join the **European Coal and Steel Community** and its more developed cousin, the European Economic Community (EEC). At the **Messina Conference** in **Italy** in 1955, Britain had been content with mere observer status and did not sign the **Treaty of Rome** (1957). Only in 1959–1960 did British prime minister **Harold Macmillan** and his government realize that the EEC, with its population of 180 million, and thrusting German, French, and Italian economies, was a vital market. Neither the Commonwealth nor the **European Free Trade Association** (1959), sponsored by Britain but much weaker in economic terms, were adequate substitutes. The United States also encouraged British membership. The failure to join the EEC in 1957–1958 cost Britain dearly. Two applications (1961 and 1967) to join the EEC were rejected because of the hostility of French president Charles de Gaulle. Only on 1 January 1973, did Britain join the EEC, after the prime minister **Edward Heath** had signed the Treaty of Accession (1972).

Lateness involved a greater British contribution to the controversial Common Agricultural Policy. This was a continuing problem for Britain in the EEC, especially when **Margaret Thatcher** was prime minister in the 1980s. The EEC changed its name to the European Community (EC) in 1986, but this did not alter Thatcher's unenthusiastic attitude toward it. There was also the fact that in the 1970s and 1980s, the EEC had lost its competitive edge. In 1980, it had a $10 billion trade deficit with **Japan**, and its growth rate was only a little more than 2 percent. Thatcher continued to complain loudly about Britain's contribution to the EC budget. It was a net contributor and imported 70 percent of its food, often from inefficient EEC farmers. In fact, the EEC reduced Britain's contribution by two-thirds in 1984.

In 1986, the EC sought to make itself more competitive through the Single European Act (SEA). Its object was to create a single market of goods, services, people, and capital by 1992. In theory, this should have been acceptable to successive British Conservative governments (1979–1997), but the existence of the SEA did not lessen Thatcher's fundamental Euroscepticism, although her successor, **John Major**, was more constructive.

EUROPEAN FREE TRADE ASSOCIATION (EFTA). Great Britain's initial reaction to the founding of the **European Economic Community (EEC)** in 1957–1958 was negative. The British government even tried to sabotage the EEC by setting up the rival European Free Trade Association (EFTA) in November 1959. It began to operate in July 1960. Alongside Britain were Denmark, Norway, Sweden, Austria, Switzerland, and Portugal. The British claimed that the EFTA would allow bridges to be built to the EEC, but this proved to be a nebulous concept. In fact, the very existence of EFTA made it more difficult for Britain to join the EEC when it eventually decided to do so in 1961. More than half of the people in EFTA were British, and the organization lacked the financial and industrial muscle of the EEC. It became redundant when Britain became a full member of the EEC in 1973. The EFTA's members, save Switzerland, also joined the EEC, demonstrating what an ill-conceived organization it was. It merely left Europe briefly at "sixes and sevens" (EFTA had seven members). Its obvious frailty brought about a revolution in British foreign policy in 1960–1961, to accommodate the first application to join the EEC.

EUROPEAN UNION (EU). In yet another transformation, the **European Community** became the **European Union (EU)** in 1991. The **Treaty of Maastricht** (1992) came into force when it was ratified by the 11 member states in November 1993 (signature precedes ratification). Britain was a signatory to the treaty, but it was forced to leave the European Monetary Union (EMU) in catastrophic fashion in 1992, when interest rates rocketed. A small but highly irritating anti-EU rump in the Conservative Party made life difficult for Prime Minister **John Major** after Maastricht and the EMU disaster. As ever, the debate was about sovereignty. Major's critics claimed that the tentacles of the EU were undermining Britain's capacity to make its own decisions. When the Conservatives lost power in May 1997, the incoming Labour government seemed friendlier to the EU. The new prime minister, **Tony Blair,** claimed to support the concept of the European common currency (euro). The euro was adopted by 11 member states in 1999, but Blair's chancellor of the exchequer, **Gordon Brown**, stuck by his mantra that conditions were not right for British involvement. This policy was also followed by the Conservative-Liberal Democrat coalition after May 2010. By then, the **Eurozone** sovereign debt crisis was already underway.

The other major issue in the EU in the 1990s concerned enlargement. **Spain** and Portugal had joined in 1986, followed by Finland, Sweden, and Austria in 1995. This suited the British, who rejected the idea of a highly centralized EU and believed that the bigger the membership, the more unlikely any form of political union would become. The adhesion of Hungary, the Czech Republic, Estonia, **Slovenia**, Slovakia, Romania, Malta, Latvia, Lithuania, **Bulgaria**, and **Cyprus** meant that by 2007, the EU had 27 member states. Increased size meant that the operation of a common EU foreign policy known as the Common Foreign and Security Policy could prove difficult. The British government was unenthusiastic. Sovereignty was again the key issue, with successive British governments not wanting their control over foreign policy subsumed by the EU. This skepticism was reflected in Gordon Brown's appointment of Kathryn Ashton in 2010 as Britain's candidate for the new EU foreign ministry. Ashton's experience was entirely domestic, with no diplomatic or foreign policy background. She remained almost invisible on British media outlets. This reflected British skepticism, or outright hostility, toward federalism in Europe.

The position of the Labour Party under **Ed Miliband** (beginning in September 2010) was only marginally more sympathetic than that of the Conservatives. The supposedly pro-European Liberal Democrats struggled to effect coalition policy toward the EU. An aura of triumphalism hung over the anti-EU majority in Britain, glad it had never joined the euro. Anglo–French intervention in Libya in 2011, under the auspices of a **United Nations** resolution, and the **North Atlantic Treaty Organization** umbrella, also pleased Eurosceptics. Defense issues impinged on sovereignty, a constant British concern. In 2007, the EU established Battle Groups, which followed the stationing of EU troops outside EU frontiers in **Bosnia** and Congo. These were meant to be ready for peacekeeping operations at short notice.

EUROZONE. The European common currency (euro) came into existence in 2000, following the 1992 **Treaty of Maastricht** and the introduction of the Single European Market. Although offered membership in the euro, Great Britain declined to join the common currency. Prime Minister **Tony Blair** was reputed to be in favor of joining, but his long-standing chancellor of the exchequer, **Gordon Brown**, was against it, and he dominated the formulation of fiscal policy from 1997–2007. Brown repeated the mantra that Britain could only join the euro when conditions were right. He held to this position when he became prime minister in June 2007. This meant that although Britain's major **European Union (EU)** partners were inside the common currency (**Germany, France, Italy**, and the BENELUX states), Britain was not. Approximately 50 percent of British trade was with the EU, and 40 percent with the Eurozone, which, by 2010, had 17 members (others included **Spain**, Finland, Austria, and Denmark).

The defeat of the Labour Party in the 2010 election brought a coalition of Conservatives and Liberals under Prime Minister **David Cameron** into office. Cameron and most of his party were Eurosceptics who permanently rejected membership of the euro, whereas the Liberal Democrats, under their leader, **Nick Clegg**, had a more open-minded attitude toward it. The **Foreign Office** found itself with a new **foreign secretary, William Hague**, who had long been skeptical about the EU, let alone the Eurozone. Conservative backbenchers, who had caused former Conservative premier **John Major** (1990–1997) so many problems, were an even more strident anti-European force in the Cameron government. This political reality caused Cameron increasing difficulties in 2011, as demands for a referendum on Britain's relationship with Europe became more vociferous. He was also embroiled in the September–December sovereign debt crisis in the Eurozone involving **Greece, Ireland**, Portugal, and, increasingly, Italy, the third-largest economy in the Eurozone. While the British favored the use of quantitative easing (printing money) by the European Central Bank, Germany, the biggest Eurozone economy, opposed this and resented, as did the French, British interference when they were not even members of the Eurozone. The **United States** also favored quantitative easing, which it, like Britain, had used to counter the dire consequences of the 2008–2009 financial crises, coming from subprime mortgage scandals and bank collapses.

Matters came to a head in December 2011. A crucial EU summit was scheduled for 8–9 December, in Paris, to save the Eurozone from potential implosion as vast bailouts to Ireland, Portugal, and especially Greece (with a sovereign debt running at 129 percent of its gross domestic product [GDP]) were exerting pressure, even on the German economy. A plan was put forth by the German chancellor, Angela Merkel, and French president Nicolas Sarkozy, whereby financial disciplines within the Eurozone were to be tightened up by a new treaty that would allow members to be fined for running up national deficits of more than 3 percent of the GDP and demanded that national budgets be submitted for EU Commission approval. This was designed to appease financial markets and credit-rating agencies, which threatened to downgrade the Eurozone and even the entire EU.

The British position was that such a fundamental revision of the Treaty of Lisbon entitled Britain to opt outs from such a treaty, in particular, to protect the financial services industry in London. France and Germany wanted agreement between all 27 EU members for the new treaty, but Cameron insisted on Britain's opt out in relation to financial services that brought in 10 percent of the GDP and was the largest such sector in Europe. When Merkel and

Sarkozy refused the British demand, Cameron used his EU veto to prevent unanimity being achieved during the night of 8 December–9 December. He claimed he was protecting Britain's national interests, but his infuriated partners accused Britain of obscurantist nationalism in the **Margaret Thatcher** mold. The other 26 members of the euro would be obliged to sign a new intergovernmental accord, leaving Britain on the outside. Cameron's action could be alternately seen as brave or rash, the worst British foreign policy blunder since the 1956 **Suez Crisis**, or a heroic stand against excessive European integration. His Franco–German EU partners wanted the new treaty to be operative by March 2012, an ambitious target. Britain remained an EU member, but it plowed a lone furrow outside the Eurozone, and even apart from the other nine non-Eurozone members of the EU. Eurosceptics inside Britain attempted to argue that it would benefit from the new arrangement.

The argument about the Eurozone underlined the whole difference of perception about the EU and its future. Britain was dedicated to protecting its national sovereignty, suspicious of EU common policies and the need for a community foreign policy. Its behavior during the **Iraq** crisis of 2002–2003 and the Libyan crisis of 2011 clearly demonstrated this, as did its behavior in the Eurozone crisis. The crisis epitomized the long-standing problems in Britain's relationship with the EU. It also placed severe pressure on the Conservative-Liberal Democrat coalition, as the Liberal Democrats had long been the most pro-EU party in Britain. On 11 December 2011, the Liberal Democrat leader and Deputy Prime Minister Nick Clegg made severe criticisms of Cameron's behavior at the Brussels summit in a BBC television interview, and he was joined by colleagues. It remained to be seen whether the coalition would hold together. Continental Europeans despaired of Britain's attitude. A complex situation was made worse on 12 December, when Clegg refused to sit next to Cameron when the prime minister was explaining his actions in Brussels in the House of Commons. Cameron appeared to defend EU membership, but many commentators were suspicious of his position, as upon his return from Brussels on 9 December, Cameron had dined with a group of extreme Eurosceptics at Chequers. The Foreign Office was also reputedly antagonized by being left out of the loop in Brussels, a traditional complaint against prime ministers who dominated foreign policy.

F

FALKLANDS WAR (1982). Between 2 April–14 June 1982, Great Britain was involved in a war (although hostilities were not officially declared) over the control of the Falkland Islands with **Argentina**. These remote islands known to the Argentines as the Malvinas are 400 miles off the coast of Argentina. They had been continuously occupied by British settlers since 1833, but Argentina disputed British sovereignty over the islands. Its point of reference for the claim of sovereignty went back to the 1760s, when the Spanish had briefly settled there. In 1982, there were some 1,700 settlers of British descent on the islands.

Argentina's interest in the islands had, in fact, wavered since it attained its independence from Spain in the 19th century, but it had been revived by dictator Juan Peron in the 1940s and became a persistent feature of Argentinian foreign policy. School maps always colored the islands in Argentina's blue. In 1981, it seemed that the **Foreign Office** was interested in a "leaseback" arrangement, whereby the Falklands would revert to Argentine sovereignty, but this stirred up such anger within the Conservative Party that the plan was dropped in 1981. Britain then seemed to signal disinterest when its defense cuts removed HMS *Endurance*, the only Royal Navy ship in the South Atlantic. This was at least the way the move was interpreted by Argentinian dictator General Leopoldo Galtieri in Buenos Aires. He ordered the invasion of the Falkland Islands on 2 April. The small British garrison could only put up token resistance, and the British governor of the islands (who carried out official duties in a black London taxicab) was obliged to surrender.

This left British prime minister **Margaret Thatcher** in a difficult situation. The islands were 8,000 miles away, and, if diplomacy failed, the only way to reclaim the islands was to send a naval task force to the South Atlantic. She was in a doubly difficult situation because in theory, as the person responsible for the overall policy on the Falklands, she had approved the withdrawal of the *Endurance*. The Argentinian invasion could therefore have been blamed on her policy, but she was saved from embarrassment by the resignation of **Foreign Secretary** Lord Carrington (1979–1982), who took the responsibility for the setback in the South Atlantic. The view of Thatcher was that, if force was needed, it would be applied, although Britain did make efforts to avoid conflict with Argentina through the **United Nations (UN)**.

The attitude of the **United States** during the Falklands conflict was vital. The Americans initially appeared to want to play a role as a neutral mediator, which infuriated Thatcher, who expected U.S. support to be forthcoming. The U.S. secretary of state, Alexander Haig, moved between London and Buenos Aires in unsuccessful attempts to resolve the situation. Although most of President **Ronald Reagan's** administration supported the United States' closest ally, a faction around Jeane Kirkpatrick, the U.S. ambassador to the UN, thought that maintaining good relations with Latin America, which supported Argentina, was more important than the **"special relationship."** President Reagan ultimately supported Britain. U.S. intelligence was made available to the British, and, by the end of April 1982, it was clear that Washington was siding with Britain in the dispute. The Royal Air Force (RAF) was allowed to use Ascension Island, a U.S. airbase halfway between Britain and the Falkland Islands.

Although it was short, the war was sharp. The Argentinian air force, equipped with French Exocet missiles and jets, was effective and sank several British warships, with considerable loss of life. Conversely, a British submarine sank the Argentine cruiser ARA *General Belgrano*. This was controversial, as the ship was moving away from the exclusion zone the Royal Navy had established around the islands. On land, British expertise and professionalism were decisive against Argentina's inexperienced conscripts, although there was a sharp action at Goose Green on 21 May. The British army captured the Falklands capital of Port Stanley on 14 June. The victory cost it and the Royal Navy 255 men, while Argentina lost 746, half of them in the ARA *General Belgrano*. After the war, a substantial British force remained in the Falklands, along with a RAF squadron. From 1982–1987, the Falklands cost Britain's taxpayers £3 billion.

The main beneficiary of the Falklands war (apart from the islanders who remained fiercely loyal to Britain), was Margaret Thatcher. She evaded responsibility for the actual circumstances that produced the invasion and was able to claim a military victory, which greatly enhanced her position as prime minister. In 1981, a year of urban rioting, strikes, and general discontent, Thatcher had been the most unpopular prime minister since polling began in Britain. The "Falklands factor" in 1983 helped her win the general election, even though the Labour Party had endorsed her interventionist stance. Britain seemed to have become a more virile, powerful nation, although informed analysts perceived a tendency to exaggerate the importance of the Falklands victory. It certainly increased the anti-**European Union** rhetoric, which was a feature of the Thatcher government. In Argentina, the war proved fatal for

Galtieri, who was swept from power as his country became a democracy. It maintained its territorial claim to the Falklands. *See also* NOTT, SIR JOHN; PONTING, CLIVE; PYM, SIR FRANCIS; RIDLEY, NICHOLAS.

FASHODA INCIDENT (1898). Egypt and the **Sudan** were areas in dispute between Britain and **France** in the late 19th century. Britain secured its dominant position in Egypt through its purchase of a majority holding in the Suez Canal Company in 1876. France retained an interest in the Sudan, and, in 1898, an expedition under Colonel Jean Baptiste Marchand reached Fashoda. Britain regarded the Sudan as being in its sphere of influence and demanded an evacuation of the expedition. The French foreign minister did not deem the Sudan worth an Anglo–French war, and Marchand's men were withdrawn. In fact, although few realized it at the time, Fashoda marked the end of centuries of intense Anglo–French rivalry. Six years later, the Entente Cordiale between Britain and France was signed.

FOREIGN OFFICE (FO)/FOREIGN AND COMMONWEALTH OFFICE (FCO). Since 1782, the Foreign Office has been one of the major departments in the British governmental structure, alongside the treasury and the Home Office. It, together with the Diplomatic Service, manages British Foreign policy through its missions abroad and policymaking apparatus in London. The two parallel branches of the foreign policy establishment were amalgamated in 1943, when **Anthony Eden** was **foreign secretary.** The Foreign Office struggled with its major accommodation in King Charles Street from its inception. The main building in King Charles Street was the work of the distinguished Victorian architect George Gilbert Scott, but it was fiercely criticized by contemporaries. Rooms had ceilings that were high and difficult to heat. Overcrowding soon became a problem, and the office presented a grubby appearance. Foreign visitors during the 20th century were dismayed to find an entrance hall with one dingy light bulb to provide light, with empty packing cases and teacups strewn around. Lord **Henry John Palmerston,** who spent much of the period from 1830–1865 as foreign secretary and prime minister (sometimes both), tried to make Foreign Office clerks work harder (even on Sundays), but working conditions were hardly encouraging. In 1968, when the Foreign Office and Commonwealth Relations Office were merged to form the Foreign and Commonwealth Office (FCO), staff still worked in as many as 11 separate buildings other than King Charles Street. A major rebuilding project was started in 1970, but it was 1995 before the project was completed, at a cost of £100 million.

In 1905, an important Foreign Office reform introduced the practice of using minuted dispatches, which moved work up a departmental hierarchy from the lowest clerk to the permanent undersecretary, the senior civil servant, and the secretary of state, the senior politician. Thus, promising juniors would have their work read by senior officials and could deal with more mundane issues by referring documents back to the registry so that senior colleagues' time would not be wasted. This hierarchal process provided historians with valuable insights into the policymaking process, albeit in a context where a 50-year rule and a 30-year rule (1968) classified many crucial documents as secret or made them unavailable for lengthy periods of time on the grounds that their disclosure might offend people still living.

In the early years, the artificial division between diplomats and officials in London caused problems. For example, **Sir Nevile Henderson**, whose diplomatic career lasted from 1905–1939, complained that he only actually spent six months in the Foreign Office itself in London and had had little idea of its workings. Conversely, Foreign Office officials often remained in London for years without any experience of working abroad in an embassy. In recent years, the Foreign Office, now often referred to as the FCO, has had to be both more flexible and more integrated into the government machine. Foreign Office officials may be seconded to **No. 10 Downing Street**, the treasury, or the Home Office, and women can be found in senior diplomatic and London posts, something that was unheard of until well after **World War II** (although there has yet to be a female permanent undersecretary or ambassador in Washington). New technology, with e-mails, faxes, and satellite telephones, has vastly accelerated diplomatic processes. The wonderfully long, sometimes arcane, handwritten comments on policy that have entertained historians in the past have long since disappeared. The Foreign Office, once a leisurely career for men who were required to have private incomes and always came from public schools, is now a bustling modern department of state. There are still claims that it is unrepresentative of British society at large, but such criticisms are now taken extremely seriously. Its representatives abroad are expected to be flagbearers for British industry and commerce as much as messengers for British diplomacy. *See also* WILTON PARK.

FOREIGN SECRETARY. The foreign secretary is the senior government representative and foreign policymaker supported by ministers of state in various capacities. During the 19th century, the post was often held in conjunction with the premiership. In the 20th century, interventionist prime ministers increasingly tried to put their personal stamp on policymaking. This process started with **David Lloyd George** from 1916–1922, when his "Garden Suburb," a secretariat based at **No. 10 Downing Street**, undermined the authority of Foreign Secretary **George Curzon**. Foreign secretaries had previously been ranked second only to the prime minister, but now they increasingly had to battle with Downing Street to preserve their power base. This characteristic was evident in the 1930s, when **Neville Chamberlain** undermined the authority of his foreign secretary, **Anthony Eden**, by using personal emissaries (including his sister-in-law) as part of his **appeasement** policy. Eden felt strongly enough about this to resign in 1938, although such unorthodox personal diplomacy was not the only reason for his departure. In fact, Eden did not learn from his own experience, running his own ultimately catastrophic policy toward **Egypt** in 1956. He had the support of the permanent undersecretary at the **Foreign Office, Sir Ivone Kirkpatrick**, but the British ambassador in Cairo was kept in the dark about the prime minister's plans. Eden even attempted to keep the BBC in line by placing a foreign-office official in Broadcasting House, but he was completely ignored by the staff. Part of the Foreign Office budget has traditionally gone to pay for the much-admired BBC World Service.

More recently, Downing Street's control of, and involvement in, foreign policy has, if anything, increased. Successive prime ministers, such as **Margaret Thatcher** and **Tony Blair** recruited foreign office officials to be part of Downing Street's staff. Under Thatcher, no one was more influential than the former **Foreign and Commonwealth Office (FCO)** man Charles Powell. In contrast, Thatcher treated her foreign secretary, **Sir Geoffrey Howe**, with such a lack of respect that he resigned and made a devastating resignation speech in the House of Commons, which contributed to Thatcher's own forced resignation in 1990.

The modern foreign secretary travels a great deal more than his or her predecessors, frequently in the company of the prime minister. This is especially true of the role within the **European Union**, where he or she represents Britain on the Council of Ministers in Brussels. European policy was a matter of acute tension between successive foreign secretaries, the Foreign Office, and Margaret Thatcher during her 10-year stint as prime minister. The relationship between foreign secretaries and ambassadors in the field can be an important one, however, here too, practice has changed. Although less common than in the **United States**, the practice of picking nondiplomats for important foreign embassies has become more of a feature in recent decades. An example of this is **James Callaghan's** selection, despite advice from the head of the Foreign Office, when he chose his son-in-law, Peter Jay, who went on to become British ambassador in Washington in 1977, a man whose previous background had been in journalism.

The foreign secretary is a member of the Cabinet, but also a politician who has to be aware of domestic political factors and constraints. At a structural level, there have been suggestions in recent years that the growing influence of the private office at No. 10 Downing Street has caused frustration at the

Foreign Office. The use of its own personnel to act as agents of successive prime ministers has caused particular frustration. The FCO's view of the **Iraq** war in 2003 did not seem to accord with that of the Downing Street staff, even if Foreign Secretary **Jack Straw** supported government policy. In contrast, his predecessor, **Robin Cook**, resigned from his government post.

British foreign secretaries are not the titans they were in the past. This reflects Britain's decline as a great power and the downgrading of their position relative to that of British prime ministers. Modern foreign secretaries have to manage the foreign relations of a medium-sized power, albeit one with a sophisticated Foreign Service tradition. This tradition was revised in a major way in 2005, when **Margaret Beckett** was created the first female foreign secretary in Tony Blair's last administration. She and her successors have to deal with a much more complex global community (in 1919, there were just two independent African states) and a large number of international organizations, for example, the International Monetary Fund, that act almost in the same way as sovereign governments. Despite this complexity, foreign secretaries continue to believe that Britain can punch above its weight in the international community. *See also* BALFOUR, ARTHUR J.; CHAMBER-LAIN, AUSTEN; DOUGLAS-HOME, SIR ALEC; HOARE, SIR SAMUEL; LLOYD, SELWYN.

FOURTEEN POINTS. On 8 January 1918, President **Woodrow Wilson** gave an address to U.S. Congress in which he laid out Fourteen Points as the basis for a lasting peace after the conclusion of **World War I**. He did this in response to an appeal by Imperial **Germany**, which thought that the American president might grant a less punitive peace than the British and French. Wilson sought international peace that could be preserved without the sinister web of secret alliances, which many thought had led to the outbreak of World War I. His most famous peace point was his last, whereby an international peacekeeping body, the **League of Nations**, would become the instrument for avoiding war and conflict. A "general association of nations" would come together to guarantee the sovereignty and independence of existing states.

British prime minister **David Lloyd George** was somewhat cynical about the League proposal, as was the **Foreign Office**. They also took exception to point two, which demanded the freedom of seas, something that seemed to present a threat to British naval power. European powers, in general, objected to points four and five, which wanted arms reduction and disarmament and the reference back of colonial disputes (which had caused tensions before 1914) for arbitration, respectively. When the armistice came into force on the Western Front on 11 November 1918, Wilson insisted that his Fourteen Points be made the basis of any peace settlement, even though the **United**

States had only entered the conflict as late as April 1917. As it turned out, Wilson's major problem with the peace settlement was domestic rather than foreign. Although the League of Nations covenant was appended to the **Treaty of Versailles** in June 1919, American public opinion and the Republican Party turned against the peace settlement. Wilson was unable to secure the needed two-thirds majority in the U.S. Senate to ratify the treaty, and the Americans refused to join the League of Nations. This had serious long-term ramifications for European peace. **France** had extracted an Anglo–American guarantee of its security in exchange for acceptance of the League (its leader, Georges Clemenceau, had wondered why Wilson had needed 14 points when the Lord God had only needed 10). America now reneged on its promise, and Britain also refused to honor its pledge to assist France in the event of a new war with Germany.

FOX, LIAM (1961–). A Conservative member of Parliament and unsuccessful candidate for the party leadership in 2005, Liam Fox was appointed defense secretary by Prime Minister **David Cameron** in 2010. Strongly pro-American and pro-Israeli, Fox had a spectacular fall from grace in 2011. He was obliged to resign on 14 October, when the irregular activities of a friend, Adam Werritty (who posed as a **Ministry of Defense [MOD]** aide), were exposed by the British media. Three days later, on 18 October, the Cabinet secretary, Sir Gus O'Donnell, produced a report, at Cameron's request, that showed that Fox had broken the ministerial code by, among other things, taking the unauthorized Werritty to a meeting with the president of Sri Lanka. Fox appeared to have been running a parallel defense policy while keeping MOD officials in the dark, a policy funded by right-wing interest groups.

FRANCE. France is Britain's oldest enemy, but, in the 20th century, also its most long-standing ally. The two countries are intimately linked by history. In 1066, the Normans conquered England, and, after the loss of mainland Normandy in 1204, the Channel Islands Jersey, Guernsey, Alderney, and Sark stayed under the English Crown. Even today, the islands, which are much closer to France than Great Britain, have their foreign relations conducted by the British government and retain **Queen Elizabeth II** as their head of state. The accession of the Angevin king Henry II in 1154 meant that England retained other lands in Anjou and Gascony. This stake in France ended with England's final defeat in the Hundred Years' War (1337–1453), although English and British monarchs maintained a claim to the throne of France. The two states remained rivals. There were periods of peace, notably in the 16th and 17th centuries, but they were unusual. In the 18th century, Britain and France fought for control of **India** and **Canada**. Britain was victorious in both instances. France got its revenge by allying itself with the **United States** in the War of Independence. A bitter Anglo–British struggle with Revolutionary and Napoleonic France (1793–1815) ended French claims to predominance in Europe. British naval power was decisive. British troops were sent to **Spain** and played a crucial role when **Napoleon Bonaparte** was defeated at Waterloo (1815). Allies in the Crimean War, the two powers were colonial rivals in Africa and almost went to war over the **Sudan** in 1898.

The process of reconciliation began with the entente, or friendship agreement, of 1904, and the two powers were allies in **World War I** and **World War II**. Throughout, however, there were misunderstandings and sometimes quite violent prejudice, as in the 1920s, when the British believed that France was seeking to dominate Europe. The **Foreign Office** and Diplomatic Service was frequently accused of being pro-French, which was an exaggeration, since its officials often complained about French paranoia over **Germany**. The French resented British unwillingness to sign a formal defense treaty or introduce conscription, leaving any land effort against a new German threat almost entirely to them. A modified form of conscription was only introduced in Britain in 1939.

Anglo–French relations were at their worst in 1940, at the time of Adolf Hitler's shattering victory in the West. Britain was the junior partner bound to go along with French decisions but anxious not to be dragged down in any military disaster. The French regarded the **Dunkirk** evacuation (May–June 1940) as a betrayal and rejected **Winston Churchill's** generous offer of an indissoluble Franco–British political union. Two weeks later, Winston Churchill, who felt he had little option, authorized the sinking of a large part of the French Fleet in North Africa to prevent it from falling into German hands. Most French people supported the collaborationist Vichy regime, which ruled in the unoccupied zone of France until 1942. A small but growing minority supported the Free French organization in Britain established on 18 June 1940 by Charles de Gaulle. Churchill found de Gaulle, with his constant sensitivity about French greatness, tiresome, but, unlike the Americans, he accepted him as France's obvious leader. De Gaulle carried a wounded pride and prejudice about Anglo–Saxons into the postwar period, when he became head of state.

Unlike Britain, France was prominent in the process of European integration after World War II. It became much more nationalistic when de Gaulle returned as president in 1958, and twice vetoed British attempts to enter the **European Economic Community (EEC)** in 1963 and 1967. Only the dedication of Britain's most pro-European prime minister, **Edward Heath**, in 1972–1973, secured its permanent place in the community.

Elsewhere, the two states had a community of interest. They joined together to invade **Egypt** in November 1956, with entirely different results.

France became more focused on Europe, and Britain quickly recovered its prized "**special relationship**" with the United States. Both states engaged in lengthy processes of decolonization, with France engaging in long, drawn out wars in **Indochina** and Algeria (1946–1954 and 1954–1962). The real focus of French foreign policy was attempting the creation of a Europe from the "Atlantic to the Urals" during the Gaullist period from 1958–1969. This meant trying to have a "special relationship" with the Soviet Union and its satellites, exclusive of the **North Atlantic Treaty Organization (NATO)**, which de Gaulle left in 1966. French influence was also applied in Latin America and even in areas traditionally regarded as British preserves, like Canada. On a memorable visit to Quebec, de Gaulle went out of his way to encourage French separatism there (the city was a relic of the period of French control that ended in the 18th century). This speech infuriated the British, who were relieved when **Georges Pompidou** (1969–1974) succeeded de Gaulle as president. It was Pompidou's warm relationship with Heath that smoothed Britain's path into the EEC in 1973.

French foreign policy thereafter followed a predictable path. France and Germany were seen to be the pillars on which the EEC, later the **European Union (EU)**, rested. France had its own independent nuclear force outside the NATO framework, and its government reserved the right to intervene forcibly in former colonies, as in Chad in the 1980s, when stability and French interests were threatened. A certain tension remained with the Americans as France followed its own independent route, recognizing, for example, the government of Communist North Vietnam well before Vietnamese unification took place in 1975. Tensions with Britain reappeared in 1982, when the French were (unfairly) accused of being the armers of **Argentina**. In fact, the French cooperated with Britain in tracking down and buying up existing stockpiles of Exocet missiles.

Even under Socialist president François Mitterrand (1981–1995), France maintained its Gaullist foreign policy. Close links with Germany remained inside the EU, and Mitterrand clashed with **Margaret Thatcher** over her attempts to claw back part of Britain's annual EU contribution. Outside Europe, Mitterrand demonstrated a new spirit of international cooperation by joining the coalition against **Iraq** in 1990–1991, when France had formerly been a major arms supplier to the Iraqi regime. The position was altered in 2003, when Mitterrand's successor, Jacques Chirac (1995–2007), refused to join the Anglo–American attack on Iraq, claiming that the action did not have full **United Nations** sanction. The tone of French policy changed when Nicolas Sarkozy became president in 2007. He flaunted his sympathy with American culture and society and rejoined NATO. In 2011, he and British prime minister **David Cameron** led the action against **Libya**, which involved NATO air forces. France was the first great power to recognize the Libyan rebels. Thus,

Sarkozy could be seen as the most Atlanticist French president since the foundation of the Fifth French Republic in 1958, with a much more friendly relationship with both London and Washington. The British Foreign Office recognized the excellence of the French Foreign Service, with an assumption that the days of discord in the de Gaulle period were over.

The old pattern of Anglo–French relations reemerged in December 2011. A bitter dispute between Prime Minister David Cameron and French president Nicolas Sarkozy arose at the EU summit in Brussels. Old French accusations about the British being bad Europeans emerged with Cameron's refusal to support the **Eurozone** fiscal package, but matters were smoothed over. In April 2012, Cameron was more worried about the possible victory of the Socialist candidate François Hollande in France's presidential election. In the event, Hollande won the election, and Cameron was left to patch up relations with a foreign leader he had refused to see weeks before, when Hollande was opposition leader.

FRANKS, SIR OLIVER (1905–1992). Sir Oliver Franks was Great Britain's ambassador in the **United States** from 1948–1952. In many respects, he was a surprising choice by the **Foreign Office**, as he was not a professional diplomat, but was appointed to what was regarded as one of the plum appointments in the service. A product of Queen's College, Oxford, Franks spent much of his career in association with that university. His service as a diplomat was therefore a break in an academic career (he was a philosopher), rather than a permanent transfer to diplomacy. He had some experience with the United States, having been a visiting professor at Chicago University in 1935. During **World War II**, like many academics, he became a civil servant, going to the Ministry of Supply in 1939, and rising to be permanent undersecretary in 1945–1946. He then returned to Queen's College for two years prior to his appointment to the Washington embassy. His task there was eased by the fact that during World War II, he got to know **Ernest Bevin** well when he was minister of labour. The two men got along well, partly perhaps because they both came from the West country. Bevin was Labour's **foreign secretary**.

Franks proved his worth in 1951–1952, by mediating between **Anthony Eden**, the new British foreign secretary, and **Dean Acheson**, the American secretary of state, over U.S. aid to Britain and defense policy. The British assumption that an increase in their rearmament program, with a £4,700 million plan during the course of three years set up in January 1951, would be helped by U.S. aid to defray any dollar shortage proved to be false. This left bruised feelings in London.

Atomic energy caused additional problems. The 1946 **McMahon Act** ended any cooperation between the United States and Britain over nuclear policy. Then, suggestions by the Americans that Britain should not make its own atomic bomb, but merely accept a supply of American ones, was rejected by Franks in September 1949. He put up a formula whereby it was agreed in October 1951 that American nuclear weapons could only be operated from British bases after joint consultation. Even **Winston Churchill** failed to extract more information about atomic weapons from President **Harry S. Truman** in 1952. Sadly, for himself, Franks inadvertently presided over one of Britain's greatest espionage disasters in 1951, which involved nuclear secrets. Two British diplomats, Guy Burgess and **Donald Maclean**, defected to the Soviet Union in May 1951, much to the embarrassment of the foreign secretary at the time, Herbert Morrison, as well as the Foreign Office and British intelligence. It turned out that Maclean had served in a senior post in the Washington embassy since 1944, leaving in August 1948, three months before Franks arrived. As first secretary, he was privy to all information coming into the embassy, including scientific material. Burgess also served in the embassy in 1950–1951. Even worse, Kim Philby, who was later unmasked as a Soviet agent, was the **Secret Intelligence Service** senior representative in the embassy from the autumn of 1949 until the summer of 1951.

As a former academic and home civil servant, Franks simply did not have the experience of vetting colleagues or security to deal with such a situation. Neither would he have had any reason to suspect Maclean, an acknowledged high flier in the Diplomatic Service, of espionage. In fact, Maclean had serious problems with alcohol, which had demanded his early recall to London, as he was on the verge of a serious psychological breakdown. Franks was unaware of this scenario, and neither was he to blame for the Burgess–Maclean fiasco when the two spies were spirited away under the noses of British intelligence. In reality, Franks deserved much credit for strengthening the Anglo–American relationship. He had an especially good relationship with **Dean Acheson** at a time of crisis with the outbreak of the **Korean War** in 1950.

Upon his return to Britain, Franks returned to academic life in Oxford, but he was still consulted, on occasion, for advice. He produced an official report on the **Falklands War** in 1983. Franks remained convinced that close cooperation with the United States was the best way of avoiding a third world war.

FREEMAN, JOHN (1915–). John Freeman was a Labour member of Parliament and junior minister in the 1945–1951 Labour government. He resigned over the issue of putting charges on teeth and spectacles from the National Health Service in 1951, along with **Aneurin Bevan** and **Harold Wilson**. He was subsequently an effective television interviewer in the well-known BBC program *Face to Face*. This varied career was preparation for Freeman's period as British ambassador in Washington from 1969–1971, in the early part of **Richard Nixon's** first term as president. In fact, Wilson, by then prime minister, had wrongly assumed that the Democrats would win the 1968 presidential election, and he appointed Freeman, an old friend of Democratic candidate Hubert Humphrey. Freeman had also been editor of the well-known left-wing periodical the *New Statesman*, in which he had made caustic remarks about Nixon's humiliating defeat in the 1962 election for the governorship of California. Wilson stuck to his guns and kept Freeman as his ambassador, much to Nixon's annoyance. The president even went as far as to say that he would have nothing to do with Freeman. In the end, Nixon made a graceful turn about where Freeman was concerned. Freeman proved to be a great success, and, in his memoirs, **Henry Kissinger** described him as one of the most effective ambassadors he had dealings with as national security advisor and secretary of state. Freeman was further praised as intelligent and perceptive, and Kissinger confessed to letting him read the early drafts of presidential speeches. Nixon, too, came to both like and trust Freeman, who went on to become one of Kissinger's closest friends. This helped the "**special relationship**," but Freeman was unable to prevent Wilson's successor, **Edward Heath**, whose priority was Europe, from distancing himself from the **United States**.

G

GAITSKELL, HUGH (1906–1963). Hugh Gaitskell was leader of the Labour Party from 1955–1963, and chancellor of the exchequer in 1950–1951. A product of Winchester School and Oxford University, he spent the early part of his career as an economics lecturer at London University. Gaitskell spent **World War II** in the Ministry of Economic Warfare. Despite his privileged background, Gaitskell was already convinced of the merits of democratic socialism. In 1945, he was elected as a Labour member of Parliament and was soon identified as a rising star. Gaitskell was a junior minister in the treasury, and he persuaded Prime Minister **Clement R. Attlee** of the merits of devaluation of the pound in 1949, when the chancellor of the exchequer, Sir Stafford Cripps, was ill. Gaitskell replaced Cripps as chancellor in October 1950.

Gaitskell proved to be a controversial choice. In his 1951 budget, he introduced a huge rearmament program of £4,700 million during the span of three years. This was intended to support the **United States** in the **Korean War**, but the plan actually meant that Great Britain, a far poorer country, was spending more on defense, 14 percent of gross national product, than the United States. Critics argued that the budget made little economic sense, as it forced Gaitskell to raise the income tax, and it also had serious political repercussions. This was because Gaitskell also put charges on teeth and spectacles, an apparent breach of the new National Health Service principle that everything should be free on delivery. **Aneurin Bevan,** the minister of health, and **Harold Wilson,** the president of the Board of Trade, resigned in protest. As a result, Gaitskell became a hated figure on the left of the Labour Party. His controversial budget stoked inflation in Britain and contributed to Labour's narrow defeat in the October 1951 election. Somewhat surprisingly, given his controversial past, Gaitskell was elected leader of the party when Attlee retired in 1955, and he moved it well to the right. He showed courage at the time of the **Suez Crisis** in 1956, by condemning the Conservative government's collusion with **France** and **Israel**, but he failed to get his party reelected in the 1959 general election.

The last phase of Gaitskell's leadership found him embattled with the left wing of the Labour Party over nuclear armaments. When the Party Conference approved unilateral nuclear disarmament for Britain in 1960, he promised to "fight and fight and fight again to save the party." A year later, he succeeded in having the policy reversed. He was equally pugnacious in opposing British entry into the **European Economic Community** when Prime Minister **Harold Macmillan** applied for entry in 1961. Some saw Gaitskell as an example of the permissive society in his private life. Already married to a divorced woman, he had a long relationship with Ann Fleming, the wife of the James Bond author Ian Fleming. His Hampstead lifestyle provoked some envy in the ranks of his party. Gaitskell died of a rare, incurable disease on the eve of an expected election victory on 18 January 1963. *See also* EDEN, SIR ANTHONY.

GENEVA CONFERENCE (1954). The Geneva Conference, held in April 1954, brought together the Soviet Union, Great Britain, **France**, the People's Republic of China, and the **United States**. Britain and the Soviet Union acted as cochairmen. Its remit was to end the **Korean War** and France's long-standing colonial war in **Indochina** (especially Vietnam, but also Laos and Cambodia). During the meeting, U.S. secretary of state **John Foster Dulles** had a negative attitude toward discussing Indochinese matters. He even refused to speak to the Chinese foreign minister, Zhou Enlai. Fortunately, the attitude of the other participants was more positive, in particular that of **Anthony Eden**, the British foreign secretary. The first part of the conference dealt with Korea, thus it was only on 8 May that the discussion of the Indochina issue began. This was the day the French suffered a final humiliating defeat when their garrison at **Dien Bien Phu** in northern Vietnam was forced to surrender.

The Geneva Accords, which flowed from the conference, ended the war in Indochina and laid down a settlement. Vietnam would be partitioned at the 17th parallel, unlike the arrangement made at the **Potsdam Conference** in July 1945. The Communist insurgents the Viet Minh would administer the territory north of the parallel, with a new non-Communist administration to the south would be under the pro-U.S. Catholic Ngo Dinh Diem. French troops would pull out of the north, while the Viet Minh would evacuate the south. All French troops were to withdraw from the south in 1956, when there were to be elections, which were supposed to lead to the reunification of Vietnam. Separate arrangements were made for Laos and Cambodia, which were not partitioned. The conference wrapped on 21 July. Its conclusions were acceptable to the Viet Minh leader Ho Chi Minh, who had to give up 20 percent of the land he had taken, because he knew, as did Dulles and Eden, that the Viet Minh would win national elections in Vietnam.

Neither Dulles nor Diem signed the accords. Instead, Diem held farcical presidential elections in what became South Vietnam, but the elections were rigged to secure his victory. More people were supposed to have voted for Diem in Saigon than were actually on the electoral register. The national elections never took place in 1956, as they were meant to. Dulles set up the **Southeast Asia Treaty Organization** in 1954, with a commitment to defend South Vietnam. In his memoirs, Eden made it clear that he regarded Dulles as being as much an obstacle to agreement at Geneva as the Russians and the Chinese. He thought that the Americans and the Chinese were adopting extreme positions, while Britain and the Soviet Union, under its new post-Stalin leadership (he died in March 1953), were more moderate. His tactic of setting up private sessions with Zhou Enlai and Soviet foreign minister Vyacheslav Molotov, a survivor of the Stalin period, proved to be effective at Geneva. *See also* DOMINO THEORY.

GERMAN REUNIFICATION (1990). The sudden collapse of the Communist satellite system in Central Europe and Eastern Europe in the fall of 1989 created a reunited **Germany** for the first time in 45 years. This involved the disappearance of the German Democratic Republic (GDR), often known as just East Germany, and its merging into the non-Communist, democratic Federal Republic of Germany (FRG). The first free elections in the GDR were held in March 1990, and these contests showed a majority desire for reunification. As East Germans were fleeing to the West in droves, it was decided to create an economic union of the two German states on 1 July 1990. The GDR gained from an overgenerous exchange rate of one GDR mark to the FRG mark for the first 21,000 marks, and 1:2 thereafter. Full merger of the five GDR states into the FRG took place on 3 October.

The key factor here was the attitude of the Soviet Union, which had 400,000 Red Army soldiers stationed in the former GDR. Soviet leader Mikhail Gorbachev agreed to reunification in a meeting with Federal German chancellor Helmut Kohl in July, in exchange for a large payment of 5 billion deutschmarks paid by the FRG. "Two Plus Four" talks between the two Germanies, the **United States**, the Soviet Union, Great Britain, and **France** (the four postwar occupying powers) produced a final treaty of agreement on reunification on 12 September. There had been some apprehension in the West about this remarkable and rapid change. **Margaret Thatcher**, in particular, who had grown up during **World War II** with all its Nazi associations, was concerned by the specter of a new, overly mighty Germany. She even convened a conference attended by right-wing historians and philosophers to discuss the issue. In the end, Thatcher and others in her Cabinet of similar a viewpoint reluctantly accepted the new reality. The new, united Germany was here to stay.

GERMANY. Great Britain has had a long association with Germany, dating back to the appearance of the Hanoverian monarchy in 1714. In the absence of a male heir for the Stuart dynasty (1601–1714), George Elector of Hanover became George I (1714–1727) of Britain. The Hanoverian link created an important continental aspect to British foreign policy. In the War of the Austrian Succession (1740–1748) and the Seven Years' War (1756–1763), Britain had to protect Hanover, as well as its growing empire. The Hanoverian connection was not always popular in Britain, especially since the first two Hanoverian kings could barely speak English. There was another dimension to British policy with regard to Germany, which in the 18th century consisted of hundreds of states and city-states. The largest was Prussia, ruled by the Hohenzollern dynasty, and, from the time of the Seven Years' War until the end of the **Napoleonic Wars** in 1815, it was a firm ally of Britain. The Prussians made a crucial contribution to the eventual defeat of **Napoleon Bonaparte** in June 1815. Prussia was an important component in the balance of power concept that dominated British policy.

Monarchical ties were strengthened in the 19th century. **Queen Victoria** (1837–1901) married Prince Albert of Saxe Coburg Gotha, and her daughter Vicky married the Prussian Crown Prince, the future emperor Frederick. During her reign, a crucial change took place concerning Germany, which, until 1866, had existed only in a cultural geographical sense rather than a political one. Prussia's military victories over Austria in 1866 and **France** in 1870–1871 completed the process of German unification. Germany was now the greatest military and industrial power in Europe.

Britain had remained neutral in the Franco–Prussian War of 1870–1871. It regarded the new Germany as a potential friend, but, by the turn of the 19th century, Anglo–German relations had worsened. Germany's great chancellor, **Otto von Bismarck** (1871–1890), admired the clever statesmanship of Britain's prime minister, **Benjamin Disraeli**, at the Congress of Berlin in 1878, but he did not seek a British alliance. He was reluctant to follow an expansionist colonial policy but was obliged by internal pressures to do so. German South West Africa (now Namibia) and German East Africa (now Tanzania) were acquired in the 1880s.

Bismarck fell from power in 1890. His successors under a young and erratic emperor William II (1888–1918) pursued an increasingly aggressive "Weltpolitik," or world policy. This involved a massive expansion of the imperial German navy from 1890 onward. It was a major concern for Britain, the premier naval power in the world. The ententes of 1904 and 1907 with France and **Russia**, which settled areas of colonial dispute, reflected British concerns. A classic exposition of Britain's anxieties was presented by a future permanent undersecretary at the **Foreign Office**, Eyre Crowe, in 1907. In this

"Memorandum on the present state of British relations with France and Germany," Crowe, who was half German himself, strongly supported the French entente. He warned against Germany's attempts to seek global domination and saw the entente as a buffer against such German ambitions. Crowe's political superiors did not share his more doom-laden predictions. **Sir Edward Grey**, the **foreign secretary** from 1905–1916, had to stand by France, but he did not believe that war was inevitable.

But German behavior did not help matters. Attempts by William II and his government to interfere in the French sphere of influence in Morocco in 1905 and 1911 only pushed Britain and France closer together. In 1911, the chancellor of the exchequer, **David Lloyd George**, made a speech at the Mansion House in London supporting France in the strongest terms and warning off Germany; however, Britain was still unwilling to abandon traditional policy and make military pacts with either France or Russia. What exactly Britain would do in the event of aggression by Germany or its ally, Austria-Hungary, against France or Russia was unclear in the absence of a clear military commitment. Even a colonial agreement with Russia, in 1907, marked progress. Britain's centuries-old commitment to the preservation of the Ottoman Empire was set aside. By 1914, it was effectively a German ally. Germany sold warships to the Turks and built the expensive Berlin to Baghdad railway.

It was German infringement of Belgian neutrality that brought Britain into **World War I** on 4 August 1914. Prussia, as it was then, and Britain had signed the 1839 Treaty of London guaranteeing Belgian neutrality. The war brought about a violent anti-German mood swing in Britain. Anything German was subjected to nationalistic abuse, and the Royal family, headed by King George V, was forced to change its name from Saxe Coburg Gotha to the more British-sounding Windsor. The Germans had spent vast sums of money on their High Seas Fleet, but it proved to be a white elephant. In the only significant naval engagement of the war in 1916, at Jutland, the Royal Navy lost slightly more ships, but its superiority in numbers allowed it to blockade the High Seas Fleet in Kiel Harbor until 1918. Britain blockaded the German coastline and reduced the German civilian population to virtual starvation by 1918. Germany replied with unrestricted submarine warfare in 1917, which threatened Britain's food supplies. On land, a bitter stalemate on the Western Front, bloody and inconclusive, cost both countries terrible losses, notably on the Somme from July to December 1916. This stalemate tempted Germany into diplomatic folly in 1917, when its enemies were almost exhausted. The Zimmermann Telegram showed Germany to be conspiring with Mexico about territories lost to the **United States**. American lives had also been lost to numerous submarine sinkings. This brought the United States into the war.

Britain's willpower had been strengthened by the appointment of the fiery Lloyd George as prime minister in December 1916. William II was sidelined in Germany by the takeover of power by the two warlords Paul von Hindenburg and Erich von Ludendorff. It availed Germany nothing. It conspired with Bolshevik enemies of Tsar Nicholas II to send Vladimir Lenin back to Russia in April 1917, after a March revolution brought down the monarchy. Britain had wanted the so-called "Provisional Government" to keep fighting. It could not and fell from power in November, thus allowing the Bolsheviks to take Russia out of the war in March 1918. The arrival of the Americans on the Western Front prevented Germany from making a decisive breakthrough. Germany's ally, **Turkey**, was defeated in the Middle East, and, through the Sykes–Picot Agreement (1916), Britain and France, not Germany, were to dominate the area following the war.

The Hohenzollern dynasty was brought down in November 1918, and William II lived out his last years in Holland. Its successor, the Weimar Republic, felt the odium of accepting a tough peace settlement, the June 1919 **Treaty of Versailles**. Although not as severe as the Germans liked to pretend, the treaty was controversial in Britain. Lloyd George warned against reducing Germany to second-class status. The famous economist **John Maynard Keynes** castigates Versailles in the book *The Economic Consequences of the Peace* (1919). This British tendency to sympathize with German grievances against Versailles was the genesis of the policy known as **appeasement**. Successive British governments were anxious to bring Germany in from the cold. **Austen Chamberlain** (foreign secretary, 1924–1929), although sympathetic to French worries about Germany, helped in the process. His counterpart, Gustav Stresemann, did so too, signing the 1925 **Treaty of Locarno**. Germany accepted the new frontiers with France and **Belgium** and, in 1926, joined the **League of Nations**. It was a tragedy for Germany and Europe when Stresemann died prematurely in 1929.

Equally tragic for Germany were the consequences of the 1929 Wall Street Crash. Germany had borrowed large sums of money from the United States, which it was in no position to repay quickly. Its banks collapsed; its industry ground to a halt; and, by 1932, 6 million Germans were out of work. The conditions were ripe for the rapid rise to power of Adolf Hitler and the Nazi Party. At the time, British governments seemed obsessed by the need for disarmament, when Germany was already secretly rearming. The Foreign Office had excellent reports from its retiring ambassador, **Sir Horace Rumbold**, who held the post from 1928–1933, about the thuggish nature of the Nazi Party. This was unwelcome news, so great was the British desire for peace. Politicians suspected the Foreign Office of being unduly pro-French; it was not. Its German equivalent was gradually Nazified when Hitler became chancellor in January 1933.

Britain now found itself with an impossible German government. Throughout the 1930s, the successive governments of **Ramsey MacDonald, Stanley Baldwin,** and **Neville Chamberlain** wanted peace and good relations with Germany. Although he claimed to admire the **British Empire**, this was not what Hitler wanted. He could never get the British to give him a free hand in Central Europe and Eastern Europe. British appeasement policy tried to turn the other cheek. When Hitler occupied the Rhineland (1936) and Austria (1938), the British protested but hoped that good Anglo–German relations could be maintained. They had to worry about aggressive behavior by **Italy** and **Japan** as well. British rearmament was slow off the mark, while Germany's was not. The **Munich Agreement** of September 1938 marked the high point of appeasement, when Hitler was granted the Czech Sudetenland without firing a shot. He proved that his word could not be trusted in 15 March 1939, when what was left of **Czechoslovakia** was also occupied by Germany. Under Chamberlain, Britain adopted a policy of collective security. Guarantees of assistance were given to **Poland**, Rumania, **Greece**, and Turkey in March and April 1939. In August, belated attempts were made to make an alliance with a suspicious Soviet Union. Hitler did not believe that Britain would fight. He believed the nonsense fed to him by Foreign Minister Joachim von Ribbentrop, a former ambassador in London. Chamberlain tried desperately to save the peace, but he could not. The Nazi state existed to promote war, and, when Hitler attacked Poland on 1 September 1939, supposedly to reclaim land lost at Versailles, he got his war. Britain declared war on Germany on 3 September. It wished, said Chamberlain, to destroy Nazism but not the German people.

Britain and Germany were at war for six years, until May 1945. **Winston Churchill**, who took over as prime minister beginning on 10 May 1940, ensured that there would be no compromise with the Nazi regime. In 1943, he and the United States demanded unconditional surrender from Germany. Churchill would not deal seriously with a German opposition, which wanted to cling to territorial gains in Czechoslovakia and Poland. The attempt on Hitler's life on 20 July 1944, by Count von Stauffenberg and others, was too little too late. Britain and the United States never made a separate peace with Germany, leaving out their Soviet ally. France was invaded in June 1944, and the last desperate German offensive in the Ardennes thrown back in December. As the Allied Forces advanced from east and west, the bestial excesses of Nazism in death camps were uncovered. British public opinion was shocked by the level of Jewish suffering at the Bergen-Belsen camp. It shamed those members of the Foreign Office who disputed early claims about the extent of the genocide. Germany's postwar fate was decided by the **Yalta** (February 1945) and **Potsdam** (July 1945) conferences. Britain was to have an occupation zone in Germany that was to be demilitarized and de-Nazified. Churchill had already rejected U.S. schemes for the pastoralization of Germany, the so-called **Morgenthau Plan,** and the British did not accept the original American concept of the "collective guilt" of the German people. The Allied Powers contributed to the 1946 Nuremberg Trials, which punished Nazi war crimes and laid down the principle of crimes against humanity.

Reparations were a major issue in postwar Germany. In their zone of occupation, the Russians took everything of value they could, forcing down living standards and increasing the flow of refugees into the British and U.S. zones. British taxpayers had to feed those refugees when they themselves had to survive one of the most severe winters in living memory in 1946–1947. The solution was Bizonia in 1947, when the British and U.S. zones were merged. Germans were encouraged to take part in the economic recovery of their shattered land. Political development soon followed. Native German Communism was encouraged in the Russian zone, but, in the British one, Kurt Schumacher, a dynamic, strongly anti-Communist leader refounded the Social Democratic Party (SPD). The SPD's rival was the Christian Democratic Union (CDU), under its leader, Konrad Adenauer. He stood as the dominant figure in the history of West Germany from 1945–1963. By 1949, Germany had become two entities, instead of the four Allied zones of occupation (British, American, French, and Russian). The old Russian zone became East Germany (the German Democratic Republic [GDR]), while the three western zones became West Germany, or the Federal Republic of Germany (FRG).

During the 1950s and 1960s, West Germany underwent an economic miracle. It owed much to the generous U.S. **Marshall Plan,** an aid program announced in June 1947, but also to the hard work and tenacity of the German people. This was demonstrated in 1948–1949, when Soviet dictator Joseph Stalin tried to force the Western allies out of Berlin, marooned inside the Soviet zone by closing down road and rail links and leaving only air corridors. Britain and its allies supplied essentials from the air for the West Berliners for 10 months, until Stalin backed down and reopened all communication links. The crisis demonstrated the resolve of Britain's Labour government under **Clement R. Attlee** to protect German democracy. Britain was still concerned about German rearmament in the new **Cold War** environment. It would not join the 1954 **European Defense Community,** which was meant to create a European army. Yet, it did keep some 50,000 troops in its Rhine Army to defend West Germany at great national cost. Conversely, Britain would not associate itself with the process of European integration, which started in 1950 with the Schuman Plan. Designed to integrate the German and French coal and steel industries, the plan provided the basis for the **European Coal and Steel Community,** which had Adenauer's enthusiastic support. Here was a way of reintegrating West Germany into Western Europe. It ended with the founding of the **European Economic Community** in 1957. Britain could only cheer from the sidelines. It would not pool sovereignty as West Germany had done. German policy was to encourage the British to abandon this isolationist attitude. European integration meant respectability for a divided and defeated nation.

In West Germany, the British could approve their handiwork. British advisors had helped to establish an industrial relations structure that proved to be much more harmonious than its strike-prone British cousin. British soldiers and airmen helped to defend the new Federal Republic. The need for this defense became obvious in June 1953, when workers in East Berlin rose up against their Communist masters, who were kept in power by Soviet bayonets. The revolt was bloodily crushed. Britain, with no diplomatic relations with East Germany, could only deplore the Communist tyranny. West Germany refused to have relations with the East or any power that recognized it. The ineptitude of Communist rule was shown by the need to build a wall to separate East Berlin and West Berlin in 1961. Beforehand, refugees had left East Berlin with embarrassing ease. Again, Britain and its allies could not risk any military riposte. Life in East Germany was made even less bearable by the knowledge that living standards in West Germany were much higher. From 1949–1989, the GDR was presided over by a series of grey, colorless Communist bureaucrats, including Walter Ulbricht (general secretary of the East German Communist Party, 1950–1971) and Erich Honecker (general secretary, 1971–1989). Ulbricht was the most enthusiastic supporter of the Warsaw Pact's crushing of Czechoslovakia's liberal experiment in August 1968.

Grim and oppressive though it was, the GDR seemed to be a permanent fixture by the mid-1970s. This brought about a change in West German policy under Willy Brandt, the SPD chancellor from 1969–1974. Brandt was a remarkable man who fought for the Resistance in Norway during **World War II**. In 1970, he embarked on a so-called "Eastern policy." This normalized relations with the GDR and secured him the **Nobel Peace Prize** in 1971. In 1973, both German states were allowed into the **United Nations (UN)**. The policy had the full support of Britain's prime minister, **Edward Heath** (1970–1974) the most pro-European of its postwar premiers. The Cold War did not go away despite Brandt's triumph. He was forced to resign in 1974, when an East German spy was discovered in his secretariat. Brandt was replaced as chancellor by Helmut Schmidt (1974–1982), another Social Democrat. Schmidt enjoyed an unusually cordial relationship with British prime minister **James Callaghan** (1976–1979), who needed German backing when Britain was beset with economic woes.

Unlike Callaghan's successor, **Margaret Thatcher**, Schmidt joined the United States in boycotting the 1980 Olympics Games in Moscow over the

Soviet invasion of **Afghanistan** in 1979. Thatcher was also at odds with Schmidt's CDU successor, Chancellor Helmut Kohl (1982–1990). Kohl was rightly celebrated as the man who presided over **German reunification** in 1990. He resented Thatcher's persistent demands for "our money back" during the 1980s, a reference to British payments to the **European Union (EU)**. Kohl, a political conservative, was an enthusiastic European integrationist. His soulmate in the EU was French president François Mitterrand. West Germany strongly supported the creation of the 1992 **Treaty of Maastricht**, which created a single EU market. Thatcher was less enthused, and she was also skeptical about German reunification in 1990. Those fears were based on a historic fear of German power. In the short run, united Germany was weakened by the economic burden of East Germany. Its aging rust-bucket economy had to be overhauled, and unemployment was high.

Even so, in the wake of Maastricht, Britain itself was forced to abandon the European Exchange Rate Mechanism (ERM) in 1992. This had been started in 1978 to allow currencies in the EU to fluctuate inside narrow limits. Britain was supposed to shadow the value of the German deutschmark. Financial market pressure forced Italy out of the ERM. Speculators then turned on the pound. The German government, with its considerable commitments after 1990, refused to support the pound, and, after a failed interest rate rise, Britain was forced out of the ERM as well. This caused some resentment against Germany in Britain, which, since December 1990, had been under the leadership of **John Major** (following Thatcher's removal from office). The British did not fully understand Germany's current problems. A currency union between East Germany and West Germany took place on 1 July 1990, and East Germany disappeared from the map of Europe on 3 October 1990. Within a year, the excitement of 1989–1990, when the Berlin Wall came down and the country was reunited, had disappeared. Kohl was chancellor of reunified Germany until 1998. During this time, he saw a change in Germany's international position. Its historical past made the issue of the use of force a sensitive one, although West Germany had been allowed to join the **North Atlantic Treaty Organization** in 1955. Germany did, under UN auspices, contribute forces to the 1991 **Gulf War** in **Iraq**. It also contributed $20 billion to the total war costs of $150 billion. Nonetheless, old memories died hard where Germany was concerned. In the Yugoslav civil war (1991–1995), there was a suspicion that Germany was pro-Croat, and, in **Serbia**, memories of the pro-Nazi World War II fascist dictatorship of Ante Pavelić in **Croatia** were still fresh. In contrast, Britain was accused of being pro-Serb. Germany and Britain were part of the Contact Group, which tried to achieve a settlement in 1994.

Germany rallied around the antiterrorist cause after the attacks in New York City and Arlington, Virginia, on 11 September 2001. It sent troops to

Afghanistan, where numerous German soldiers died in the struggle against the Taliban. This policy was masterminded by the new SDP chancellor, Gerhard Schröder (1998–2005). Schröder's period as chancellor was notable for a pro-Russian slant in German foreign policy. He maintained good relations with Russian president Vladimir Putin. Schröder approved a deal in 2005, whereby the nationalized Russian oil corporation Gazprom would directly supply Germany with oil. In contrast, the German chancellor refused to join Britain in its support of the U.S.-led invasion of Iraq in March 2003. Schröder, supported by German public opinion, expressed his opposition to the war in strong terms. This put a considerable strain on Anglo–German relations.

In 2005, Schröder was replaced as chancellor by Angela Merkel, the daughter of an East German Protestant minister, and Germany's first woman leader. This was a watershed, as was the fact that Merkel came from the East German CDU. Merkel proved to be an adroit operator, developing a close relationship with French president Nicolas Sarkozy. Relations with Britain were more problematic. Like her predecessors, Merkel was a strong supporter of the euro, whereas her British counterparts, **Gordon Brown** and **David Cameron**, were Eurosceptics. Germany, with its strong manufacturing base, was less affected by the economic crisis of 2008–2010, but it was fully committed to saving the euro. Merkel clashed with Cameron in December 2011, over the EU intergovernmental treaty during the Brussels summit. Earlier in the year, Germany had shown its foreign policy independence by declining to join Britain and France in their intervention in **Libya**. As 2012 began, Germany was the dominant player in the struggle to preserve the existing membership of the EU. Merkel was adamant that Germany would not allow the European Central Bank (ECB) to permit quantitative easing. Such printing of extra money by its Central Bank was forbidden by the German constitution. At German insistence, a clause preventing the ECB from doing so was written into the Treaty of Maastricht. Germany led those who insisted that Greece institute a draconian austerity program to qualify for an EU loan in March 2012. *See also* ANSCHLUSS; BERLIN BLOCKADE; BERLIN CRISIS.

GIBRALTAR. One of Britain's oldest colonies, Gibraltar came into British possession in 1713, at the end of the War of the Spanish Succession. A heavily fortified rock that sits astride an entrance to the Mediterranean Sea, Gibraltar has long been a matter of dispute with Britain's **European Union** partner **Spain**, especially during the dictatorship of Francisco Franco (1939–1975).

GLADSTONE, WILLIAM EWART (1809–1898). Along with his great rival **Benjamin Disraeli**, William Gladstone was one of the most dominant figures of 19th-century British politics. He was prime minister four times, the last time at the age of 84, in 1893. Gladstone was a reluctant imperialist who preferred to settle international disputes by arbitration. In 1872, his first administration paid out $15.5 million to the **United States** in compensation for damage done by the Confederate commerce raider the *Alabama* during the American Civil War. Gladstone's last years were spent in a valiant attempt to obtain home rule, with a degree of autonomy, for **Ireland**. He failed on two occasions in 1886 and 1893, and the issue split his Liberal Party. A faction known as Liberal Unionists defected to the Conservatives.

GREECE. The first part of the Ottoman Turkish Empire to free itself of Turkish rule in the Balkans, Greece relied a good deal on Great Britain to achieve this feat. The Royal Navy took part in the destruction of the Ottoman fleet at Navarino Bay in 1827. There was much sympathy with the Greek cause when the anti-Turkish revolt broke out in 1821, but they failed to capitalize on it. It involved British intellectuals like the poet Byron. The combination of Britain, **France**, and **Russia** proved too much for the Ottomans. The Treaty of Adrianople (1829) gave Greece its independence. British aid to Greece marked an unusual move away from its traditional pro-Turkish stance. Relations between Britain and Greece were difficult at times, most notoriously over the **Don Pacifico** affair (1847–1850). This centered on the ill treatment of a British citizen in Athens whose house was attacked by an anti-Jewish mob. The Greek government had refused to pay compensation, and Lord **Henry John Palmerston**, acting as **foreign secretary**, sent out the Royal Navy. The fleet appeared off the port of Piraeus on 15 January 1850, and it blockaded Athens. The Greeks gave way. In other situations, Britain was sympathetic. In 1880, British prime minister **William Gladstone** ensured that Greece and **Montenegro** received all the territory promised to them by **Turkey** in the Congress of Berlin (1878).

In 1897, a war between Greece and Turkey settled little at a time when British foreign policy was moving away from its age-old pro-Turkey stance. Britain did not intervene on Turkey's side when a Greek–Serb-led coalition routed the Turks in 1912. Greece's national territory doubled in size as a result of this victory. In **World War I**, the Greek king Constantine I, of German descent himself, sided with the Central Powers. The parliamentary government, under Eleutherios Venizelos, favored the Western allies. In 1916, Anglo–French troops set up a great base at Salonika, with Greek permission. They then failed to use it to drive into Austria-Hungary, but Constantine I was forced into exile. This pro-Allied Greek stance paid dividends at the Treaty of Sèvres (1920). Greece obtained much of defeated Turkey's territory in Asia Minor. British premier **David Lloyd George** was a great admirer of Venizelos, and he encouraged his aspiration to control most of Asia Minor.

The French and Italians were less enthusiastic. In the Greco–Turkish War of 1921–1922, the Greeks overreached themselves and were routed by Kemal Ataturk. The capture of the largely Greek city part of Smyrna was accompanied by a terrible bloodbath. The Treaty of Lausanne (1923) reversed what had been conceded at Sèvres. One million Greeks who had lived in Turkey were forced out in an exchange of population, and they had to be integrated into Greek society. This was done effectively through land distribution.

During the interwar period, Greek politics were unstable. The monarchy came back (1920–1924) but was then replaced by a republic (1924–1935). The proroyalist Joannis Metaxis then ruled Greece from 1936–1941. Greece had poor relations with Fascist **Italy**, which seized neighboring Albania in April 1939. In the last days of its **appeasement** policy, Britain responded by giving Greece a guarantee of assistance if it were attacked. The attack duly came when Benito Mussolini invaded Greece in 1940. Britain came to its assistance when **Germany** joined in the attack in 1941, after Mussolini had been driven back. Greece then suffered the terrors of Nazi occupation during **World War II**, including the mass murder of its Jews. It was because of an agreement between **Winston Churchill** and Joseph Stalin in October 1944, that Greece was allocated to the British sphere of influence in Europe. British intervention saved Greece from a Communist takeover by 1949, but not from a protracted civil war from 1943–1949, and not from political instability. In the postwar era, Greece was dominated by two men, Georgios Karamanlis (prime minister, 1955–1963, 1974–1980) and Andreas Papandreou (prime minister, 1944,1963, 1964–1965), and also Papandreou's son, Georgios, and grandson, George. Karamanlis also came back as president from 1980–1985, and again from 1990–1995.

In the 1960s, democracy was briefly overthrown. This was because a military coup in 1967 set up the so-called "regime of the colonels," with authoritarian, fascist trappings. King Constantine II was exiled from Greece by the colonels. They also fatally conflated Greek politics with those of **Cyprus**, where Britain still had sovereign bases. In 1974, the regime made the fatal error of trying to annex Cyprus and overthrow the government of Archbishop Makarios, who himself had been exiled during the British colonial era. This provoked the Turkish invasion of Cyprus. It brought down the military regime and allowed the return of Karamanlis from exile. He himself had been heavily criticized for accepting the terms on which Britain conceded independence to Cyprus in 1960. Although King Constantine II had been allowed to return, on 8 December 1974, a plebiscite saw 69 percent of the Greek people vote for the abolition of the monarchy. Constantine II went into permanent exile in Britain.

Another major change came in 1981, when Greece, with British support, was allowed to join the **European Economic Community**. Relations with

Turkey remained bad, with as much as one-third of the Greek budget being spent on armaments. Georgios Papandreou (prime minister, 1981–1989, 1993–1996) was now prime minister as head of the Panhellenic Socialist Movement (PASOK). Georgios Papandreou Jr. was a U.S. citizen who had been a celebrated economist at the University of California, Berkeley, in his years of exile, but he was still unable to deal with endemic corruption in Greece. The economy was under the control of two dozen families, and, by 1996, when Papandreou ended his second term, half of Greece's wealth was a product of the black economy. In foreign policy, he was a maverick. He signed the Single European Act in 1986, but supported the Palestine Liberation Organization and condemned the 1982 **Israeli** invasion of Lebanon.

Papandreou was even put on trial for corruption when the right-wing New Democracy Party came back in power in 1990, but he was eventually acquitted. The Greek government massaged the economic data to allow Greece to enter the **Eurozone** on 1 January 2001. Nepotism remained a strong national feature. Kostas Karamanlis, the nephew of Georgios, became premier in 2004, and George Papandreou, the grandson of Andreas, did the same in 2009. Taxes were not paid by most Greeks, and the country was devastated by the effects of the 2007–2008 credit crunch in Europe. PASOK was blamed for the financial crisis in the general election of 2011, and it was voted out of office. A government of technocrats held the fort until May 2012, when the two main parties, New Democracy and PASOK, were severely punished at the polls. Another technocratic government headed by a senior judge took office until a second election on 17 June. There was a danger that the Greek electorate would vote against the **European Union (EU)** fiscal package of December 2011, for a second time, and reject "bailout" terms. Britain, not a member of the Eurozone, observed this from the sidelines. On 21 May, Prime Minister **David Cameron** warned the Greek people that the June election was effectively a referendum on EU membership. His message was not well received in Greece. The British perception was that a Greek withdrawal from the Eurozone was almost inevitable.

GREEK CIVIL WAR (1944–1949). From 1944–1949, Greece, which had obtained its freedom from the Ottoman Turkish Empire during the 19th century, was engulfed in a bitter civil war. It was between the Communist Party, which had set up the National Liberation Front (EAM) to organize resistance at the time of the German invasion in 1941, and the non-Communist resistance forces, which favored a monarchy. In October 1944, British prime minister **Winston Churchill** put Greece at the top of the British agenda in his meeting with Joseph Stalin in Moscow. This "**percentages agreement**" recognized that Britain would have a 90-percent interest in Greece, to the

Soviet Union's 10 percent. In the end, Stalin kept his word and did not assist the Communists in the civil war, while Britain helped the monarchists. The British ordered EAM to disband its forces in November 1944, but it refused. On 3 December, fighting broke out between the British and the Communists, who received aid from **Yugoslavia, Bulgaria,** and Albania.

On 21 February 1947, the Labour government, led by **Clement R. Attlee,** told the Americans that Britain could no longer afford to assist the anti-Communist side in the Greek Civil War. The response was clear-cut and decisive. On 12 March 1947, the U.S. Congress authorized a payment of $300,000 to Greece, which was approved by President **Harry S. Truman.** This move, in parallel with aid to **Turkey,** was enshrined in the **Truman Doctrine,** which promised aid to those who were threatened by Communism. The Communist response was to attempt to seize control in Greece before help from the **United States** became meaningful. By October 1948, the Communists held most of Northern Greece, but U.S. air power was ultimately decisive. Trained and equipped by the Americans, the Greek army defeated the military wing of EAM, the National People's Liberation Army, which was driven over the Albanian border. In October 1949, the Greek Communists stated that they had given up the struggle. Greece became a constitutional monarchy under King George II of the Hellenes.

A significant role in the civil war was played by the British ambassador to Greece from 1943–1946, Sir Reginald Leeper. He liaised with the Greek government in exile in London and was consulted by all parties about the return of King George. At one point in 1944, Leeper and his staff were besieged in their embassy in Athens by the Communists. Leeper's memoirs, entitled *When Greek Meets Greek,* contains a graphic account of Churchill's visit to the embassy at Christmastime 1944, when the prime minister came close to being shot by Communist snipers.

GRENADA (1983). The invasion of the **British Commonwealth** island of Grenada on 25 October 1983, by U.S. forces, was a massive shock for Prime Minister **Margaret Thatcher,** who prided herself on the closeness of her relationship with U.S. president **Ronald Reagan.** She had not been consulted by the Americans beforehand and condemned their action. For their part, they thought Thatcher's reaction to be out of proportion, given the aid that the **United States** had given Britain in the 1982 **Falklands War.** Reagan's administration was alarmed by the appearance of Marxist regimes under prime ministers Maurice Bishop and Bernard Coard. Its concerns were matched by neighboring islands, including Jamaica, Barbados, and Bermuda, who asked the United States to intervene on 19 October 1983. The campaign was swift and only cost 19 American lives, and it resulted in Coard's government being overthrown. Free elections followed in 1984, after U.S. troops had left the area. Grenada caused the worst short-term Anglo–American animosity since the 1956 **Suez Crisis**.

GREY, SIR EDWARD (1862–1933). Sir Edward Grey was Britain's Liberal **foreign secretary** at the outbreak of **World War I** in August 1914. After the massive Liberal election victory in 1906, Grey presided over a foreign policy designed to safeguard British security without treating war with **Germany** as inevitable. Grey held the post of foreign secretary until 1916. He was famous for allegedly remarking upon the outbreak of war that the "lights are going out all over Europe." He was created Viscount Grey of Fallodon.

GULF WAR (1991). On 2 August 1990, the forces of Iraqi dictator Saddam Hussein invaded the small Gulf kingdom of Kuwait. **Iraq** claimed Kuwait, part of the old Ottoman Turkish province of Basra since 1935. Seriously in debt at the time, as a result of his long war with **Iran** (1980–1988), Hussein coveted Kuwait's oil fields. British prime minister **Margaret Thatcher** was visiting the **United States** at the time and urged President **George H. W. Bush** to take action against Hussein. This required a **United Nations (UN)** mandate, although Thatcher thought that the right to self-defense under Article 51 of the UN Charter entitled Kuwait and its likely allies to make a military response. The tiny kingdom was officially annexed by Hussein on 8 August, after his much larger army had overrun it.

The U.S. secretary of state, James Baker, believed that a new UN resolution was required, and, after much diplomatic work in New York, it was obtained on 29 November 1990. UN Resolution 678 gave Iraq until 15 January 1991 to withdraw its forces from Kuwait or face armed intervention. Great Britain contributed 43,000 troops to a 33-nation coalition force, although three-quarters of it was American. Britain was the largest European contributor. Hussein prevaricated and tried to subsume the issue of Kuwait in the long-standing **Palestine** one to gain support in the Arab world, but the deadline ran out with no Iraqi withdrawal. **John Major** had replaced Margaret Thatcher as prime minister by the time the House of Commons approved Britain's military involvement by 534 votes to 57 on 15 January. The war began on 17 January, with air attacks on military targets inside Iraq and its infrastructure. A ground invasion of Kuwait was launched on 24 February and lasted just four days. The Iraqi army was routed, and the United States decided unilaterally to cease hostilities without consulting other coalition members.

There was a debate about whether coalition forces should have pressed on to Baghdad and brought down Hussein's regime. Bush and his advisors argued that UN Resolution 678 did not provide such legal cover and that

Arab members of the coalition, for instance, **Egypt** and Syria, would not be likely to support such an extension of the war. Major managed to persuade the United States that "safe havens" should be established for the Kurds, long in revolt against Hussein in the north of Iraq. Britain and the United States had worked closely together during the Gulf War. This was most evident in the close working relationship between the United States; UN coalition force commander General Norman Schwarzkopf; and Britain's commanding general, Sir Peter de la Billière. Britain's Diplomatic Service emerged with credit from the crisis, whereas the U.S. ambassador to Iraq, April Glaspie, had wrongly implied in July 1990 that the United States had no interest in Hussein's border dispute with Kuwait. This may well have encouraged Hussein's reckless invasion, although his precarious financial situation might have brought about an invasion anyway.

H

HAGUE, WILLIAM (1961–). Great Britain's current **foreign secretary,** William Hague, was appointed to his post by Conservative prime minister **David Cameron** on 12 May 2010. He formerly served as Welsh secretary (1995–1997) in the administration of **John Major** and was party leader from 1997–2001. Hague's background is unusual among current Conservative leaders. He comes from humble origins and was educated at a comprehensive school in Yorkshire, but this did not prevent him attending Oxford University and obtaining a first-class honors degree. A significant development in his Oxford years was Hague's securing of the position of president of the Oxford Union. This debating society has provided a political pathway for many Conservative leaders. It enabled Hague to develop the debating skills for which he is noted. He went on to obtain a master of business administration and worked as a management consultant. Politics was always Hague's first love, and, in 1987, he made a first unsuccessful attempt to get into Parliament. In 1989, he succeeded in winning a by-election for the seat in Richmond, Yorkshire. Promotion was rapid for Hague, and, in 1990, he was made parliamentary private secretary to the then-chancellor of the exchequer, Norman Lamont. In 1993, the highly thought of newcomer was promoted to parliamentary undersecretary of state, and, in 1994, he became minister of state at the Department of Social Security. He did well as Welsh secretary from 1995–1997, before the catastrophic Conservative election defeat.

In a dark hour for the Conservatives, Hague opted to stand for the party leadership when Major stood down. He was just 36 years of age, and some thought him to be too young. Hague failed as leader, as the Conservatives were even more heavily defeated in the 2001 election. His profound Euroscepticism was not a vote winner, and, although he opposed British membership of the European common currency (euro) in 2000, any potential here was neutralized by the similar opposition of Labour's chancellor, **Gordon Brown,** who dictated economic policy. There was also an impression of gaucheness. Hague was involved in public relations disasters involving baseball hats and admissions about excessive teenage drinking. His attempt to shift the Conservatives to the right on social issues also produced few benefits.

Hague reverted to being a backbencher when he decided to stand down as leader in 2001. From 2001–2005, he was variously a company director, a broadcaster, and an after-dinner speaker. He was then appointed shadow foreign secretary in 2005, having served his political exile. Conservatives are not usually kind to failed leaders, but, in his new role, Hague pulled the Conservatives out of the European People's Party group in the European Parliament on 30 January 2006. This was a significant move that distanced the Conservatives from their usual center-right allies in favor of an arrangement with extreme right-wing Polish and Czech parties. Hague's shadow experience made him the obvious candidate for foreign secretary when the Conservative-Liberal Democrat Coalition was formed in May 2010.

Hague's first overseas visit took him to Washington, D.C., where he visited U.S. secretary of state Hillary Clinton. He has not developed the close rapport with Clinton achieved by his Labour predecessor, **David Miliband**. Just as his predecessor, **Robin Cook**, had spoken of the need for a moral foreign policy in 1997, Hague stressed the importance of human rights in a speech in August 2010. He received criticism in the **United States** and **Israel** for meeting with **Palestinian** demonstrators against Israel's security barrier on the West Bank of the River Jordan. During the so-called "Arab Spring" in 2011, there were one or two gaffes in Hague's handling of the **Libya** crisis, most notably when the **Foreign Office** seemed slow to pull British citizens out of a war-torn Libya and an inept attempt to liaise with Libyan dissidents in eastern Libya ended with the arrest of eight British diplomats and Special Air Services men. Although Cameron and Hague wanted a no fly zone in Libya, it was noted that defense cuts meant Britain had no aircraft carriers to use.

In practice, Britain began readopting the sort of interventionism practiced by **Tony Blair** in Sierra Leone, **Kosovo**, **Afghanistan**, and **Iraq**. The difference was that no combat troops were involved in Libya, and that Britain and **France**, rather than the United States, were leading the **North Atlantic Treaty Organization** intervention. Hague would not commit Britain to automatic intervention against dictators, and, in a speech on 22 April 2011, he recognized that there had to be constraints for British foreign policy. In the case of Syria, where the regime was butchering its demonstrating citizens, Hague demanded political change but would not promise active help Libya-style for dissidents. In contract, the overthrow of the regime of Muammar al-Gaddafi was presented as a victory for British foreign policy. In Afghanistan, where Britain had maintained a military presence beginning in 2001, Hague claimed that it was Britain who had persuaded the administration of U.S. president **Barack Obama** to open talks with the Taliban. Britain had lost 374 soldiers in Afghanistan by June 2011.

As it has for so many of his predecessors, Europe proved to be a thorny problem for Hague. As a politician who had been a hardened Eurosceptic for decades, Hague could expect institutional resistance in the Foreign Office, which had tended to favor ties with the **European Union**. Hague was a trenchant critic of the **Eurozone** who strongly supported Cameron's veto in Brussels on 9 December against a new intergovernmental treaty. Hague believed that the Eurozone was a folly that was bound to fail.

During his years as a politician away from front benchwork, Hague developed skills as an acclaimed biographer. Both of his books, one about **William Pitt the Younger,** and the other about William Wilberforce, were well-received in Britain.

HALIFAX, LORD (1881–1959). Edward Wood, 3rd Viscount Halifax, was a key player during the period when **appeasement** was the dominant theme in British foreign policy during the 1930s. Halifax was viceroy in **India** (1926–1931), **foreign secretary** under both **Neville Chamberlain** and **Winston Churchill** (1938–1940), and British ambassador to the **United States** (1941–1946). Prior to his appointment as foreign secretary, Halifax, then the Lord Privy Seal, had been sent to **Germany** in November 1937, to meet Adolf Hitler and Hermann Göring, head of the German Air Force. Halifax nearly caused a diplomatic incident by mistaking Hitler for a footman and attempting to give the German dictator his hat. He was warned off by the German foreign minister but then criticized at home for appearing to adopt too friendly a posture in his talks with the Nazis. Just before the **Munich Agreement** in September 1938, Halifax was a mainstay of appeasement as foreign secretary. He then staged a brief revolt against the terms produced by Hitler's meeting with Chamberlain at Godesberg a week before Munich. Halifax ultimately went along with the agreement, and his reputation suffered accordingly, as independent **Czechoslovakia** disappeared within six months in March 1939.

Halifax was retained as foreign secretary when Winston Churchill became prime minister on 10 May 1940. The two men fell out over the issue of whether a negotiated peace with Germany was feasible after **France** had surrendered. Churchill did not believe that it was, and he used their disagreement on this issue to remove Halifax from his post and send him to the United States as Britain's ambassador in January 1941. It would be wrong to see Halifax as a defeatist. Once in the United States, he did his best to explain the danger that Britain was in, often to unsympathetic audiences when isolationist feeling was still strong. President **Franklin D. Roosevelt**, who was reelected president in November 1940, had pledged to keep the United States out of any European struggle. Along with the famous economist **John Maynard**

Keynes, Halifax played a key role in negotiating the **Anglo–American Loan Agreement** in 1945, and he was Britain's delegate at the **San Francisco Conference,** which established the **United Nations.** Halifax was nicknamed "Holy Fox" by Churchill, because of his tendency to suggest that he had divine approval for subtle changes of attitude on major issues. His achievements came despite an artificial arm, which he maneuvered with some skill.

HARLECH, LORD (1918–1985). David Ormsby-Gore, 5th Baron Harlech, was a Conservative member of Parliament from 1950–1961, when he was appointed British ambassador in Washington. Ormsby-Gore held the appointment until 1965, and he had a close personal relationship with President **John F. Kennedy.** The two men had known each other since the 1930s, when Kennedy's father, **Joseph P. Kennedy,** was ambassador in London, and he was also briefly a student at the London School of Economics and Political Science. It has been suggested that President Kennedy personally requested that Ormsby-Gore, a nondiplomat, be sent to Washington. They were, in fact, distantly related, and Kennedy's sister, Kathleen, married Ormsby-Gore's cousin.

Ormsby-Gore did not have diplomatic experience, but he was minister of state for foreign affairs in **Harold Macmillan's** government, with special responsibility for disarmament. Kennedy learned a great deal from him about disarmament planning during the 1960 U.S. presidential election. Ormsby-Gore was an outstanding success as ambassador, although his closeness with Kennedy caused some irritation within the rest of the diplomatic corps. The two men went sailing with one another and shared a healthy skepticism about hackneyed **Cold War** thinking. Yet, at no time did Ormsby-Gore (he became Lord Harlech upon the death of his father in 1964) fail to stand up for British interests. Nevertheless, his personal rapport with Kennedy gave him a special influence during the perilous **Cuban Missile Crisis** in October 1962. Ormsby-Gore is credited by one of Kennedy's biographers with suggesting the release of aerial photographs of the Cuban missile sites, and with convincing the president that the interception point for U.S. warships should be much closer to Cuba. This would give the Soviet leadership the maximum amount of time to turn back its missile supply ships and avoid confrontation. Ormsby-Gore remained in post for two years after the assassination of his lifelong friend on 22 November 1963. His appointment created something of a trend for appointments to Washington, with nondiplomats **John Freeman** and Peter Jay following him.

HARVEY, OLIVER (1893–1968). Starting out as **Anthony Eden's** private secretary in January 1936, Oliver Harvey's career was closely associated with the **foreign secretary**. When Eden resigned in February 1938, Harvey continued to work as private secretary for his successor, Edward Wood, **Lord Halifax**, until December 1939, when he was sent as minister, second only to the ambassador, to the Paris embassy. While acting in that capacity, he was an eyewitness to the Fall of **France** in June 1940. The French collapse obliged him to return to London, where he took up a post at the Ministry of Information until June 1941, when he again became Eden's private secretary at the **Foreign Office**. On his own admission, he was rather too old for this particular post, and, in November 1943, Harvey became an assistant undersecretary at the Foreign Office. Eden's successor at the Foreign Office, **Ernest Bevin**, sent Harvey on an important mission to Paris in 1946, which helped to secure the signing of the Dunkirk Treaty in March 1947. Harvey was created Lord Harvey of Tasburgh.

HEALEY, DENIS (1917–). Denis Healey was secretary of state for defense from 1964–1970, and chancellor of the exchequer from 1974–1979, in successive Labour administrations. A robust right-winger, Healey failed to become party leader but did win a famously fierce battle for the deputy leadership in 1981. He had been a Communist as a student at Oxford University, but, after serving in the military in **World War II** (he was a beachmaster on **D-Day** in 1944), he swung strongly to the right. He became a Labour member of Parliament in 1952, after service at the party headquarters at Transport House. Healey was now a strong supporter of the **North Atlantic Treaty Organization** and the Western Alliance. As defense secretary under **Harold Wilson**, he had to preside over severe defense cuts, which included the cancellation of the TSR-2 aircraft. In 1968, Healey was at the heart of the decision to withdraw British troops East of Suez, the **East of Suez Decison**. His period as chancellor of the exchequer was turbulent, coming to a head in 1976, when he and Prime Minister **James Callaghan** had to negotiate a loan from the International Monetary Fund. The terms were stringent, and Healey was booed at the podium at the Labour Party Conference in Blackpool. Healey was an abrasive performer in the House of Commons, describing an attack by his Conservative counterpart **Sir Geoffrey Howe** as like being "savaged by a dead sheep."

HEATH, EDWARD (1916–2005). Edward Heath was leader of the Conservative Party from 1965–1974, and prime minister from 1970–1974. He was the most pro-European of British postwar prime ministers, and rather indifferent to the "**special relationship**" with the **United States**. Unusual for the Conservative Party of his era, Heath came from humble origins. His father was a master carpenter. He was still able to win an organ scholarship to Oxford before distinguished war service. Heath was clearly a rising star in **Harold Macmillan's** Conservative government, and, in 1961, he was put in charge of Great Britain's first unsuccessful attempt to enter the **European Economic Community (EEC)**. As prime minister, Heath took charge of the negotiations during the third application. He succeeded in securing British entry into the community on 1 January 1973. After his fall from power in February 1974, Heath was a notable critic of the anti-European tendencies of his successor, **Margaret Thatcher**. In office, he was infuriated by President **Richard Nixon's** decision to call a nuclear alert on 25 October 1973, during the Yom Kippur War. Britain had not been consulted beforehand, and this did little to strengthen a lukewarm Anglo–American relationship. The EEC was always the primary focus of British foreign policy under Heath.

HENDERSON, SIR NEVILE (1882–1942). Nevile Henderson, who became notorious as an allegedly pro-Nazi ambassador in **Germany** between 1937–1939, was of Scots descent. He attended **Eton College** but did not go to university, instead following the traditional route of cramming for the foreign languages needed for entrance into the **Foreign Office**. He entered the Diplomatic Service in 1905.

Henderson had a typical British diplomatic career, which meant that by the time he was appointed ambassador to Germany, he had spent virtually no time in his native land. Once in Berlin, Henderson tried to improve relations with the Nazis, as he had been instructed, but he was accused in the Foreign Office of having exceeded his brief to the extent of being nicknamed "our Nazi Ambassador in Berlin." This was an exaggeration, but it was true that Henderson believed that he had an almost divine mission to improve Anglo–German relations, even though he loathed the German foreign minister, Joachim von Ribbentrop (1938–1945). Henderson's mission to Germany ended on 3 September 1939, when he took the British ultimatum to the German Foreign Ministry, which expired at 11:00 a.m. that day. *See also* APPEASEMENT; CHAMBERLAIN, NEVILLE.

HENDERSON, SIR NICHOLAS (1919–). Nicholas Henderson was British ambassador to the **United States** from 1979–1982; therefore, he was in post at the time of the **Falklands War,** and helped to ensure that Britain had the support of the administration of President **Ronald Reagan**. "Nico," as Henderson was known in the Diplomatic Service, had been in the Washington embassy as a junior diplomat during the Burgess and Maclean spy scandal of the early 1950s. He had the favor of **Margaret Thatcher** as ambassador, a rarity, as she had a low opinion of the **Foreign Office**.

HMS *PRINCE OF WALES*. *See PRINCE OF WALES*, HMS.

HOARE, SIR SAMUEL (1880–1959). British **foreign secretary** briefly in 1935, Samuel Hoare was at the center of the notorious Hoare–Laval Pact, which was intended to hand a large slice of **Ethiopia** over to Benito Mussolini on a plate. When the plan was leaked, the British public was outraged, and Hoare was obliged to resign. Strongly associated with the **appeasement** policy of the 1930s, Hoare resumed his career as First Lord of the **Admiralty** from 1936–1937, and home secretary from 1937–1940. **Winston Churchill** sent him packing to Madrid as British ambassador when he became prime minister on 10 May 1940, a post Hoare held until 1944. Hoare was created Viscount Templewood in 1944.

HOLY LOCH NAVAL BASE. During the **Cold War,** Great Britain had persistent difficulty in developing an independent nuclear delivery system. This problem was resolved in March 1960, when Prime Minister **Harold Macmillan** met his old wartime colleague, President **Dwight D. Eisenhower.** They agreed that the **United States** would provide the British with **Polaris missiles** in exchange for the lease to the United States of a naval base at Holy Loch in Scotland. The agreement was unpopular in Scotland, because Holy Loch was close to major population centers, and the Campaign for Nuclear Disarmament also campaigned strongly against the presence of U.S. nuclear submarines at Holy Loch. The base was closed in 1992, at the end of the Cold War.

HONG KONG. The Crown colony of Hong Kong came under British rule in 1842, after the first Opium War. Kowloon, on the Chinese mainland, was obtained in 1860, and the New Territories, which makes up 92 percent of Hong Kong, was added in 1898, on a 99-year lease. Hong Kong rapidly became an important commercial and financial center in the **British Empire.** In December 1941, Hong Kong was seized by imperial Japanese Forces, and it remained under their control until 1945, when **Japan** was defeated by the **United States** and Britain. In 1949, the Communist takeover in **China,** which brought with it a strident nationalism, made Hong Kong vulnerable. This contributed to the more conciliatory approach taken with Communist China by the Labour government of **Clement R. Attlee.**

Some problems were created for the Hong Kong authorities in the 1980s, when an influx of Vietnamese refugees produced Anglo–American disagreement about their fate. By the 1990s, the looming issue of the end of the British lease on the colony became paramount. The last British governor, Chris Patten, ceded more democratic rights to the Hong Kong population, although his policy from 1992–1997 was open to criticism that it was rather late in the day. In Beijing, this extension of democracy was fiercely resented and led to a strained period in Anglo–Chinese relations. Britain's 99-year lease on Hong Kong expired on 30 June 1997. It had refused British nationality to Hong Kong residents, thus there was a mass exodus of Hong Kong Chinese to Western countries, including **Canada**.

HOON, GEOFF (1953–). Made secretary of state for defense by **Tony Blair** in 1999, Geoff Hoon was in charge of British operations in Sierra Leone in 2001, **Afghanistan** in 2001, and **Iraq** in 2003. Not considered an outstanding appointment, Hoon was lampooned in the British media as "Buffoon."

HOWARD, ESME (1863–1939). Esme Howard was a British delegate at the **Paris Peace Conference** in 1919, and then ambassador in Washington from 1924–1930. He was instrumental in allowing Prime Minister **Ramsay MacDonald** to have successful conversations with President Herbert Hoover in October 1929. These led to the successful London naval conference of January to April 1930.

HOWE, SIR GEOFFREY (1926–). Geoffrey Howe served as chancellor of the exchequer under **Margaret Thatcher** from 1979–1983, and then as her **foreign secretary** from 1983–1989. Howe had previously been solicitor general and minister for consumer affairs in **Edward Heath's** administration from 1970–1974. As chancellor, he was strongly associated with monetarism, an economic doctrine fashionable in Britain in the 1980s. This maintained that inflation could be kept down by restricting the money supply. It formed the focus for Howe's notorious 1979 budget, which sparked the worst recession in Britain for 50 years and doubled unemployment. Nearly a quarter of Britain's industrial capacity was destroyed by Howe's policy between 1979–1983. Howe and Thatcher refused to budge from their unsuccessful economic policies.

After her 1983 election victory, Thatcher moved Howe to the **Foreign Office** as someone she could rely on. The prime minister had regarded the Foreign Office as the home of pro-European dreamers who did not stand up for British interests. Howe did good work there, notably in reaching agreement with China about **Hong Kong** in 1984. The colony was to revert to Chinese administration in 1997. Howe also rather surprisingly persuaded Thatcher to agree to the Single European Act in 1986, which abolished a member state's right of veto over much of **European Union (EU)** law. Thatcher had previously been a robust defender of British rights in the EU. In June 1989, Howe and his successor as chancellor, **Nigel Lawson**, forced a reluctant Thatcher to accept British membership of the Exchange Rate Mechanism. This was a bridge too far as far as Howe was concerned, as Thatcher now found him a bore with unpalatable views. In July 1989, she moved him out of the Foreign Office into the meaningless post of deputy prime minister, but there was still to be a twist in the story of relations between Howe and Thatcher. In November 1990, Howe, who was generally regarded as colorless and submissive, resigned from the government and savaged Thatcher in his resignation speech in the House of Commons. There was speculation at the time about whether Howe's wife Elspeth, who was known to loathe Thatcher, had a hand in the speech. The speech was doubly significant because it precipitated the challenge from Michael Heseltine, a former defense secretary, to Thatcher's leadership. She was obliged to resign in December 1990.

HURD, DOUGLAS (1930–). Douglas Hurd, a product of **Eton College** and Oxford, was a diplomat before being appointed **foreign secretary** by **Margaret Thatcher** in 1989. He retained the post until 1995, under Thatcher's successor, **John Major.** Hurd had also been a close aide of **Edward Heath** in the early 1970s. His period as foreign secretary was a difficult one. He oversaw the British response to Saddam Hussein's invasion of Kuwait in 1990, which ended with 45,000 British troops being sent to the Persian Gulf in 1991. Hurd was unhappy about President **George H. W. Bush's** decision not to move on to Baghdad once Saddam's army had been routed by the Allied coalition. Britain had not been consulted about Bush's decision beforehand.

There was further Anglo–American dissension over policy in **Bosnia-Herzegovina.** Hurd rejected the plan put forward in 1995, by President **Bill Clinton,** to lift an international arms embargo on the Bosnian Muslims. In his view, this would only increase the potential for slaughter in a civil war already four years old. Instead, Hurd wanted the **United States** to join the **United Nations** peacekeeping operation in Bosnia and create safe havens for the Muslims there. The tensions created were even worse than those that resulted from the **Grenada** crisis a decade before. Hurd produced a thoughtful study of Britain's foreign secretaries in 2010, entitled *Choose Your Weapons.* In it, he stresses the perils of historical ignorance in diplomacy.

HYDE PARK MEETING (1942). The family home of **Franklin D. Roosevelt** in New York, Hyde Park was the location for a meeting between President Roosevelt and **Winston Churchill** from 19–20 June 1942. It was designed to discuss the course of **World War II** and Anglo–American priorities. In particular, it was decided that the European theater of operations would take priority over the war in the Pacific. The two leaders also agreed to pool resources for the development of an atomic bomb, which became known as Operation Manhattan.

I

IMF CRISIS (1976). The International Monetary Fund (IMF) was the product of the 1944 **Bretton Woods Agreement**. In 1976, the IMF was called upon by the British Labour government to assist the pound sterling, whose value had begun to slide against the U.S. dollar. The crisis began in March, and, in June, the government, led by **James Callaghan**, appealed to the U.S. government for help. A loan was arranged, whereby the **United States** provided £2 billion, while a standby credit of $5.3 billion was made available with central banks. There was a six-month time limit on the loan, which had to be repaid in full. Problems persisted in Britain, and the pound was still in trouble in September 1976. The industrial disputes, a feature of 1970s Britain, had been a problem in the public corporation British Leyland. A seaman's strike, which had been catastrophic in 1966, was also threatened. This forced the British government to apply to the IMF for a rescue package, which involved severe cuts in public spending. Defense cuts, which contemplated scrapping **Polaris**, were opposed by the administration of Gerald R. Ford in Washington, because they would weaken the **North Atlantic Treaty Organization**. Even so, there was little sympathy in Washington for Callaghan's problems, which were attributed to British financial mismanagement and chronic industrial turmoil. A direct appeal from Callaghan to President Ford for more sympathetic treatment failed, and Callaghan's government had to accept IMF terms for a loan of £2.3 billion. The IMF loan was extremely controversial in Britain and was bitterly attacked by the left-wing of the Labour Party in the House of Commons. In retrospect, it is questionable whether the approach to the IMF was the best solution. Those countries that took IMF loans, like Britain, and complied with IMF terms, did not ultimately perform any better than those that did not. In the shorter run, the Callaghan government began to pioneer the monetarist approach, albeit in a milder form, followed by **Margaret Thatcher** and her government after 1979. *See also* HEALEY, DENIS; HOLY LOCH NAVAL BASE.

INDIA. Often referred to as Great Britain's "jewel in the crown," India was the single most important part of the **British Empire**. It was acquired as a result of the military genius of Robert Clive during the Seven Years' War, when **France** was defeated. The British relied heavily on the cooperation of native Indian princes. They continued to rule over approximately two-fifths of India. From 1756–1857, the East India Company (founded in 1600) was the instrument of British power, ruling over a complex mixture of Hindus, Muslims, Sikhs, and other minorities. In the early days of British rule, East India Company officials often adopted Indian customs and dress. This fraternization largely ended following the crisis of the Indian Mutiny in 1857. The conflict had its origins in rumors about the use of a mixture of beef and pork grease to clean cartridges, the first animal, the cow, being sacred to Hindus, and the second, the pig, deemed unclean by Muslims. The crisis resulted in a revolt by the native troops, or sepoys, against the British. Only 45,000 out of 277,000 Company troops were Europeans. Large tracts of northern and central India were lost to the rebels. The mutiny was ultimately put down with draconian brutality by the British. Indians were burned alive and blown up by British artillery. The British reacted to this shock by altering the structure of British rule. In November 1858, the British Crown became responsible for India, working through the India office in London. A viceroy represented the Crown.

Lessons were learned after 1857. The British distanced themselves from native Indians and concentrated on material development, notably railways. By 1900, the railway system was 24,700 miles long. The British increasingly spoke of the burden of empire. At its apex was **Queen Victoria**, made empress of India by Prime Minister **Benjamin Disraeli** in 1876. Native Indians were regarded as children in the charge of British imperial officials. The greatest fear of officials in the last half of the 19th century was that **Russia**, which was expanding its empire into Central Asia, would overrun **Afghanistan** and threaten British India. In 1885, Russia effectively controlled northern Afghanistan and was thought to be intriguing against Britain at the Afghan Court. The North West Frontier of India, with its turbulent tribes, was recognized to be Britain's most vulnerable one. The diplomatic revolution in Europe between 1904–1907, which saw Britain settle colonial issues with France and Russia, was crucial. British anxieties about the defense of India were allayed.

When **World War I** broke out in 1914, India was not a concern, although its natives were not consulted about being involved. Hindus, Muslims, and Sikhs fought courageously for Britain. One million Indians were sent overseas. They were deemed suitable to die for Britain, but the mother country was slow to cede any degree of autonomy. In 1917, the Morley–Minto Reforms began the process of limited Indian self-government. In 1919, the Amritsar Massacre was a savage British reprisal against a peaceful demonstration. Mohandas K. Gandhi, the emerging leader of Indian nationalism, called the British "satanic." They were fortunate that Gandhi and his Indian National Congress subsequently adopted nonviolent tactics. The British were too thin on the ground to deal with an all-India mass uprising. In response to Gandhi's campaign, successive viceroys recognized the need for concession. In 1935, the **India Act**, passed by the government of **Stanley Baldwin**, extended the powers given to Indian provincial governments, while reducing those of British governors. There was also a new two-chamber legislature, although the Indian National Congress thought that the princes were overrepresented. The new leader of the congress, Jawaharlal Nehru, epitomized Indian nationalist attitudes. Privileged and educated at Harrow School (he kept a photo of it in his wallet) and Cambridge, Nehru spent nine years in British jails. Gandhi, too, was frequently imprisoned for civil disobedience, but he still regarded the British as righteous people. The Congress dominated in the elections of 1937, but, already, the shadow of Muslim separatism had appeared. Gandhi was horrified by the **Pakistan** Resolution of 1940, and the prospect of partition.

During **World War II**, British policy was ambivalent about Indian independence, largely because **Winston Churchill** bitterly opposed it. His Labour coalition partners favored independence, and their election victory in July 1945 brought the prospect nearer. Labour prime minister **Clement R. Attlee** recognized that an India that had mobilized 2.5 million men for the British war effort deserved independence. In 1946, he sent a cabinet mission to India, but it foundered on the issue of a separate Muslim state. In 1947, **Lord Louis Mountbatten** was sent to accelerate the independence process, because Attlee and his colleagues knew that Britain now lacked the resources to garrison the subcontinent. Mountbatten fortunately got along with both Gandhi and Nehru. Independence was conceded to both India and Pakistan on 15 August 1947. At Nehru's request, Mountbatten remained as India's first governor general. Gandhi was devastated by partition, dying at the hands of a Hindu extremist on 30 January 1948. His disciple, Nehru, was India's first prime minister (1947–1964).

Britain still had hopes where independent India was concerned. As late as March 1946, the Chiefs of Staff of the British Armed Forces still expected to access the huge reserves of Indian manpower. There was also the hope that British bases might be kept. Nehru preserved a rigorous neutrality instead. India did not join the **Southeast Asia Treaty Organization** in 1954, or sign the Baghdad Pact in 1955. Even worse from the British viewpoint was Nehru's rigorous criticism of Britain at the time of the **Suez Crisis** (1956). India voted with the Soviet Union at the **United Nations (UN)**. Nehru rejected force in international relations, but he used it in 1961, to seize the Portuguese enclave of Goa. Britain's premier, **Harold Macmillan**, pointed out the inconsistency in his policy. He was unable to bring India and Pakistan together over the thorny issue of Kashmir, two-thirds of which stayed under Indian rule. An even more serious problem arose in 1962, when the People's Republic of China invaded Indian territory. It had never accepted the old MacMahon line imposed by the British. The Indian army was defeated, and Nehru appealed desperately to Macmillan for help. Some automatic weapons and small arms were sent by the British, but **China** retained some of the disputed land. As Nehru had spent much time cultivating Chinese friendship, it was a major embarrassment for him. A year after Nehru's death in 1964, a second Indian–Pakistan war over Kashmir settled nothing. India was now as close to the Soviet Union as it was to Britain, and it was Soviet mediation that ended the war in 1966. India was a member of the **British Commonwealth**, but it was a republic severing the link with the Crown.

At home, India was dominated by the Nehru–Gandhi dynasty. In 1966, Nehru's daughter, Indira Gandhi, became prime minister, a post she retained until 1977. The most important development during this 11-year period was India's involvement in the creation of an independent **Bangladesh** in 1971. The role of the Indian army was decisive, leaving just a rump Pakistan state. The atrocities carried out by the Pakistani army in the former East Bengal meant that India won the sympathy of Britain and its government. In other respects, Indira was controversial. Her style was authoritarian, and she acted as a tutor for **Margaret Thatcher**. Before becoming premier in 1979, Thatcher had visited Gandhi and was impressed. She, too, adopted an imperious governing style and admitted to being influenced by Gandhi. The Indian leader was accused of election abuses in 1977, and she tried to survive by declaring a state of emergency. In the subsequent election, the Indian National Congress was defeated, and Gandhi subsequently set up her own branch of congress.

Restored to power in 1980, Gandhi faced the problem of Sikh separatism. Sikh extremists wanted to set up separate Khalistan, and there were accusations that Britain was harboring Sikh **terrorists**. There was a large emigrant Sikh community there. When extremists occupied the Golden Temple in Amritsar, the holy city of the Sikhs, the Indian army was ordered to storm it in 1984. In a reprisal, Gandhi was assassinated by members of her own Sikh bodyguard. The dynastic element in Indian government surfaced when Rajiv Gandhi was selected to be prime minister (1984–1989). Rajiv was a former airline pilot with no political experience. He had failed to complete an engineering degree at Cambridge, where his grandfather had studied. The most notable development in this Gandhi's premiership was his decision to intervene in the Sri Lankan civil war in 1987. The Tamil minority there had many ethnic compatriots in Southern India. The number of troops soon increased to 100,000. This decision cost Gandhi his life. In 1991, he was assassinated by a Tamil Tiger suicide bomber while electioneering.

India long had aspirations to become a nuclear power. It attained this status in 1998. The event, which was strongly criticized in Britain and the **United States**, left the country in some diplomatic isolation. This ended after the 9/11 terrorist attacks, when the Indian government was able to portray jihadist activity in Kashmir as part of the war against terrorism. Britain and India began to evolve closer defense links. One was the joint Indo–British exercise in India, in March 2005. This resulted in the biggest presence of British troops on Indian soil since independence. Britain also supported India's long desire to become a permanent member of the UN. There was cooperation in security and technology matters, although India protected its own interests. In 2011, Britain was somewhat embarrassed when a 10-billion-pound fighter aircraft contract was awarded to France over a British bid. Still, formal links remain close. Indian presidents paid state visits to Britain in 1963, 1990, and 2009. **Queen Elizabeth II** paid reciprocal visits to India in November 1963, April 1990, and October 1997.

INDIA ACT (1935). The British government had long recognized the need for some devolution of power in **India**. The 1935 India Act, which was steered through Parliament by **Sir Samuel Hoare** as secretary of state for India, was a step forward. It set up a provincial administration, a division between central and local government that could be adapted to Indian needs, and a system of justice updated and developed by the act. The nature of the Indian Civil Service was also defined and reinforced. Indian nationalists were not satisfied with the agreement, as it still left reserve powers over defense and foreign policy with the British viceroy in New Delhi. Indian representatives were not consulted about the decision to go to war with **Germany** in September 1939. Even so, Conservative right-wingers like **Winston Churchill** objected to the concession of any real autonomy to India.

INDOCHINA. Indochina, with its component parts of Vietnam, Laos, and Cambodia, was under French colonial rule for a century. Great Britain briefly played a significant role in its history in 1945–1946, when British troops occupied southern Vietnam, Laos, and Cambodia in the wake of the **Potsdam Conference** in July 1945. Some British soldiers were killed in actions with Vietnamese nationalists, who wished to establish an independent Vietnamese state. The 20th Division of the British Army was withdrawn in March 1946, as French colonialism reimposed itself. **France** was involved in a full-scale colonial war by December 1946. *See also* DIEN BIEN PHU; EDEN, SIR ANTHONY.

INTELLIGENCE AND SECURITY COMMITTEE. Along with its sister organization, the Overseas and Defense Committee, the Intelligence and

Security Committee has a key role in Whitehall. It prepares and circulates intelligence assessments from British intelligent sources.

IRAN. The ancient kingdom of Iran (formerly Persia), dating back 2,500 years, had been of interest to Great Britain since the 19th century. Its strategic position between **Russia** and British **India** made its neutralization essential. This was achieved in the 1907 Triple Entente agreement between Britain, **France**, and Russia. Persia, as it was then called, would be divided into zones of influence, Russian in the North and British in the South. Most importantly, the agreement allowed the Anglo–Iranian Oil Company a dominant role, which it retained for almost 50 years. The British embassy also dominated native Persian affairs through its then-minister, Sir Cecil Spring-Rice (1906–1908) and his tiny staff. In 1907, it was made up of just the minister, the counselor, two diplomatic secretaries, the oriental secretary, the military attaché, and the doctor. In 1914, **Winston Churchill**, as First Lord of the **Admiralty**, approved the purchase of a controlling 51 percent of the Anglo–Persian Oil Company, soon to be the Anglo-Iranian Oil Company at the cost of £2.2 million. This guaranteed the delivery of 6 million tons of oil during the course of 20 years. This was vital, as the Royal Navy had made the switch from coal to oil in its battleships in July 1913. By 1947, Britain was getting twice as much oil revenue from Iran as the Iranians.

Between 1918–1939, Iran, ostensibly independent, was ruled by the dictator Reza Khan, founder of the short-lived Pahlavi dynasty, which he tried to link with his country's ancient past. His flirting with the Nazis led to the Anglo–Soviet invasion in 1941, and joint control lasted until 1946. By then, British exploitation of Iranian oil was sharpening Iranian nationalist opposition. The key figure was Muhammed Mossadegh, an eccentric intellectual educated in the West who mounted a campaign against corruption and British oil policy. He opposed the new shah, or emperor, Mohammed Reza Pahlavi (1941–1979), and demanded that the oil industry be nationalized. When the British candidate for prime minister was assassinated in 1950, Mossadegh was forced on an unwilling shah. He promptly nationalized the Anglo–Iranian Oil Company. Mossadegh was not a Communist, but the British were able to arouse U.S. fears of possible Soviet infiltration. A joint operation by the Anglo–American secret services brought down Mossadegh's government on 19 August 1953. Mossadegh was imprisoned for three years but remained a hero to many Iranians who did not forget Britain's treachery. Churchill, Britain's prime minister from 1951–1955, was delighted both by Mossadegh's overthrow and the shah's return. He congratulated the Central Intelligence Agency operative who organized the coup against Mossadegh.

The shah proved to be a reliable ally of Britain and the West. Britain failed to recognize his dictatorial tendencies, enforced by a sinister secret police organization, Savak. As late as 1977, the shah, with an army of 400,000 men, seemed secure. This was the view of the British government of **James Callaghan**, which, like other Western governments, failed to predict the overthrow of the shah's regime by the fundamentalist movement of Ayatollah Khomeini and its secular allies. In December 1979, a huge protest march of 2 million people converged on the Shahyad monument in Tehran, which the shah had built to commemorate 2,500 years of Iranian monarchy. On 16 January 1979, the shah left Iran for good. On 1 February, Khomeini returned from exile in France. He immediately announced the establishment of an Islamic state.

Subsequent Anglo–Iranian relations proved to be difficult. If the **United States** was the "Great Satan" (the Iran hostage crisis of 1979–1981 effectively brought down President Jimmy Carter), Britain was next in the demonology. Iranians still remembered Mossadegh. In 1980, an attempt by Iranian opponents of the new Islamic Republic to seize the Iranian Embassy in London obliged the British to use their special forces to regain control. The dissidents held the embassy for six days. Britain, although it did not provide military equipment, like the United States, France, and the Soviet Union, certainly supported **Iraq** in its eight-year war with Iran (1980–1988). The war was a bloody stalemate that was followed by an immediate crisis in Anglo–Iranian relations. In 1989, Khomeini issued a fatwa, or religious decree, condemning the British writer Salman Rushdie to death for allegedly insulting Islam in his novel *The Satanic Verses* (1988). The fatwa also encouraged Muslims to kill Rushdie. **Margaret Thatcher** was not the kind of prime minister to tolerate this sort of threat, and, for years, Rushdie was provided with elaborate security. Britain had suspended all diplomatic relations with Iran after the overthrow of the shah in 1979. Only in 1988 was the British Embassy reopened in Tehran. In 1989, diplomatic relations were broken off by Iran on the orders of Khomeini, in the wake of the Rushdie affair. They were only normalized in 1998. And, in 2001 **Foreign Secretary Jack Straw** visited Tehran. He was the first senior British politician to do so since the 1979 revolution.

If the visit was supposed to create a new harmony in Anglo–Iranian relations, this proved to be an illusion. In 2002, eight British sailors were seized by Iran in international waters. They were subsequently released, but another crisis escalated. The Iranians rejected the newly appointed British ambassador, claiming that he was a spy. An especially thorny issue was the projected Iranian nuclear program, which they claimed was for peaceful purposes only. The **European Union (EU)** and the United States did not accept this, and Britain was part of the EU team that tried to negotiate on the issue. Some progress was seemingly to be made, but the Western powers were convinced that Iran was trying to manufacture a nuclear bomb. In April 2006, British newspapers reported on a secret defense establishment meeting in London about an attack on Iran. The high level of tension between Britain and Iran was heightened by a second crisis over Royal Navy personnel in 2007. On 23 March, 15 sailors (one woman) were seized by Iranian Revolutionary Guard naval units for allegedly straying into Iranian waters. A week later, there were large demonstrations outside the Tehran Embassy. The episode seemed to have a serious potential for conflict, but, on 3 April, the Iranian authorities released the sailors. Outside observers believed that the episode reflected internal power struggles in Iran. This seemed to be the case again in 2008. Statements from the Iranian Foreign Ministry suggested that London be targeted in an effort to deter any attack by the United States and **Israel** on Iran's nuclear plants. This was a bluff, but the 2009 Iranian elections, which should have seen the defeat of the eccentric hard-line president Mahmoud Ahmadinejad, were rigged. There were widespread antigovernment demonstrations. The regime responded by blaming foreigners for the protests. Britain, in particular, was blamed for sending in spies to stir up trouble. Two British diplomats were expelled in June 2009, and the **Foreign Office** responded by expelling two Iranians in the standard fashion. When more British staff were arrested, the EU acted by demanding their release, showing the value of Britain's EU link.

The seemingly endless cycle of provocations continued in 2011. On 29 November, the British Embassy in Tehran was stormed by demonstrators while the police stood by. There seemed to be a direct link between this event and the announcement of joint American–Canadian–British sanctions on the regime over the nuclear issue and a bill in the Iranian parliament expelling the British ambassador. Documents were burned, pictures of **Queen Elizabeth II** were defaced, and the British flag was replaced with an Iranian one. Britain's foreign secretary, **William Hague**, responded by expelling all Iranian diplomatic staff in London. The start of the year 2012 proved no different. When Iran threatened to block the Strait of Hormuz, an important international waterway, Britain responded on 7 January by threatening to send naval reinforcements to aid U.S. naval units in the area. In February, the Iranians produced a new anti-British tactic by making personal attacks through the media on staff at the Persian language service in the Foreign Office–funded BBC World Service. As ever, the British problem was discerning which faction in the Iranian regime was responsible. The tensions between the mullahs and President Ahmadinejad made this difficult.

IRAQ. A former province of the Ottoman Empire, Iraq became a British mandate at the **Paris Peace Conference** in 1919, under the auspices of the **League of Nations**. It was a colonial construct that amalgamated Kurds in the north, with Sunni in the center and Shia in the south, a clumsy territorial compromise. During the 1920s and 1930s, the Kurds were especially resentful of British control, and, in 1927, the Royal Air Force bombed Kurdish land. This strengthened Britain's determination to maintain a foothold in Iraq. The British had a controlling interest in the Iraq Petroleum Company until 1961, and U.S. interest in Iraq sharpened after **World War II**, also because of its oil resources. The pro-Western regime of Nuri as-Said had been overthrown on 14 July 1958, and a period of instability followed before Saddam Hussein established his dictatorship in 1969. During the long, drawn out war between Iraq and fundamentalist **Iran** (1980–1988), Britain, like the **United States**, supported Hussein. He was seen as a stabilizing influence in the region, a considerable irony in light of future events. The shadow of Iraq's inception as a nation lay over the **Gulf War** of 1991, for Kuwait was also a British construct to which successive Iraqi governments laid claim after 1935. Kuwait was an important supplier of oil to Britain, even after North Sea oil supplies became available in the 1970s.

IRAQ WAR (2003). After suffering defeat in the 1991 **Gulf War**, **Iraq** was required under **United Nations (UN)** Resolution 687 to destroy its chemical, biological, and nuclear weapons. These were generally known as weapons of mass destruction (WMD). In the West, there was a suspicion by 2002 that Iraqi dictator Saddam Hussein had not observed these cease-fire conditions. British prime minister **Tony Blair** was convinced that Hussein was a threat to regional security, even though the UN arms inspection team, led by the Swede Hans Blix, had failed to find any WMD stockpiles. Blair's American ally, **George W. Bush**, tried to link the Iraqi regime with the attacks on New York City and Arlington, Virginia, in 2001, even though there was no real evidence to sustain this theory. Hussein was an Arab secularist, not a Muslim fundamentalist of the type that had attacked the **United States** on 9/11.

A series of meetings between Bush and Blair determined policy in 2002–2003, although whereas the Americans wanted to force Hussein out of power, Blair maintained that this line would be unacceptable in the House of Commons. Instead, the British would have to emphasize the threat from the WMDs to justify intervention. Intelligence sources were used in both Britain and the United States to provide some sort of legal cover for intervention. Blair wanted a second UN resolution to underpin UN Resolution 1441, which the Security Council had passed on 8 November 2002. Bush and his administration deemed it sufficient to allow an attack on Iraq. It became clear during negotiations at the UN headquarters in New York that **France, Russia,** and **China** would not support military action. The United States proceeded with their move, and the British were ultimately prepared to support it. There was no dissension in the British Cabinet. The overseas aid minister, Clare Short, threatened to resign but was persuaded to stay on, and the **foreign secretary, Jack Straw,** went along with government policy. A key role in securing the passage of UN Resolution 1441 had been played by Britain's ambassador at the UN, Jeremy Greenstock, but a second resolution was never going to be attainable. Diplomacy had failed.

On 17 March 2003, the House of Commons authorized intervention after being convinced that WMDs did exist, and Britain was second only to the United States in the size of its commitment, with 46,000 men being sent. They had responsibility for securing Basra in southern Iraq. As it turned out, British Armed Forces found this task much more difficult than expected. Hussein's field army was routed, but the war changed into an urban guerrilla insurgency. The religious divisions, which had been forced underground under the Hussein dictatorship, reemerged to plague both the British in charge in the Shia South, and the Americans in the Sunni central area, although it had a substantial Shia minority. It was 2009–2010 before Britain was able to begin to disengage from Iraq, and many lives were lost in the interim.

IRELAND. Part of the **British Empire** until the Anglo–Irish Treaty of 1921, Ireland was partitioned by that agreement. Six northern counties remained part of Great Britain, while the remaining 26 made up the Irish Free State, which remained part of the **British Commonwealth.** King George V remained the head of state of the Irish Free State. Relations, if not amicable, remained on a reasonable basis throughout the 1920s, but there was a sharp worsening of Anglo–Irish relations in 1932, when Eamon de Valera became prime minister. He was a convinced republican who wanted to break ties with Britain, and, during **World War II**, he preserved Irish neutrality. This resulted in fierce attacks on the Irish Free State by **Winston Churchill,** who assumed, somewhat unreasonably, that Ireland should be on Britain's side. Only 20 years earlier, de Valera and his colleagues had been involved in a bloody war of independence with the British. In fact, neutral Ireland's position was slanted in favor of the Allies. Fire engines were sent to Belfast when the Germans bombed it in 1941, and Allied fliers crashing in the Irish Free State were returned to the North, whereas German ones were imprisoned. Neither did de Valera prevent thousands of southern Irishmen from joining the British forces, as they had done before independence. In a final irony, it was not de Valera, but his political opponent, John Costello, who broke the constitutional link with Britain in 1949, by declaring Ireland a republic outside the Commonwealth. The response of the British Labour government, under **Clement R. Attlee,** was to reiterate that Northern Ireland would remain part of Great Britain until its population decided otherwise. Attlee knew that the Protestant majority in the six northern counties outside the new Irish Republic had no desire to be part of the largely Catholic state to their south.

The discriminatory policies of the separate Northern Ireland government against Catholics led to the civil disturbances of 1968–1969. This forced a reluctant British government to send troops to Northern Ireland in 1969. This actually escalated the situation in the long run, as republican and loyalist paramilitaries outdid one another with bombings and shootings. An attempt by the British government of **Edward Heath** to cross the religious divide in 1973, with the Sunningdale power-sharing executive, failed miserably, as northern Protestants went on strike. It would have given the Republic a role in the North, which the majority of Protestants could not stomach. Neither would they share power with Catholics. Sectarian atrocities continued into the 1990s, along with attacks on the British military and the Royal Ulster Constabulary. A notable victim in 1979 was **Lord Louis Mountbatten**, a member of the British royal family whose yacht was blown up in County Donegal. Diplomatic support from the **United States** was essential in setting up the 1998 Good Friday Agreement, when prime ministers **Tony Blair** and Bertie Aherne were able to announce a new Anglo–Irish agreement. This allowed for a new Northern Ireland assembly and an executive on which all Northern Ireland parties were represented. By 1998, interest in the Republic in Northern Ireland affairs had lessened, partly as a result of the Irish Republic's entry into the **European Economic Community (EEC)** in 1973, which changed the focus of Irish policies.

Ireland's entry into the EEC greatly assisted in the development of the economy, so that in the years after 2000, there was a tremendous boom. There was talk of Ireland being a "Celtic Tiger," and it, unlike Britain, entered the **Eurozone** in 2000. In fact, the boom proved to be unsustainable, based as it was on massive property speculation and rather reckless behavior in the financial services sector, which invested heavily in Britain. Ireland was badly hit by the financial crisis of 2007–2008, and it was clear that the stewardship of Prime Minister Aherne (1997–2007) was open to serious criticism. His Fianna Fáil (Ourselves Alone) Party, now led by former finance minister Brian Cowan (2007–2011), was routed at the polls in 2011. It was replaced by the main opposition party Fine Gael (Soldiers of Ireland). The new government faced a massive sovereign debt crisis, although Britain, mindful of its historic links with Ireland, loaned it £4 billion in 2010. Under the tutelage of the International Monetary Fund and the **European Union (EU)**, Ireland had to impose a severe austerity package to qualify for a massive EU "bailout" package. There was sympathy in Britain for Ireland's predicament, and Anglo–Irish relations were more cordial than they had been for many years. In 2011, **Queen Elizabeth II** visited the Irish Republic, the first British monarch to do so since George V prior to **World War I**. This would have been unimaginable only 20 years before, and the symbolism of the visit for an intensely republican Ireland was clear for all to see. *See also* IRISH REPUBLICAN ARMY.

IRGUN ZVAI LEUMI. Irgun Zvai Leumi was a Jewish **terrorist** group responsible for blowing up the King David Hotel in Jerusalem on 22 July 1946. The hotel was the headquarters of the British mandatory forces. The explosion killed 91 people and influenced the decision by British **foreign secretary Ernest Bevin** to refer the question of **Palestine** to the **United Nations (UN)** in February 1947. In November 1947, the UN approved a three-way partition of Palestine: a Jewish state, an Arab state, and an international zone around Jerusalem. The British mandate ended on 15 May 1948, but the day before the state of **Israel** was declared. Irgun Zvai Leumi was also responsible for a notorious massacre of Arab villagers at Deir Yassin in April 1948, just before the mandate ended. The first Arab–Israeli War in 1948–1949 rendered the UN partition plan inoperable and left the Jews in possession of virtually all of Palestine. The plan itself had left the Arabs, who previously held 89.4 percent of Palestinian land, with just 43.5 percent, while the Jews, with only 10.6 percent before 1948, received 56.5 percent.

IRISH REPUBLICAN ARMY (IRA). The Irish Republican Army (IRA) was a paramilitary organization with the aim of creating a united **Ireland** through the use of **terrorist** bombings, shootings, and targeted assassinations. Its roots can be found in the 19th Fenian Brotherhood, formed after the catastrophic potato famine that lasted from 1846–1849, widely believed in Irish republican circles to be a deliberate act of Anglo–Saxon genocide. Attempts by Charles Stewart Parnell to achieve home rule for Ireland through constitutional means lessened the attraction of militant republicanism in the years before 1914, although there was a strong cultural revival stressing the use of the Irish language and distinctive sports like Gaelic football and hurling.

When **World War I** came in 1914, the Irish National Party, under John Redmond, generally dropped its demand for internal autonomy within the British Isles for the duration of the hostilities. Militant republicanism seemed to have been sidelined, but, in 1916, republican militants staged an uprising against the British in Dublin. The revolt, which devastated the city center and was quite easily put down by the British, was highly unpopular in the Irish capital, but the British administration made an extraordinary error by then shooting the leading rebels in batches during a period of days, which allowed the republicans to portray them as martyrs for the cause of Irish Freedom. A lost cause thus became a vibrant one.

In the general election of 1918, the Republican Party Sinn Fein (Ourselves Alone) swept the country outside the largely Protestant northeast. Its members of Parliament refused to take up their seats at Westminster, and the party founded a rival parliament that did not recognize the authority of the British Crown in Ireland. Sinn Fein's military wing was the IRA, which came to prominence during the War of Independence from 1918–1921, and, which, like its political wing, believed that only a 32-county united Ireland was acceptable.

It launched a bloody campaign against the police and military, which was countered by equally brutal British reprisals. These acts of retaliation angered many people living in the **United States**, with its large population of Irish immigrants. When the British government gave way in 1921, and agreed to the creation of a partly independent Ireland, the perception was that violence had worked for the IRA. Yet, it then split over the issue of independence, the hard-liners refusing to accept the partition of Ireland under the 1921 Anglo–Irish Treaty. A moderate faction accepted partition under Michael Collins and set up the Irish Free State.

This bitter division led to a civil war in 1922–1923, which was won by those in favor of the treaty, under Collins, who himself was a victim of the struggle. The defeated faction refused to accept this reality and continued to wage bombing campaigns in Northern Ireland and the British mainland into the 1990s. The early campaigns were spasmodic and ineffective, and, during **World War II**, the Free State government itself took draconian measures against IRA militants.

A serious upsurge in IRA violence came in 1970–1971, when a largely Catholic civil rights campaign had been repressed by the Protestant Unionist Northern Ireland government. The IRA split once again, with its core militant wing forming the Provisional IRA (PIRA), which was fully committed to the use of violence on both sides of the Irish Sea, the aim being to force the British government to abandon its jurisdiction in the six northern counties, which remained part of Great Britain. The following decades saw a pattern of bombings and shootings of Crown Forces, intermixed with Protestant loyalist outrages against Catholics. The IRA also killed many civilians, most notably in horrific bombings in England in 1974. It also accepted arms from its republican supporters in the United States, while also going as far afield as **Libya** and Eastern Europe to acquire stocks of Semtex explosive and sophisticated machine guns.

The IRA strategy failed. The British government was never going to give up its position in the six counties unless the majority of the population so stipulated. Eventually, in the 1990s, the Sinn Fein leadership, often interchangeable with that of the IRA, realized that the "armed struggle" would have to be abandoned in favor of a political solution. Evolution was slow, and spasmodic violence was still a feature, especially in 1996, when PIRA abandoned a cease-fire. The impetus for a solution was thought impossible to stop, involving, as it did, the efforts of successive British premiers **John Major** and **Tony Blair**, their Irish counterparts, and President **Bill Clinton**, who visited Belfast.

The crucial date was 10 April 1998, when the Good Friday Agreement, signed by the respective political leaders in Britain and Ireland, and the representative of President Clinton, **George Mitchell**, returned devolved government, which Britain had put on hold in 1971, to Northern Ireland. There was still much haggling about the surrender of IRA arms, but its leaders agreed that the Sinn Fein leaders Gerry Adams and Martin McGuiness could engage in the power-sharing process.

The only cloud on the horizon was the reappearance of republican violence in 2009–2010, carried out by small IRA factions that could not accept the new political treaties. The mainstream PIRA had accepted peace and disarmed itself, an unimaginable scenario as recently as 1990.

IRON CURTAIN. The phrase the "Iron Curtain" is associated with **Winston Churchill**, who used it in a celebrated speech at Fulton, Missouri, in March 1946, warning about the onset of the **Cold War**. It was not original. Nazi propaganda minister Joseph Goebbels is credited with using it as early as 1943.

ISMAY, SIR HASTINGS (1887–1965). A distinguished soldier, Hastings Ismay, commonly nicknamed "Pug," was chief staff officer to the **Ministry of Defense** and deputy secretary (military) to the War Cabinet from 1940–1945. In those roles, he worked closely with **Winston Churchill** on wartime planning. *See also* WORLD WAR II.

ISRAEL. The origins of the state of Israel lay with the 19th-century Zionist movement, which demanded the establishment of an independent Jewish state. Its aspirations were recognized by the British government in the Balfour Declaration of 1917, which conceded the right of Jews to establish a "national home" in **Palestine**. It did not allow the founding of a state, an important distinction. Thousands of Jews immigrated to Palestine during the interwar period, a development that antagonized local Palestinian Arabs. In 1936, there was an Arab uprising in Palestine, which was put down by the British with some severity. The British authorities in Palestine often seemed to favor Jews over Arabs, but, in 1939, the Jewish cause suffered a setback when the British issued a White Paper proposing the creation of an independent state of Palestine within 10 years, with the limitation of Jewish immigration to 15,000 Jews per year for the next five years. After this period, Jewish immigration would stop, unless the Palestinian Arabs agreed to it. By this point, two-thirds of the population of Palestine was Arab. **World War II** presented the Jews with something of a dilemma. They mostly believed that they should support Britain against the evils of National Socialism. A minority, however, notably the **terrorist** Stern Gang, continued to attack Arab and British targets.

When World War II ended, the Jewish defense force Haganah, under the leadership of David Ben Gurion, began to target the British forces in Palestine. Sympathy for the Jews began to erode in the Labour government, and in the **Foreign Office**. Officials there had some disinclination even to believe the first accounts of Holocaust atrocities. **Ernest Bevin**, the **foreign secretary**, was accused of anti-Jewish prejudice, and he may have been influenced by the pro-Arab sentiment of some of his officials. Bevin ultimately decided that a cycle of Jewish and Arab atrocities, sometimes aimed at the British, made the position in Palestine untenable. He therefore handed the problem over to the **United Nations (UN)** and announced that the British mandate would end on 15 May 1948, the day after the state of Israel was declared by Ben Gurion. Many Arabs fled from the new Israel, which was immediately attacked by its Arab neighbors, **Egypt**, Syria, **Iraq**, and Lebanon. The kingdom of **Jordan** seized Arab Jerusalem, but the rest of the Arab lands were swallowed up by the Jews. This created an ongoing problem of displaced Palestinian Arabs. The First Arab–Israeli War ended in January 1949, when Egypt was defeated. Three further wars in 1956, 1967, and 1973 failed to resolve the question of Arab–Israeli relations. The 1967 war, often called the "Six-Day War," made the situation even worse, as Israel occupied the whole of Jerusalem, the West Bank of the River Jordan, and the Golan Heights. UN Resolution 242 demanded that Israel evacuate those Occupied Territories. To date, it has failed to do so, apart from the restitution to Syria of part of the Golan Heights and the Sinai Desert to Egypt.

The war of October 1973 presented a severe crisis for Israel when it was attacked by Egypt and Syria. The eventual Israeli victory precipitated the oil crisis of 1973–1974, when Arab oil producers used their resource to influence Western policy. Britain suffered less because of its North Sea oil fields, and it did not abandon its policy of insistence that UN Resolution 242 should be implemented. The government of **James Callaghan** applauded in 1977, when Anwar Sadat, the Egyptian president, went to Israel as part of a peace initiative. This ended with the 1978 Camp David peace agreements between Israel and Egypt, which returned the entire Sinai desert and secured Egyptian diplomatic recognition of Israel. The surprising feature about the events of 1977–1978 was that Israel prime minister Menachem Begin (1977–1983) had been a member of **Irgun Zvai Leumi**. He had taken part in several terrorist attacks on the British in the 1940s. Begin's party, Likud, was a rightist, nationalistic grouping in sharp contrast to the Israeli Labour Party, which had strong links with European democracies.

Terrorism aimed at the Israelis in London became an increasing problem. Feeble attempts to use firebombs in Oxford and Regent Street in 1969 only needed to be dealt with by the Metropolitan Police Special Branch. Then the situation escalated. On 19 September 1972, an agricultural advisor at the Israeli Embassy was killed by a letter bomb sent by a member of Black September, a branch of the Palestine National Liberation Movement. Israel remained a target for all Arab terrorist groups. In June 1982, Shlomo Argov, the Israel ambassador in London, was shot in the head outside the Dorchester Hotel by a member of the Abu Nidal Organization. Britain's position was simple: It wanted to implement UN Resolution 242. On the other hand, it fully accepted Israel's right to exist and would protect its diplomatic and consular staff in Britain. Britain was also a provider of arms to Israel. In the 1967 war, its aging Centurion tanks in the Israeli Defense Force had outshot their Soviet-supplied Egyptian counterparts.

Israel attracted a good deal of international odium by invading Lebanon in 1982. British prime minister **Margaret Thatcher** was not a vocal critic. She was an admirer of Jewish culture and a friend of the chief rabbi in Britain. Only during the premiership of her successor, **John Major**, was there more overt criticism of Israeli policy in the Occupied Territories, notably by a junior **Foreign and Commonwealth Office (FCO)** minister, David Mellor, while on a visit to the Gaza Strip in the 1990s. Such criticism got nowhere with Begin's successor, Yitzhak Shamir (prime minister, 1983–1984, 1986–1992). He, like Begin, had been a member of Irgun Zvai Leumi, and then of the even more extreme Stern Gang, which was responsible for the assassination of the British politician Lord Moyne in 1944. The U.S. secretary of state, James Baker, got British support in 1991 for an international conference aimed at bringing Middle Eastern peace based on UN Resolution 242, but Shamir sabotaged it. He agreed to take part but later admitted that his plan was to drag talks out for 10 years. Shamir stood down as Likud leader after losing the 1993 election to Labour.

Later, under the leadership of Yitzhak Rabin (prime minister, 1992–1995), Israel began to adopt a more conciliatory policy. Israeli recognition of the Palestine Liberation Organization as the representative of the Palestinian people won British approval in 1994. It was a profound shock when Rabin was assassinated by a far-right Jewish extremist in 1995. Thereafter, Israeli governments took on a more right-wing hard-line perspective under Benjamin Netanyahu (1996–1999), Ehud Barak (1999–2001), and Ariel Sharon (2001–2006). Barak was prepared to make concessions about the status of Jerusalem, but he was voted out of office as a result. In Britain, the government of **Tony Blair** favored a two-track policy, whereby there would be a separate Palestinian state. Military pragmatism caused Sharon to withdraw Israeli troops from Gaza in August 2005, which split his party, Likud. Sharon set up a new party, Kadima, before being immobilized by a stroke in 2006. British governments continued to be critical of Israeli policy in the West Bank, where the number of Israeli settlements increased by the year, although they were illegal under international law.

The complexities of Israeli policy caused the British government some difficulty from 2009–2011, when Netanyahu was again prime minister. This was linked to the Gaza War of 2008–2009, caused by the firing of missiles by the Hamas terrorist group in Gaza into Israel. Israel invaded, and many civilians died. Its then-foreign minister, Tzipi Livni, had an arrest warrant for war crimes issued against her in a British court in December 2009. Livni called off a visit to Britain, much to the embarrassment of the FCO. British foreign secretary **David Miliband** (2007–2010) indicated that the British government would not allow such harassment of Israeli officials. Livni was out of office at the time and so not covered by diplomatic immunity. She did visit Britain in 2011, and was protected from possible prosecution by a special certificate issued by the new foreign secretary, **William Hague**. British law remained in a state of flux about alleged war criminals.

Despite those underlying tensions, Britain and Israel maintained reasonable relations. Hague visited Israel in November 2010, and bilateral trade amounted to £3.75 billion ($6 billion) in 2011. There were problems regarding the importation of Palestinian products from the West Bank into Britain, but, in 2012, the British ambassador, Matthew Gould, spoke about how attempts to boycott Israeli goods had little impact on bilateral trade.

ITALY. Like other European countries, Great Britain had the imprint of Roman civilization firmly upon it long before the legions left forever in A.D. 410. The eventual collapse of the Roman Empire meant that a unitary Italian state would cease to exist until 1870. While England was evolving a primitive diplomatic service, it had to deal with such individual Italian states as Venice, Genoa, Florence, Naples, and the Papal States. To quote the Austrian statesman Prince von Metternich, Italy itself was a "geographical expression," ruled variously by Spaniards, the French, Austrians, Byzantines, and Arabs. The French Revolutionary Wars (1792–1802) and **Napoleonic Wars** (1799–1815) brought about a massive transformation. French administration was more efficient, and French despotism encouraged Italian nationalism. In 1814–1815, the European Great Powers ignored this national feeling when the Napoleonic Wars ended. Reactionary Austria was in charge in northern Italy. The Papacy ruled in much of Central Italy. The Kingdom of Naples and the Kingdom of the Two Sicilies dominated the South, a byword for reaction and oppression.

Despite all this, the Italians, although strongly attached to localities, began to develop a desire for self-government, which was generally supported by successive British governments. There were revolts in the northern state of Piedmont and the southern kingdom of Naples in 1820 and 1821. Further revolts took place in 1831, stimulated by secret societies and led by Giuseppe Mazzini, one of modern Italy's founding fathers. The cataclysm of 1848 threatened the authority of all Italian states. Remarkably, there was even the liberal Pope Pius IX (1846–1878), who was so unnerved by the nationalist uprisings that he abandoned liberalism. Britain's **foreign secretary**, Lord **Henry John Palmerston**, favored reform in the Papal States and opposed Austrian desire to intervene against it. Britain made it known that it would also discourage other states from intervening; however, as ever, there was no intention of sending British redcoats to fight in Italy. British policy was to cheer on Italian liberals from the sidelines. Britons were pleased by Piedmontise victories in 1848, as they tried to free Lombardy and Venetia from Austrian rule. When Austria reversed these victories, Britain would not intervene in 1849.

Ten years passed. In 1859, the great Piedmontise statesman Count Camillo di Cavour found **France** a willing ally against Austria. Palmerston, now prime minister, and his foreign secretary, Lord John Russell, feared too much French influence in northern Italy, although they wanted Austria out. Austria was defeated by the Franco-Piedmontese in 1859, and Piedmont gained Lombardy, less than it had hoped for. The situation was then transformed by the appearance of the great romantic nationalist hero Giuseppe Garibaldi, the third of Italy's founding fathers. Garibaldi was tremendously popular among all classes in Britain (he visited in 1862), as the number of public houses named after him shows. He landed in Sicily in 1860, with his "Thousand Redshirts," and defeated the Neapolitan forces there. Russell was converted to Garibaldi's cause, which was to end the tyranny of the kings of Naples. So important were Britain's diplomatic representatives Henry Elliot (in Naples) and Sir James Hudson (in Turin), that they immediately demonstrated how dramatically Russell could influence British foreign policy. Under their influence, Russell refused to agree to a French plan to convene a European conference to stop Garibaldi from crossing over the straits to mainland Italy. Other European powers risked Britain's opposition to any intervention. Russell adopted a classic British policy as its foreign secretary (1859–1865). He stated that Britain would adopt any position to assist Italian unification, which did not clash with British vital interests. He knew that Prime Minister Palmerston shared this view.

Garibaldi did cross the straits with his Redshirts, and the Kingdom of Naples was conquered. Rather late in the day, 600 British volunteers arrived to help Garibaldi. They spent too much time overindulging on cheap Italian wine, but the gesture was significant. On 27 October 1860, Russell stated that Britain would support the union of Naples with the Kingdom of Piedmont under its king, Victor Emanuel II. Russell became wildly popular in Italy. Garibaldi, a republican, was less happy. In 1861, all of Italy, apart from Rome and Austrian Venetia, united with Piedmont. The British role in this achievement was important, although no British blood had been shed (the volunteers did no real fighting). The unification process continued in 1866, when Austria was forced to give up Venetia. Rome followed in 1870, when a French garrison protecting the pope was withdrawn. Successive popes refused to recognize the new Italian state. Victor Emanuel II was king of Italy.

Anglo–Italian relations after 1870 followed a less glamorous path. Italy joined the Triple Alliance with **Germany** and Austria-Hungary in 1882, but there were no obvious areas of dispute between Britain and the new state. Indeed, Britain encouraged Italy to acquire a colonial empire in North Africa. In 1887, Prime Minister Lord Salisbury (1886–1892) sponsored the 1887 Mediterranean Agreement, whereby both powers recognized one another's rights in that sea. Austria-Hungary, not Britain, was Italy's natural enemy, but animosity toward France, a more successful colonial power, made a German alliance important. Britain did not object when Italy conquered **Libya** in 1912. In many ways, an alliance with Britain was attractive to the Italians. When **World War I** broke out in 1914, Italy was not immediately involved, but Britain and France could bribe her more effectively than Germany and Austria-Hungary. The secret Treaty of London in April 1915 promised Italy the Brenner Pass, Trieste (both belonged to Austria), and land along the Dalmatian Coast. Colonial territory was also promised in Africa and Asia Minor (modern **Turkey**). On 23 May 1915, Italy entered the war as Britain's ally. It was a costly struggle for the Italians along a frontier with Austria-Hungary where the enemy had the advantage of high ground. Britain tried to help in a small way, and a force was sent to help. One of its officers was **Hugh Dalton,** a future **Foreign Office** minister and chancellor of the exchequer in British Labour governments. The Italians suffered a devastating defeat at the hands of both the Germans and Austrians at Caporetto in 1917, but recovery followed. Substantial Anglo–French aid secured a decisive victory at Vittorio Veneto, and, on 4 November 1918, the Austrians asked for a cease-fire. The war resulted in 700,000 Italian casualties. The postwar settlement disappointed Italy. The **Treaty of Versailles** did not give it what it expected under the terms of the Treaty of London. The colonial gains were modest, and much wrangling was needed to get Trieste back from **Yugoslavia.**

Disillusionment with the peace settlement was certainly a factor in the rise to power of the Fascist dictator Benito Mussolini (1922–1943). He posed as the defender of Italy against Communism and had his admirers in Britain. One of them in the early days was **Winston Churchill,** who went on record as saying that had he been Italian, he would have supported Mussolini. Disillusionment later set in. The dictator had a major success in 1929, when the Lateran Treaty set up the Vatican state. In exchange, the Catholic Church recognized the Italian state. Mussolini's foreign policy was more low key in the

1920s, although he ludicrously tried to claim the **Nobel Peace Prize** for setting up the **Treaty of Locarno** (1925). It was true that Italy and Britain were guarantors of that treaty, by which Germany accepted its borders with France and **Belgium**. In the 1930s, Mussolini turned into an international braggart. He had been condescending to Hitler in 1934, and, in April 1935, he formed the Stresa Front with Britain and France. This was meant to stop Hitler from interfering in a much weakened, pro-Italian Austria. The British government was anxious to preserve good relations with Italy, seeing Mussolini as a possible counterweight to Hitler. This policy was undermined by Mussolini's invasion of **Ethiopia** in October 1935, which was deplored by the British. British foreign secretary **Sir Samuel Hoare** had to resign for appearing to take a pro-Italian line. His successor was **Anthony Eden** (1935–1938), who disliked Mussolini and his policies. This brought him into conflict with Prime Minister **Neville Chamberlain**, who still saw Mussolini as a potential friend. Eden resigned over Italian policy in February 1938.

Mussolini was able to pose as a European statesman at the **Munich Agreement** in September 1938. An attempt to lure him away from his new ally, Hitler, failed in January 1939. Mussolini and his foreign minister, Count Galeazzo Ciano, regarded Chamberlain and his foreign minister, **Lord Halifax,** as effete defenders of a newly defunct **British Empire**. Chamberlain could only deplore Italy's invasion of tiny Albania in April 1939. Only the fact that his armed forces were so weak kept Mussolini out of **World War II** until June 1940. He had grandiose plans but also a new tough opponent in Winston Churchill. According to fascist propaganda, the Mediterranean was "our sea," but this was a delusion. The Italian fleet was routed at Cape Matapan in 1940, and the army driven out of **Egypt** by much smaller British forces. German assistance was needed in North Africa. On 28 October 1940, another catastrophic Italian adventure started in **Greece**. Mussolini's invasion failed, and Hitler again had to be summoned to his aid. A share in occupied Yugoslavia was a sop to Italian pride. Britain, too, was defeated in Greece, and Crete in 1941, but it was always able to defeat the Italians if they lacked German help. By 1943, Mussolini was, in his own words, the "most hated man" in Italy. Churchill saw Italy as a weak reed and a chance for an easy success. He persuaded the **United States** to launch a joint invasion of Sicily, prior to invading the mainland. While the Italian campaign proved to be much tougher than Churchill expected, it did bring down Mussolini on 25 July 1943, as his own colleagues turned on him. Germany refused to accept the defeat of its fascist ally. Britain recognized the new Italian government, but it had no power with Germans in Northern and Central Italy. Mussolini was rescued by German parachutists, and he became the puppet ruler of the so-called "Republic of Salo." A hard, grinding campaign to conquer Italy showed that Churchill's hope that the country would be a "soft underbelly" of the fascist–Nazi alliance was misconceived.

Mussolini was captured by Communist partisans while attempting to flee into Switzerland. He was executed on 28 April 1945. Some 200,000 Italians had been involved in the Resistance to fascism. They were assisted by the British **Special Operations Executive**. Britain and its allies were in a difficult position where postwar Italy was concerned. Italy had been an enemy (1940–1943), but it had also technically been an ally during the last two years of World War II. This may account for the relatively lenient treatment of those associated with the former fascist regime. The chief victim was King Victor Emanuel III (1900–1946). He had helped Mussolini to power in 1922, but he also helped to eject him in 1943. The Italian monarchy, tarnished by its links with fascism, was abolished by a referendum on 2 June 1946. Traditional British sympathy was seen in the decision to waive any reparations (the United States did the same). This helped in the recovery of a war-torn country.

Immediate postwar Italian politics were dominated by Alcide de Gasperi as prime minister (1948–1953). He was a great supporter of the ideal of European unity, which the British encouraged from a distance. Like the United States, Britain feared that the powerful Italian Communist Party might seize power. It supported de Gasperi's Christian Democrat (CD) Party as a **Cold War** ally. De Gasperi had to preside over the postwar territorial settlement as it affected Italy. In February 1947, it lost Dalmatia, Istria, and Fiume to Yugoslavia and its colonies in Africa. The thorny issue of Trieste was not settled until 5 October 1954, when it returned to Italian control. The agreement between Italy and Yugoslavia was brokered by British foreign secretary Anthony Eden (1951–1955). He regarded the agreement as a classic example of effective British diplomacy. Yet, Eden opposed British entry into the **European Coal and Steel Community (ECSC)** in 1951, as well as the **European Economic Community (EEC)** in 1957. Italy joined both organizations and continued to hope that Britain would alter its policy. Both states were members of the **North Atlantic Treaty Organization (NATO)**, founded in 1949.

The other major figure in Italian politics was Aldo Moro (prime minister, 1963–1968, 1974–1976). His career was notable for two things. Moro recognized the need to bring the Italian Communist Party, which had much support by the early 1970s, into government. He did not achieve this, but he was behind the so-called "historic compromise," an agreement that managed to keep the Communists from opposing CD measures in Parliament. The end of Moro's career was tragic. This was an era of urban **terrorism** in Italy, and Moro was its most high-profile victim. On 16 March 1978, he was kidnapped by the notorious Red Brigades. They wanted an exchange of prisoners, but when the government would not agree to this, Moro was murdered on 9 May.

British prime minister **James Callaghan** (1976–1979) could empathize, as Britain had its own problems with the Provisional Irish Republican Army. His successor, **Margaret Thatcher** (1979–1970), was, according to a Foreign Office official, extraordinarily ignorant about Italian politics and history before her appointment as prime minister in 1979.

Anglo–Italian relations had no obvious pitfalls. Both states had been members of the EEC since Britain finally joined in 1973. Italy tended to see Britain as a useful counterweight to Franco–German domination in the community. It also ceased to be a net contributor to the EEC when Britain joined. The Italians were not, however, part of the ongoing wrangle between Thatcher and the French and Germans over EEC affairs. They were gratified in 1987, when, during the Thatcher era, Italy's national income per head passed that of Britain. Abroad, Italy, like Britain, was a participant in the **Gulf War** of 1991, when Giulio Andreotti was prime minister for the fourth time (1989–1992). Italy was firmly embedded into the Western Alliance system.

This continuity contrasted with what was happening at home. In 1992–1993, the Italian political establishment imploded. CD support nosedived to only 10 percent as a result of persistent scandals about mafia links, and the Socialists decreased to 2 percent. Instead, a right-wing alliance led by Silvio Berlusconi (prime minister 1994–1996, 2001–2006), which included a neofascist party, won power. A turbulent period followed, with center-left governments in power, before Berlusconi returned to power in 2001. He was a firm ally of British prime minister **Tony Blair** and U.S. President **George H. W. Bush** during the war in **Iraq** in March 2003. Berlusconi needed foreign friends, as he was constantly embroiled in domestic scandals. In April 2006, he was ejected from power after parliamentary elections, and between 17 May and 21 February, Romano Prodi's government was in power. Prodi's term as prime minister ended with his resignation, but he was asked to form a second administration, which survived until 24 January 2008. Italy then became enmeshed in the **European Union (EU)** financial crisis. Berlusconi returned to power after the 2008 general elections. Surrounded once again by sex scandals, he was unable to deal with Italy's financial crisis. Italy signed the December 2011 EU treaty agreeing to budgetary constraints, but, by 2012, it had to appoint a government of technocrats under Mario Monti. The British government, under **David Cameron** (2010–), refused to sign the new EU treaty, and there was much criticism in Britain in 2012 of how Italy had ceased to be a real democracy. The Italians, by contrast, seemed relieved to have stability under Monti. There had also been a clear difference over foreign policy in 2011 regarding the war in Libya. As the former colonial power, Italy would not join Anglo–French action against the dictatorship of Muammar al-Gaddafi. It did, however, allow NATO aircraft to use its airfields en route to bomb Libya. The difference was a rare one in the history of Anglo–Italian relations since World War II.

J

JAMESON RAID (1896). The Jameson Raid was a daring but unsuccessful raid into the Transvaal led by Doctor Storm Jameson, an associate of Cecil Rhodes, the great British imperialist, in 1896. The raid was a disaster and merely contributed to a worsening of Anglo–Boer relations. *See also* SOUTH AFRICA.

JAPAN. The Japanese imperial monarchy, which had modernized itself in the 19th century, with British assistance, made a formal alliance with Great Britain in 1902. This was aimed at **Russia**, which seemed to be a threat to both powers in the Pacific. The British assisted Japan during the Russo–Japanese War of 1904–1905, by closing the Suez Canal to Russian warships. This forced the cumbersome Russian Baltic Fleet to sail around Africa before meeting its end off the Japanese islands. Britain and Japan remained allies from 1902–1922, when U.S. pressure forced the British to reluctantly abandon the 1902 Anglo–Japanese Friendship Treaty. The Americans were concerned about the growing Japanese naval presence in the Pacific, and Britain regarded friendship with the **United States** as a priority. The 1921–1922 **Washington Naval Conference** determined that Britain, the United States, and Japan could build warships at the ratio of 5:5:3. These were ships weighing more than 10,000 tons, and the Japanese felt aggrieved by that treatment. By the 1930s, Japanese policy had taken on an aggressive, militaristic posture, starting with the invasion of Manchuria in 1931. This was a Chinese province, and there was strong sympathy for **China** in the Far Eastern Department of the **Foreign Office**. Neither Britain nor the United States felt able to do anything more than protest Japanese behavior. The British were severely understrength in the Far Eastern theater, and they put undue reliance on their Singapore naval base. When Japan attacked Britain's imperial possessions in Burma, Malaya, **Hong Kong**, and Singapore in 1941–1942, they fell with alarming ease. The surrender of Singapore in February 1942 was a particular humiliation for the British. Recovery came largely through U.S. efforts in the Pacific, although the British 14th Army did recover Burma in 1944–1945. After Japan's surrender in August 1945, the task of administering it was undertaken entirely by the United States, demonstrating the change in the balance of power in the Pacific.

Although Britain was not to be involved in the occupation and governance of Japan, it did have some concerns. There was strong feeling in Britain about the role of Emperor Hirohito (1926–1989), for example, in **World War II**. In 1945, the newly elected Labour member of Parliament, **James Callaghan**, a future prime minister, devoted his first speech in the House of Commons to the subject of getting rid of Hirohito. In the end, the Foreign Office decided to support the U.S. decision to preserve Hirohito in the interest of stability. This angered **Australia**, which had put Hirohito seventh on a list of 64 Japanese war criminals. War criminals continued to be a controversial issue in Britain. There was also anger in Australia and **New Zealand** about the use of defeated Japanese troops in a law and order function in **Indochina** and the Dutch East Indies. This was caused by a shortage of British, French, and Dutch troops on the ground. Another issue was the question of adequate compensation for abused British and **British Commonwealth** prisoners of war. A modest settlement had been agreed in 1951, and Japan caused resentment, especially when it became prosperous, by refusing to budge on the issue, nor would it show any sign of contrition over atrocities committed in the 1930s and 1940s by its armed forces, for example, the infamous Nanjing Massacre in 1937 in China.

The **Cold War** actually assisted in Japan's postwar recovery. It was a base for American and other forces in the **Korean War** (1950–1953). British involvement with Japan was largely confined to matters concerning trade and commerce. Japan was in a state of devastation in August 1945, but, with U.S. assistance, it made a spectacular recovery. The automobile industry offered a spectacular example. In the 1950s, Japan could not challenge the domination in markets of British makes like Morris and Austin. Yet, by 1970, the country was producing 5 million cars and undercutting Western models. In 1990, less than 50 years since World War II, Japanese car manufacturers were making reverse agreements to move their technology westward. Rover in Birmingham was a British example, which was linked up with Honda. Japan was also able to improve on Western camera and machine-tool technology. In contrast, Britain had constant problems in the 1970s and 1980s in getting access to Japanese markets because of their bureaucracy and obstructive protectionist policies.

Conversely, Japan gained from its absence of defense spending for much of the postwar period. Japan was dependent on the United States through the 1951 Japan–U.S. Security Pact, and it had no armed forces for years. In 1960, a revision of the agreement made the Americans responsible for defending Japan, while its forces were now subject to Japanese law. The slow evolution of Japanese defense forces saved the state a great deal of money and assisted in economic recovery. In 1983, the average Briton was paying $439 a year toward defense costs. The average Japanese citizen paid just $98. Unlike Japan, under the governments of **Harold Macmillan** (1957–1963) and **Harold Wilson** (1964–1970, 1974–1976), Britain had no proper corporate strategy. Japan was not a key player in British diplomacy but did broadly support the British position in the opening stages of the **Suez Crisis** (1956). After the Yom Kippur War of 1973, Japan adopted the same Middle Eastern policy as Britain, but for different reasons. Britain was critical of **Israel's** permanent occupation of the West Bank and the other Occupied Territories. Japan opposed Israeli policy because it was dependent on Arab oil producers. It thus showed a rare independence in rejecting U.S. views on Israeli policy.

At home, Japan was dominated from 1946–1998 by the Liberal Democratic Party (LDP). This apparently unhealthy dominance was not as serious as it might appear. The Japanese government was neither dictatorial nor authoritarian, if prone to corruption. For many years, foreign policy was operated under the doctrine laid down by Shigeru Yoshida (prime minister, 1946–1954). This emphasized Japan's neutrality and rejection of war and belligerency under Article 9 of its 1947 constitution. The Yoshida Doctrine was kept in place by prime ministers Hayato Ikeda (1960–1964) and Eisaku Sato (1964–1972). Thereafter, it was a story of stability under the LDP, with growth rates at an average of 6 percent in the 1970s and 1980s. Prime Minister Yasurhiro Nakasone (1982–1987) tried to open up Japanese markets to British and other foreign imports but failed. He also broke away from the postwar Japanese tradition by expanding the military. The fruits of this change were seen in 2003, when Japanese troops were sent to support the Anglo–Americans in **Iraq**. This was during the premiership of Junichiro Koizumi (2001–2006), who effectively abandoned Japan's pacifist tradition. The nuclear threat from North Korea, which also alarmed successive British governments, caused Japan's parliament to change the constitution. Japanese servicemen were no longer banned from serving abroad.

The royal families of Britain and Japan have remained close, even when Hirohito was threatened with exposure as a war criminal. In 1971, Hirohito visited Britain, where there were protests by former servicemen. **Queen Elizabeth II** went to Japan in 1975. Hirohito's successor, Akihito (1989–present), visited Britain in 1998 and 2007. In 2011, Britain sent special dog rescue teams to Japan to assist after the terrible Fukushima earthquake. Relations remain cordial, despite remaining issues about Japanese conduct during World War II. The **Foreign and Commonwealth Office** emphasized the closeness of Anglo–Japanese relations in 2011.

JAY, MICHAEL (1946–). Michael Jay became permanent undersecretary at the **Foreign and Commonwealth Office (FCO)** on 14 January 2002, and he retired from the FCO on 21 July 2006. He was thus in post at the height of the wars in **Afghanistan** and **Iraq**. His earlier career was somewhat unusual in that he moved from the Overseas Development Department to the FCO after 11 years (1969–1981). Thereafter, he was a counselor in the Paris embassy (1987–1990), before becoming ambassador there from 1996–2001. While serving as permanent undersecretary, Jay did the spadework in setting up the 2005 Gleneagles Summit in Scotland, and he acted as Prime Minister **Tony Blair's** personal representative. The day after the summit opened on 7 July 2005, London suffered terrible **terrorist** bombings, in which 52 people died. After his retirement from the FCO, Jay was created Baron Jay of Ewelme on 18 September 2006.

JEBB, SIR GLADWYN (1900–1996). A classic **Foreign Office** entrant who was educated at **Eton College** and Magdalene College, Oxford, Gladwyn Jebb entered the Foreign Office in 1924. He subsequently served in the British embassy in **Iran**, before being appointed private secretary to the Labour undersecretary at the Foreign Office, **Hugh Dalton**. This appointment lasted from 1929–1931. Jebb then served in Rome until 1935, during the heyday of the fascist government of Benito Mussolini. Thereafter, he served in senior positions in the Foreign Office in London from 1935–1950. Although he is critical of **appeasement** in his memoirs, Jebb was not so in the 1930s, as the documentary record reveals. In 1944–1945, Jebb played a significant role in establishing the **United Nations (UN)** Secretariat, which helped get the organization on its feet. From 1946–1948, Jebb was undersecretary at the Foreign Office, under **Ernest Bevin**, the new Labour **foreign secretary**, with whom he got along well. He and other Foreign Office officials took part in singing the choruses of popular songs, which Bevin enjoyed crooning in his suite after dinner. During this period, Jebb had special responsibility for the treaties with such former enemy powers such **Italy, Bulgaria**, and Romania. He also dealt firsthand with Soviet foreign minister Vyacheslav Molotov, who was notorious for his suspicion of the Western powers. In 1950–1951, Jebb served as Britain's permanent representative at the UN with such effectiveness that at one point American polls showed him to be second only to Bob Hope in popularity. This was because Jebb was able to disclose in a speech the attempts by the Russian president of the UN Security Council to remove its previous condemnation of North Korean aggression in June 1950. He continued his stint at the UN until 1954, when he was appointed Britain's ambassador in Paris. While in Paris, Jebb was able to form a good working relationship with President Charles de Gaulle when the latter returned to power in 1958. In his post, Jebb became convinced that Britain's future must lie with the **European Economic Community,** which had come into existence on 1 January 1958. Jebb retired from the Paris embassy and the **Foreign and Commonwealth Office** in 1960. He was created Baron Gladwyn.

JEROME, JENNIE (1854–1921). A famous beauty and the daughter of a rich American businessman, Leonard Jerome, Jennie Jerome was the mother of **Winston Churchill.** She had married Lord Randolph Churchill, a future chancellor of the exchequer, after a whirlwind romance. Lord Randolph was the son of the Duke of Marlborough, a descendant of the great 18th-century British general John Churchill. Tragically, he died young in 1895, leaving his widow, Jennie, and his son, Winston, with a strong sense that his work as a Conservative reformer be continued. Jennie used her links with the aristocratic and political establishment to further Winston's career, as he was the first to acknowledge. In old age, Jennie had a leg amputated after gangrene set in after a fall resulted in a broken leg. This followed a third marriage at the age of 64. Winston was always acutely aware of his American heritage, which he used to strengthen Anglo–American relations.

JOHNSON, LYNDON BAINES (1905–1973). A formidable domestic politician from Texas, Lyndon B. Johnson became president of the **United States** when **John F. Kennedy** was assassinated in Johnson's home state on 22 November 1963. Johnson did not have the close family ties with Great Britain of his predecessor, but he professed admiration for Britain's doughty resistance to Nazism in **World War II.** Still, relations with British prime ministers remained problematic. He had little in common with the old Etonian aristocrat and former **foreign secretary Sir Alec Douglas-Home,** nor were relations between him and Home's successor **Harold Wilson,** who became prime minister in October 1964, any easier. Wilson had been a big admirer of Kennedy, but he could not be induced by an increasingly angry Johnson to make a military commitment in the **Vietnam War.** Rumor had it that Johnson would have settled for a symbolic band of Scots bagpipers, but Wilson, sensing domestic outrage, would not be tempted.

There was some Anglo–American cooperation, notably over the creation of an Atlantic Nuclear Force in December 1964. Johnson also agreed to support the vulnerable pound sterling when Wilson unwisely refused to devalue the currency until 1967. Johnson was again angered by the British decision on 16 January 1968 to withdraw all forces from the Far East (save **Hong Kong**) on 31 March 1971. Economic reality gave Wilson little choice, but Johnson felt betrayed, believing that Britain had left the United States to be a global policeman. Johnson, with an impressive record of domestic achievement, was left to rue the Vietnam legacy.

JOINT INTELLIGENCE COMMITTEE (JIC). The Joint Intelligence Committee (JIC) is an important body in Whitehall. It is a subcommittee of the Chiefs of Staff Committee, the Chiefs of Staff of Britain's Armed Forces being an integral part of defense planning. In many instances, the JIC has produced invaluable intelligence appraisals for the British government. In February 1947, for example, at the height of **Cold War** anxiety on both sides of the Atlantic, the JIC produced a perceptive and invaluable report on Soviet future intentions. The committee correctly took the view that the Soviet Union would not engage in a major war in the next five years. The experience of the JIC at the time of the **Iraq War** in 2003 was not as happy. There were suggestions that it had been improperly pressured by **Tony Blair's** government.

JONES, THOMAS (1870–1955). A Welshman, Thomas Jones was a civil servant and close ally of **David Lloyd George**, and later of another prime minister, **Stanley Baldwin**. Jones was deputy secretary to the Cabinet from 1916–1930, and a leading member of the so-called "Cliveden Set," which met at **Nancy Astor's** country house in Berkshire. It is now accepted that the Cliveden group had much less influence on government policy than was once thought. Jones went with Lloyd George on his ill-advised visit to see Adolf Hitler in 1936. He became disillusioned with **appeasement** in 1938. Jones produced an influential diary entitled *A Diary with Letters* in 1954, which covered the period from 1931–1950.

JORDAN. Often referred to in the 1940s as Transjordan, this small Arab kingdom has played a pivotal role in the politics of the Middle East. A greater Jordan, which included Arab Jerusalem, emerged from the first Arab–Israeli War of 1948–1949. Its king, Abdullah, of the Hashemite dynasty, was assassinated in 1951, and his son, Talal, had to be replaced after a year because he suffered a complete nervous breakdown. Thus it was that the 17-year-old King Hussein came to the throne. He was to dominate the postwar history of his small kingdom.

Hussein had strong links to Great Britain, being educated at Harrow School and the Royal Military Academy Sandhurst. A British officer, Sir John Glubb, commanded the Arab legion, the well-disciplined force that emerged with credit from the war of 1948–1949. Glubb's sacking by Hussein in February 1956 infuriated British prime minister **Anthony Eden**, who wrongly assumed that President **Jamal Abd al Nasser** of **Egypt** was behind it. In reality, it was an attempt by Hussein to free himself of the influence of the much older Glubb. He also closed down Britain's bases in the country. Jordan was not directly involved in the **Suez Crisis** of 1956, but it faced a real crisis from 1967–1971. Together with its allies Egypt and Syria, Jordan was defeated in the 1967 Six-Day War. As a result, it lost Arab Jerusalem and the West Bank of the River Jordan.

In the aftermath of this catastrophic Arab defeat, the Palestine Liberation Front (PLF) set up bases in Jordan, which threatened the authority of the Hashemite dynasty. Hussein used his army to smash the PLF. He stayed out of the Yom Kippur War in 1973. A persistent problem remained, and, by 1988, there were still 750,000 Palestinian refugees in Jordan, many of whom had been displaced from their homes in 1948–1949. Most had been integrated into Jordanian society, but 200,000 remained in camps. The unsettled **Palestine** problem (the Arab states refused to recognize **Israel**) put pressure on Hussein to adopt radical positions. British influence and aid had largely disappeared. Hussein supported the dictatorial regime of Saddam Hussein in the war with **Iran** from 1980–1988. He also refused to join the coalition against **Iraq** in the **Gulf War** of 1991, a decision that left Jordan dangerously isolated. It was this, perhaps, that persuaded him to sign a peace treaty with Israel in 1994. The Hashemite monarchy experimented with a degree of democracy, with multiparty elections being held in 1993. This may have saved it from the fierce revolutionary protests in the Arab world in the spring of 2011. Protests took place, but the monarchy was not endangered.

KELLOGG–BRIAND PACT (1928). The Kellogg–Briand Pact, a multilateral pact signed in Paris on 27 August 1928, was named after the U.S. secretary of state in the Calvin Coolidge administration, Frank B. Kellogg, and French foreign minister Aristide Briand. Briand had been instrumental in creating the **Treaty of Locarno** in 1925. The pact was designed to outlaw war as an instrument of national policy and signed by representatives of **Australia, Canada, Germany,** Great Britain, and the Irish Free State. The Kellogg–Briand Pact failed in its objective of preventing war, but it did influence later thinking, which was subsumed in the **United Nations** Charter, about preventing aggression in the international system.

KENNEDY, JOHN FITZGERALD (1917–1963). Despite his Irish background, John F. Kennedy had strong links with Great Britain, both personal and political. They were to be significant when he became president of the **United States** in January 1961. His sister, Kathleen, married the Marquis of Hartington (both died during **World War II**), and his father, **Joseph P. Kennedy,** was U.S. ambassador at the Court of St. James. Kennedy briefly attended the London School of Economics and wrote an undergraduate thesis entitled *While England Slept*, a critique of British **appeasement** policy. It was published in 1940. This background was valuable for Kennedy in his conduct of U.S.–British relations when he became president, and he rapidly established a close relationship with British prime minister **Harold Macmillan.** This was aided by the British ambassador in Washington, David Ormsby-Gore (later **Lord Harlech**), to whom Kennedy was also distantly related.

Kennedy supported Macmillan's efforts to get Britain into the **European Economic Community** from 1961–1963. He also had a "Grand Design" for the United States and Europe, supposedly about copartnership, but, in reality, giving primacy to the United States. The problem of British dependence on U.S. nuclear technology was reiterated when the Kennedy administration cancelled the Skybolt missile. Anglo–American relations were at a low ebb when Kennedy met Macmillan at Nassau, in the Bahamas, in December 1962. Kennedy had found Macmillan a loyal ally during the **Cuban Missile Crisis** of October 1962, and the older man supported the concept of the **Nuclear Test Ban Treaty,** which was signed in August 1963.

The British people joined in the mourning for the fallen president on 22 November 1963. In May 1965, a memorial to Kennedy was dedicated at Runnymede, in Surrey, where the Magna Carta had been signed in 1215.

KENNEDY, JOSEPH PATRICK (1888–1969). A successful businessman and supporter of President **Franklin D. Roosevelt,** Joseph P. Kennedy was the father of President **John F. Kennedy** and ambassador in London from 1938–1940. Kennedy was a strong supporter of the **appeasement** policy of British prime minister **Neville Chamberlain.** At the time of the **Munich Agreement** in September 1938, President Roosevelt also appeared to endorse Chamberlain's policy toward **Germany.** Events changed this perspective, but Kennedy did not move with them. He caused great offense in the summer of 1940 by suggesting that Great Britain was finished and would soon be occupied by the Germans. Kennedy also opposed **Winston Churchill's** requests for military equipment and supplies during the Battle of Britain. His subsequent withdrawal as U.S. ambassador was welcomed on all sides in Britain.

KEYNES, JOHN MAYNARD (1883–1946). The most well-known British economist of the 20th century, John Maynard Keynes played key roles in the events following **World War I** and **World War II.** In 1919, Keynes was a member of the British delegation at the **Paris Peace Conference,** from which he resigned to write a famous polemic against the **Treaty of Versailles** entitled *The Economic Consequences of the Peace* (1919). It was fiercely critical of the punitive reparations policy of the Allied Powers against **Germany.**

While based at King's College, Cambridge, Keynes was later associated with the theory of "deficit spending," which advocated that governments should spend their way out of recession through public works schemes, which would stimulate demand. This was controversial in the 1930s, when economic theory dictated that budgets should be balanced and recession dealt with by cuts in public expenditure. After 1945, Keynes was the dominant voice in British financial policy for 30 years. It was he who achieved the financial settlement with the **United States** in 1946 that obtained a massive loan at a time when the demands of World War II meant that Britain had overseas debts of £3,355 million, making it the largest debtor nation in the world. It is said that the strain of the Anglo–American negotiations for the loan in 1945–1946 killed Keynes. It was his last service to his country. He was created Baron Keynes. *See also* BRETTON WOODS AGREEMENT.

KIRKPATRICK, SIR IVONE (1897–1964). Born in **India,** Sir Ivone Kirkpatrick was a product of the Catholic public school Downside who went on to become permanent undersecretary at the **Foreign Office** from 1953–1957. He entered the Diplomatic Service in 1919, where he served in various foreign postings, most notably under **Sir Nevile Henderson** in Berlin in 1937–1938. Thereafter, he rose rapidly through the Foreign Office ranks, while also serving as United Kingdom high commissioner for **Germany** from 1950–1953.

Kirkpatrick's term as permanent undersecretary was most notable for the **Suez Crisis** of 1956, during which he, like Prime Minister **Anthony Eden**, was strongly in favor of military action against the Egyptian leader **Jamal Abd al Nasser**. Kirkpatrick did not exercise sufficient caution on Middle Eastern policy, and he encouraged the temperamental Eden to slide into excess, with catastrophic consequences.

KISSINGER, HENRY (1923–). Henry Kissinger came from German Jewish origins, and his family fled to the **United States** in the 1930s to escape Nazi persecution. He was a distinguished academic at Harvard University before becoming special assistant for national security affairs (1969–1973) and then secretary of state (1973–1977) under presidents **Richard Nixon** and Gerald Ford. Kissinger was an admirer of British prime minister **Edward Heath** (1970–1974), but he was disappointed by Heath's overtly pro-European stance, which downplayed the "**special relationship**" with the United States. Kissinger became noted for his shuttle diplomacy after the 1973 Yom Kippur War, which achieved a degree of stabilization in the Middle East. That same year, he was awarded the **Nobel Peace Prize**. He was heavily involved in the diplomacy designed to secure the U.S. withdrawal from Vietnam, and in normalizing U.S. relations with the People's Republic of China in 1971–1972. Despite some Anglo–U.S. tensions, Kissinger played a pivotal role in establishing a six-nation plan toward black majority rule in Britain's former colony, **Southern Rhodesia** (Zimbabwe), in 1980.

KOREAN WAR (1950–1953). On 25 June 1950, the forces of the Communist republic of North Korea crossed the 38th parallel into South Korea. This was a geographical line of latitude that delineated the border between the two Koreas, which had been under Japanese rule from 1910–1945. The North Korean invasion was almost certainly encouraged by Joseph Stalin, the leader of the Soviet Union. In response, the **United States** organized a coalition through the **United Nations** to assist South Korea. Great Britain, under its Labour prime minister, **Clement R. Attlee**, was a robust supporter of intervention, the British sending 63,000 men to fight in Korea by 1953. Attlee was alarmed when President **Harry S. Truman** appeared to be considering the use of atomic weapons when the People's Republic of China intervened in the conflict on 30 November 1950. The British prime minister flew to Washington to express his anxiety to Truman. An alarming feature of the crisis was that Britain had only recently sanctioned the stationing of B-29 bombers at U.S. air bases in Britain and assumed that it would be consulted about the use of atomic weapons being flown from those bases. Attlee was reassured; however, part of British public opinion was not. British forces served with distinction in Korea, notably the 29th Infantry Brigade, which mounted a heroic defense of the Imjin River from 22–25 April 1951. Britain lost 1,109 soldiers in the three-year conflict, which ended in a stalemate with Korea, still divided by the 38th parallel. It was unsatisfactory from the British point of view that Truman was only willing to keep America's allies informed about any future use of the bomb. *See also* FRANKS, SIR OLIVER; GAITSKELL, HUGH.

KOSOVO (1999). The province of Kosovo was the site of a historic defeat of the Serbs by the Ottoman Turks in 1389. It was a paradox, then, that the Serbs clung so fiercely to a province that, by 1998, was largely Albanian Muslim. At the time, the threat of "ethnic cleansing" by Serbian dictator Slobodan Milošević seemed real. Under Prime Minister **Tony Blair**, Great Britain was to be intimately involved in the Kosovo crisis. Britain's American allies noted that Blair was far more proactive in dealing with the Serbs than the previous Conservative government. He became persuaded that military intervention was needed against **Serbia**. His **foreign secretary, Robin Cook** (1997–2001), already had a deep commitment to the Balkans and its problems. On 23 March 1999, Blair told the House of Commons that failing to act on behalf of the Kosovo Albanians would be a breach of faith. He also let it be known that he considered Milošević to be a deeply evil man. His U.S. counterpart, President **Bill Clinton**, was unenthusiastic about intervention, but he was ultimately persuaded to allow U.S. aircraft to bomb Serbia as part of a **North Atlantic Treaty Organization (NATO)** operation. President Clinton was not willing to allow U.S. ground forces to take part. NATO air forces bombed Serbia intensively from 24 March to 11 June 1999. On the previous day, 10 June, Milošević agreed to withdraw his army from Kosovo, allowing a peacekeeping force, which now included U.S. forces, to enter the province under the NATO masthead.

The success of the Kosovo operation was a considerable coup for Blair, who was greeted as a hero by Albanians in Kosovo. Critics of his later record detected the beginnings of hubris in Blair, who allegedly became obsessed with interventionism as a solution to international problems. He certainly had not solved Kosovo's problems. In 1999, there were 200,000 refugees in Kosovo. Another 850,000 had fled over the province's border. A **United Nations (UN)** peacekeeping force (initially commanded by the British general Mike Jackson) had 19,000 British troops attached to it. The task of the UN force, known as KFOR (Kosovo Force) was to keep Albanians and the Serb minority separated. The presence of the UN force did at least allow free elections in Kosovo in 2000. They were won by the moderate Kosovo Democratic League, and Ibrahim Rugova became interim president. Albanian Kosovars wanted full independence. In 2007, a UN plan made provision for more autonomy, but Serbia bitterly opposed it. Kosovo declared its independence from Serbia on 17 February 2008, and Great Britain recognized its sovereignty on 18 February. A British embassy was established in the Kosovo capital of Pristina as early as 5 March 2008. Kosovo established its own embassy in London in October 2008. Serbia refused to accept full Kosovar sovereignty.

KYOTO PROTOCOL (1997). The Kyoto Protocol, agreed to in **Japan** in December 1997, was an addition to the **United Nations** Framework Convention on Climate Change. The treaty came into force on 16 February 2005, and was intended to reduce greenhouse gas emissions with targets for reduction set for state signatories of the treaty. Great Britain was an enthusiastic supporter of the treaty and one of the most committed nations with regard to dealing with global climate change. In contrast, the **United States** refused to ratify the treaty, thus seriously weakening its impact worldwide. Unusually, Prime Minister **Tony Blair** was at odds with President **George W. Bush** on this issue. President **Bill Clinton** had signed the treaty, but it could not be ratified because of opposition in the U.S. Senate.

L

LAWSON, NIGEL (1932–). One of **Margaret Thatcher's** chief aides, Nigel Lawson was chancellor of the exchequer from 1983–1989. Educated at Oxford University, Lawson began his career as a speechwriter for **Sir Alec Douglas-Home** in 1963–1964. He then spent a decade in journalism before becoming a Conservative member of Parliament in 1974. When the Tories returned to power in 1979, Lawson was variously financial secretary to the treasury (1979–1981) and then energy secretary (1981–1983). He replaced **Sir Geoffrey Howe** after the Conservative election victory in 1983. As chancellor in 1984, Lawson wanted to join the Exchange Rate Mechanism (ERM), but Thatcher opposed the move. Lawson countered by shadowing the value of the German deutschmark, in effect creating his own ERM at a parity of three deutschmarks to the pound. Lawson also sponsored a deregulation boom, which privatized state industries and elevated living standards. Conversely, it created a credit boom with debts from credit cards, bank overdrafts, and mortgages rising sharply from £43 billion in 1980 to £235 billion in 1987. This ultimately led to a recession, as Lawson failed to control the credit boom. Rising inflation, 10 percent by the autumn of 1990, was a symptom of this. By then, Lawson was gone, having resigned in November 1989, because of the alleged interference of Thatcher's financial advisor, Alan Walters. He was created Baron Lawson in 1992.

LEACH, SIR HENRY (1923–2011). Admiral of the British fleet, Sir Henry Leach was first sea lord at the British **Admiralty** at the time of the **Falklands War** in 1982. He had ascended through the Royal Navy since 1941, when His Majesty' ship, was sunk off the Malayan coast on 10 December. After distinguished war service, he became director of naval plans in 1968, and then assistant chief of naval staff and vice chief of defense staff by 1976. Leach was promoted to admiral in 1977, and first sea lord two years later.

His later career was a classic exposition of naval against political priorities. Leach opposed the cuts to the Royal Navy introduced by the British defense secretary, **John Nott**, in 1981–1982, which included the withdrawal of Britain's sole naval vessel in the South Atlantic. His robust advocacy of an expeditionary force when **Argentina** invaded the Falklands impressed **Mar-**

garet Thatcher, who much preferred admirals and generals to her political colleagues. Nott favored diplomacy over sending a task force some 8,000 miles away, but he was overruled. Leach disputed Nott's policy, even attempting to beard him in his **Ministry of Defense** office on 31 March 1982, while in full naval uniform. When Thatcher agreed to see Leach, she concurred with his analysis, and the task force was sent. Leach continued to fight naval reductions until his retirement in November 1982.

LEAGUE OF NATIONS. President **Woodrow Wilson's Fourteen Points** placed before to U.S. Congress on 8 January 1918 includes a 14th point that advocated a **League of Nations.** Enshrined in the **Treaty of Versailles,** the League of Nations Covenant was designed to preserve international peace. All sovereign states were entitled to become members, although **Germany** was not allowed to join until 1926, or the Soviet Union until 1934. The **United States** refused to ratify the Treaty of Versailles or join the League of Nations when the treaty was signed in June 1919. *See also* LLOYD GEORGE, DAVID.

LEND–LEASE ACT (1941). In 1940–1941, Great Britain was chronically short of war materials and equipment. The Lend–Lease Act of March 1941 permitted the **United States** to provide such goods to Allied states. It did so without breaking official American neutrality. The Lend–Lease Act was a result of lobbying by **Winston Churchill,** and it indicated where the sympathies of President **Franklin D. Roosevelt** lay. The aid provided continued to be crucial to Britain after the United States entered **World War II** on 7 December 1941. In all, $50 billion was allocated to the British and other Allied states during the war under Lend–Lease. Thousands of aircraft, vehicles, and ships, as well as thousands of tons of food, also flowed across the Atlantic.

LIBYA. The North African state of Libya was part of the Ottoman Turkish Empire from 1551–1911. The war of 1912 between the Ottomans and **Italy** resulted in Libya becoming an Italian colony. In 1939, Libya was directly incorporated into the Italian state by the Italian dictator Benito Mussolini. He had designs on British **Egypt,** but an Italian invasion from Libya was easily defeated by British forces in 1941. German forces, under Erwin Rommel, were sent to the Libyan desert in 1941, and they went on to capture the British base at Tobruk, before Axis Forces surrendered in 1943. Libya then came under British military rule. A newly democratic Italy renounced all claims to Libya in 1947, although Libya, under King Idris I (1947–1969), remained heavily dependent on Britain. The Labour prime minister, **Clement R. Attlee,** and his **foreign secretary, Ernest Bevin,** agreed that Britain must retain control of its military bases in eastern Libya. The country remained poor and lacked resources until vast oil deposits were found in 1959.

Belated attempts to modernize Libya resulted in the overthrow of Idris I on 1 September 1969, by military officers led by Muammar Gaddafi. He closed down foreign bases and rapidly became a rogue elephant in the international system. Britain had particular concern over Gaddafi's encouragement of the **Irish Republican Army (IRA)**. He regarded the IRA as an anticolonialist movement and supplied it with Semtex explosive and other sophisticated weapons. The British helped French customs officials seize the MV *Eksund* in 1987. The vessel was carrying £15 million in armaments to the IRA. Gaddafi's involvement in **terrorism** reached throughout Europe, and he ignored the norms of diplomacy. In 1984, British police constable Yvonne Fletcher was shot dead by a member of the Libyan embassy in St. James Square, London, while guarding the embassy against anti-Gaddafi demonstrators. Only in 2011 was the **Foreign and Commonwealth Office (FCO)** able to determine that the culprit had died in the interim. Gaddafi's government went on to antagonize the **United States** when a bomb planted by its agents in a Berlin nightclub killed several American servicemen in 1986.

President **Ronald Reagan** wanted to take retaliatory action by means of an air strike. The use of aircraft carriers off the Libyan coast was deemed perilous, and Reagan approached British prime minister **Margaret Thatcher** about flying U.S. F-111 bombers from bases in Britain. This presented Thatcher with something of a dilemma. She was on the record as saying that such strikes were against international law. Yet, she persuaded herself that Article 51 of the **United Nations (UN)** Charter, which had been used with Korea in 1950, could justify U.S. action. Leading members of the Thatcher Cabinet, including Foreign Secretary **Douglas Hurd** and the chancellor of the exchequer, **Nigel Lawson**, were reportedly horrified by the U.S. plan to bomb the Libyan capital of Tripoli. Thatcher insisted that the United States must be supported, even though the bombing in April 1986 was very unpopular in Britain. In fact, there was a decrease in Libyan terrorism after 1986. Thatcher used Gaddafi's involvement to justify U.S. action using British bases. Another crisis in Anglo–Libyan relations took place in December 1988. In this instance, Libyan agents were accused of bombing Pan Am Flight 103 over Lockerbie, in Scotland, when hundreds died, both on the ground and in the air. Scotland had its own legal jurisdiction, but, as this was clearly a case of terrorism, the case against two Libyans was tried by Scottish judges at the International Court of Justice at The Hague in the Netherlands. One conviction was obtained in 2001, and Gaddafi agreed to hand over the individual to the Scottish authorities. This was part of an attempt to rehabilitate his regime after 9/11. Gaddafi dropped his support for the IRA, and, in 2003, the government of **Tony Blair** joined the United States in welcoming Libya back into the international community. This change ended abruptly in 2011, with the so-called "Arab Spring." Eastern Libya, which had always resented al-Gaddafi's rule, broke into revolt. Britain's prime minister, **David Cameron**, came out strongly in favor of the rebels, and British jets took part in the bombing of Tripoli and other centers of al-Gaddafi backing. An important UN sanction was obtained to authorize this.

Britain was thus instrumental in bringing down al-Gaddafi; however, policy during the period from 2003–2011 came back to haunt it. There had been accusations that Britain had been involved in U.S. rendition of terrorist suspects from 2001 onward. On 19 April 2012, such accusations were formalized when a Libyan jihadist, Abdel Hakim Belhaj, took out a legal case in Britain against former foreign secretary **Jack Straw** and MI6 head of counterterrorism Mark Allen. Belhaj claimed that he and his pregnant wife had been physically mistreated as part of the rendition process, in which British agents had been involved. Documents discovered by Libyan rebels in Tripoli in 2011, of whom Belhaj was one, showed Allen talking in effusive terms about intelligence cooperation between Britain and the al-Gaddafi regime. Doubts about MI6 competence had already emerged in 2011, when, now assisting the rebels, some of its operatives with Special Air Services men were arrested outside Benghazi while trying to make contact with the new rebel government. This was a major embarrassment for Foreign Secretary **William Hague** and the FCO, which had overall control of MI6. *See also* LIBYA, BOMBING OF (1986); LIBYA, BOMBING OF (2011).

LIBYA, BOMBING OF (1986). The strength of the relationship between **Margaret Thatcher** and **Ronald Reagan** was demonstrated on 14 April 1986, when Royal Air Force bases were used by the **United States** to bomb Libya. This was a response to the involvement of the Libyan president Muammar al-Gaddafi's regime in acts of **terrorism**. The worst were in Rome and Vienna, when 16 passengers were murdered at the respective airports. Thatcher's decision was highly controversial in Great Britain and did not have the approval of most of the British public. In contrast, **France** and **Spain** had refused to allow U.S. F-111 bombers to fly in their airspace. In the raid, one of al-Gaddafi's daughters was killed when his personal compound was bombed. Thatcher felt that the American response and British support for it was entirely justified and a recognition of U.S. help given during the **Falklands War** in 1982.

LIBYA, BOMBING OF (2011). The center point of the so-called "Arab Spring" between February and June 2011 was the struggle in Libya. A revolt against the regime of Muammar al-Gaddafi in eastern Libya evoked a ferocious response from the regime, and there were real fears that al-Gaddafi's forces might massacre the population of Benghazi. It was the focal point for resistance to the Libyan government. At this moment, Britain and **France**, followed by a more reluctant **United States**, decided that international action was needed. British prime minister **David Cameron** and French president Nicolas Sarkozy sponsored the idea of a "no-fly zone" over Libya to prevent al-Gaddafi from bombing his own people. Their efforts also secured a **United Nations (UN)** resolution on 20 March 2011, which authorized a no-fly zone and measures to enforce it. American backing was secured, although **Russia** and **China** abstained in the vote at the UN Security Council. Cameron, who came into office as a reluctant interventionist, secured a huge majority for British action in the House of Commons on 21 March, by 557 votes to 13. Intensive bombing of al-Gaddafi's power center in Tripoli began, which saved the rebels from the threat of defeat.

LLOYD, SELWYN (1904–1978). A Conservative Party stalwart, Selwyn Lloyd served **Winston Churchill** as **foreign secretary** from 1951–1954. When Churchill stood down as prime minister in 1955, Lloyd then served **Anthony Eden** as foreign secretary and survived the foreign policy disaster of the **Suez Crisis** in 1956. This second term at the **Foreign Office** lasted from 1955–1960. He was sacked rather brutally by **Harold Macmillan**, who had been one of the chief supporters of the Suez fiasco. During that crisis, Lloyd was sidelined by Eden and the permanent undersecretary at the Foreign Office, **Sir Ivone Kirkpatrick**.

LLOYD GEORGE, DAVID (1863–1945). The man who went down in British history as the "man who won the war," David Lloyd George was prime minister from 1916–1922. The first two years, 1916–1918, covered the end of **World War I**. Lloyd George was of Welsh nonconformist background, and he made a reputation for himself as a Liberal Party opponent of the Second **Anglo–Boer War** (1899–1902). He then became a member of the famous reforming Liberal government, which won a landslide election victory in 1906. He was appointed chancellor of the exchequer in 1909, a post he retained until being appointed prime minister. A brilliant parliamentary orator, Lloyd George pushed through the controversial People's Budget of 1909, which imposed a wealth tax and resulted in the constitutional crisis of 1910–1911, which in turn greatly reduced the powers of the House of Lords. Initially opposed to British involvement in World War I, Lloyd George became one of the most effective members of the War Cabinet. His reputation secured his appointment as prime minister in December 1916, presiding over a

Liberal-Conservative coalition. This process wrecked the Liberal Party, as part of it opposed the coalition.

Lloyd George's dynamism and leadership helped to secure an Allied victory in November 1918. He was one of the "Big Four" at the **Paris Peace Conference** in 1919, but he was skeptical about President **Woodrow Wilson's** utopianism about the **League of Nations**. He secured Britain's war aims. The German fleet was handed over and subsequently scuttled, and British war pensions were paid for by the Germans. Their colonies in Africa became British, and South African mandates came under overall control of the League of Nation. Lloyd George later warned in prescient fashion against treating defeated **Germany** too harshly, but he won a decisive election victory for his coalition in 1918, using anti-German propaganda. His prestige was badly damaged by a savage war of independence in **Ireland**, when he unwisely boasted that, "we have murder by the throat," but he had to concede independence to southern Ireland. Then the Chanak Crisis with **Turkey** led to the fall of the Lloyd George Coalition in November 1922. Lloyd George never held political office again, although he remained a considerable political force. His reputation was tarnished later in life by a visit to Adolf Hitler in Germany in 1936, and an apparent willingness to concede a negotiated peace with Nazi Germany in 1940. As prime minister, Lloyd George set a precedent for the sidelining of the **Foreign Office** in the formulation of British foreign policy. He was created Earl of Dwyfor in 1945. **Winston Churchill** called him the greatest Welshman in history. *See also* STEVENSON, FRANCES.

LOCARNO, TREATY OF (1925). The greatest achievement of **Austen Chamberlain's** time as British **foreign secretary** from 1924–1929 was the signing of the Treaty of Locarno in 1925. Working with French foreign minister Aristide Briand and his German counterpart, Gustave Stresemann, Chamberlain secured, through the treaty, German agreement to crucial aspects of the 1919 **Paris Peace Conference**, most notably German acceptance of the existing Franco–German and Belgian–German borders by voluntary agreement, not through the threat of coercion, as in the **Treaty of Versailles**. Along with his French and German colleagues, Chamberlain was awarded the **Nobel Peace Prize** in 1925. Thereafter, many ballrooms and cinemas in Great Britain were named after Locarno, and the newspapers wrote about the "spirit of Locarno."

LOCKHART, SIR ROBERT BRUCE (1887–1970). In the murky events surrounding the Bolshevik Revolution in November 1917, Robert Bruce Lockhart was a key British player. Lockhart was the first British diplomat sent to Moscow to deal with the Bolsheviks, and he cooperated with the notorious British secret agent **Sidney Reilly**, the so-called "Ace of Spies." In the 1930s, Lockhart developed strong links with **Czechoslovakia**, and he got to know the Czech leaders Thomas Masaryk and Eduard Beneš quite well. In 1941, during **World War II**, he became an assistant secretary of state in the **Foreign Office**, having worked with **Hugh Dalton**, the minister of economic warfare, to set up the **Special Operations Executive**, which **Winston Churchill** wanted to "set Europe ablaze." Dalton highly valued him as a colleague.

LOTHIAN, LORD (1882–1940). Philip Henry Kerr, later 11th Marquis of Lothian, was a key aide of British prime minister **David Lloyd George** at the **Paris Peace Conference** of 1919. Lloyd George later wrote about his "priceless help." Kerr succeeded to the family title in Scotland in 1930. As Lord Lothian and a member of the Liberal Party, he was undersecretary of state for **India** in 1931–1932. He became closely associated with British **appeasement** policy in the 1930s, and his country house, Blickling, in Norfolk, was a meeting place for those with a similar outlook, including **Nancy Astor, Waldorf Astor, Thomas Jones,** and Geoffrey Dawson, the editor of the *Times*. Lord Lothian made visits to **Germany** but was regarded by the **Foreign Office** as an interfering nuisance. In 1938, he had a dramatic change of mind about appeasement, confessing that he had got it wrong. He was British ambassador in Washington in 1939–1940.

LUSITANIA, **RMS.** One of the most infamous attacks by a German U-boat submarine in **World War I** was on the Cunard liner RMS *Lusitania* off the coast of **Ireland** on 7 May 1915. It resulted in the deaths of 1,200 noncombatants, including 128 Americans. The sinking swayed U.S. public opinion in favor of the Allied Powers, although the **United States** did not enter the war until April 1917.

M

MAASTRICHT, TREATY OF (1992). Ratified by the eleven **European Union (EU)** member states, the Treaty of Maastricht entered into force in November 1993. The treaty laid down a timetable for the Economic and Monetary Union (EMU) and planned to abolish control on capital movements so EU economies could converge. Convergence would be measured by inflation, which had to be within 1.5 percent of the three lowest EU rates. British prime minister **John Major** was able to secure the removal of a Social Chapter on working conditions from the treaty. It appeared as a separate protocol to the treaty, signed by the remaining 10 members. Britain also secured the right to opt out of the final binding stage of the EMU because of its general reluctance to cede more national sovereignty. The EMU would lead to a common currency (the euro) by 2002, a move welcomed by big business, because it would remove the need to insure against currency fluctuations. The signature of even a watered down treaty was still highly controversial in Britain, where anti-EU sentiment was strong on the right wing of the Conservative party. *See also* EUROZONE.

MACDONALD, RAMSAY (1866–1937). The first prime minister provided by the British Labour Party, Ramsay MacDonald headed minority governments in 1924, and from 1929–1931. MacDonald came from humble origins and had been a conscientious objector during **World War I**. He became prime minister in 1924, as a result of the split in the Liberal Party, which allowed Labour to replace it as the second main party in Great Britain. MacDonald, who was always keenly interested in foreign policy, presided over the London Reparations Conference of August 1924, which set up the **Dawes Plan**. In his second period as prime minister, he was responsible for the appointment of **Sir Robert Vansittart**, his former private secretary, as permanent undersecretary at the **Foreign Office** in 1929. His protégé became a key figure in policy formulation in the 1930s.

MacDonald was unfortunate enough to be in office at the time of the Wall Street Crash in October 1929. He supported the deflationary policies of his chancellor of the exchequer, Philip Snowden, which alienated Labour Party colleagues. In 1931, at the height of the economic crisis, MacDonald and a rump of Labour ministers were persuaded by King George V to form a National Government with the Conservatives. This split the Labour Party, which regarded MacDonald as a traitor. He presided unhappily as prime minister of the National Government from 1931–1935, a shadow of his former self. MacDonald was associated with the beginnings of the **appeasement** policy. Unlike most of his Labour colleagues, he disliked the **League of Nations** and mistrusted Britain's ally, **France**. He had visited the **United States** in 1930 and believed in the "**special relationship.**"

MACLEAN, DONALD (1903–1983). The son of a Liberal minister in the National Government of 1931, Donald Maclean became one of the notorious "Cambridge Spies" and defected to the Soviet Union in 1951. He was recruited by a Soviet spymaster in the 1930s as a student at Trinity Hall, Cambridge, before joining the **Foreign Office** in 1935. A high flyer, Maclean brought about rejoicing in Moscow when he was promoted to the post of first secretary at the Washington embassy. This gave him access to atomic secrets, which were copied for his Soviet controllers. Maclean's dual existence as a top diplomat and espionage agent eventually undermined his fragile personality. He developed a serious drinking problem and had to be sent back to London for medical treatment. Now under suspicion in both the Foreign Office and MI5, Maclean was something of a liability to colleagues in his spying circle in Britain. Extremely lax surveillance by MI5 allowed "Homer," as Maclean was known to Soviet intelligence, to be spirited away to **France** on 25 May 1950. It was the work of his fellow spy and former Foreign Office colleague Guy Burgess. Both men ended up in Moscow, where Maclean remained until his death. While in Soviet exile, he wrote an extremely critical appraisal of British foreign policy in 1963. He, like the other members of the Cambridge spy ring, Kim Philby, Guy Burgess, Anthony Blunt, and Alec Cairncross, were convinced Marxists who were prepared to betray their own country without scruple. The Maclean–Burgess defection was a serious blow to a Foreign Office, which had tended to assume that public school Oxbridge products were ideologically reliable.

MACMILLAN, HAROLD (1894–1986). The British prime minister in the wake of the 1956 **Suez Crisis**, Harold Macmillan was a successful leader. He held the post of premier from 1957–1963. Macmillan was an Oxford graduate with a distinguished record during **World War I**. He went on to become Conservative member of Parliament for Stockton-on-Tees and an opponent of the **appeasement** policy of Great Britain in the 1930s. Macmillan claimed to have burned **Neville Chamberlain** in effigy after the 1938 **Munich Agreement.** During **World War II**, Macmillan joined **Winston Churchill's** government and became a member of the Cabinet as minister resident in North Africa in 1942. He returned to government after the Conservative election of 1951 and became a successful minister of housing. From October 1954 until April 1955, Macmillan was minister of defense, a job in which he admitted he had been a failure. **Anthony Eden** moved Macmillan to the **Foreign Office**, where he rejected overtures to get Great Britain to join the **European Economic Community (EEC)** in 1955–1956.

At the time of the **Suez Crisis** in 1956, Macmillan was a hawk, but by then he was chancellor of the exchequer. It fell to him to warn Eden that Britain could not survive financially in the teeth of American disapproval. "First in, First out" was one description of Macmillan's role in the Suez conflict. He was the main political beneficiary, replacing Eden as prime minister in January 1957. Like Winston Churchill, Macmillan had an American mother, and he used this to repair the **"special relationship"** with the **United States**. Wartime links with **Dwight D. Eisenhower** were useful, and Macmillan got along well with the youthful **John F. Kennedy.** Kennedy was in close contact with Macmillan at the time of the **Cuban Missile Crisis** in 1962, although the British prime minister sometimes felt that the United States pursued its own agendas. Macmillan's greatest disappointment was his failure to get Britain into the EEC, despite his efforts to persuade his wartime colleague, French president Charles de Gaulle. Intensive talks from 1961–1963 failed to secure British membership. Conversely, Macmillan was a sensible realist where the **British Empire** was concerned. His speech before the white-only **South African** parliament in 1960, which recognized a "wind of change" in Africa, was courageous.

Macmillan's government was badly tainted by the Profumo Scandal in 1963, when his war minister resigned over a sex scandal. Macmillan resigned due to health issues in September 1963, but he remained a public figure for another 25 years. An accusation from Macmillan that **Margaret Thatcher** had "sold off the family silver" through a series of privatizations demonstrated his disillusionment with her government. Macmillan was created 1st Earl of Stockton in 1984, at the age of 90.

MAJOR, JOHN (1943–). Great Britain's prime minister from 1990–1997, John Major rose rapidly from relative obscurity. He had been **Margaret Thatcher's** chancellor of the exchequer in 1989–1990, before the Conservative Party rejected her as leader. Major was a very different personality, seen by many as rather colorless, who was elected because he was able to pose as a common man, where those with a grander pedigree, like **Douglas Hurd,** who remained **foreign secretary** under Major, could not. Major himself had spent just three months as foreign secretary in 1989, which meant that he lacked foreign policy experience. He came into **No. 10 Downing Street** in the middle of the **Gulf War** crisis and acquitted himself quite well. It was Major who persuaded President **George H. W. Bush** to enforce no-fly zones in **Iraq** to protect the Kurdish minority from Saddam Hussein. He worked well with Bush, but tensions were provoked with Bush's successor, **Bill Clinton**, when Major's Conservative Party, against convention, had appeared to support Bush's Republican Party in the November 1992 presidential election. The two men initially disagreed about policy over **Bosnia**, with Clinton apparently being reluctant to intervene.

Major had an alarming experience when the Provisional Irish Republican Army (PIRA) landed mortar shells in the garden of No. 10 Downing Street while the Cabinet was in session, yet it was he who set up the Downing Street Declaration in November 1993. The Provisionals subsequently broke their cease-fire in 1996, but it was Europe that caused Major the greatest anguish. "Eurosceptics" in his party had opposed the **Treaty of Maastricht** in 1992 and obliged him to negotiate an opt-out from the Social Chapter. Relations became so fraught that, in 1995, Major briefly stood down as leader and ran for reelection against the Eurosceptic John Redwood. He easily won, but he could not prevent the worst defeat in Conservative history in the general election of May 1997.

MAKINS, ROGER (1904–1996). Roger Makins, later 1st Baron Sherfield, served as British minister in Washington from 1945–1947, before being promoted to be ambassador in 1952. He remained in that post until 1956. Makins had been in the Central Department of the **Foreign Office** in the 1930s, and, in 1938, he had the thankless task of being the British representative on the International Commission adjudicating the post-Munich frontier of **Czechoslovakia**. In 1943, Makins joined **Harold Macmillan's** staff in North Africa, where he was minister resident, and Macmillan had a very high opinion of his abilities. In 1945–1946, Makins had been in the Washington embassy in charge of atomic energy negotiations, and, in this area, he developed an expertise lacking in the majority of Foreign Office diplomats. He subsequently became known as "Mr. Atom." The British ambassador in Washington, **Lord Halifax**, formed as high an opinion of Makins's abilities as Macmillan. In 1947, as an assistant undersecretary at the Foreign Office, he contributed to the influential **Russia** Committee.

As ambassador himself, Makins had a somewhat frosty relationship with U.S. secretary of state **John Foster Dulles**, but his atomic expertise came to the fore in negotiating the Anglo–American Atomic Agreement of 15 June 1955. He was in place during the **Suez Crisis** (1956) but left his post on 11 October. His successor did not arrive until 8 November, a strange gap that may have been deliberately contrived by **Anthony Eden** when Anglo–French troops invaded **Egypt**. It was Makins who had warned the British government of the fateful U.S. decision to withdraw the offer to subsidize the building of Egypt's **Aswan Dam** on 19 July. Makins, who had married the daughter of Senator Dwight F. Davis, was a convinced Atlanticist who would have been distressed by the breakdown in the "**special relationship**" with the **United States** at the time of the Suez Crisis.

MALAYAN EMERGENCY (1948–1960). Only three years after the Japanese occupation of Malaya had been ended in 1945, Great Britain faced a domestic insurgency in the country. This was largely associated with the Chinese minority, the Malay majority remaining loyal to the British. The rebels were Communist in their political orientation, but their strength never amounted to more than 10,000 men at any one time. Nevertheless, they pinned down 250,000 men of the Malayan security forces, of whom 50,000 were British troops. The British tried but failed to secure U.S. aid in Malaya, at a time when the Americans were largely funding **France's** war in **Indochina**. They crushed the revolt by creating 600 large, fortified camps with their own education and welfare services to deprive the Communists of support. This, linked to intelligence work supervised by counterinsurgency expert **Sir Robert Thompson**, effectively ended the uprising by 1954, although a rump of insurgents remained near the border with Thailand. The emergency lasted until 1960. Some 1,500 **British Commonwealth** troops died during the Malayan Emergency, along with 10,000 Communist insurgents and 5,000 civilians. Thompson's advice on counterinsurgency was sought by the Americans during the **Vietnam War**. Malaya emerged as an independent state in 1957. *See also* MALAYSIA.

MALAYSIA. Former British Malaya was transformed in September 1963 into the Federation of Malaysia, whose component parts were Malaya, Sabah, Sarawak, and Singapore. The island of Singapore, a former British naval base with a mostly ethnic Chinese population, seceded from the federation in August 1965. The federation remained part of the **British Commonwealth** of Nations but soon found itself in confrontation with Indonesia, the former Dutch East Indies. Indonesia refused to accept the union of Malaysian territories and pronounced a "state of confrontation" with it. Britain was obliged to honor defense promises it had extended in exchange for bases in the new federation. Troops from Britain, **Australia**, and **New Zealand** engaged Indonesian guerrilla forces from 1963–1966. As was the case during the **Malayan Emergency**, the **United States** refused to get involved in the conflict (just as Britain had stayed out of the **Vietnam War**). Britain was obliged to send

30,000 men to Malaysia. Its leaders, **Harold Macmillan** and **Harold Wilson,** argued that this considerable commitment meant that Britain was in no position to afford aid to the United States elsewhere in Southeast Asia. A trend toward Islamization emerged during the premiership of Dato Seri Mahathir Mohamad. It went hand in hand with massive economic growth. In the 1980s, Malaysia had the second-highest growth rate of any Asian country. Mohamad behaved in an increasingly authoritarian manner, which disturbed Britain and other Commonwealth states. He suffered a landslide defeat in the general election of 2004, and was succeeded by Abdullah Badawi.

MANNING, SIR DAVID (1949–). The career of Sir David Manning has exemplified the growing tendency for **Foreign and Commonwealth Office** diplomats to be seconded to **No. 10 Downing Street,** where Manning served from 2001–2003. He developed a close relationship with **Tony Blair,** but also with the U.S. national security advisor, **Condoleezza Rice,** during the **Iraq** crisis in 2002–2003. Manning is credited with having considerable influence over Blair in regards to Iraq policy, and he was sent to Washington in 2002 to persuade President **George W. Bush** to use the **United Nations** route in dealing with the Iraqi government. This background secured his appointment as British ambassador in Washington in 2003.

MARSHALL, GEORGE CATLETT (1891–1967). The name General George C. Marshall became synonymous with American generosity after **World War II** because of the massive aid plan associated with his name. Marshall had been chief of staff of the U.S. Army during the conflict. He disagreed with his British allies about the timing of the Allied invasion of northern **France,** which he wanted to occur in 1943, at the latest. From 1947–1949, Marshall was secretary of state in the administration of **Harry S. Truman,** and, in this capacity, he sponsored the European Recovery Program. *See also* MARSHALL PLAN.

MARSHALL PLAN (1947). In 1946–1947, economic conditions were so dire in Western Europe that the administration of **Harry S. Truman** realized that something must be done. In Great Britain, the terrible winter of 1946–1947 reduced coal supplies to industry by half. Food had to be rationed, and 6 million people were unemployed. Conditions in continental Europe were even worse. The European Recovery Program, otherwise known as the Marshall Plan, was authorized by the U.S. Congress after Marshall's celebrated speech at Harvard University on 5 June 1947. European states were asked to present a list of their requirements, and Britain, although one of the victorious allies, had substantial needs. It received $3 billion in aid, more than any other European state, and it was gratefully received by British prime minister **Clement R. Attlee**. The British had been disappointed by the terms of the **Anglo–American Loan Agreement** in 1945. Marshall aid continued from 1947–1952, and, in its early years, it accounted for 10 percent of the U.S. budget and up to 2 percent of American national income. Under its generous terms, 90 percent of the aid did not have to be repaid. The Marshall Plan was subsumed into the Organization for European Economic Cooperation in 1948. British **foreign secretary Ernest Bevin** was an enthusiastic supporter of the plan, which he saw as a way of holding back the expansion of Communism. The **Foreign Office** saw it as a means of defending "Western civilization." *See also* COLD WAR.

MASSIVE RETALIATION. In the specialized terminology of the **Cold War**, the term *massive retaliation* occupied a special place. It was first used by U.S. secretary of state **John Foster Dulles** in a speech in January 1954. It implied that the **United States** would respond to a Soviet attack, be it conventional or nuclear, with a massive nuclear strike. A nuclear-based strategy would avoid the sort of ground combat commitment made by both the United States and Great Britain in the **Korean War**, but it was fraught with peril, hence the later switch to a policy of "flexible response," in which Western ground forces would be used as a trip wire to register the nature of the Soviet threat. As it was, the British and U.S. governments disagreed about the monolithic nature of world Communism. *See also* NUCLEAR NONPROLIFERATION TREATY.

MAU MAU. Perhaps the most difficult colonial struggle in which Great Britain was engaged after 1945 was that in Kenya, where a state of emergency existed from 1947–1960. Mau Mau fighters, who were obliged to take a secret oath by their Kikuyu leaders, numbered around 25,000 at the height of the emergency. Their target was the white European minority of 30,000 settlers who owned most of the land in the so-called "White Highlands." Land shortage was at the root of the problem in Kenya, which created resentment among the 5 million blacks, especially those of the majority Kikuyu tribe. The Kikuyu leader, Jomo Kenyatta, was imprisoned for seven years, although the evidence that he inspired Mau Mau was inconclusive. The British authorities herded 80,000 Kikuyu into special camps and resettled hundreds of thousands of others. Many Kikuyu died of ill treatment, and the release of Colonial Office documents in 2011 demonstrated that Crown forces had used torture and even castration as weapons of intimidation. The unconvincing official **Foreign and Commonwealth Office** response to Kenyan survivors' compensation claims was that the passage of time now meant that this was a matter for the government of the current postcolonial Kenyan government. Kenya received its independence in 1963, and Kenyatta became its first president.

MCMAHON ACT (1946). In August 1946, U.S. Congress passed an act that made it against the law for the **United States** to share its nuclear research with other friendly states, for example, Great Britain. It took the name of its sponsor, Congressman Brien McMahon. President **Dwight D. Eisenhower** was a critic of the act, and he promised Britain's prime minister, **Harold Macmillan**, that he would urge Congress to renew previous Anglo–American nuclear cooperation. In 1958–1959, U.S. legislation renewed the flow of information between the two allies. None of the United States' other allies were so privileged.

MESSINA CONFERENCE (1955). In November 1955, the Messina Conference, which paved the way for the founding treaty of the **European Economic Community (EEC)**, was held at Messina, in Sicily. Although it was invited to become a founding member of the EEC, Great Britain only sent an observer to Messina. Prime Minister **Anthony Eden** said that Britain should keep out of "far-reaching schemes." Britain did not sign the **Treaty of Rome** in 1957.

MEYER, SIR CHRISTOPHER (1944–). An influential British ambassador in Washington from 1997–2003, Christopher Meyer was in post at the time of the 11 September 2003 **terrorist** attacks on the World Trade Center in New York City and the Pentagon in Arlington, Virginia. He was also Great Britain's representative at the time of the outbreak of the **Iraq War**. His memoirs offer interesting insights into the relationship between **Tony Blair** and **George W. Bush**. Meyer, like other officials, was critical of Blair's broad-brush approach, which was not based on detailed background knowledge. Like many **Foreign Office** officials in the past, he felt that prime ministers allowed the Foreign Office to be marginalized too readily.

MI6. *See* SECRET INTELLIGENCE SERVICE.

MILES, SIR OLIVER (1938–). In 1984–1985, Oliver Miles was British ambassador in **Libya** during a dramatic phase in Anglo–Libyan relations. In 1984, a London police constable Yvonne Fletcher was shot dead by rogue elements in the Libyan embassy during a demonstration against Libyan leader Muammar al-Gaddafi. As a result, **Margaret Thatcher's** government broke off diplomatic relations with Libya, and Miles was recalled from his embassy in Tripoli. He was a Middle Eastern specialist who had joined the

Diplomatic Service in 1970, serving variously in Amman, **Jordan**, and Aden, Yemen. Named private secretary to the British ambassador, he then secured the important post of ambassador to Saudi Arabia (1975–1977), moving to Athens two years later. The immediate period (1980–1984) before Miles went to Libya saw him holding the important post of head of the **Foreign and Commonwealth Office** North East and North African Department. Miles finished his career with ambassadorial posts in Luxembourg and **Greece** (1985–1996). He is much in demand as a television pundit about Libya.

MILIBAND, DAVID (1965–). The son of a well-known academic at the London School of Economics, Ralph Miliband, David Miliband was **foreign secretary** in **Gordon Brown's** Labour government (2007–2010). He is member of Parliament for South Shields. Miliband was educated at Oxford University and the Massachusetts Institute of Technology. Known as a strong supporter of **Tony Blair**, he was his head of policy when Labour was in opposition. He helped draft Labour's winning election manifesto in 1997. Blair then created him head of the Prime Minister's Policy Unit at **No. 10 Downing Street** (1997–2001). Junior posts followed, most notably at the Department for Education and Skills in June 2002. A reshuffle of the government in December 2004 saw Miliband moved to the Cabinet Office. After Blair's third electoral victory in May 2005, he became minister of state for communities and local government, a post that carried a Cabinet seat. On 5 May 2006, Miliband was promoted to be secretary of state for the environment. He spoke strongly in favor of creating a balance between consumers and producers. Miliband also campaigned for increased awareness of the impact of climate change. Britain ratified the **Kyoto Protocol**, and, in 2006, the British economist Nicholas Stern warned strongly about the costs of ignoring this peril. This experience gave Miliband insights into the foreign policy ramifications of climate change policy. When appointed secretary of state for foreign and commonwealth affairs on 28 June 2007, he had not held a foreign policy portfolio. He was also the youngest person to be appointed foreign secretary since **David Owen** held the position in 1977.

One of Miliband's successes as foreign secretary was his strengthening of the "special relationship" with the **United States**. The U.S. secretary of state, **Hillary Clinton**, thought highly of his abilities. Tensions existed, notably over the U.S. facility at Guantanamo Bay, Cuba. Miliband made a House of Commons statement on 5 February 2009, drawing U.S. attention to the plight of British citizen Benjamin Mohammed. He antagonized the Indian government in 2008 by calling for a settlement in Kashmir, which he suggested would contribute to winning the conflict against international **terrorism**. **India** resented interference by a third party, especially the former colonial power. In 2009–2011, Miliband drew attention to human rights abuses against the Tamil minority in Sri Lanka, where the long-standing civil war (1983–2010) was drawing to a close. Miliband lost his government post as a result of Labour's election defeat in May 2010. He stood for the party leadership in September, and it was a major surprise when he lost the contest to his younger brother, **Ed Miliband**. He opted not to accept a post in his brother's Shadow Cabinet. Miliband remains a backbench member of Parliament.

MILIBAND, ED (1969–). The younger brother of **David Miliband**, the former Labour Party **foreign secretary**, Ed Miliband became leader of the party on 25 September 2010. He was educated at Oxford University and the London School of Economics. Unlike the coalition leaders **David Cameron** and **Nick Clegg**, he was educated at a state comprehensive school rather than a public school. As a child, he spent a year in Boston, Massachusetts, when his father taught at a university in the **United States**. In other respects, Miliband's political career followed a classic path. He was a special advisor to the then-chancellor of the exchequer, **Gordon Brown**, from 1997–2002. Brown was his political mentor. Miliband then spent a 12-month unpaid sabbatical at Harvard University (July 2002–September 2003) teaching economics. The spell was extended to January 2004, when Miliband returned to Britain as chairman of Her Majesty's Treasury Council of Economic Advisors. He resigned from this post in 2005 to stand in the general election.

Miliband was elected member of Parliament for Doncaster North. His first government post found him working as minister for the Third Sector, responsible for voluntary and charity work. When Brown became prime minister in June 2007, Miliband became minister for the Cabinet Office and chancellor of the Duchy of Lancaster (a portfolio with no departmental responsibility that allows its holder to act as a troubleshooter). This post had Cabinet rank, meaning that Miliband and his brother David were the first brothers to hold cabinet rank since 1938. On 3 October 2008, Miliband was given the important post of secretary of state for energy and climate change. This put him at the heart of an important aspect of policy with strong international implications. Miliband represented Great Britain at the 2009 Copenhagen Summit. It produced a global commitment to fight the effects of climate change with appropriate international funding. No enforcement machinery emerged, a fact that Miliband blamed on Chinese obstruction.

Labour lost the May 2010 election, and Brown resigned both as prime minister and leader of the Labour Party. David Miliband announced his candidacy for the leadership, and he was the favorite to secure the post. To the surprise of many, so too did Ed Miliband. He received a crucial endorsement on 23 May, when former leader Neil Kinnock came out in his favor.

Just fewer than a quarter of the Parliamentary Labour Party endorsed the younger Miliband. The key factor was the support of the trade unions, which enabled him the slightest victory over his elder brother David (by 1.3 percent) on 25 September. It was a major political shock in Britain. As leader, Miliband continued to show the skepticism about the **European Union (EU)**, and especially the **Eurozone**, that had marked his mentor, Brown. He supported Britain's military intervention in **Libya** in 2011, but, although not in parliament at the time, he criticized the 2003 invasion of **Iraq**. Conversely, Miliband fully backed continued British involvement in **Afghanistan**. He thought the austerity program of the **David Cameron** coalition government to be too severe and called for a commitment to growth both in Britain and the EU in 2012. There was also talk of Labour offering a referendum on Europe, an indication of its problematic status in the party's thinking. In June 2012, his brother, David, still remained outside the Shadow Cabinet.

MINISTRY OF DEFENSE. *See* DEFENSE, MINISTRY OF.

MITCHELL, GEORGE (1933–). George Mitchell played a key role in the Northern **Ireland** peace process as an envoy of President **Bill Clinton**. A former Democratic senator, Mitchell used his political experience to support Prime Minister **Tony Blair** in the tough negotiations required to secure an all-party settlement via the 1998 Good Friday Agreement. Mitchell was subsequently used as peace envoy in the Middle East.

MONROE DOCTRINE (1823). Although the Monroe Doctrine is a central plank in U.S. foreign policy, its announcement by President James Monroe in 1823 relied upon support from Great Britain. Monroe stated that the **United States** would regard interference in the Americas by a non-European power as a hostile act. Yet, it owed its inception to the decision made by British foreign secretary George Canning, who had just returned to the **Foreign Office**, that Britain would resist by force any attempt by European powers to reassert control in South America, which revolted against Spanish colonial rule. He disliked the interventionist pronouncements by the Holy Alliance and realized that the infant United States was too weak to prevent interference by **France** or any other European power. President Monroe rejected any formal alliance with Britain, but his doctrine relied upon the strength of the British fleet at the time. Only later in the 19th century did the U.S. have the naval strength to enforce the Monroe Doctrine's constraints on its own. In the short run, Britain gained the most in commercial terms. It opened formal commercial relations with **Argentina**, Mexico, and Columbia in 1824.

MONTENEGRO. The small former Yugoslav republic of Montenegro remained in union with **Serbia** until 4 June 2006, when it achieved independence. Montenegro has a complex racial mixture, with Macedonians making up 67 percent of the population, Albanians 20 percent, and Serbs 2 percent. The poorest of the former Yugoslav republics, it needed the Serb link on economic grounds but suffered accordingly when economic sanctions were imposed on Serbia during the **Kosovo** crisis in 1999. Great Britain has tried to strengthen ties with Montenegro. The British Council, which focuses on cultural ties, has been in Montenegro since 1994. It administers Chevening scholarships for Montenegrin citizens. In 2002, the British **foreign secretary Jack Straw** signed an agreement in the Serb capital of Belgrade on cooperation in science, education, and sport with **Yugoslavia**. This was applied directly to Montenegro by its government when independence was attained in 2006. The Embassy of the Republic of Montenegro, London, opened in September 2007. There are regular contacts at the intergovernmental level. The Montenegrin finance minister, Milorad Katnic, met representatives of the **Foreign and Commonwealth Office** and Her Majesty's Treasury during a visit to London from 10–12 October 2011. Britain's minister for Europe, David Lidington, also visited Montenegro on 8 June 2011.

MORGENTHAU PLAN (1944). For Great Britain and the **United States** in 1944–1945, the focus was on the shape of postwar Europe, in particular, what should be done with a defeated **Germany**. The U.S. treasury secretary, Henry Morgenthau, produced a plan for the deindustrialization of Germany in 1944, which would have reduced it to a fragmented, pastoral status. It was an extreme solution that was rejected by both President **Franklyn D. Roosevelt** and the U.S. military. On the British side, **Ernest Bevin**, then the minister of Labour, wanted to break Germany up into several smaller states, whereas the **foreign secretary, Anthony Eden**, wanted a more moderate approach. Germany was ultimately fragmented into zones of occupation at the **Potsdam Conference** in July 1945.

MOUNTBATTEN, LORD LOUIS (1900–1979). A member of the British royal family who was appointed supreme commander of Allied Forces in the South-East Asia Command in 1943, Lord Louis Mountbatten was a highly controversial figure. Some members of the British military establishment believed that Mountbatten had been promoted because of Prime Minister **Winston Churchill's** weakness for royalty, rather than as a result of his own abilities. His headquarters at Kandy, in Ceylon, was regarded as being far too lavish, and he was also criticized for surrounding himself with sycophants. There was a major clash with **Foreign Office** representative Esler Dening in 1946, over Dening's right to report directly to the Foreign Office, and he was scathing about Mountbatten's pomposity and inefficiency.

Mountbatten was a master of self-publicity; however, on some issues, his instincts were sound. One was the need for other colonial powers, like **France** and the Netherlands, to recognize the aspirations for independence of the people of **Indochina** and the Dutch East Indies. In this respect, he was probably the right man to be appointed Great Britain's last viceroy in **India** in 1947. The original British intention was to make India and **Pakistan** independent in 1948, but Mountbatten steamrollered the independence process through by August 1947. This achievement, which resulted in hundreds of thousands of deaths during the transfer of power, also opened Mountbatten to serious criticism. He subsequently became first sea lord at the **Admiralty**, in which capacity he was critical of Prime Minister **Anthony Eden's** operation during the **Suez Crisis** in 1956, although his doubts were not aired in public. Mountbatten, who had overall responsibility for the brief British involvement in Vietnam in 1945–1946, came to believe that the massive U.S. involvement in that country in the 1960s was a catastrophic blunder. He was killed by the Provisional Irish Republican Army in County Donegal in the Irish Republic, in 1979, when **terrorists** blew up his yacht, *Shadow V*. It was characteristic of Mountbatten, who did not lack personal courage, to ignore Irish police concerns about his lack of security.

MUGABE, ROBERT (1924–). The unilateral declaration of independence made by **Southern Rhodesia**, in 1965, placed Great Britain in considerable difficulty. It was only in 1980, when Robert Mugabe became the first prime minister of what was then Zimbabwe, that the position was resolved after a lengthy guerrilla war. Mugabe became president of the Zimbabwe African National Union beginning in 1976, and commander of its military wing. He reluctantly attended the Lancaster House talks in London, as he regarded the British as imperialist exploiters of his country. After a conciliatory beginning, when he promised not to confiscate the land of white farmers, Mugabe became more and more tyrannical. Political opponents were eliminated and the economy collapsed because of the ineptitude of his government. The British position remained consistently noninterventionist, with Britain fearing that interference by the former colonial power would antagonize other African countries. Mugabe, who became president in 1987, increasingly blamed Zimbabwe's problems on Britain, even making bizarre accusations of homosexuality against **Tony Blair** and his government after 1997. Under Mugabe, Zimbabwe, despite its natural resources, became one of the poorest countries in the world with one of its most odious regimes.

MULTILATERAL FORCE (MLF). A great deal of attention and money was lavished by Great Britain during the 1940s and 1950s on preserving an independent nuclear deterrent. U.S. president **John F. Kennedy** tried to wean the British away from this concept, toward the idea of a mixed-manned multilateral force (MLF). It would be a naval force made up of sailors provided by the **North Atlantic Treaty Organization** but would have American-owned nuclear weapons. Unsurprisingly, the MLF concept did not win favor with the British, whose military chiefs argued in favor of retention of the nuclear deterrent because Britain was so much more vulnerable to a Soviet nuclear strike. Plans for a MLF were scrapped in 1964.

MUNICH AGREEMENT (1938). In September 1938, Prime Minister **Neville Chamberlain** flew to **Germany** on three occasions to talk to German chancellor Adolf Hitler. The third and definitive meeting was at Munich, on 29–30 September. It decided the fate of the Czech Sudetenland. The Italian dictator Benito Mussolini, together with French prime minister Eduard Daladier, was also present. Seen as the nadir, or high point, of **appeasement**, the agreement ceded to Germany 11,000 miles of Czech territory and transferred 800,000 Czech citizens to German rule, along with the 3 million ethnic Germans in the Sudetenland. Hitler grudgingly signed the Anglo–German Declaration with Chamberlain, whereby Britain and Germany promised not to fight one another in the future. After returning triumphantly to London, Chamberlain boasted about achieving "peace in our time." Posterity never forgave him, but, at the time, President **Franklin D. Roosevelt** sent a congratulatory two-word telegram, reading, "Good man." Peace only lasted a year, however, and Munich became synonymous with weakness and defeatism. More recent research has provided a more nuanced analysis of the British appeasement policy that led to Munich.

MURROW, EDWARD R. (1908–1965). Rarely has a foreign journalist won the hearts of British people as did Edward Murrow in 1940–1941. At the time of the "Blitz" in London, Murrow was broadcasting nightly from Britain's bombed-out capital to tell his fellow Americans that the spirit of the Londoners remained intact. This raised the morale of Londoners and may well have influenced the attitudes of the many Americans who heard his broadcasts for CBS. His broadcasts always began with the catchphrase, "This is London." Murrow was also admired by the British center-left for the way he stood up to the frantic anti-Communist rhetoric of Senator Joseph McCarthy in the 1950s. It was a mark of the esteem in which Murrow was held in Britain that he was invited to recreate his Blitz-time role in the 1958 British war film *Sink the Bismarck*.

N

NAPOLEONIC WARS (1799–1815). Following the French Revolutionary Wars from 1792–1798, the continuing struggle between **France** and the other European powers took the name of the French dictator **Napoleon Bonaparte**. He had become first consul in the former republican government in 1799, and he soon eclipsed his rivals. Bonaparte crowned himself emperor of France in 1804. Great Britain was his chief enemy, and it was the Royal Navy that put an end to Bonaparte's attempt to conquer **Egypt** in 1798, and he never solved the problem of invading the British Isles. The French naval defeat at Trafalgar, on 21 October 1805, put an end to any naval threat to Britain. Bonaparte won a series of brilliant victories against Britain's continental allies Austria, Prussia, and **Russia** from 1805–1807, but the problem of Britain—the funder of the continental powers—remained. Napoleon's Continental System, designed to ruin Britain's trade by closing European harbors to it, only managed to provoke Russia. British intervention in **Spain** and Portugal from 1808–1814 provided France with another costly problem, combined as it was with national uprisings. After the catastrophic Russian campaign in 1812, Bonaparte never recovered. Britain joined the Austrians, Prussians, and Russians in invading France in 1814. Brilliant defensive tactics by Bonaparte could not save him, and he was forced to abdicate his throne.

Exile on the small Mediterranean island of Elba preceded Bonaparte's last adventure, when he returned to France in March 1815. His last decisive defeat was at Waterloo, on 18 June 1815. Bonaparte believed that the British commander, the Duke of Wellington, was a "bad general" and the British troops were "bad troops," but they were not, and Britain played a decisive role in bringing an end to the Napoleonic Wars. British **foreign secretary** Lord Castlereagh played a key role in the intricate diplomacy needed to keep the Allied coalition together in 1813–1814, and again in 1815.

NARVIK EXPEDITION (1940). The only successful part of the Anglo–French intervention in Norway in April 1940, during **World War II**, was the capture of the north Norwegian part of Narvik. It subsequently had to be evacuated because of the Allied defeats in **France** and **Belgium**. **Winston Churchill**, who had planned the Norway Expedition, survived its failure, as did **Anthony Eden,** who at the time was secretary of state for war, before his return to the **Foreign Office.**

NASSAU AGREEMENT (1962). Great Britain's persistent failure to evolve its own nuclear delivery system resulted in the Nassau Agreement between the **United States** and Britain. Prime Minister **Harold Macmillan** met with President **John F. Kennedy** at Nassau, in the Bahamas, from 18–21 December 1962. Under the terms of this agreement, the United States agreed to provide Britain with **Polaris missiles,** which gave it a submarine-based nuclear deterrent. **Holy Loch** was the chosen Polaris base in Scotland. Nassau was not just of military importance. Its signature took place weeks before President Charles de Gaulle of **France** vetoed Britain's attempt to secure membership in the **European Economic Community.** In his veto statement in January 1963, de Gaulle argued that Britain's "**special relationship**" with the United States, proved by Nassau, demonstrated that the British could not be good Europeans.

NASSER, JAMAL ABD AL (1918–1970). Egypt's president at the time of the 1956 **Suez Crisis,** Jamal Abd al Nasser won the diplomatic struggle with Great Britain's prime minister, **Anthony Eden.** Nasser was a fervent Pan-Arab nationalist who used the Egyptian army to further his career. He helped overthrow the Egyptian monarchy in 1952, to become prime minister of the new Egyptian republic and then president in 1954. Nasser negotiated the British withdrawal from the Suez Canal Zone in 1954.

NATIONAL ARCHIVES, THE. The most important repository of government papers in Great Britain can be found in Kew, London, at The National Archives, the former Public Record Office. The personal papers of former prime ministers, **foreign secretaries,** foreign office officials, and diplomats can be found here, along with Cabinet minutes and other important papers.

NEUTRALITY ACTS (UNITED STATES). British **appeasement** policy in the 1930s was formulated around the hope that the **United States** would abandon its neutrality in favor of cooperation with the Western democracies. This was prevented by the Neutrality Acts of 1935, 1937, and 1939, which circumscribed President **Franklin D. Roosevelt's** attempts to make U.S. foreign policy more actively anti-fascist. On the British side, **Neville Chamberlain** was skeptical about the degree to which the United States could be relied upon in the struggle against fascism. As late as November 1940, Roosevelt was reelected on an isolationist platform. The Neutrality Acts prevented the United States from selling arms and other munitions to belligerent states. *See also* WORLD WAR II.

NEW ZEALAND. New Zealand was discovered by Captain James Cook on 6 October 1769. The youngest of Great Britain's white dominions in historical terms, New Zealand's indigenous Maori population came from Polynesia, probably around 900 A.D. It was declared a British colony on 21 May 1840, after the signing of the Treaty of Waitangi. Afterward, Anglo–Scots migration to the North Island and South Island, which make up New Zealand, increased rapidly. New Zealand, like the other white dominions **Australia, Canada,** and **South Africa,** began the slow evolutionary process toward full independence. It was given dominion status in 1907, and its independence was fully recognized by Britain in the Statute of Westminster (1931). Remote and small as it was, New Zealand seemed reluctant to sever ties. Only in 1947 did its parliament ratify the Statute of Westminster. In other respects, the island country was progressive, giving women the right to vote in 1893, well ahead of its concession in Britain. Its troops fought bravely for Britain in **World War I,** particularly at Gallipoli in 1915–1916, as part of the Australian–New Zealand contingent. New Zealand lost 16,000 men in the conflict. Kinship with the mother country remained strong in the 1920s and 1930s, as did defense dependence. In 1937–1938, New Zealand only contributed 0.8 percent of its gross national product to imperial defense. Despite this, its leaders continued to warn about the threat of Japanese aggression in the 1930s.

During **World War II,** New Zealand was steadfast. In December 1939, a New Zealand warship helped the Royal Navy sink a German pocket battleship in the Battle of the River Plate. New Zealand troops were sent to **Egypt** at a crucial time in 1940, and, afterward, they fought in many theaters. The blood tie with Britain was strong, but New Zealand increasingly looked to the **United States** as its key defense partner. In the **Cold War** era, the country supported British exclusion from the Anzus Treaty (1951). But old ties still meant that New Zealand sent soldiers to help Britain in Malaya in the 1950s. In the **Suez Crisis** of 1956, it supported Britain when most **Commonwealth** countries would not. Britain's decision to apply for membership of the **European Economic Community** dismayed New Zealanders who knew how dependent their country's dairy products were on British markets. While Britain fought for membership from 1961–1963, New Zealand was a stumbling block. At the time of the third British application in 1971, the issue of New Zealand butter still had the possibility of causing deadlock in Brussels. British membership in 1973 was a watershed. In 1958, when **Harold Macmillan** visited New Zealand on a Commonwealth tour, he was delighted to find that British influence was still great in the country. Even in 1973, 65 percent of New Zealand's exports went to Britain. In 1989, only 4 percent of New Zealand's goods were exported to Britain, while 18 percent were exported to **Japan.**

In other respects, New Zealand showed an independent spirit. Its Labour leader, Norman Kirk (prime minister, 1972–1974), reversed policy on the **Vietnam War** and withdrew New Zealand troops. David Lange (prime minister, 1984–1989) went further in adopting antinuclear policies and stopping a U.S. nuclear warship from docking in New Zealand. The island produced two female prime ministers, Jenny Shipley (1997) and Helen Clark (1999–2006). Another premier, Jim Bolger (1990–1997), challenged the old constitutional relationship with Britain by calling for the abolition of the monarchy. Some judicial functions remained with the Privy Council in London. This ended in 2004, when New Zealand acquired its own Supreme Court. **Elizabeth II** remained as the country's symbolic head of state, and intergovernmental links remain close. In September 2008, Meg Munn, parliamentary undersecretary at the **Foreign and Commonwealth Office (FCO)**, visited New Zealand, together with Sir Peter Ricketts, its permanent undersecretary. Chris Bryant, parliamentary undersecretary at the FCO, followed up this visit in July 2009. Murray McCully, New Zealand's minister of foreign affairs, visited Britain in July 2009 and January 2010. At the time, Britain was supportive at the time of the catastrophic Christchurch earthquake in New Zealand in 2011. There was admiration in Britain for the way New Zealand was able to host the 2011 Rugby World Cup. No nation was more devoted to the sport of rugby, which British settlers had brought to New Zealand, and in which its Maori population figures prominently.

NEWTON, BASIL (1889–1973). Basil Newton was the British minister in Prague, in 1937–1938, just as German pressure on **Czechoslovakia** began to mount. Newton had previously been first secretary in the Berlin embassy, when Nazi intentions would have been all too clear. He was promoted to minister in Berlin, in 1935, before his Prague posting. His view that Czechoslovakia, with its large German minority, was not a viable state in the long run undoubtedly influenced British policy. He was ambassador in **Iraq** from 1939–1941.

NICOLSON, SIR HAROLD (1886–1968). A distinguished diplomat, historian, and diarist, Harold Nicolson played a significant role in hammering out the details of the Central and Eastern European Settlement at the 1919 **Paris Peace Conference**. He remained with the Foreign Office until 1929, serving in Teheran and Berlin. He then went into journalism, before becoming a National Labour member of Parliament from 1935–1945. He was an opponent of **appeasement** who gloried in the fact that he possessed a "Foreign Office mind." Nicolson believed that Great Britain's task was to set a moral example for other European powers and protect the balance of power. He was a celebrated diarist (two volumes covering the period from 1931–1945) and the author of *Peacemaking, 1919* (1933), one of the greatest works on diplomacy ever written. He was married to the well-known writer Vita Sackville West and was the father of the artist Ben Nicolson. *See also* WORLD WAR I; WORLD WAR II.

NIXON, RICHARD M. (1913–1994). President of the **United States** between 1968–1974, Richard Nixon served as **Dwight D. Eisenhower's** vice president from 1953–1961. Nixon got along well enough with Great Britain's prime minister, **Harold Wilson,** but relations with his Conservative successor, **Edward Heath,** were lukewarm. Heath's priority was getting Britain into the **European Economic Community,** and he thus put less effort into the "**special relationship**" with the United States. Nixon was frustrated by Heath's apparent lack of interest. There were also differences over the Middle East following the Arab–Israeli War of October 1973. Heath refused to allow British bases to be used to refuel U.S. aircraft, which were flying supplies to **Israel.** Conversely, Nixon's worldwide nuclear alert at the time of the Arab–Israeli War was regarded with suspicion in Britain, where it was thought to be a device to distract attention from the disastrous Watergate scandal, which brought Nixon down in 1974.

Nixon's economic policies had a significant effect on Britain. In 1971, inflationary pressures resulting from the **Vietnam War** created a large U.S. trade deficit. Nixon's response was to abandon the fixed exchange rate of the dollar, which allowed it to float and then be devalued. This move effectively destroyed the monetary system set up by Britain and the United States at **Bretton Woods** in 1944.

NO. 10 DOWNING STREET. *See* DOWNING STREET, NO. 10.

NOBEL PEACE PRIZE. One of a series of international awards instituted by the Swedish armaments magnate Alfred Nobel, the Nobel Peace Prize traditionally recognizes those who have worked to avert international conflict. In 1925, Great Britain's **foreign secretary, Austen Chamberlain,** was awarded the prize. **Sir Norman Angell,** Labour member of Parliament from 1929–1931, also won the prize in 1933.

NOEL-BAKER, PHILIP (1889–1982). Philip Noel-Baker was the Labour member of Parliament for Coventry and a long-standing member of the party executive. He became secretary of state for **Commonwealth** relations in the 1945–1951 Labour government. Prior to his entry into Parliament, Noel-Baker had been in the Political Intelligence Department of the **Foreign**

Office at the time of the 1919 **Paris Peace Conference**, and also parliamentary private secretary to Arthur Henderson. He became a strong supporter of the **League of Nations** in the 1920s and 1930s, and was a leading figure in the League of Nations Union.

NORMAN, SIR MONTAGUE (1871–1950). The governor of the Bank of England at the time of the Wall Street Crash in 1929, Montague Norman was an advocate of the unsuccessful deflationary policies adopted by successive British governments to combat the Great Depression. In 1925, he was primarily responsible for persuading the new chancellor of the Exchequer, **Winston Churchill**, to return Great Britain to the gold standard, a decision that Churchill later admitted to have been a serious blunder. Norman's advice meant the acceptance of gold's prewar parity of $4.86, and a slump in overpriced British exports followed.

NORTH ATLANTIC TREATY ORGANIZATION (NATO) (1949). One of the lessons of the 1930s had been the need for effective collective security, and the North Atlantic Treaty Organization (NATO) provided this in 1949. Great Britain's **foreign secretary, Ernest Bevin**, was the strongest proponent of NATO as the answer to the apparent threat from the Soviet Union in 1947–1948. A striking feature of the new organization was the way in which it brought the **United States** and **Canada** in as players in the defense of Europe. The North Atlantic Treaty was signed in Washington on 4 April 1949. Signatory powers included **Belgium**, Canada, Denmark, **France**, Great Britain, Iceland, **Italy**, the Netherlands, Norway, Portugal, and the United States.

The end of the **Cold War** in 1989–1990 changed NATO's role, but its forces (including those of Great Britain) intervened in **Kosovo** in 1999 and **Libya** in 2011. It was in **Afghanistan**, in August 2003, that NATO took over responsibility for the international force, which remains the organization's greatest responsibility. Under a **United Nations** mandate, NATO led the International Security Assistance Force that tried to deal with the Taliban threat. Britain was a prominent player in the NATO force. The length of the NATO mandate remained a crucial issue, and this was the subject of a NATO summit in Chicago, on 21–22 May 2012, at which British prime minister **David Cameron** and U.S. president **Barack Obama** were present. It was agreed with Afghan president Hamid Karzai that when British and U.S. troops are pulled out in 2014, a force will remain to help with training. It was suggested that such a force will require a contribution of $4.1 billion (£2.6 billion) from member states. Britain promised to contribute $110 million per year, a considerable burden at a time of massive domestic austerity.

There has been a great extension of NATO membership since 1949. **Greece** and **Turkey** joined in 1952, and West Germany in 1955. **Spain** joined in 1986, while the Czech Republic, Hungary, and **Poland** did so in 1999. In a final demonstration that the Cold War was over, **Bulgaria**, Estonia, Latvia, Lithuania, Romania, Slovakia, and **Slovenia** became members in 2004.

NORTON, SIR CLIFFORD (1891–1990). Clifford Norton was educated at Rugby and Oxford and entered the Diplomatic Service in 1921. He was a "fond private secretary" to **Sir Robert Vansittart**, the permanent undersecretary at the **Foreign Office** from 1929–1937. As a diplomat in the Warsaw embassy from 1937–1939, Norton demonstrated deep sympathy for a **Poland** in peril. He dealt effectively with a difficult situation in **Greece** as ambassador from 1946–1951. Norton ended his career as a British delegate to the **United Nations** in 1952–1953.

NOTT, SIR JOHN (1932–). Secretary of state for defense at the time of the **Falklands War** in 1982, John Nott was fortunate to remain in post. It was his defense cuts that resulted in the removal from the South Atlantic of HMS *Endurance*, the sole Royal Navy vessel. Unlike British **foreign secretary** Peter Carrington, Nott chose not to resign, although he bore the greater responsibility along, with Prime Minister **Margaret Thatcher**, for precipitating the invasion of the islands by **Argentina**. As it was, Nott was more hawkish about the war than some other colleagues, and he was supportive of Thatcher's hard-nosed stance. Nott left British politics after the 1983 general election. He subsequently wrote a memoir that was praised for being better written and more incisive than most in the genre.

NUCLEAR NONPROLIFERATION TREATY (1968). The process of nuclear disarmament in the 1960s achieved a notable turning point with the 1968 Nuclear Nonproliferation Treaty. Great Britain, the **United States**, and the Soviet Union were the signatory powers. The object of the treaty was to prevent the spread of nuclear weapons to other states. The treaty came into force in 1970, and the signatories promised not to give nuclear weapons, or the technology whereby they might be created, to other powers. Nonnuclear powers that later signed the treaty pledged that they would not produce or obtain nuclear weapons. When the treaty came into force, it had been signed by 97 states. *See also* MASSIVE RETALIATION; NUCLEAR TEST BAN TREATY.

NUCLEAR TEST BAN TREATY (NTBT) (1963). Signed by Great Britain, the **United States**, and the Soviet Union, the 1963 Nuclear Test Ban

Treaty was a recognition of just how close the world had come to war at the time of the **Cuban Missile Crisis** of October 1962. It outlawed nuclear testing in the atmosphere, underwater, and in outer space, but did not prevent underground testing. In fact, more nuclear tests were carried out in the 10 years after 1963 than in the decade before. **France** and **China** would not sign the treaty, but 90 other states did so by 1965. British prime minister **Harold Macmillan** had been active in trying to persuade President **John F. Kennedy** to sign such a treaty, even before the Cuban Missile Crisis. It was part of the slow process of Soviet–Western **détente** in the 1960s and 1970s, designed to decrease **Cold War** tensions.

NUTTING, SIR ANTHONY (1920–1999). Minister of state at the **Foreign Office** at the time of the 1956 **Suez Crisis**, Anthony Nutting had been close to British prime minister **Anthony Eden** for 11 years prior to the crisis. He was regarded as the most pro-Arab minister in Eden's government and was appalled by the prime minister's growing paranoia about President **Jamal Abd al Nasser** of **Egypt**. Eden's personal fondness for him meant that he was kept in post even when he was known to oppose the Anglo–French Suez intervention. Nutting ultimately resigned on 31 October, although his resignation did not become public until 5 November. The Parliamentary Conservative Party viewed Nutting's resignation as a personal betrayal of Eden. There was also some prejudice against him because of his pending divorce, even though Eden himself divorced in 1950 and then married **Winston Churchill's** niece, Clarissa. Nutting and Eden did not speak again after November 1956, even though Eden had remarked to him that, "Everything is wrecked except friendship." Nutting was as much of a loser in the Suez Crisis as Eden himself. He resigned from his parliamentary seat at the same time that he gave up his ministerial position, and he never had the career in the Conservative Party that his early promise suggested. A subsequent attempt to secure selection for a parliamentary seat in 1964 failed, and Nutting had to accept that his political career was over. His memoir *No End of a Lesson: The Story of Suez* (1967) is an important source for the period.

O

OBAMA, BARACK HUSSEIN (1961–). The first African American president of the **United States**, Barack Obama was elected to the White House in November 2008. His election won a good deal of approval among the increasingly multicultural British public; however, there was some speculation about the course Anglo–American relations would take with Obama as president. Relations between former prime minister **Tony Blair** and President **George W. Bush** had been close. This was less true of Blair's successor, **Gordon Brown**, but the "**special relationship**" was still very much intact.

President Obama had a Kenyan father who had some difficulties with British colonial authorities during the **Mau Mau** period (1952–1959); therefore, his attitude was likely to be somewhat different where Great Britain was concerned, with more attention being given to countries like **Germany**. Nevertheless, when **David Cameron** succeeded Brown as prime minister in May 2010, events soon underlined the value of Anglo–American friendship. Obama and Cameron cooperated in the campaign against **Libya** in 2011, and they tried to get a hamstrung **United Nations** to be more proactive in the emergency over Syria in 2011–2012. The extraordinary gaffes made by Obama's Republican Party opponent Mitt Romney while on a visit to Britain in July 2012 only appeared to enhance Obama's value as a partner and his chances of reelection in November 2012.

OLIPHANT, SIR LANCELOT (1881–1965). Deputy undersecretary at the **Foreign Office** from 1936–1939, Lancelot Oliphant was a mentor to many young diplomas, including **Nevile Henderson**. Oliphant was Britain's ambassador in the Netherlands in 1939–1940, and he was captured and interned in **Germany**. He was released in October 1941 and resumed his duties at the Foreign Office. He chronicles his experience as a German prisoner in a memoir entitled *An Ambassador in Bonds* (1946).

O'MALLEY, SIR OWEN (1887–1974). The son of Sir Edward O'Malley, a judge of the supreme court in **Egypt** and of northern Irish extraction, Owen O'Malley was educated at Magdalen College, Oxford. He entered the **Foreign Office**, which he later described as the "brotherhood," in 1911. In 1928,

O'Malley was involved in a scandal over speculation in francs, but he was cleared by a government board of inquiry and his career prospects were not blighted. He became head of the Southern Department of the Foreign Office and was a supporter of the emollient line taken by **Sir Nevile Henderson** as ambassador in Berlin toward the Nazis from 1937–1939. O'Malley was a Francophobe who also preached about the lack of wisdom in assuming that British democratic practice could transfer itself to other European states. After his time in the Southern Department, O'Malley served as minister and ambassador to the Polish government in exile, and to Mexico, Hungary, and Portugal. While in Lisbon from 1945–1947, he got along well with dictator António Salazar. O'Malley was married to the well-known novelist Anne Bridge.

O'NEILL, SIR CON (1912–1988). Con O'Neill took the traditional road from **Eton College** and Balliol College Oxford to the **Foreign Office**. An additional distinction was his fellowship at **All Souls College** from 1935–1946. He joined the Foreign Office in 1936 and was posted as a third secretary to Berlin. O'Neill resigned his post in 1938, in protest of the **Munich Agreement**. During **World War II**, he served in the Intelligence Corps of the British Army, joining the *Times* newspaper as a lead writer in 1946. Unusually, he returned to the Foreign Office in 1947. After service in **Germany,** O'Neill was appointed head of the News Department at the Foreign Office in 1954–1955. He was chargé d' affaires in Beijing from 1955–1957, and ambassador to Finland in 1961. As ambassador to the **European Economic Community** in 1963, O'Neill was involved in the events surrounding Great Britain's first unsuccessful attempt to join the organization.

OSBORNE, GEORGE (1971–). The current chancellor of the exchequer, George Osborne was appointed to his post by the Conservative prime minister **David Cameron** in May 2010. Osborne comes from Anglo–Irish roots and is the heir to the Osborne baronetcy (of Ballentaylor in County Tipperary, and Ballylemon in County Waterford, both in the Irish Republic). Upon the death of his father, Sir Peter Osborne, he will become the 18th Baronet. This background enabled Osborne to be educated at St. Paul's School, London, and Magdalen College, Oxford, where he read history. It was at Oxford that Osborne made his most important political friendship with Cameron. Osborne was also a Dean Rusk scholar at Davidson College, in North Carolina. Like Cameron, Osborne worked for the Conservative Research Department, starting in 1994. From 1995–1997, he worked as a special advisor to the minister of agriculture, Douglas Hogg, a classic route to promotion in modern British politics. Osborne's next post was as a speechwriter to the Conservative leader **William Hague** from 1997–2001, when Hague stood down. He had also acted as Hague's political secretary before his election as a Conservative member of Parliament in the 2001 general election. Osborne won the Tatton, Cheshire, seat, which had forced out the previous Conservative member of Parliament in 1997 for financial misdemeanors.

After three years in the House of Commons, Osborne obtained a crucial promotion from the new Conservative leader Michael Howard, becoming shadow chief secretary. This developed his career path in financial governance, and, in 2005, at the young age of 33, Howard made Osborne shadow chancellor of the exchequer. When Howard stood down as leader following his 2005 election defeat, Osborne chose not to use this senior post as a base to run for leader himself. Instead, he became Cameron's campaign manager, and his old friend became leader (the two men are even godfather to one another's children).

It cannot be said that Osborne's period as shadow chancellor was especially innovative. He fully supported the Labour policy of light-fingered regulation of London, where the boon in financial services was out of control by 2007. His idea of a general flat tax of 22 percent was not pursued, although a promise to reduce inheritance tax was popular within the Conservative ranks. Like Cameron, Osborne was a Eurosceptic.

In 2009, Osborne was implicated in the British parliamentary expenses scandal affair after he designated his second home as his first to avoid paying capital gains tax. He played a minor role in the 2010 election campaign, partly because of his unpopularity, but also because London doubted his capacity to run the British economy. He was appointed chancellor of the exchequer on 12 May 2010. One of his first acts was to establish the Office of Budget Responsibility (OBR), which was supposed to offer independent advice and predictions on fiscal policy (even though the OBR was located in Osborne's own treasury building). Osborne's major objective was to deal with Britain's massive deficit, £40 billion of which derived from the need for the previous Labour government to partly nationalize the Royal Bank of Scotland, Lloyds Bank, and Northern Rock. In July 2010, Osborne demonstrated his intent by cutting government expenditure by 25 percent. Yet, paradoxically, he was still prepared to pay £20 billion to pay for the cost of four new Vanguard-class submarines.

Osborne's strategy was to reduce the deficit by 2015, the next general election, and be in a position to make tax cuts, but events in 2010–2011 actually resulted in increased government borrowing, by £158 billion. Osborne tried to link this occurrence to the 2011 **Eurozone** crisis, but this line of argument did not convince anyone. Unemployment soared as a result of the coalition government's austerity program, and the lack of growth in Britain meant that in 2011, the economy flatlined for two successive quarters (the definition of a recession). Osborne constantly referred to Britain as a safe haven during a global crisis, but his deflationary policies, with the barest nod to growth, risked the danger of a double-dip recession in 2012. Some lessons were learned. On 19 December 2011, Osborne announced the acceptance of Sir John Vickers's report on British banking. Retail and investment banking were to be ring-fenced by 2019, more slowly than many would have liked, in an attempt to prevent the sort of reckless banking bonanza that had caused the "credit crunch" of 2007–2009, and almost brought down the British financial system. Osborne remained Cameron's chief ally and supporter in the Conservative Party, and a potential future leader.

OWEN, DAVID (1938–). Great Britain's youngest **foreign secretary** since the appointment of **Anthony Eden** in 1935, David Owen held the post from 1977–1979. He owed his surprise appointment to the premature death of his Labour predecessor, Anthony Crosland, in 1977. Owen worked effectively with U.S. secretary of state **Cyrus Vance** to solve the problems posed by white minority rule in **Southern Rhodesia**. The issues were resolved in 1980, when Owen's Labour Party lost power. Owen and Vance were colleagues again when they tried to resolve the **Bosnia** crisis in the 1990s. The Muslims in Bosnia thought him to be pro-Serbian in his approach and nicknamed him the "Serbian doctor." Owen was pro-European in outlook, which was one of the reasons why he was one of the so-called "Gang of Four," led by Roy Jenkins, that left the Labour Party in 1981 and founded the Social Democratic Party. He was created Lord Owen.

P

PACIFICO, DON. The most prominent of a series of complaints by Great Britain against **Greece** in the 1840s concerned a Jewish man named Don Pacifico, who was born in **Gibraltar** and held a British passport. In 1847, his house in Athens was attacked by an anti-Semitic mob, and his appeal for compensation to the Greek government was ignored. Lord **Henry John Palmerston**, the British **foreign secretary**, arranged for a British fleet to sail to Athens to obtain compensation from the Greeks. When they refused to comply, a blockade of the city was imposed by the Royal Navy. In the House of Lords, on the night of 25–26 June 1847, Palmerston gave a grandiose defense of his conception of British foreign policy. Comparing Great Britain to the Roman Empire, he claimed that a British subject, no matter where he was, must know that the "watchful eye and strong arm of England" would protect him. In contrast, Palmerston's opponent, **William Gladstone**, said that British foreign secretaries should not be like mediaeval knights, but rather behave with dignity while seeking compromise. Pacifico received his compensation and returned to obscurity. **Queen Victoria** was disgusted by Palmerston's behavior.

PAKISTAN. Pakistan, which obtained its independence from Great Britain on 15 August 1947, had been part of British **India** since the early 19th century. The name is an acronym for the constituent peoples of the new state, which include Punjabis, Afghans, Kashmiris, Sinds, and the inhabitants of Baluchistan. The Northwest Frontier tribes were a considerable problem for the British, who accorded them considerable autonomy. There were millions of Muslims in India, but they were concentrated in the Northwest and East Bengal. Resentment against British rule began to emerge before **World War I,** and the foundation of the Muslim League reflected this. The founder of the Pakistan state, Muhammad Ali Jinnah, joined the Muslim League in 1913. He was also a member of the All-India Congress Party. In the 1920s and 1930s, Jinnah increasingly began to move away from the Congress. The Muslim League had limited electoral support, but, on 27 March 1940, the league put forth the so-called "Lahore Resolution," also known as the "Pakistan Resolution," demanding a separate Muslim state in the Punjab and East Bengal.

There were suspicions that the British viceroy Lord Linlithgow encouraged Muslim separatism to break the power of the Congress Party. Muslims fought bravely for Britain in **World War II**.

During 1942, British prime minister **Winston Churchill** sent Sir Stafford Cripps to India to seek a solution. Cripps failed in this, partly because of Churchill's adamant refusal to endorse the concept of Indian, let alone Pakistani, independence. In 1946, the Labour prime minister, **Clement R. Attlee**, much more sympathetic to Indian aspirations, sent the so-called "Cabinet Mission" to the subcontinent. It suggested that Pakistan should not be given independence, but that two Muslim majority areas should have autonomy. Britain would retain responsibility for foreign policy, defense, and communications. Jinnah flatly rejected the proposal on behalf of the Muslim League. He could dictate events, because, in the 1945–1946 provincial elections, the league got 75 percent of the Muslim vote. Attlee had doubted whether Pakistan would be viable in economic terms, but he had changed his mind. In 1947, **Lord Louis Mountbatten** was sent out as viceroy to accelerate the process of independence. Pakistan received its independence on 15 August 1947. Jinnah had been appointed governor general, the representative of the British Crown, on 14 August. Partition was a disaster. Unknown numbers of Muslims died while trying to flee from India to Pakistan. Others died in communal rioting in cities like Bombay. Jinnah was a British-educated secularist, free of religious prejudice. It was a tragic loss for Pakistan when he died on 1 September 1948. Proper constitutional and administrative structures had not yet been formed.

This lacking became clear in the years that followed. Matters were made even more complex by geography. West Pakistan was 1,000 miles from East Pakistan, where the population was more homogenous. Politics and religion also intruded. Kashmir, a Muslim majority state, was divided by the British. War threatened between the two new states, and the **United Nations** had to get involved. On 1 January 1949, a truce line was established. Pakistan only got one-third of the state. Kashmir was a running sore in Indian–Pakistani relations. Some of the responsibility for the unsatisfactory settlement rested with Britain. Pakistan, however, was a reliable regional British ally. Both countries joined the **Southeast Asia Treaty Organization** in 1954, and the Baghdad Pact in 1955. British **foreign secretary Anthony Eden** visited Pakistan the same year. The two countries fell out over Eden's botched invasion of **Egypt** in 1956, when Pakistan threatened to leave the **Commonwealth**. This crisis was resolved. **Harold Macmillan** noted Pakistani anxieties about British efforts to enter the **European Economic Community (EEC)** (1961–1963). Pakistan's president, Ayub Khan, wanted better terms for its textiles and thought India was being treated too generously in the EEC talks.

Britain was unable to prevent its former colonies from falling out over Kashmir. War broke out in 1965. Both the Pakistani and Indian generals had been educated at Britain's premier military academy, Sandhurst, and sounded like public school products. It was a sign of the times that the settlement following the Indian victory was presided over in Tashkent, in January 1966, by Soviet prime minister Alexei Kosygin. Pakistan increasingly fell into the U.S. orbit, as did India into the Soviet Union's. Britain was sidelined. Its major involvement with Pakistan increasingly focused on the movement of ethnic Pakistanis to Britain to seek work. At home in Pakistan, democracy failed. There were military coups in 1958, 1977, and 1999, and the influence of the Pakistani army was unhealthy. In 1971, it was defeated again by India, and, long resentful, East Pakistan seceded to become **Bangladesh.**

The career of Zulfikar Bhutto (president, 1971–1973; prime minister, 1973–1977) was symptomatic of most of what was wrong with Pakistan. An Oxford graduate and immensely wealthy Sind landowner, Bhutto tried to foster democracy through his Pakistan People's Party. Yet, his power was based on wealth and privilege, one of 22 families that dominated the country. Bhutto was overthrown by a military coup in 1977, and hanged in 1979 for electoral abuses. His daughter, Benazir Bhutto, another Oxford graduate, also held the title of prime minister (1984–1986, 1990–1996) before being assassinated in 2008. Zulfikar Bhutto Sr. was overthrown by the military dictator Zia-ul-Haq (1977–1988), who tried to move the country in the direction of Sharia law. His death in a plane crash in 1988 brought back Benazir Bhutto (1990–1996), whom British observers hoped would restore real democracy. Benazir Bhutto was a liberal-sounding exile while in Britain, but her highly privileged Sind-based background meant that her record as a reformer was poor. It was hard to preserve law and order, even in Bhutto's own province of Sind, especially among the turbulent Northwestern tribes. There was much corruption, as well as an overly powerful army, lavishly aided by the **United States.** Bhutto's successor, Nawaz Sharif (1996–1999), was no more successful. In 1999, Pakistan's instability was demonstrated by yet another military coup by Pervez Musharraf. Under Musharraf's government, Islamic extremism flourished, encouraged in religious schools whose zealotry alarmed Westerners.

Pakistan has maintained links with Britain through its membership in the **Commonwealth.** George VI was its head of state from 1947–1952, when **Elizabeth II** became queen. In 1956, Pakistan became a republic and, in 1962, the Islamic Republic of Pakistan, thus severing the link with the Crown. Elizabeth II paid a state visit to Pakistan in October 1997. Interstate relations became more complex and fraught after the Soviet invasion of **Afghanistan** in December 1979. Britain and Pakistan encouraged anti-Soviet resistance, which ultimately brought about Soviet withdrawal in 1989. In encouraging such mujahideen opposition, Britain made a rod for its own back. Particularly after Anglo–American intervention in Afghanistan in 2001, and **Iraq** in 2003, the British involvement in Afghanistan made the country a target for jihadist activity, which was not always picked up by the British authorities. The bombing outrages in London, on 7 July 2005, were carried out by four individuals, three of whom were of Pakistani origin. British suggestions that they were directed by a jihadist mastermind in Pakistan were rejected by the high commissioner for Pakistan in London. The huge Pakistani immigrant population of almost 1 million kept close links with the mother country, but the Pakistani government continued to deny any link between **terrorism** in Britain and Pakistan. Britain and the United States were constantly suspicious of the role of the Interservices Intelligence (ISI) organization in the Pakistani armed forces, which was known to have close links with the Taliban in Afghanistan. Relations with India over Kashmir fermented more instability as jihadist activity spread there.

The British government was generally reluctant to speak publicly about suspicions of collusion between the ISI and the Taliban, who became a serious security problem inside Pakistan itself. On 28 July 2010, Britain's new premier, **David Cameron**, went against this trend and stated that Pakistan encouraged the export of terrorism. This outraged the people of Pakistan, where it was pointed out that it suffered far more from internal terrorism than Britain. Matters were patched up when Cameron subsequently met President Asif Ali Zardari (the husband of Benazir Bhutto) and spoke of an "unbreakable relationship" with Pakistan. Zardari reciprocated in friendly language, but suspicions remained nonetheless.

In December 2010, Cameron suggested a state visit to Pakistan in the wake of a visit to British soldiers in Afghanistan. The Pakistanis rejected this afterthought as insulting. For its part, Britain was dismayed by the sudden discovery and execution by U.S. Special Forces of Osama bin Laden inside Pakistan in 2011. Bin Laden had been hunted since 2001, but the Pakistani government had always denied knowing his whereabouts. Both British and U.S. intelligence agencies believed this to have been impossible. It was a fragile balance. Pakistan was still deemed to be an essential partner in the war against terrorism, but it remained a dangerous environment for Britons. In April 2012, Foreign Secretary **William Hague** described the murder of a British Red Cross worker in southwest Pakistan as senseless.

PALESTINE. Great Britain's relationship with Palestine dates from the 1917 Balfour Declaration, in which His Majesty's Government declared its support for a national home for the Jews, but not a state in Palestine. British forces conquered the area by defeating the Ottoman Turks in 1918. The San Remo Conference of the **League of Nations** made Palestine a British mandate in 1920, and their administration took over in 1923. Severe communal tensions between Jews and Arabs were a feature from the start, and the British mandatory authorities were perceived to be pro-Jewish. Zionists—those who wished to create a Jewish state in Palestine—were adept at convincing the British that this was a desirable solution. The Arab revolt of 1936 was no surprise, and the British had difficulty suppressing it. During **World War II**, Arab nationalists flirted with Nazism, while the Zionists joined Crown forces fighting **Germany**, thus gaining valuable military experience. The situation was transformed, however, by the Holocaust, which created a displaced Jewish population of 250,000 people, many of whom wished to immigrate to Palestine. In April 1946, the British agreed to allow just 100,000 more Jews into Palestine. At the time, the mandatory authorities faced both Jewish and Arab **terrorism**. In July 1946, the King David Hotel, Britain's military headquarters in Jerusalem, was blown up by Jewish terrorists and its resolve to remain in Palestine greatly weakened. The British Labour government, led by **Clement R. Attlee**, agreed on 15 February 1947 to hand over the Palestine problem to the new **United Nations (UN)** organization, which had replaced the League of Nations. The British mandate ended on 14 May 1948, and Israel declared itself an independent state. The UN partition plan, which divided up Palestine between Jews and Arabs, was set aside as a result of the Arab–Israeli War of 1948–1949. Thousands of Palestinian Arabs became stateless as a result. Britain had voted to accept Israel's independence at the UN. *See also* BEVIN, ERNEST; IRGUN ZVAI LEUMI.

PALLISER, SIR MICHAEL (1922–2012). Michael Palliser was permanent undersecretary and head of the Diplomatic Service from 1975–1982. Between April and July 1982, he was a special advisor to Prime Minister **Margaret Thatcher** at the time of the **Falklands War**. Beforehand, Palliser had a classic Foreign Office career after joining the service in 1947. He was a private secretary to **Harold Wilson** in the 1960s and had to mediate in the sometimes-volatile relationship between Prime Minister Wilson and his **foreign secretary, George Brown**. Palliser subsequently served in the Paris embassy and as ambassador and permanent representative to the **European Economic Community (EEC)**. He married Marie Marguerite Spaak, the daughter of Belgian statesman Paul-Henri Spaak, one of the founding fathers of the EEC.

PALMERSTON, HENRY JOHN 3RD VISCOUNT (1784–1865). The son of an Irish peer, Henry John Palmerston was probably the most flamboyant prime minister and **foreign secretary** Great Britain has ever had. He won his last general election victory in 1865, at the age of 80. Palmerston was foreign secretary continuously from 1830–1841, and he stood for robust interventionism in Europe wherever British naval power could be applied. When it could not, Palmerston's diplomacy failed, notably over the thorny issue of Schleswig-Holstein in 1863–1864. Palmerston encouraged Denmark to expect help from Britain against Austria and Prussia, but this was a bluff. The Danes were easily defeated by the Austro–Prussians in 1864, and the provinces of Schleswig and Holstein were taken from them. Palmerston's attitude was typically casual. He claimed that only three people understood the Schleswig-Holstein problem: the husband of **Queen Victoria**, Prince Albert, who was dead; a Danish professor who was in a lunatic asylum; and he himself, and he had forgotten all about it. Yet, Palmerston could represent a noninterventionist tradition in British foreign policy when he chose to. During his last spell as prime minister from 1859–1865, the American Civil War broke out, and Palmerston, who seems to have sympathized with the South, was careful to keep Britain uninvolved, refusing to even act as a mediator, as his foreign secretary, Lord Russell, and his chancellor of the exchequer, **William Gladstone**, wanted. Even in old age, Palmerston was a notorious womanizer, which partly accounts for Queen Victoria's antagonism toward him. Upon hearing of his death in 1865, she remarked, "I never liked him." *See also* PACIFICO, DON; UNITED STATES.

PAN-ARABISM. Pan-Arabism is a doctrine associated with President **Jamal Abd al Nasser** of **Egypt** that sees the Arab world as an ethnic and religious community. Nasser tried unsuccessfully to unite Egypt and Syria from 1958–1961, and an intervention in Yemen also failed. The British **Foreign Office** tended to confuse Pan-Arabism with Communism in the 1950s and 1960s. It was a curiosity that Nasser, an Egyptian, was himself not actually an Arab.

PARIS PEACE CONFERENCE (1919). The settlement at the end of **World War I** was negotiated in Paris in 1919. It began on 18 January 1919, and work continued for more than a year, with Great Britain being represented by its prime minister, **David Lloyd George**. A series of treaties emerged from the Paris Peace Conference, the most important being the **Treaty of Versailles**, dealing with defeated **Germany**, which was signed on 28 June 1919. The Treaty of Saint-Germain dealt with Austria-Hungary, the Treaty of Trianon with Hungary, and the Treaty of Neuilly and Treaty of Sèvres with **Bulgaria** and **Turkey**. The locations were all suburbs of Paris.

PEARL HARBOR (1941). On 7 December 1941, the Imperial Japanese Navy launched a devastating aerial attack on the U.S. naval base at Pearl Harbor, in Hawaii. Carrier-based Japanese aircraft sank five U.S battleships and damaged others. The tragedy, in which 2,400 Americans died, brought the **United States** into **World War II** on the side of Great Britain and the Soviet Union. Fortunately, the U.S. aircraft carriers were at sea at the time. Conspiracy theories that suggest that President **Franklin D. Roosevelt** knew in advance of the attack and allowed it to unite public opinion in the United States have little substance. The Japanese intended to present a declaration of war before the attack, but incompetence at the Japanese embassy in Washington prevented transmission of the war declaration in time. Suggestions that **Winston Churchill** withheld British intelligence about the Japanese attack are also fanciful.

PERCENTAGES AGREEMENT (1944). In October 1944, British prime minister **Winston Churchill** flew to Moscow to discuss postwar Europe with Soviet leader Joseph Stalin. The **"percentages agreement"** that emerged gave Great Britain a predominant influence in **Greece** but acknowledged the greater Soviet influence in **Bulgaria** and Romania. Stalin honored his deal with Churchill in regards to Greece and did not assist the Communists in the **Greek Civil War.**

PERSIA. *See* IRAN.

PETERSON, SIR MAURICE (1889–1952). Great Britain's ambassador in Moscow from 1946–1949, at the onset of the **Cold War**, was Maurice Peterson. He arrived in Moscow in May 1946. Before doing so, Peterson had attended an important **Foreign Office** briefing on 18 March, about the state of Anglo–Soviet relations. There was a good deal of confusion among officials about Soviet intentions and pessimism. Once settled in Moscow, Peterson told his superiors that a firm attitude represented the best way of dealing with the Russians, who could be persuaded to put their policies into reverse. He attempted to persuade the notoriously intransigent Soviet foreign minister Vyacheslav Molotov that the Polish elections of January 1947 must be free and democratic, but, like his American colleague, he was ignored. They were, in fact, wholly fraudulent. Peterson was quite unable to prevent the marked worsening of East–West relations, which ended with the **Berlin Blockade** of 1948–1949, and the formation of the anti-Soviet **North Atlantic Treaty Organization.**

Peterson had previously been British ambassador in Madrid in 1939–1940, and he was embittered by his sudden removal when **Winston Churchill** wanted to get his old adversary and appeaser **Sir Samuel Hoare** out of the way by sending him to **Spain**. Peterson subsequently served in Cairo and became an undersecretary of state at the Foreign Office.

PHIPPS, SIR ERIC (1875–1945). A product of Kings College, Cambridge, Eric Phipps was British ambassador in Berlin from 1933–1937, and then ambassador in Paris until 1939. He was the brother-in-law of the permanent undersecretary at the **Foreign Office, Sir Robert Vansittart,** but the two did not always see eye to eye. Phipps later claimed that Vansittart undermined him when he was ambassador in Paris. In Berlin, Phipps was an acerbic and astute critic of National Socialism and was removed in 1937 because he was deemed too anti-German. By contrast, in Paris, Phipps became much more sympathetic to the British government's **appeasement** policy. He caused dismay in the Foreign Office at the time of the 1938 **Munich Agreement** by suggesting that all the best elements in French society favored appeasement of **Germany**. Phipps had served in Paris, Petrograd, and Madrid earlier in his career, which started in 1889. He was minister in Vienna, a minor posting that did not merit an ambassadorship, from 1928–1933.

PITT, WILLIAM THE YOUNGER (1759–1806). The son of William Pitt, Earl of Chatham, who had led Great Britain to victory in the Seven Years' War (1756–1963), William Pitt the Younger became prime minister at the age of 23. He was in **No. 10 Downing Street** for nearly the entire span of the French Revolutionary War and **Napoleonic Wars** from 1793–1806, when Britain was at war with **France**. Pitt tried to keep unwieldy anti-French coalitions in place while passing draconian laws against republican subversion. Upon hearing the news of **Napoleon Bonaparte's** sweeping victory over Britain's land allies at Austerlitz in December 1805, Pitt is alleged to have told colleagues to roll up the map of Europe because it would not be needed for a decade. He died in January 1806, weighed down by the burdens of office.

PLEVEN PLAN. Named after the French foreign minister René Pleven, this plan of October 1950 called for an integrated, multinational European army responsible to a European assembly and also a European defense minister. Great Britain rejected the idea for a **European Defense Community** as an unacceptable breach of national sovereignty. Prime Minister **Clement R. Attlee** described it as unworkable. *See also* EUROPEAN COAL AND STEEL COMMUNITY; EUROPEAN ECONOMIC COMMUNITY/EUROPEAN COMMUNITY.

POINCARÉ, RAYMOND (1860–1934). President of **France** from 1913–1920, Raymond Poincaré was prime minister at the time of Franco–Belgian intervention in the Ruhr in January 1923. This followed a German default on reparations payments, which had been enforced under the terms of the 1919 **Treaty of Versailles**. This move was strongly opposed by Great Britain. British intelligence was reading French diplomatic communications at the time, and the foreign secretary, **George Curzon**, was reduced to tears by the violence in Poincaré's language about Britain.

POLAND. A reunited Poland came back into existence in 1919–1920, as a result of the **Treaty of Versailles** and the Treaty of Saint-Germain. It was divided yet again by the Nazi–Soviet Pact of 23 August 1939, between the Soviet Union and Nazi **Germany**. Poland suffered terribly in **World War II**, with 6 million causalities, the highest loss per head of population for any European state. Great Britain went to war on 3 September 1939, pledging to restore an independent Poland, and many Poles joined their government in exile in Britain. Ostensibly independent after the German defeat in 1945, Poland was, in reality, a satellite of the Soviet Union. Communism was intensely unpopular in a strongly Catholic Poland, which revolted against Communist rule in 1956 and 1980 through the non-Communist trade union movement Solidarity. Two years earlier, in 1978, the election of the Polish pope John Paul II was a notable development in Poland's national struggle. Repression merely strengthened Polish nationalism, and the Communists were ejected from power, amid much national rejoicing in 1989. Poland subsequently became a member of both the **European Union** and **North Atlantic Treaty Organization**. *See also* POLISH CORRIDOR.

POLARIS MISSLE. The submarine-launched Polaris missile was based at **Holy Loch**, in Scotland, as a result of talks between Prime Minister **Harold Macmillan** and President **Dwight D. Eisenhower** in March 1960. The missiles were solely under U.S. control, a concession that angered many in Great Britain at the time. Holy Loch became a target for antinuclear protests.

POLISH CORRIDOR (1919). The newly recreated **Poland** of 1919–1920 needed access to the Baltic Sea to avoid being a landlocked state. This access was granted under the terms of the 1919 **Treaty of Versailles**, which drove a corridor of Polish territory through eastern **Germany** and isolated East Prussia from the rest of the state. The Poles were also allowed to use the port of Danzig (now Gdansk), which was under overall **League of Nations** control. This settlement caused bitter resentment among both the majority German population in the Polish Corridor and Danzig, and the rest of the German population. It was this crisis over Danzig and the Polish Corridor that forced Great Britain and **France** into war with Germany in September 1939.

POMPIDOU, GEORGES (1911–1974). The second president of the 5th French Republic, Georges Pompidou had succeeded Charles de Gaulle in 1969. He reversed de Gaulle's foreign policy by withdrawing French objections to Great Britain's membership in the **European Economic Community (EEC)**, thus setting the stage for its entry to the EEC on 1 January 1973.

PONTING, CLIVE (1944–). In 1984, Clive Ponting, a senior civil servant at the **Ministry of Defense,** was asked to gather the highly sensitive material relating to the sinking of the Argentinian battleship the ARA *General Belgrano* by a Royal Navy submarine during the **Falklands War** of 1982. He was later at a meeting presided over by the secretary of state for defense, Michael Heseltine, when it was decided to effectively mislead Parliament about what had happened. The ARA *General Belgrano* had, in fact, been sailing away from the Falklands when it had been sunk on government orders. Ponting found this decision unacceptable and made the truth known to the public. He was then tried under Section 2 of the 1911 Official Secrets Act because he had broken an undertaking not to divulge government secrets. Ponting's trial defense was that he had the call of a duty higher than just obeying his minister as a civil servant. The trial jury agreed with him, and he was acquitted, much to the embarrassment of the government of **Margaret Thatcher.** It had been desperate to preserve the story of the Falklands War as a heroic adventure that nothing must detract from. Ponting subsequently became an author and historian.

"POSITION OF THE UNITED KINGDOM IN WORLD AFFAIRS" (1958). In the aftermath of the 1956 **Suez Crisis,** there was a painful reexamination of Great Britain's foreign policy priorities. A policy review paper entitled "The Position of the United Kingdom in World Affairs" was published in June 1958. This accepted Britain's reduced status in world affairs while still claiming that it could have an influential role. Britain's dependence on the **United States** was fully recognized and the primary importance of the American alliance rather than **Commonwealth** links accepted. Unlike two papers produced by former foreign secretary and prime minister **Anthony Eden** in 1952 and 1956, the 1958 paper recognizes Britain's economic weakness and chronic balance of payments problems. Yet, it still refuses to see Britain as a purely European power. The nuclear deterrent had to be retained and the British military presence in **Germany** maintained at existing levels. Savings would have to be made in civil rather than military expenditure, so that Britain's status as a great power was not threatened. This reflected the views of Prime Minister **Harold Macmillan** on Britain's future foreign policy role. His strong pro-Americanism con-

trasted with Eden's tendency to mistrust the United States. This had allegedly led to the "Suezide" of November 1956.

POTSDAM CONFERENCE (1945). The Potsdam Conference of July
1945 was the last of the great wartime conferences involving Allied leaders
in **World War II**. Great Britain was initially represented by Prime Minister
Winston Churchill, but he had to be replaced by **Clement R. Attlee** when
the Labour Party won a sweeping victory in the 1945 general election. The
United States was represented by President **Harry S. Truman** and the Soviet Union by General Secretary Joseph Stalin. The conference, which lasted
from 17 July to 2 August, finalized the plans to defeat **Japan** and divided
defeated **Germany** between the victorious powers. **France** joined the other
three Great Powers in running a zone of occupation in Germany. During the
conference, President Truman was told about the successful detonation of
an atomic bomb in the New Mexico desert. He told Stalin about the device,
but the Soviet dictator already knew about its existence, thanks to espionage
activity in Britain and the United States. Relations between Stalin and his
Western allies were already starting to fracture.

POWELL, CHARLES (1941–). Charles Powell was seconded to **No. 10
Downing Street** from the **Foreign Office** when **Margaret Thatcher** was
prime minister. He became her close confidant and Baron Powell of Bays-
water.

PRINCE OF WALES, HMS. The sinking of the battleship HMS *Prince of
Wales* by the Japanese was one of the most devastating losses suffered by the
Royal Navy in **World War II**. On 10 December 1941, the HMS *Prince of
Wales* and its sister ship, the HMS *Repulse*, were attacked by Japanese air-
craft off the coast of Malaya. Six hundred British sailors were lost. **Winston
Churchill**, who had authorized the sending of the ships to the Far East, was
deeply shocked.

PROTHERO, GEORGE (1848–1922). George Prothero was the long-
standing director of the **Foreign Office** historical section. A traditionalist,
he felt that Prime Minister **David Lloyd George** was the wrong person to
represent Great Britain at the 1919 **Paris Peace Conference** because he was
a "cad."

PYM, SIR FRANCIS (1922–2008). Sir Francis Pym replaced Lord Peter
Carrington as British **foreign secretary** when he took responsibility for Great
Britain being surprised by **Argentina's** invasion of the **Falkland Islands** in

April 1982 and resigned. There was a sharp difference of approach to the Falklands problem between Pym and Prime Minister **Margaret Thatcher**. He believed in taking the diplomatic track, while Thatcher, egged on by Admiral **Sir Henry Leach**, thought force should be used. Like his predecessor Carrington, and unlike Thatcher, Pym had seen distinguished military service in **World War II** and was therefore of the view that war should be avoided at all costs. Relations between Pym and Thatcher worsened rapidly when he did not appear to share the prime minister's enthusiasm for the conflict. His instincts in favor of diplomacy generally mirrored those of the **Foreign Office**. Pym was prepared to accept increased Argentine involvement in Falkland affairs and long-term talks about the status of the islands, but Thatcher was not. She sacked Pym shortly after her sweeping election victory in May 1983. Pym had previously served as secretary of state for defense in the Thatcher Cabinet but was already regarded as a "wet," a term used for those who did not share Thatcher's robust inclinations in economic defense and foreign policies. In fact, in November 1980, Pym had threatened to resign from the government when Thatcher and her monetarist supporters wanted deep cuts in the defense budget. He was punished by being moved laterally to serve as leader of the House of Commons. It was an irony that Thatcher-inspired defense cuts led to the Argentine invasion, which in turn led to Pym's demise. His great ancestor, John Pym, had led the parliamentary side in the English Civil War (1642–1645).

QUEBEC AGREEMENT (1943). On 19 August 1943, Prime Minister **Winston Churchill** and President **Franklin D. Roosevelt** signed an agreement relating to nuclear cooperation between Great Britain and the **United States**. Beforehand, the British had considered producing their own atomic bomb before cost issues intruded. Britain certainly had research scientists of sufficient caliber. As it was under the code name "Operation Manhattan," British research was subsumed into the American program. Both parties agreed not to pass nuclear research on to third parties without the other partner's consent, or to use the research against one another. Unfortunately, at least one British scientist, Alan Nunn May, who was subsequently arrested for espionage, was passing nuclear secrets to the Soviet Union.

QUEBEC CONFERENCE (1943). The Quebec Conference, from which the Anglo–American nuclear agreement emerged in August 1943, also dealt with other matters. At the meeting, **Winston Churchill's** reservations about "Operation Overlord" (the invasion of northern **France**) were made clear. He wanted a guarantee of Allied air and ground superiority before the operation was launched. Churchill had also made clear to his Chiefs of Staff that he feared a disaster worse than **Dunkirk** if the operation was launched prematurely. President **Franklin D. Roosevelt** was told about the defects of such a plan, which, in Churchill's view, ought to be subordinated to the invasion of **Italy** and entry into the Balkans.

QUEEN ELIZABETH, RMS. In July 1954, Prime Minister **Winston Churchill** and his **foreign secretary**, **Anthony Eden**, traveled home from a trip to Washington on the liner RMS *Queen Elizabeth.* It was the occasion for a big row between the two men about whether Churchill should send Soviet foreign minister Vyacheslav Molotov a telegram proposing that he visit Moscow for talks with the new Soviet leader, Georgii Malenkov. Eden strongly opposed the idea, partly because the Americans were known to oppose it, but also because he doubted its wisdom. In the hot and oppressive conditions on the liner, a compromise was hammered out, whereby Eden would not oppose the proposal if the telegram was shown to the British Cabinet first, but, once the two men were ashore, the compromise fell apart. Fortunately, the Russians solved the problem by suggesting a bigger meeting of European leaders.

QUINLAN, SIR MICHAEL (1930–2009). A civil servant in the **Ministry of Defense** under **Margaret Thatcher's** administration, Michael Quinlan came to her attention because of his ability in providing a justification for Great Britain's nuclear deterrent. He contributed to a key speech on disarmament that Thatcher made during a **United Nations** conference in June 1982. Quinlan was one of a number of senior civil servants described by Thatcher as "one of us."

R

REAGAN, RONALD (1911–2004). As president of the **United States** (1981–1989), Ronald Reagan worked closely with Prime Minister **Margaret Thatcher** on foreign policy issues. They had similar political philosophies, both being strong believers in free market economics and opponents of Soviet Communism. Reagan started out as a strident critic of the Soviet Union, which he famously described as the "evil empire," but, in his second term as president, he was more disposed to negotiate with the new Soviet leader, Mikhail Gorbachev, on nuclear disarmament. Thatcher played a key role acting as a sort of mediator between Washington and Moscow. She did not, however, agree with Reagan's desire for a "Star Wars" defensive system in outer space, which she deemed unworkable. Reagan supported Great Britain at the time of the **Falklands War** in 1982, even though there were elements in his administration that thought the links with **Argentina** and Latin America to be more important than the **"special relationship."** American satellite intelligence played a vital role in the British victory.

The two friends fell out over Reagan's decision to invade the **Commonwealth** island of **Grenada** in 1983. Reagan had not informed Thatcher first, and she inflicted a ferocious rebuke on him. The easygoing Reagan, who relied a great deal on charm and presentational skills, was taken aback. He and other members of his administration assumed that British gratitude for U.S. assistance over the Falklands War would somehow make clearance of the invasion with Thatcher unnecessary. This proved to be a blip in generally cordial Anglo–American relations. In 1986, Thatcher allowed U.S. aircraft to refuel at Royal Air Force bases while on their way to bomb **Libya**. The personal chemistry between the two leaders remained strong, and they met no fewer than 15 times from 1981–1989, when Reagan was president. Both were convinced that their tough stance on the Soviet Union had won the **Cold War**, although internal changes had been at least as important. When Reagan died in 2004, Thatcher recorded a eulogy for the president in which she reiterated her view about his contribution to the end of the Cold War. In 2011, a statue of Reagan was erected in London.

REILLY, SIDNEY (1874–1925). Possibly the most remarkable agent the British **Secret Intelligence Service** has ever had, Sidney Reilly was born Sigmund Georgievitch Rosenblum, the son of a rich Jewish landowner. He left his native **Russia** in the 1890s and settled in London, where he changed his name to Reilly. Charismatic, resourceful, and fearless, Reilly was recruited by the British Secret Service, which made use of his flair for languages. Most of his activities are shrouded in mystery, but it is probable that Reilly was able to provide the British with information on the movements of the Russian Far Eastern Fleet when it was sent to Port Arthur. As was typical of people with his background, he attended Trinity College, Cambridge, in 1905, on a bogus certificate and left without a degree, although he later claimed to have a doctorate from the University of Heidelberg. Although a fantasist, Reilly had many admirers, one of whom was **Winston Churchill**.

Reilly's principal obsession was Russia, and he spent two and a half years in the **United States** during **World War I** as a purchasing agent for the Tsarist government. When it fell, he joined Britain's Royal Flying Corps, before returning to Russia in 1918 as a British agent. He became involved with **Robert Bruce Lockhart**, a British diplomat, in an attempted coup that planned to use the Latvian personal guard of Vladimir Ilyich Lenin, the Bolshevik leader, to overthrow him and his government. The plot failed, and the Bolsheviks condemned both Reilly and Lockhart to death. Reilly managed to escape across the Finnish border. The British awarded Reilly the Military Cross. The British Secret Service, known as the Secret Intelligence Service beginning in 1921, regarded Reilly as a hero. The **Foreign Office**, which funded SIS, thought him to be an unreliable adventurer.

The last phase of Reilly's erratic career began in the United States, where he used his business acumen to fund anti-Bolshevik plotters. He was ultimately outsmarted by the head of the Cheka (Russian secret intelligence), Felix Dzerzinsky, who created a bogus organization called "The Trust" to lure anti-Bolshevik leaders and their supporters back to Russia. Reilly was a victim of this elaborate plot. He crossed the Finnish border in September 1925, to attend a Trust meeting, and was arrested. Disowned by the Foreign Office, Reilly was shot by OGPU, the successor to the Cheka, in November. He would have expected nothing better, as he was a consummate assassin himself. *See also* SPEARS, GENERAL SIR EDWARD.

REILLY, SIR PATRICK (1909–1999). Patrick Reilly served as British ambassador in Moscow and Paris. He was educated at Winchester College and New College, Oxford, before joining the Diplomatic Service in 1933. During **World War II**, Reilly was variously chief of staff officer to the head of the **Secret Intelligence Service** with a brief of representing the **Foreign**

Office interest, and an official in the Ministry of Economic Warfare. He then worked under **Harold Macmillan** in North Africa, before being posted to Athens from 1945–1948, while the **Greek Civil War** raged. In 1950, after a stint at the Imperial Defense College, Reilly became an assistant secretary at the Foreign Office, and then deputy undersecretary in 1953. His appointment to the Moscow embassy as ambassador in 1957 meant that he played a key role in setting up the Anglo–Soviet Summit of 1959, when Macmillan and **Selwyn Lloyd** met the Russian leaders. Upon his return to the Foreign Office in 1960, Reilly spent most of his time dealing with Great Britain's first application to join the **European Economic Community** and Franco–British relations. This formed the background for his posting to Paris as ambassador in 1965. His three-year service there was abruptly terminated in 1968, by the somewhat volatile **foreign secretary George Brown**, who decided that he was not the right man for the post. Others disagreed, and Reilly's service to Franco–British relations was recognized by the award of the Legion d'Honneur in 1979.

RENDITION FLIGHTS. During the **Iraq War**, which started in 2003, the British government, headed by **Tony Blair**, was accused of complicity in the alleged U.S. practice of "extraordinary rendition." This involved the secret movement of **terrorist** suspects arrested in **Iraq** or **Afghanistan** to third countries for interrogation. These states, which included **Egypt** and Morocco as examples, condoned the use of torture. Rendition Flights began under President **Bill Clinton**, and detainees complained that British intelligence operatives were present at interrogations, if not torture sessions.

In 2005, controversy arose in Great Britain when the Central Intelligence Agency was accused of using British airports, like as Prestwick in Scotland, as part of the rendition operations. Detainees imprisoned in Guantanamo Bay, Cuba, who were British citizens, subsequently brought cases against the government of the United Kingdom.

REVIEW COMMITTEE ON OVERSEAS REPRESENTATION (1969). Chaired by Sir Val Duncan, the 1969 Review Committee on Overseas Representation imposed drastic staff cuts on the **Foreign and Commonwealth Office (FCO)**. Many diplomats were forced to take early retirement as foreign missions were cut. The committee also recommended that the FCO centralize its London staff to save money. At the time, there were no less than 17 separate buildings where its staff worked. This recommendation was accepted.

RHINELAND REOCCUPATION (1936). On 7 March 1936, Adolf Hitler sent 22,000 German troops into the demilitarized Rhineland, thus breaking both the **Treaty of Versailles** and **Treaty of Locarno**. Both agreements prohibited the stationing of German troops in the zone east of the river Rhine. At the time, the British and French governments contented themselves with diplomatic protests and action through the **League of Nations**. Hitler effectively got away with his act of illegality. In their memoirs, written after **World War II**, both **Winston Churchill** and **Anthony Eden** deplored the lack of action by the two governments. In fact, as Churchill had recognized at the time, neither the Conservative-dominated government nor the Labour opposition, still less British public opinion, had any appetite for action over the Rhineland, which was German territory. It was clear from German documentation that they were prepared for last-ditch resistance to any move by the French army. Eden, who was **foreign secretary** at the time, worked hard to prevent any response by the Locarno powers—Britain, **France**, and **Italy**—that would involve the use of force. This behavior mysteriously avoided any reference in his 1962 memoir, *Facing the Dictators*. Churchill was not in office at the time of the Rhineland Reoccupation.

RHODES SCHOLARS. The great British imperialist Cecil Rhodes left a generous financial settlement, whereby scholars from the **British Commonwealth** and the **United States** could attend Oxford University. The scheme began to operate after Rhodes died in 1902, with students spending at least one year at an Oxford college. Future secretary of state **Dean Rusk** and future president **Bill Clinton** were Rhodes Scholars in their time, as was Australian prime minister Bob Hawke (1983–1991).

RICE, CONDOLEEZZA (1954–). Condoleezza Rice was the first African American woman to be appointed U.S. national security advisor in 2001, and then secretary of state in 2005. An academic by background, her expertise was in Soviet studies, and she tended to bring **Cold War** attitudes to international relations. As secretary of state, she worked effectively with Great Britain's foreign secretary, **Jack Straw**, on such issues as **Afghanistan** and **Iraq**.

RIDLEY, NICHOLAS (1929–1993). A junior minister at the **Foreign Office**, in 1979, Nicholas Ridley was given the thankless task of reexamining the long-standing problem of the Falkland Islands and Great Britain's claim to sovereignty over them. Prime Minister **Margaret Thatcher** allowed Ridley to go on a mission to the islands in November 1980, to see how the Falklanders reacted to the idea of a transfer to Argentinian sovereignty, followed by a long-term leaseback of the islands to Britain. This was designed to protect the British way of life of the islanders, and some islanders were prepared to accept the leaseback concept. In December 1980, Ridley put his plan before the House of Commons but, in a torrid half hour, was attacked by both Labour leaders and the right wing of the Conservative Party. He was forced to abandon the leaseback plan. Although the Thatcher government reined back on this issue, it continued defense cuts in 1981, which encouraged the military government in Buenos Aires to invade the Falklands in 1982. Ridley was a free market ideological ally of Thatcher, so his Falklands fiasco did not harm his career. He had resigned from the **Edward Heath** government over industrial policy and shared Thatcher's hostility toward nationalized industries. By 1985, Ridley was a Cabinet minister. He was created Baron Ridley of Liddesdale.

RIFKIND, MALCOLM (1946–). Malcolm Rifkind is of Scots origin and served as secretary of state for defense from 1992–1995. He was later appointed **foreign secretary** (1995–1997) by Prime Minister **John Major.** Rifkind had served as a junior minister at the **Foreign and Commonwealth Office** under **Margaret Thatcher,** and it was his visit to Moscow, in January 1983, that opened the way for the later improvement in Anglo–Soviet relations.

ROBERTS, SIR FRANK (1907–1999). A British ambassador to Moscow (1960–1963) and the West German capital Bonn (1963–1968), Frank Roberts was an influential figure in the Foreign and Diplomatic Service. He entered the Diplomatic Service in 1930, following an education at Rugby School and Trinity College, Cambridge. Roberts served variously in Paris from 1930–1932, and Cairo beginning in 1937, and then in the **Foreign Office** Central Department beginning in 1938. It was he who, as desk officer, rejected the last desperate attempts by Nazi German intermediaries to restart talks in August 1939. Roberts was a man of great energy whose small stature earned him the nickname the "Pocket Hercules of the Foreign Office."

Roberts's greatest contribution was in **Russia.** He advised **Winston Churchill** at the **Yalta Conference** in February 1945, and served as chargés d' affaires in Moscow until 1947. In 1946, Roberts sent the Foreign Office a series of important telegrams on Soviet intentions, which are often compared to the American **Cold War** diplomat George Kennan's famous "long telegram." Roberts believed that a search for security was still the basis of Soviet policy. The Soviet Union needed to recover from its wartime catastrophe and would not engage in foreign policy adventures in the near future. The West, Roberts believed, should adopt a policy of "containment," which would involve respecting the spheres of influence concept established at the **Potsdam Conference.** This would make coexistence with the Soviet Union possible, although Roberts accepted that Anglo–Soviet relations would be difficult for many years to come. The Marxist nature of the USSR made a friendly relationship with Great Britain and its allies virtually impossible. Some of Roberts's Foreign Office colleagues took an even more pessimistic view. It was accepted by both Roberts and his colleagues in London that a joint Anglo–American policy toward the Soviet Union was desirable.

Although both **Anthony Eden** and **Harold Macmillan** recognized Roberts's talent when they ran the Foreign Office, he never attained the position of permanent undersecretary, which might have been expected. Some colleagues clearly thought that his industry could result in his being overzealous and domineering. After Moscow, Roberts served as assistant undersecretary in 1951, British representative to the **Brussels Treaty** Commission from 1952–1954, ambassador to **Yugoslavia** from 1954–1957, and permanent United Kingdom representative to the **North Atlantic Treaty Organization** from 1957–1960. He wrote a memoir entitled *Dealing with Dictators* (1991), which contains interesting insights into the life of a British ambassador in a totalitarian state.

ROME, TREATY OF (1957). The founding treaty of the **European Economic Community (EEC)** was signed in Rome, in 1957, by **France**, West Germany, **Italy**, **Belgium**, Holland, and Luxemburg. Its most important creation was the common external tariff, which removed tariffs between the six member states, while putting up a tariff wall against nonmembers. This included Great Britain, which had rejected an invitation to join the EEC, just as it had turned down an opportunity to join the **European Coal and Steel Community (ECSC)** in 1950–1951. The ECSC was subsumed inside the EEC under the Treaty of Rome. The EEC was to be run by the Commission, the Council of Ministers representing the national rather than the EEC interest, and the European Parliament, the EEC's legislature.

ROOSEVELT, FRANKLIN DELANO (1882–1945). As president of the **United States** for four terms, from 1933–1945, Franklin D. Roosevelt set a record that has never been challenged (U.S. Congress subsequently passed legislation limiting presidents to two terms). Roosevelt became president after an unhappy period in Anglo–American relations, during a succession of Republican presidencies. Roosevelt first met **Winston Churchill** when he was assistant navy secretary during **World War I**. As president from 1933 onward, he was generally sympathetic to Great Britain in its efforts in dealing with **Germany** and **Japan**, but he was hamstrung by the **Neutrality Acts**. In January 1938, his initiative to preserve the international peace was rejected by British prime minister **Neville Chamberlain**, who thought that Roosevelt was guilty of impractical rhetoric. In September 1938, Roosevelt sent Chamberlain his famous two-word telegram, "Good man," which implied approval of Chamberlain's role in establishing the **Munich Agreement**.

A year later, in September 1939, Roosevelt was able to amend the Neutrality Acts to provide the British with much-needed war supplies. When Churchill became premier on 10 May 1940, he worked hard on his personal relationship with Roosevelt, frequently writing under the heading "former naval person." Roosevelt was clearly sympathetic to the British cause, although he was forced to stand for reelection in 1940 on an isolationist platform for political reasons. In January 1941, Roosevelt got the crucial **Lend–Lease** bill through the U.S. Congress, authorizing more aid to be sent to Britain. Roosevelt also had his first face-to-face meeting with Churchill when they met on a warship off the coast of Newfoundland and approved the **Atlantic Charter**. The increasing likelihood of U.S. involvement in **World War II** was made certain by Japan's surprise attack on the United States at **Pearl Harbor** on 7 December 1941, which Roosevelt famously denounced to congress as a "day of infamy." Churchill later recorded that upon hearing the news of Japan's attack, he was sure that Britain and its allies, the United States and the Soviet Union, would be victorious. Hitler saved Roosevelt the bother of declaring war on Nazi Germany by declaring war on the United States on 10 December.

Relations between the two Anglo–Saxon powers were not always easy during World War II. Although he admired Churchill's fighting spirit, Roosevelt tended to regard him as a hopelessly outdated Edwardian imperialist. He went along with Churchill's obsession with the Mediterranean against the better judgment of U.S. military leaders, who saw **France** as the greater priority. Roosevelt also accepted that the German war, rather than war with Japan, should be the primary Anglo–American objective, although American generals and admirals in the Far East resented the role of British South-East Asia Command, which they nicknamed "Save England's Asian Colonies." Roosevelt took a strong line on French **Indochina**, which he believed to have been badly administered and wanted to be put under some form of international trusteeship. In this sense, Roosevelt was a proponent of decolonization some time before the European powers agreed to start it in 1947–1948. At the wartime conferences at **Tehran** (1943) and **Yalta** (1945), Roosevelt also convinced himself that Churchill and Britain were rather superfluous to the arrangements he was making with the Soviet dictatorship of Joseph Stalin. By the time of Yalta, contemporary photographs showed that Roosevelt, or "FDR," as he was commonly known, was a dying man. He died at Palm Springs, Florida, on 10 April 1945. Churchill told the House of Commons that Roosevelt was Britain's greatest friend. This was true, but he could drive hard bargains.

RUMBOLD, SIR HORACE (1866–1941). As Great Britain's first ambassador in Berlin (1928–1933) during the Nazi period, Horace Rumbold was a keen observer of the new regime. He summarized his anxieties in a celebrated memorandum known in the **Foreign Office** as his "Mein Kampf" [My Struggle] dispatch. This analyzed Adolf Hitler's ideology and concluded that the Nazi leader was an unbalanced pathological case. Rumbold's warnings were not entirely welcome to the British government in the **appeasement** era. Berlin was Rumbold's last posting. He had previously served as ambassador in Constantinople (1920–1924) and Madrid (1924–1928). In 1923, Rumbold had signed the Treaty of Lausanne, which rearranged postwar arrangements with **Turkey** on behalf of Britain.

RUNCIMAN, SIR WALTER (1870–1949). As Prime Minister **Neville Chamberlain's** envoy to **Czechoslovakia** in August 1938, Walter Runciman failed to achieve a settlement to the problem of the ethnic German minority's status and role in the country. The Czechs believed that Runciman was too pro-German in orientation. Runciman began a career in politics by defeating **Winston Churchill** in 1899, and becoming Liberal member of Parliament for Oldham. He had several posts in the Liberal government elected in 1906, finishing as president of the Board of Trade in 1914. Losing his parliamentary seat in 1918, Runciman was out of the House of Commons until he returned to hold office in the National Government in 1931. Upon his resignation from his second stint at the Board of Trade in 1937, he was selected the following year by the **Foreign Office** to go to Czechoslovakia. He was created Viscount Runciman of Doxford.

RUSK, DEAN (1909–1994). Dean Rusk served for a long period (1961–1969) as secretary of state to both presidents **John F. Kennedy** and **Lyndon B. Johnson**. He had been a **Rhodes Scholar** at Oxford University at the time of the **appeasement** policy of the 1930s in Great Britain. This experience may have influenced his later hard-nosed attitude toward Communism. It made him critical of British prime minister **Harold Wilson's** decision not to provide any military support for U.S. intervention in Vietnam in the 1960s. Rusk and his leader, President Johnson, were desperate to obtain some sort of British involvement, however symbolic. Rusk is alleged to have remarked that a single regiment of the Black Watch would have done.

RUSSIA. England's links with Russia go back to at least the reign of Tsar Ivan the Terrible (1530–1584). Ivan, a bloody and ruthless tyrant, is known to have corresponded with Queen Elizabeth I, and, during his reign, the English explorer Richard Chanceller arrived at the mouth of the River Dvina.

An envoy, Sir Giles Fletcher, was sent to represent England in Muscovy, the original core of the evolving Russian state. Fletcher reported to his queen that the tyrant Ivan allowed his parliament, the so-called Assembly of the Land, virtually no say in governance. For the English (Great Britain only evolved by 1707), Russia was a remote and barbaric place. It was not perceived to be a threat, lacking any naval power until the 18th century. Instead, England was a school for the westernizing Tsar Peter the Great (1696–1725), who studied shipbuilding techniques there. Within 70 years, the rise of Russian power begun by Peter would create frictions between Britain and Russia for the first time. It was Russian expansion toward the Black Sea that threatened the Ottoman Empire and created anxiety in London. Britain was a traditional ally of the Ottoman Turks.

In 1783, Catherine II (1762–1796) annexed the **Crimea**, which brought Russia and Britain into direct conflict. Catherine seized the Fortress of Ochakov in 1791, and British prime minister **William Pitt the Younger** protested. Rude cartoons about the empress appeared in British papers. She responded by making links with the opposition in the House of Commons. Pitt was bluffing. He did not want a war with Russia when war with revolutionary **France** threatened. On her side, Catherine turned down the offer of U.S. privateer John Paul Jones to attack British ships on their way to **India**. He had been in imperial Russian service since 1788. The Ochakov Crisis was a straw in the wind. Britain and Russia were allies against **Napoleon Bonaparte** and France (1799–1815), but the new British **Foreign Office** increasingly viewed Russia as a threat to the balance of power in Europe. In 1814–1815, Russian troops were in Paris, and Tsar Alexander I (1801–1825) was the arbiter of Europe.

Anglo–Russian antagonism was disguised to a degree. Russia and Britain were on the same side in the war, which freed **Greece** from Turkish rule (1827–1829). After this, clashes were only avoided because of the inherent conservatism of Tsar Nicholas I (1825–1855), Alexander's youngest brother. Nicholas put preservation of the existing European state structure ahead of any antagonism toward Muslim **Turkey**. This policy ended with the Crimean War (1854–1856). Russia's long-term aim was the fragmentation of the Ottoman Empire and the seizure of Constantinople and the Straits between the Black and Mediterranean Seas. Nicholas I visited Britain in 1844, and he seemed to have misunderstood Britain's likely reaction to any move against Turkey. The crisis, which led to war with Britain and France in 1854, was sparked by a dispute over the custody of the Holy Places in Jerusalem. In 1853, Nicholas was unwise enough to tell the British ambassador that Russia regarded itself as the protector of the Christians in the Turkish Empire. The role of Lord Stratford de Radcliffe, the British ambassador, in thwarting

Nicholas's demands was significant. In an age of much slower communications, Lord Stratford was the last of a breed of influential British ambassadors. The Tsar's own ambassadors abroad served him badly in underestimating foreign hostility toward Russia. Regardless of this, Nicholas ordered his army to cross the Pruth River into Moldova and Wallachia, modern Romania, in July 1853. When the Russians refused to withdraw, Turkey declared war on 23 October. The Turkish Black Sea fleet was destroyed by Russia at Sinope on 30 November. In Britain, this was called the "massacre of Sinope," and it did much to arouse anti-Russian feeling. On 4 January, Anglo–French warships entered the Black Sea, and, given Russia's refusal to withdraw from Moldova and Wallachia, Britain declared war on it on 27 March 1854. Russia had now to fight against Britain, France, and Turkey.

The Crimean War was a disaster for Russia. Its army proved to be even more inept than the British one, which was commanded by the relic from the **Napoleonic Wars**, Lord Raglan. The tsarist regime proved unable to fight an effective war, even on its own soil. The key battle was for the great Russian naval base at Sebastopol in the Crimea. A series of Russian defeats near the fortress contributed to the death of the tsar in 1855. His heir, Alexander II (1855–1881), soon realized that the struggle had to be ended. The Treaty of Paris (1856), the last great European treaty to be written in French, the language of diplomacy until then, was a humiliation for Russia; however, it was not as punitive, as had been feared. The Anglo–French wanted all warships to be banned in the Black Sea, but Alexander's diplomats said that this would be unnecessary, as the Russian Black Sea Fleet had already been destroyed. Sebastopol had already been largely demolished by the allies as well. The treaty was signed on 30 March 1856.

Russia also lost its self-allocated role of protector of the Christians in the Turkish Empire. In most respects, the Crimean defeat did not lead to any serious decline in Russian power. The massive territorial expansion, which characterized Russian foreign policy in the second half of the 19th century, went on. By 1859, Alexander II had acquired all the lands between the Black Sea and the Caspian. Russia broke a treaty with Britain concerning the neutrality of Turkestan and conquered it. Its capital, Samarkand, fell in 1868. There was also success in Europe. The Franco–Prussian War of 1870–1871 allowed Russia to declare null and void the part of the Treaty of Paris that closed the Black Sea to all warships. Britain, under its Liberal prime minister, **William Gladstone**, was in no position to intervene without its former French ally. It looked as if Alexander II had isolated Britain by joining the Three Emperors League (1872) with Austria and **Germany**. A further triumph seemed to have been achieved in 1876–1877. In 1876, the Turkish authorities in **Bulgaria** crushed a revolt with great severity. Gladstone, by then in opposition, denounced the "Bulgarian horrors," embarrassing his old rival, Prime Minister **Benjamin Disraeli**, who wished to preserve the Turkish Empire and resist Russian power. In Russia, Pan-Slav feeling, in favor of the Slav race, the Bulgars swept the country. In the war of 1877, Russian troops defeated Turkey and created a so-called "Big Bulgaria." This was unacceptable to Britain, which assumed, wrongly, as it turned out, that Bulgaria would become a Russian satellite state. With the support of the German chancellor **Otto von Bismarck**, Disraeli convened the 1878 Congress of Berlin. Bulgaria was greatly reduced in size, and Britain got **Cyprus** as a reward from the grateful Turks. This time, Russia was isolated. None of the other Great Powers wanted to see further Russian territorial expansion in Eastern Europe. Russia and Britain continued with the "Great Game" of trying to impose their influence in Persia and **Afghanistan**.

From 1878–1914, Russia concentrated on eastward expansion to Vladivostok and the Pacific coast. It built the great Trans-Siberian Railway to link Moscow and Saint Petersburg to Central Asia and beyond. This expansionist policy was generally successful, until Russia got involved in Korea during the reign of Nicholas II (1894–1917), the last of the tsars. Korea had timber and coal, and, most important, the warm-water, ice-free port that Russia wanted at Port Arthur. The problem was that a newly industrialized **Japan**, with modern forces, was eyeing the same territory. In 1902, it had made an alliance with Britain, the creator of its modern fleet. Russia made the fatal error of underestimating Japan. In the war of 1904–1905, Russian land and naval forces were routed, and Port Arthur fell. Britain played its part by closing the Suez Canal. This forced the Russian Baltic fleet to sail around the world (the Black Sea fleet was bottled up there) to Japan. It was a bizarre episode, creating a diplomatic incident with Britain when incompetent Russian leadership caused the fleet to fire on British trawlers in the North Sea. They were somehow deemed to be hostile vessels. When the Russians arrived in the Straits of Tsushima, every Russian vessel was sunk by the Japanese in 20 minutes. It was a shattering Russian humiliation that coincided with the 1905 revolution at home. Under the Treaty of Portsmouth (New Hampshire), Russia lost Port Arthur and all influence in Korea. A further Russian humiliation took place in 1908, when the Russian foreign minister was deceived into accepting the annexation of **Bosnia-Herzegovina** by Austria-Hungary. The provinces had technically been part of the Turkish Empire since 1878, but they had been administered by the Austrians. In exchange, Austria-Hungary said that it would have no objections to Russia securing Constantinople and the Straits. It knew full well that France, and especially Britain, would be likely to object to such a change, together with Turkey's new ally, Germany. In 1907, Britain had agreed to sharing zones of influence in Persia with Russia, and the two states were part of the Triple Entente. The fiasco over Bosnia-Herzegovina meant that Russia could not tolerate another humiliation of the type that followed its 1905 defeat without losing face as a Great Power. Russia could take some consolation from the fact that Britain, as part of a policy realignment, had actually supported Russia's demand for a conference on the Straits.

The Balkan Wars of 1912–1913 seemed to leave Russia with an advantage. Its small Slav neighbors, **Serbia**, Bulgaria, **Montenegro**, and non-Slav Greece, wanted to defeat Turkey. In the second war, Bulgaria, too greedy about territory, was defeated by its recent allies. As Bulgaria was now under German influence, its defeat was not a blow for Russia. There was some Russian rejoicing over the two victories of its main Slav ally, Serbia.

War came for Russia in July 1914, because it had to stand by its fellow Slav kingdom, Serbia. Britain went to war for an altogether different cause, **Belgium**. Both nations played a vital role in aiding their ally, France. Two Russian army corps invaded Eastern Germany in August 1914 to divert German forces from the West. They succeeded, but at a price. Russia suffered a catastrophic defeat at Tannenburg. Afterward, a pattern set in. Russia did well against the **Austro-Hungarian** army; many of its soldiers were Slavs anyway. Against Germany, the Russian army fared badly, and another serious defeat followed at the Masurian Lakes in 1915. In 1915–1916, Britain and France tried to aid Russia by attacking Germany's ally, Turkey, and opening up the route to the Black Sea. This was the brainchild of **Winston Churchill**, the first lord of the **Admiralty**. His Gallipoli campaign failed, and Russia remained isolated from its Western allies. Its industries struggled to provide enough munitions, and its leadership was poor, as in the Crimea. In 1916, a talented leader, Alexei Brusilov, was found, and he won some sweeping victories against the Austro-Hungarians.

By then, internal factors were starting to dominate. There was strong feeling against the German-born empress Alexandra and her monkish favorite, Rasputin. Nicholas II was incompetent and did not improve matters by going to the Front and trying to act as commander in chief of his army. In Britain, there was ambiguity about having the tsar as an ally, even though Nicholas II was the cousin of George V. In March 1917, the parliament, or duma, demanded the abdication of Nicholas II. He was replaced by the Provisional Government, a mixture of Liberals, Social Democrats, and moderate Socialists. There was rejoicing in Britain over Russia's switch to democracy. The Provisional Government pledged to stay in the war, but this proved to be its undoing. In April 1917, Vladimir Lenin, the leader of the Bolshevik party, returned to Russia from Switzerland, with German assistance. He promised the Russian people "bread, land, and peace." The leader of the Provisional Government, Alexander Kerensky, tried to launch new offensives in the summer of 1917. They failed, although a premature Bolshevik rising also failed in July, and Lenin had to flee to Finland. When the Bolsheviks seized power in November 1917, they implemented their peace policy. In March 1918, the Treaty of Brest Litovsk took Russia out of **World War I**, to the annoyance of its British, French, and U.S. allies. Much territory and industry was lost to Germany, but Russia's former Western allies supported attempts by so-called "white counterrevolutionaries" to overthrow Lenin's government. The Bolsheviks reneged on debts to the West (especially France), and Britain, France, the **United States**, and even Japan intervened by force in Russia. A bloody civil war dragged on from 1918–1920, long after Germany and its allies sued for peace in November 1918.

Since his downfall, Nicholas II and his family had been moved from one place of detention to another. His cousin, George V, had refused to grant refuge to Nicholas, although the British government was willing. He allegedly feared that the late tsar's presence would be a threat to the British monarchy. Nicholas and his entire family were murdered by Bolsheviks in Siberia in 1918. Three hundred years of rule by the Romanov family had ended in 1917. Surrounded by enemies both internal and foreign, the Bolsheviks somehow secured victory by 1921. Russia became the Soviet Union, a state driven by ideology and a belief in international revolution. Bolshevik hopes of Communist victories in Germany and Hungary were destroyed in 1919–1920. An invasion of **Poland** by the Red Army in 1920 reached the gates of Warsaw, but it had been provoked by a Polish invasion of Ukraine. The Poles defeated the Russians, and Lenin realized that his new Communist Party would have to concentrate on internal consolidation. As it was, the new Soviet Union (the full title was the Union of Soviet Socialist Republic [USSR]) was an international pariah. It was not asked to attend the **Paris Peace Conference** of 1919 and did not join the **League of Nations** until 1934. Churchill called the Bolsheviks "ferocious baboons." He was equally suspicious of Britain's new Labour Party, which came into power as a minority government in 1924. Its heavy election defeat was attributed to the notorious Zinoviev letter, supposedly a letter from the head of the Comintern (the international wing of the Soviet Communist Party) trying to stir up revolution in Britain. Although now largely accepted as a forgery involving either the British **Secret Intelligence Service** or the Conservative Party, the Zinoviev letter provoked anti-Soviet hysteria in Britain. It was reciprocated in the USSR when Joseph Stalin replaced Lenin as Soviet leader by the mid-1920s. Stalin was pathologically suspicious of the West, although he was in need of its technical expertise to drive his five-year modernization plans. In March 1933, six British engineers from Metro-Vickers were arrested on fabricated charges of spying in the Soviet Union, a classic example of Stalin's paranoia about foreigners.

From 1928–1934, Stalin imposed a totally inappropriate foreign policy. Fascism was on the rise throughout Europe (Benito Mussolini had come to power in **Italy** in 1922), but Stalin rejected cooperation with social democrats in Europe, who were denoted "social fascists." He believed in the fantasy of fascism as the highest stage of capitalism, to be followed by a coming to power of Communists. When applied in Germany, where the Nazis came to power in 1933, the result was the destruction of the German Communist Party. Soviet foreign policy then changed to one of seeking alliances with non-fascist states like France and **Czechoslovakia**. The policy lasted from 1934–1938. Stalin supported the Spanish Republic in its war with right-wing nationalists (1936–1939). While no absolute proof is available, he appeared willing to aid the Czechs against Germany in 1938. When Britain and France were not, Stalin abandoned collective security, sacking his foreign minister, Maxim Litvinov, who was closely associated with attempts to improve relations with Britain and France, in May 1939. There was then a complete turnabout in Soviet foreign policy. Anglo–French overtures were rejected, and, on 23 August, a nonaggression pact was agreed to in Moscow between the USSR and Germany. A secret protocol to this Nazi–Soviet pact partitioned Poland between Germany and the USSR. On 17 September 1939, just a little more than two weeks after Adolf Hitler had invaded Poland, the Red Army invaded Poland from the east. In the opening phase of **World War II**, from 1939–1941, Nazi Germany and the Soviet Union were allies, albeit uneasy ones. Stalin tried to buy time, not least because his 1937 purge of the Red Army had devastated its command structure. He also tried to make Leningrad, the former Soviet Petersburg, more secure by seizing Finnish territory. The resulting Winter War (1939–1940) was an embarrassment, as the Red Army had the greatest difficulty in defeating the small, but highly effective, Finnish forces. In 1940, the USSR took advantage of German preoccupations in the West to annex the Baltic Republics of Lithuania, Latvia, and Estonia. Southward, Bessarabia was annexed from Romania. In the Soviet zone in Poland, a deliberate attempt was made by the USSR to destroy any elements that were viewed to be anti-Communist. Some of its citizens had joined the Free Polish Government in Britain in 1939–1940.

British warnings in 1941 that the Soviet Union was about to be attacked by Hitler were ignored. Stalin thought that such warnings were an imperialist plot to get his country involved in a war with the Nazis. The predictable German invasion under the code name "Barbarossa" was launched on 22 June 1941. The Russians suffered devastating losses as the Ukraine was overrun, Kiev captured, and Moscow threatened in the late autumn of 1941. Winston Churchill withdrew none of his criticisms of Communism but promised all the aid Britain could offer. The British military was pessimistic about Soviet chances. On 6 December 1941, the Red Army proved them wrong. The Germans were close to Moscow, but extreme winter conditions were slowing their advance. The Red Army divisions brought from Siberia under Marshal Georgii Zhukov suddenly attacked them, forcing the Germans to retreat. Even though Soviet fortunes varied afterward, the Germans would never menace Moscow again, although they besieged Leningrad until 1944.

Britain had a high-caliber ambassador in the Soviet Union in Sir Stafford Cripps, who went on to be a chancellor of the exchequer. In 1942, Cripps was replaced by **Sir Archibald Clark Kerr** as ambassador. He got along remarkably well with Stalin and advised the Foreign Office to accept the annexation of the Baltic Republics. Little reference by either was made to the thorny issue of Poland, and, on 26 May 1942, an Anglo–Soviet Treaty was signed. Britain tried, as did the United States after 7 December 1941, to supply the USSR via the perilous Arctic route to North Russia.

The issue that most obsessed Stalin and his obdurate foreign minister, Vyacheslav Molotov, was when Britain and the United States would open a second front in Western Europe. The Red Army won a remarkable victory at Stalingrad in January 1943, and another at Kursk in July, but Stalin persisted in accusations of British and American cowardice. He was also canny enough to play President **Franklin D. Roosevelt** off against Winston Churchill, who was more nervous about any projected landing in France. The victories of the Red Army in 1943 actually made the USSR less dependent on Western aid. In November 1943, Stalin and Molotov turned down a British offer to place Royal Air Force bases in the Caucasus. By that stage, it was clear that the United States, USSR, and Britain were going to defeat Germany. The big question became the fate of postwar Germany and Europe. In 1944, the Red Army advanced eastward through Poland, Anglo–U.S. bombers pounded German cities, and the **D-Day Landing** took place in June. The most controversial Soviet action in 1944 was the failure to assist the rising by the Polish underground against the Germans. The Polish Home Army was smashed, it was non-Communist led, and the suspicion remained that Stalin wanted to eliminate any non-Communist threat to a Communist takeover in Poland. In the early months of 1945, the Red Army swept into Eastern Germany and drove toward Berlin. Anxious for revenge, the Red Army committed atrocities, but they paled in comparison with the German ones in Russia.

Twenty-seven million Soviet citizens died in World War II. Stalin would exact his pound of flesh. In February 1945, at the **Yalta Conference**, the USSR obtained Anglo–American agreement to permanent Soviet annexation of the Baltic Republics. It was also agreed that the USSR would retain the Polish territory it had obtained in August 1939. The Poles were compensated with German territory so that their western frontier would be shifted westward. Britain had gone to war in 1939 over Polish independence, and Churchill was not happy about the arrangements. Like Roosevelt, he felt that the Western allies had little choice, since, by February 1945, the Red Army had overrun much of Eastern Europe. In April, the Red Army fought for Berlin, and, on 8 May, Victory Europe Day, Nazi Germany surrendered. After a catastrophic start, Stalin had shown himself to be a most effective war leader, and, by the time of the **Potsdam Conference**, Roosevelt was dead and Churchill was on the verge of a massive electoral defeat. Faced with the inexperienced **Harry S. Truman**, the new U.S. president, and British prime minister **Clement R. Attlee**, Stalin secured an occupation zone in Germany and a veto on the Security Council of the new **United Nations (UN)** organization. During the Potsdam Conference, Stalin learned of the explosion of the first atomic bomb in New Mexico, but it was not a surprise. Soviet agents were deeply embedded in the British scientific diplomatic and secret service establishments.

In the post-1945 world, the USSR wanted security while also wanting ideological domination of the states surrounding it. Stalin would compromise on occasion. In 1944, for example, he had recognized Britain's paramount influence in Greece. The USSR did not subsequently aid the Communists during the **Greek Civil War** (1944–1949). Soviet troops also withdrew from **Iran** in 1946. Against this, Stalin imposed surrogate Communist regimes in Bulgaria, Romania, Hungary, and Poland and, in February 1948, Czechoslovakia. He did this by infiltrating the supposedly democratic regimes with Communists and fellow travelers. An attempt to pressure the Western allies into leaving their sectors of Berlin in 1948–1949 failed, but, in 1949, the Russian zone in Germany was transformed into the German Democratic Republic, or East Germany. The **Cold War** between the USSR and the Anglo–Americans was well underway. Stalin almost certainly encouraged the North Korean Communist dictator Kim Il Sung to attack the South in June 1950. The previous year, 1949, had seen the final victory of the Chinese Communists in the civil war with the nationalists. Stalin was not especially enthusiastic, fearing the appearance of a rival giant in the Communist world.

Britain had watched all these developments with alarm. The left-leaning 1945–1951 Labour government had not established a cordial relationship with the USSR. It assisted the United States during the **Berlin Blockade** and sent troops to Korea. There was agreement between Labour and the Conservative opposition on the line to take with the Russians. The former Conservative **foreign secretary, Anthony Eden**, admired his Labour counterpart, **Ernest Bevin**, a leading proponent of the **North Atlantic Treaty Organization (NATO)**, founded in 1949. Upon his return to office in 1951, Winston Churchill hoped to open a dialogue with the new Soviet leadership once

Stalin died, which occurred in March 1953. He did not succeed in arranging a summit because of U.S. opposition, but Soviet leaders Nikita Khrushchev and Nikolai Bulganin visited Britain in 1955. Animosity between Britain and the USSR reemerged in November 1956, at the time of the **Suez Crisis**, when the Soviet Union threatened to use missile technology in support of **Egypt**. By then, Khrushchev had emerged as general secretary of the Soviet Communist Party and denounced the horrors of the Stalin period in a secret speech to the Party Congress in February 1956. There was a sharp change in direction, which affected foreign policy. It was now the Soviet Union's intention to pursue "peaceful coexistence" with the West. Relations with **China**, which were close until that point, worsened in 1959, when Khrushchev made tactless criticisms of China's five-year plans. Neither would the Chinese leader Mao Zedong accept Khrushchev as the heir of Lenin and Stalin. While visiting the United States in 1959, Khrushchev boasted that the USSR would outstrip the Americans in consumer goods production. This was a fantasy, given the overcentralized nature of Soviet industry, but, in space, the USSR was ahead. In 1957, Sputnik, the first space satellite, was launched, and, in 1961, Yuri Gagarin became the first man in space. Equally alarming from a Western point of view was the way in which the USSR had caught up with the U.S. lead in nuclear weapons. In 1949, the Soviet Union had exploded its first atomic bomb, and it followed with its first hydrogen bomb test in Siberia in August 1953, after the U.S. test in 1952. Anxious to remain at the nuclear table, Britain exploded its own hydrogen bomb in 1957. These weapons were ruinously expensive for the inefficient Soviet economy. This was one reason why Khrushchev wanted peaceful coexistence.

His vulnerable point was the ramshackle, repressed nature of the Soviet empire in Eastern Europe. In 1953, Soviet tanks had to be used against rioting workers in East Berlin, and, in November 1956, the Red Army again had to be used to put down a serious uprising in Hungary. There were also protests against Communist rule in Poland. The attempts of the East Berlin population to flee forced East Germany, with Soviet support, to build a wall in Berlin in 1961. There was a brief, dangerous confrontation between Soviet and U.S. forces at the well-known "Checkpoint Charlie" in Berlin. The United States, Britain, and the other NATO allies could not risk a war over Berlin when both sides had nuclear weapons. Berlin seemed like a Soviet success and may have encouraged Khrushchev, possibly under pressure from the Soviet military, to risk using Soviet power in the backyard of the Americans.

In 1959, Fidel Castro came to power, and he soon alienated the Americans, who unwisely tried to overthrow his regime by force in April 1961. The Bay of Pigs fiasco might have encouraged Khrushchev to be more reckless and send nuclear missiles to Cuba, ostensibly to protect Castro from another U.S.

invasion. This was the USSR acting as a global superpower, in breach of the Monroe Doctrine. The coolheaded reaction by President **John F. Kennedy** prevented the 1962 **Cuban Missile Crisis** from escalating into a world war. The USSR removed its missiles, although Khrushchev also secured the covert removal of aging U.S. missiles from Turkey. Along with Britain and the United States, the USSR subsequently signed the 1963 **Nuclear Test Ban Treaty**, which prevented nuclear testing in the atmosphere. There was no doubt, however, that the Cuban Missile Crisis seriously damaged Khrushchev. In October 1964, his enemies removed him from power. It was a mark of changed times in the Soviet Union that he was allowed to live out his last seven years in obscurity rather than face execution, as in Stalin's day.

Khrushchev, a warmhearted extrovert, was replaced by the colorless Leonid Brezhnev, beginning what were later referred to as the "years of stagnation" in the USSR. **Indochina** came to be a focus for Soviet policy. In 1954, the USSR and Britain had been cochairmen of the **Geneva Conference**, which had granted independence from France to Vietnam, Laos, and Cambodia. The USSR continued to support Ho Chi Minh and the Democratic Republic of Vietnam (DRV), while even the British would have accepted a Ho Chi Minh victory in All-Vietnam elections. This was not the position of the United States, and its commitment to non-Communist South Vietnam continued until 1975. During the 1960s, Britain continued to try to mediate between the United States and the DRV, generally called the North Vietnamese, without success. The USSR for its part was the major arms provider for North Vietnam. Vietnam became part of the complex Great Power global struggle. The People's Republic of China had long supported the Vietnamese nationalist movement, but relations with the USSR had significantly worsened during the 1960s. There was even fighting along the common Soviet–Chinese border in 1969. The United States sought to take advantage by opening the line to China in 1971–1972. Conversely, this forced the USSR to seek **détente** with the United States, lest it be isolated by the new Sino–American friendship. In 1972, President **Richard Nixon** visited Moscow to agree to both the sale of U.S. wheat to the USSR, whose agriculture system was notoriously inefficient, and the Strategic Arms Limitation Talks. The agreement limited antiballistic systems in the USSR and United States.

Despite détente, the USSR still found itself supporting opposite sides from the United States in the Angolan Civil War. In the 1973 Yom Kippur War in the Middle East, the Soviet Union supported Egypt and Syria, which made initial gains until Israel defeated them. The USSR continued to see the Middle East as in its sphere of influence, although it suffered a setback in 1971, when Soviet advisors were ejected from Egypt. The Soviet Union also tried to secure influence in **Ethiopia** and Somalia. In a real sense, it had replaced

Britain as a regional influence. The big exception was **Israel**. Starting with voting for an independent Israel in 1948, the USSR was consistently pro-Arab thereafter. Its hostility toward Israel prevented the Soviet Union from playing any mediatory role.

Soviet–Western détente suffered a serious blow in December 1979, when the USSR, reluctantly, according to the British ambassador Roland Braithwaite, invaded Afghanistan. The Afghan experience proved to be a bloody exercise designed to preserve the native Communist government. It failed to do so, and relations were fractured with Britain and the United States. Under Prime Minister **Margaret Thatcher**, Britain strongly opposed the Afghan invasion, but it was acute enough to sense the opportunity offered by the coming of a new dynamic Soviet leader, Mikhail Gorbachev, as general secretary in 1985. In power until 1991, Gorbachev offered "openness" (glasnost) and "restructuring" (perestroika) at home. These reforms largely failed. Gorbachev was much more successful abroad and became a hero in Western Europe. He pulled Soviet troops out of Eastern Europe and made a series of important arms agreements with the United States. A serious internal disaster took place at the nuclear plant at Chernobyl, in the Ukraine, in 1986. Inept attempts to cover up the seriousness of the nuclear accident infuriated foreign countries like Britain, which was affected by radiation fallout from Chernobyl. This was the old-style Soviet secretiveness that Gorbachev was trying to stop. Gorbachev's experiment at home failed, but he courageously allowed Poland, Czechoslovakia, East Germany, and Hungary to go their own non-Communist ways in 1989. He could not have realized that the USSR was living on borrowed time. Nationalism in the USSR's republics was reawakened by the principle of openness. All three Baltic Republics broke away in 1991; the idea of the Union of Sovereign States failed; and Byelarus, Moldova, Kyrgyzstan, Tajikistan, Ukraine, Turkmenistan, and Uzbekistan had declared themselves independent in 1990. Georgia also declared itself sovereign. Thus, the British Foreign Office, used to dealing with one USSR, now found itself dealing with 11 new sovereign entities. The Russian Federation also emerged to represent the old territorial core of the USSR. Its president was Boris Yeltsin, an old rival of Gorbachev who was left redundant when the old Soviet Union and the Soviet Communist Party all disappeared at the end of 1991. Gorbachev had been discredited when the August 1991 attempted coup by Communist conservatives on the ruling Politburo seemed to implicate him (although he was arrested in his Black Sea villa).

Supposedly about democracy, the Yeltsin period in Russia (1991–2000) was something of a disaster. A rushed economic liberalization in the early 1990s pauperized many ordinary Russians. This contributed to another attempted coup by Soviet-style conservatives in Moscow in September 1993.

Yeltsin showed some personal courage in crushing this, but he became involved in a bloody war in 1994, when the Chechen Republic (largely Muslim) tried to leave the Russian Federation. Seen as a democrat in both Britain and the United States, Yeltsin survived the reports of bad behavior by Russian troops, but his regime was increasingly mired in corruption. So-called "oligarchs" made vast fortunes from the sell-off of old Soviet industries. Many, like Roman Abramovitch, bought huge mansions in London. He ended up owning Chelsea Football Club.

In 1999, traditional Russian policy reasserted itself over Serbia. Its regime was accused of atrocities in the largely Muslim province of **Kosovo**. Britain's prime minister, **Tony Blair**, took the lead in sponsoring NATO intervention in Kosovo after Serbia had been intensively bombed between March and June 1999. Russian sympathies were entirely with the Orthodox Serbs, but Yeltsin dared not intervene against NATO. The Serbian army was forced out of Kosovo. It was one of an increasingly large number of issues between Russia and Britain. The two states were on opposite sides regarding the 2003 war in **Iraq**, a traditional ally of the old USSR.

The new Russian president, Vladimir Putin (2000–2007), was a strong nationalist who had gained from the perception in the West that he was part of the war against **terrorism**. In reality, the Chechen struggle, which Putin renewed, was an age-old struggle against the Russian state. Chechen terrorists (in the eyes of Putin) seized hostages in a theater in Moscow in 2002, and, in a botched security operation by the Russian security forces, many hostages died. An uneasy Anglo–Russian relationship under Putin broke into crisis in 2006. First, when British diplomats in Moscow were involved in a bizarre spy episode in Moscow, they were filmed putting a radio transmitter into a hollowed-out rock. Then, in 2007, a Russian defector, Alexander Litvinenko, was poisoned in London with radioactive polonium by a Russian secret police agent. Attempts to extradite the culprit failed because Russia refused to extradite any of its citizens. The British ambassador in Moscow, Tony Benton, was intimidated by members of the Putin-funded neofascist youth group Nashi. Talks between Soviet foreign minister Sergei Lavrov and British foreign secretary **David Miliband** did little to alleviate Anglo–Russian tensions.

British media were critical of Putin's decision to stay in office as prime minister (2007–2012), while his protégé, Dmitry Medvedev, became president. Medvedev was normally in charge of foreign policy, but there was no discernible change. Medvedev was the public front of Russia when its forces invaded Georgia in 2008, following unwise Georgian provocations in response to a territorial dispute. In 2001, Russia was sharply critical of Anglo–French intervention in **Libya,** and even more so of British and **European Union** attempts to get the UN to do something about the carnage in Syria in

2011–2012. In February 2012, Russia used its UN veto to prevent any further sanctions against Syria, a traditional ally. British foreign secretary **William Hague** was critical of Russian policy, which tried to suggest that any Western intervention would cause civil war. Putin's domination of Russian policy was ensured by his victory in the March 2012 presidential election. Medvedev did not stand against him, thus creating a scenario whereby Putin would be in power continuously from 2000–1017 (the presidential term having been reduced to five years). *See also* RUSSIA COMMITTEE.

RUSSIA COMMITTEE. The onset of the **Cold War** in 1945–1946 made the **Foreign Office** aware of the need for a specialist **Russia** Committee, especially as it lacked the linguistic and cultural specialists that were a feature of the U.S. State Department. **Frank Roberts**, whose dispatches influenced British thinking about the Soviet Union, was unable, like many British diplomats posted there, to speak Russian. The Russia Committee was formed on 2 April 1946, under the leadership of the head of the Foreign Office Northern Department, **Christopher Warner**. This was an abbreviation of the longer title "Committee on Policy Toward Russia." Roberts had some claim to have originally suggested the need for such a committee.

S

SANDYS, DUNCAN (1908–1987). The son-in-law of **Winston Churchill** who married his daughter, Diana, Duncan Sandys joined the **Foreign Office** in 1930. He served in Whitehall and the Berlin Embassy before resigning from the Diplomatic Service in protest over the British government's **appeasement** policy toward **Germany**. Sandys was elected as a Conservative member of Parliament in 1935, and he became part of Churchill's group of antiappeasement supporters in the House of Commons. He was seriously wounded in **World War II** and then became financial secretary at the treasury. He was junior minister at the War Office from 1941–1943. As minister of works in 1944–1945, Sandys was in charge of Great Britain's massive rebuilding program after the intensive German bombing. He had previously coordinated "Operation Crossbow," which dealt with the German V1 and V2 rocket attacks on London. Out of government from 1945–1951, Sandys was appointed minister of supply by Churchill upon his return to power, and Sandys served in the position until 1954. He was then minister of housing and local government (1954–1957) and minister of defense (1957–1959). In this post, he sponsored the important 1957 Defence White Paper, which recognized Britain's finite military resources. Sandys ended his political career as secretary of state for **Commonwealth** Relations in 1960, following a short period as minister of aviation (1959–1960).

SAN FRANCISCO CONFERENCE (1945). Convened between 15 April and 26 June 1945, during which time **World War II** in Europe ended on 8 May, the San Francisco Conference provided the foundation for the new **United Nations (UN)** organization and was attended by 50 states. It was held in the **United States** because the refusal of the United States to join the old **League of Nations** had been a fatal weakness in that organization. Thus it was that the new UN headquarters was situated in New York City. Great Britain, not always a strong supporter of the League of Nations, gave its full support to the UN, with its vital task of preserving international peace. The UN Charter was signed on 26 June 1945, and its initial session, prior to its permanent transfer to New York, was held in London on 24 October. The charter was ratified by the new UN General Assembly.

SARGENT, SIR ORME (1884–1962). A product of Radley School, Orme Sargent became deputy undersecretary at the **Foreign Office** (1939–1946) and then permanent undersecretary, and thus head of the Foreign and Diplomatic Service from 1946–1949, the onset of the **Cold War**. Sargent worked his way up the Foreign Office hierarchy in the classic fashion after entering the service in 1906. He was a member of the British delegation at the **Paris Peace Conference** in 1919 and served briefly in the Paris embassy in 1920. Otherwise, Sargent was based in the Foreign Office in London, where he rose to be an assistant undersecretary of state (1936–1939). He was noted for his opposition to the **appeasement** policy of **Stanley Baldwin** and **Neville Chamberlain,** acquiring the nickname "moley," a comment on his burrowing activities against official foreign policy. Sargent was always strongly anti-Soviet, warning as early as 1945 that the Russians were creating a security belt on their western frontier against a new **Germany**. A minute by Sargent on 2 April suggested that the West ought to have a political showdown with the Russians, and this rapidly made the attitude of Sargent's colleagues more hostile toward them. Foreign Secretary **Anthony Eden** broadly agreed with Sargent's analysis. He was open to the accusation that, unlike his colleague, **Frank Roberts,** in Moscow, he could not see beyond the Soviet Union's Marxist–Leninist ideology to the traditional Russian nationalist interests beneath. In old age, Sargent came to assess, not always favorably, his colleague's careers for the premier biographical work of reference the *Dictionary of National Biography.*

SECRET INTELLIGENCE SERVICE (SIS). Using passport control officers (PCOs), the British Secret Service, known since 1921 as the Secret Intelligence Service (SIS), and commonly known as MI6, obtained information abroad that was filtered through the official embassy system. A **Foreign Office** representative was attached to the small SIS headquarters in London. When the system of PCOs was established in 1921, 23 out of 28 officials were based in Europe. Initially, there was no PCO in Moscow because it was considered too hostile an environment for an SIS station to operate effectively. Instead, SIS operations in the Soviet Union were operated from the Baltic states and Finland. Foreign Office control of the PCO system had begun in August 1919, when the Cabinet of Prime Minister **David Lloyd George** sanctioned the creation of a Passport Control Department there. It was funded from the Foreign Office budget. *See also* VENLO INCIDENT; VIVIAN, MAJOR VALENTINE.

SERBIA. Serbia was the largest component in the old **Yugoslavia,** but its dissolution in 1991 owed much to Serb nationalism. In 1989, Slobodan

Milošević became president of Serbia (1989–1992; president of Yugoslavia, 1992–2000), and he pressed for a "Greater Serbia." This would include the Serb areas in **Bosnia** and **Croatia**. He therefore backed Serb separatism in Bosnia and Croatia during the civil war. Britain's reluctance to intervene may have inadvertently assisted Serbian chauvinism in the short run. Its former foreign secretary, Lord **David Owen**, contributed to a **United Nations–European Union** plan in January 1993, to divide Bosnia. Milošević, canny when it suited him, accepted the plan, which was rejected by the Bosnian Serbs. By then, he was technically president of Yugoslavia, a state that had largely disappeared from the map. Milošević was then persuaded to sign the Dayton Agreement (1995), which formalized the end of the Bosnian War.

A new issue then arose with the revolt in the Serb province of **Kosovo** by the Albanian ethnic majority. Kosovo had great historical significance for Serbs, just as the persecution of Serbs by the Pavelić fascist dictatorship in **World War II** explained their attitudes to Croatia. Milošević's attempt to impose ethnic cleansing in Kosovo was challenged head on by British prime minister **Tony Blair**. He was instrumental in organizing **North Atlantic Treaty Organization (NATO)** air strikes against Serbia's infrastructure on 24 March 1999. The Royal Air Force took part in 73 continuous days of bombing of Serbia. On 10 June, under the pressure of this concerted bombardment from NATO, Milošević agreed to withdraw Serb forces from Kosovo. There was intense bitterness in Serbia against Britain and all the other NATO states involved. This anger was also turned against Milošević, who was ejected from power in 2000. He was then placed under house arrest by the new Serbian government and, on 28 August, was extradited to face the International Criminal Tribunal for the Former Yugoslavia (ICTY) at The Hague. He died in custody in 2002. Milošević's successor, Zoran Djindjić (2001–2003), was assassinated by members of the Serb criminal underworld and security forces. He had begun the process of trying to deal with other Serb war criminals from the 1990s, especially the Bosnian Serb leaders Radovan Karadžić and General Ratko Mladić. Britain made it clear that Serbian acceptance into the European Union depended upon the arrest of those men. Mladić's trial before the ICTY began in 2012. Serbia had remained in union with its small neighboring republic, **Montenegro**, until 2006, when it secured its own independence.

SHINWELL, EMMANUEL (1884–1986). A veteran member of the Labour Party, Emmanuel Shinwell was minister of fuel and power during the terrible winter of 1947 in Great Britain. He was generally deemed to have been a failure in this key role. Shinwell was a strong opponent of British moves to enter the **European Economic Community** in the 1960s and 1970s. He was created Baron Shinwell.

SHORE, PETER (1924–2001). Elected as a Labour Party member of Parliament in October 1964, Peter Shore became a parliamentary private secretary to Prime Minister **Harold Wilson**. He was a vehement opponent of British membership in the **European Economic Community (EEC)**. When Wilson held a referendum on the issue of membership in 1975, Shore was one of those prominent members of the Labour Party who campaigned against remaining in the EEC on existing terms. He was created Baron Shore.

SINCLAIR, SIR ARCHIBALD (1890–1970). Archibald Sinclair was a product of **Eton College** and the Royal Military Academy Sandhurst. He served under **Winston Churchill** in the trenches during **World War I**, the start of a lifelong friendship. He was Churchill's personal secretary at the War Office from 1919–1921, and again at the Colonial Office in 1921–1922. Elected as a Liberal member of Parliament in 1922, Sinclair was briefly secretary of state for Scotland in the 1931 National Government under **Ramsay MacDonald**. He became leader of the opposition Liberals in 1935, and joined Churchill in his criticisms of the government's **appeasement** policy. When **World War II** broke out in September 1939, Sinclair refused to bring his party into coalition with **Neville Chamberlain's** wartime government. In May 1940, Churchill appointed Sinclair secretary of state for air. After Churchill's defeat in 1945, Sinclair, whose Liberal Party had been decimated in the general election, never held office again. He was created 1st Viscount Thurso in 1952.

SKYBOLT CRISIS (1962). The crisis over the Skybolt missile in December 1962 was part of Great Britain's ongoing difficulties with a nuclear delivery system. In February 1960, it had become apparent to the Cabinet Defense Committee in **Harold Macmillan's** government that the British-designed Blue Streak liquid-fuelled rocket would have to be abandoned, as its 15-minute response time would put Britain at a disadvantage in the event of a Russian attack. The cost of Blue Streak, estimated by the chiefs of the Defense Staff at more than £600 million, was also prohibitive. In March 1960, Macmillan visited Washington, and it was agreed that Britain could purchase the Skybolt missile, an air-to-ground weapon, which gave the Royal Air Force bomber force an extra lease of life. The Royal Navy wished to keep its existing carrier force and rejected the alternative option of the **Polaris** submarine-launched missile. The Skybolt deal meant a derogation from Britain's defense sovereignty, as it was now totally dependent on the **United States**. Yet, members of Macmillan's Conservative Party perpetuated the myth that Britain's nuclear deterrent was somehow independent. Skybolt, the public was told, was independent because it was under British control.

Macmillan got along well with President **John F. Kennedy,** which was as well, because, on 7 November 1962, acting on Pentagon advice, Kennedy decided to cancel Skybolt. The reasons given were a cost overrun and poor missile performance in tests. This put Macmillan and his government in an embarrassing position, but, fortunately, Kennedy was willing to sanction an alternative, Polaris. Macmillan needed this badly, because the cancellation of Skybolt left Britain without even the pretense of a nuclear deterrent. When he met Kennedy at Nassau, in the Bahamas, in December 1962, Macmillan insisted on Polaris as the alternative to appease angry Conservative members of Parliament. There were other alternatives to Skybolt, but Kennedy realized that Polaris was a political imperative for his ally. He therefore rejected objections from the U.S. Department of State. The Polaris deal was confirmed in April 1963, and it was a recognition that the **"special relationship"** between Britain and the United States was important. Britain was allowed to buy Polaris on specially favorable terms at cost price, with only a 5 percent contribution to the development of the nuclear submarine program. Such terms were not available to the United States' other allies.

SLOVENIA. The former Yugoslav republic of Slovenia declared itself independent on 25 June 1991. Diplomatic relations between Great Britain and Slovenia were rapidly established. The Slovenes opened an embassy in London, on 29 April 1992, and the British opened one in the Slovene capital of Ljubljana on 25 August. Britain's relationship with Slovenia was entirely different from those with the sister republics of **Croatia, Bosnia,** and **Serbia.** It did not involve military intervention or campaigns against war criminals. Slovenia was fortunate to be largely homogenous, with 90 percent of the population being Slovene, and only 2 percent Serb. There was no common border with Serbia, and, after a brief intervention by the federal Yugoslav army in 1991, Slovene independence was accepted. Britain strongly supported Slovenia's applications to join the **European Union (EU)** and **North Atlantic Treaty Organization (NATO).** Slovenia became a full member of both organizations in 2004. Britain also tried to assist Slovenia in the preparations for its EU presidency in 2008. Slovene officials were seconded to Whitehall departments in 2005 to gain experience when Great Britain itself held the presidency. **Queen Elizabeth II** visited Slovenia in October 2008.

SMUTS, JAN (1870–1950). A man who fought against the British as a leader of his Boer community, Jan Smuts was a remarkable individual who was in the British War Cabinet. He was also a key player at the 1919 **Paris Peace Conference** and a prime minister of his native **South Africa.** Smuts was extremely critical of the treatment of **Germany** by the Allied Powers in 1919, and he encouraged **John Maynard Keynes** to write his famous attack on the **Treaty of Versailles**. Smuts was prime minister of South Africa from 1920–1924, and deputy prime minister from 1933. He agreed with the statement of neutrality by Prime Minister James Barry Munnik Hertzog at the time of the **Munich Agreement** in 1938, but, in 1939, as prime minister, Smuts declared war on Germany to join Great Britain in **World War II**. He attended the Cairo Conference with **Winston Churchill** in 1942, and urged a change in British leadership for the North African campaign. He went with Churchill to **France** after the D-Day invasion in June 1944, and attended the **San Francisco Conference** as South Africa's representative in 1945. Although thought of as a liberal by some, Smuts approved the principle of white supremacy in South Africa, his United Party adhering to traditional Afrikaner attitudes. In 1948, Smuts was defeated in the general election by the National Party, losing his seat in the Transvaal. There is a statue of him in London's Parliament Square.

SOAMES, SIR CHRISTOPHER (1920–1987). The son-in-law of **Winston Churchill** who married his youngest daughter, Mary, Christopher Soames was a Conservative member of Parliament, diplomat, and colonial administrator who played a key role in the creation of independent **Southern Rhodesia** (Zimbabwe) in 1980. After serving in the military in **World War II**, Soames was assistant military attaché in Paris. He then entered parliament as Conservative member of Parliament for Bedford (1950–1966), serving as undersecretary of state for air in the government of **Anthony Eden** from 1955–1957. During the premiership of **Harold Macmillan**, Soames served as financial secretary to the **Admiralty** in 1957–1958. He was then promoted to the Cabinet as secretary of state for war (1958–1960), before being appointed minister of agriculture (1960–1964). Soames then went into opposition as the Labour Party came into power, and it was their prime minister, **Harold Wilson,** who appointed him ambassador in Paris in 1968. This was a key posting during a period when Great Britain was trying to get into the **European Economic Community (EEC)**, and, in 1969, the new ambassador became involved in what became known as the "Soames Affair."

In February 1969, President Charles de Gaulle told Soames in an interview that Britain and **France** should end their feuding over EEC membership and Europe's future. De Gaulle then allegedly said that existing EEC institutions needed to be reappraised and replaced by a series of multilateral collaborations. Ultimately, de Gaulle argued, an inner group of France, **Germany,** Britain, and **Italy** should lead the community. De Gaulle suggested that Britain could take the initiative in proposing bilateral talks with France. The **Foreign Office** suspected a French plot to undermine the support of the other five members of the EEC for British membership. It decided to ignore de Gaulle's initiative, lest it sabotage Britain's pending third application to join EEC (which was successful in 1971–1972). There was never any suggestion that Soames himself had acted improperly.

Soames served in Paris until 1972, and he then became a vice president of the European Commission (1973–1976). When **Margaret Thatcher** became prime minister, she made Soames governor of Southern Rhodesia, a post he held from 11 December 1979–18 April 1980. In this capacity, he helped steer through the process whereby the former Southern Rhodesia became Zimbabwe. Created Baron Soames in 1978, he served as leader of the House of Lords between May 1979 and September 1981, while doubling as governor of Southern Rhodesia.

SOUTH AFRICA. European links with South Africa stretch back to 1652, when the Dutch East India Company founded a settlement in the Cape Colony. The company went bankrupt in 1806, and Great Britain assumed control. The presence of two rival white entities, the British and the Boers (literally "farmers"), along with the native Bantu, complicated South Africa's history. The Boers spoke Afrikaans, an African version of Dutch, and they increasingly resented British control. In 1835 and 1836, in what Boers called the "Great Trek," 14,000 Boers migrated northward. Their settlements became known as the Orange Free State, independent after 1854, and Natal, which became a British Crown colony in 1856. The South African Republic, later known as the Transvaal, became independent in 1852. Nonetheless, the tentacles of British imperialism followed the Boers. It had its uses, as when the Transvaal became a Crown Colony in 1877, and needed to protect itself from the powerful Zulu kingdom. The war between the British and the famous Zulu king Cetewayo, in 1879, was initiated by British officials without London's approval. After an early and embarrassing defeat, the British crushed Zulu power at Ulundi. The Boers were not grateful. The Transvaal revolted in 1881, and a British defeat caused Prime Minister **William Gladstone** to concede independence.

The big issue in the following years was minerals. In 1886, huge deposits of gold were discovered in the Witwatersrand, along with diamonds. The British government thus wanted to secure control of the Orange Free State and the Transvaal. A forward policy in South Africa was encouraged by the colonial secretary, Joseph Chamberlain (1895–1903). The Boers objected to the presence of foreign prospectors in their republics. The reckless **Jameson Raid** (1896) was a result of the British desire to acquire the vast mineral resources of South Africa. Anglo–Boer tensions resulted in the Second Boer War (1899–1902). Britain needed all its imperial might to crush a few hundred thousand Boer farmers. Its policy of imprisoning Boer women and children in so-called "concentration camps" was not easily forgiven. In the aftermath of the war, British policy was magnanimous. The Orange Free State and the Transvaal became British colonies in 1902, but their independence was restored in 1907. Along with Natal and the Cape Colony, they became part of the Union of South Africa in 1910.

British policy was successful in winning over Boer leaders like **Jan Smuts**. He led South African forces in German East Africa during **World War I** and, in June 1917, was appointed a member of the British War Cabinet. Smuts also played a significant role as part of the British peace delegation at the **Paris Peace Conference** of 1919. Britain recognized South Africa's contribution to the Allied war effort by securing a **League of Nations** mandate for it over former German South West Africa (modern Namibia). Smuts and the other main leader of the Boer community, Louis Botha, wanted to maintain links with the **British Empire**, while achieving the greatest possible degree of autonomy. In the Statute of Westminster (1931), the British conceded South Africa's right to run an independent foreign policy. The seeds of future trouble lay in the new state's undemocratic nature. The majority black community had no vote, and the mixed race Cape Coloreds lost their existing voting rights. In 1924, Afrikaans was recognized as an official language, alongside English.

Entry into **World War II** was controversial in South Africa. Many Afrikaans speakers sympathized with the racist attitude of Nazi **Germany**. It was the influence of Smuts, as effective father of the nation, that secured a parliamentary majority for war in 1939. In World War II, as in World War I, Afrikaners and English speakers fought alongside blacks and coloreds. The illusion persisted postwar that Smuts was South Africa's dominant figure. He certainly played a major role in establishing the **United Nations** in 1945, and was widely admired in Britain. There was now, however, a new, more virulent strain of Afrikaner nationalism. Although as prime minister Smuts got more votes in the 1948 general election, his United Party was defeated by the National Party of Daniel Malan (prime minister, 1948–1954). Malan brought into operation the concept of apartheid, or separate development, whereby blacks were treated as second-class citizens in their own country. He had opposed support for the British war effort in World War II. He used the **Cold War** as an excuse to discriminate against his black population. Communism was no real threat to the apartheid regime, but Malan used the Suppression of Communism Act (1950) to outlaw any form of civil dissidence.

In the 1950s, successive British governments, Labour and Conservative, made little response to South Africa's racist policies. One factor was Britain's desire to hang on to the Simonstown naval base. Another was Britain's need for South African uranium and gold, which was extracted with the aid of British capital. The high priest of apartheid was Hendrik Verwoerd (prime minister, 1958–1966), who had been in charge of native African education under Malan and was openly pro-Nazi in World War II. Under Verwoerd, Anglo–South African relations reached a crisis point. Britain was involved in the process of decolonization in Africa, and 1960 was the year of **Harold Macmillan's** "Winds of Change" speech in Cape Town. It was also the year of the bloody massacre of blacks at Sharpeville that shocked British and international opinion. Verwoerd moved to break existing links with Britain, sensing that the Macmillan government was increasingly out of sympathy with his policies. South Africa decimalized the rand, which replaced sterling. A referendum was held that narrowly endorsed Verwoerd's desire to make South Africa a republic. When the **British Commonwealth** condemned apartheid in 1961, Verwoerd withdrew from it. In doing so, he probably avoided expulsion. Verwoerd was assassinated in 1966.

Little changed under his successor, Johannes Vorster (prime minister, 1966–1978). The British governments of Harold Macmillan and **Harold Wilson** had little time for South Africa's regime. It worsened relations by providing the outlaw regime of Ian Smith, in **Southern Rhodesia**, with supplies after 1965. The antiapartheid movement in Britain was strong and focused on breaking sporting links with South Africa (sport being an Afrikaner obsession). It was successful. The 1969–1970 rugby tour to Britain was sabotaged by persistent demonstrations. The 1970 cricket tour by South Africa did not take place at all. Commonwealth members, including **Australia**, **New Zealand**, and the West Indies, joined in the boycott. South Africa tried to pose as the defender of Western values against Communism. When the Portuguese empire in Mozambique and Angola collapsed in 1974–1975, Vorster supported rebel anti-Marxist movements. He conflated Communism with black rights. A second massacre of black South Africans took place at Soweto on 16 June 1976. The African National Congress (ANC) now had much international support and training camps in black African states. In 1978, Vorster was replaced by the equally obdurate Pieter Botha (prime minister, 1978–1989).

Botha seemed to have found a friend in Britain's new premier, **Margaret Thatcher**. Appointed in 1979, Thatcher consistently opposed Commonwealth sanctions on South Africa. At Nassau in 1985, when Commonwealth heads met, South Africa dominated the agenda. Britain seemed to be at loggerheads with other Commonwealth states on the issue. Thatcher claimed to detest apartheid. She opposed economic sanctions on the grounds that Britain's trade would suffer and black South Africans would lose their jobs. Thatcher seemed to triumph at Nassau when it was merely agreed that there would be a ban on the import of gold Krugerrands and government help for trade delegations visiting South Africa. She was widely criticized in Britain for alleged triumphalism. Even **Queen Elizabeth II** was reported to be concerned about how Thatcher's South African policy was dividing the Commonwealth. Thatcher claimed that Botha would phase out racist legislation, for example, the need for blacks to carry passbooks. He did not. The **Foreign and Commonwealth Office** did not share Thatcher's analysis. Her **foreign secretary, Sir Geoffrey Howe**, knew South Africa from personal experience. On 12 June 1986, black discontent in South Africa resulted in the imposition of a state of emergency. Thatcher refused to alter her policy. She believed that it reflected the view of most British voters.

The period of 1989–1990 proved to be a turning point. Botha's time as prime minister ended in 1989, and Thatcher's in 1990. Frederik de Klerk (prime minister, 1989–1994) was a more liberal premier. In 1990, he ended South African control of Namibia. Recognizing that apartheid was unsustainable, he also released the ANC leader, Nelson Mandela, from imprisonment on the notorious Robben Island in 1990, where he had been held since 1963. In 1993, a new constitution was instituted, and, in 1994, general elections were held. They were the first multiracial elections in South Africa's history. The ANC won more than 60 percent of the vote. These changes had the approval of British prime minister **John Major** and his government. Mandela's refusal to bear grudges won widespread admiration in Britain. He was South Africa's first truly national president (1994–1999). During this time, he visited Britain and offered his support to black youths in inner city London who complained of police harassment. It was a triumph for multiracialism when South Africa won the 1995 Rugby World Cup, rugby being the most Afrikaner of sports. Mandela strongly associated himself with the team, playing a game brought to South Africa by the British colonialists. Blacks historically favored soccer.

In 1999, Thabo Mbeki, a British-educated ANC veteran, succeeded Mandela as president. This was a time when relations between Britain and **Robert Mugabe's** Zimbabwe were very poor. White farmers were being expropriated, and Mbeki was unwilling to criticize a former anticolonial leader. The British government of **Tony Blair** was unhappy with this policy, as Robert Mugabe also savagely repressed his black political opposition after 2000. There was also criticism in Britain of Mbeki's attitude toward the HIV virus. In 2006, estimates put the number of South Africans affected at 15 percent. On the positive side, Anglo–South African relations were improved by the establishment of the South Africa–UK Bilateral Forum in 1997. This was designed to improve political and economic relations between the two countries. The forum has provided for top-level meetings. In June 2001, Mbeki met Blair at **No. 10 Downing Street,** and he visited the British prime minister again in May 2006, at the conclusion of the seventh forum at Lancaster House. South Africa received Foreign Secretary **David Miliband** and a British delegation for the eighth biannual forum on 7 July 2008.

There was continued British unhappiness with Mbeki's attitude toward Zimbabwe, where persecution of the opposition was rampant. The killing of white farmers (1,500 since 1991) in South Africa itself was also a concern for the Blair government. Mbeki resigned as president on 25 September 2008. He was replaced by Kgalema Motlanthe. It was understood that Motlanthe would only be a caretaker president. He was appointed by the South African National Assembly on 25 September 2008, and was to remain in place until the national elections were held on 22 April 2009. Jacob Zuma was elected president and sworn in on 9 May 2009. The ninth biannual South Africa–UK Bilateral Forum took place in London, on 9 June 2011. After visiting South Africa in December 2011, the parliamentary undersecretary of state at the FCO, Henry Bellingham, stated that bilateral trade between Britain and South Africa should double by 2015. Britain remains one of the two top foreign investors in South Africa, and South Africa is one of the 20 top exporters to Britain.

SOUTHEAST ASIA TREATY ORGANIZATION (SEATO). At the height of the **Cold War**, the Southeast Asia Treaty Organization (SEATO) was created by an agreement signed in Manila, the capital of the Philippines, in September 1954, to defend the region against Communism. The signatory powers were Great Britain, **Australia, France, New Zealand, Pakistan,** the Philippines, Thailand, and the **United States**. A separate protocol to the SEATO treaty extended protection to Cambodia, Laos, and Vietnam, the former constituent parts of French **Indochina**. The Americans thought that the protocol justified their subsequent intervention in Vietnam, which only ended in 1975; however, Britain did not and refused to provide the United States with any military support during the **Vietnam War**. The U.S. retreat from Vietnam removed the relevance that SEATO had once seemed to have, and it was phased out. *See also* DOMINO THEORY.

SOUTHERN RHODESIA (ZIMBABWE). Taking its name from Cecil Rhodes, Southern Rhodesia was a so-called "white dominion" with rights of self-government from 1922. Like Great Britain's other African colonies, it was in line for independence in the early 1960s, but the British government insisted that there must be black majority rule. This was unacceptable to Rhodesian prime minister Ian Smith, a veteran Royal Air Force pilot from the Battle of Britain. Smith declared that black majority rule would not come to his country in 1,000 years, and, on 11 November 1965, Armistice Day, he made a Unilateral Declaration of Independence. His aim was to preserve power for the white settler minority. This placed the Labour government of **Harold Wilson,** which had only come to power in October 1964, in considerable difficulty. Force was an option, and most people in Britain, apart from right-wingers in the Conservative Party, deplored what Smith had done. As the former colonial power, however, Britain was reluctant to take the military option, and Wilson handed the issue of Southern Rhodesia over to the **United Nations (UN)**. In 1966, the UN voted for economic sanctions to be used against Smith's regime, but they were not entirely successful, as Smith was supplied with essentials by the apartheid regime in **South Africa**, and through Portuguese Angola and Mozambique. There were even suggestions that some British firms were breaking the sanctions regime. A guerrilla war was launched against Smith by black African fighters, led by **Robert Mugabe** and Joshua Nkomo. The **Foreign Office** was obliged, grudgingly, to accept the mediation of U.S. secretary of state **Henry Kissinger** in 1976. He provided a six-step plan leading to black majority rule, which Smith, beset by a bloody guerrilla war, accepted. Britain's prime minister, **Margaret Thatcher**, whose natural instincts were against revolutionary insurgencies, was persuaded by the Foreign Office to convene a conference at Lancaster House in September 1979, which accepted an all-party solution for Southern Rhodesia. After elections, Zimbabwe, as Southern Rhodesia had become, was granted its independence from Britain in April 1980, and it became a member of the **Commonwealth**.

SOVIET UNION. *See* RUSSIA.

SPAIN. Links between Spain and Great Britain are ancient ones, stretching back to the marriage of Henry VIII (1509–1547) to Catherine of Aragon and beyond. The Spanish king, Philip II, who married Henry's daughter, Mary Tudor, was briefly king of England (1555–1558) as well. But this closeness was short-lived. Religious differences and commercial rivalry meant that by 1588, Catholic Spain was launching a great invasion fleet, the Armada, against England. The Armada failed, and Anglo–Spanish relations remained poor throughout the 17th century. Britain, as it had become, was heavily involved in the War of the Spanish Succession, which prevented a French Bourbon from inheriting the Spanish throne (1702–1714). During the struggle, Britain seized the crucial naval base of **Gibraltar** at the entrance to the Mediterranean Sea in 1704. Afterward, Gibraltar remained a persistent problem in Anglo–Spanish relations. It was so in a new context of Spanish decline as the treasure fleets from South America brought less and less valuable cargo. Spain itself was invaded by **Napoleon Bonaparte** in 1808, and it had to turn to its old enemy, Britain, for assistance. Tenacious resistance by the Spanish people and the generalship of Britain's Arthur Wellesley (later Duke of Wellington) ejected the French from Spain by 1813. The end of the **Napoleonic Wars** coincided with revolts against Spain in her Latin American colonies.

Britain regarded these as important outlets for trade and warned off the Congress Powers (**France**, Austria, and **Russia**), who threatened to reverse the verdict of the Latin American revolutions. In essence, the U.S. **Monroe Doctrine** of the 1820s, which was supported by Britain, prevented any comeback by Spanish imperialism in Latin America. Spain retained toeholds in Cuba and the Philippines. Cuba was also lost in a war with the **United States** in 1898. Spain increasingly became an obscurantist Catholic backwater in Europe. It did not take part in **World War I**.

Spain returned to the center of the European stage only during the Spanish Civil War (1936–1939). The Republican government, which had overthrown the monarchy in 1931, was challenged by military rebels led by General Francisco Franco. In a bloody struggle in which 1 million Spaniards died, Franco secured both German and Italian help. This proved decisive, as Britain and France opted for nonbelligerency, a doctrine shamefully ignored by the Nazis and fascists. There was much sympathy for the Republicans in Britain, and many left-wingers and trade unionists fought in the famous International Brigades. The British government had no intention of becoming involved in the era of **appeasement**. The struggling Republic was not assisted by the British decision to refuse refueling facilities to the Republican navy at Gibraltar. Franco was no friend of democracy as his behavior after his victory in 1939 demonstrated. He was, however, canny enough to keep out of **World War II**. This neutrality saved his regime, which was still viewed with much distaste by the postwar British Labour government (1945–1951). The coming of the **Cold War** in the late 1940s changed the view of Franco's neofascist regime, especially in the United States, where an enemy of Communism was seen as a friend of the West. Britain and Spain were still, and continued to be, at loggerheads over Gibraltar. Unsurprisingly, Spain regarded the Rock as part of its sovereign territory. The British saw it as key to their control of the Mediterranean, even though this was on the wane by the 1950s. In 1969, Franco revived the issue when, following the failure of Anglo–Spanish talks in 1966, he closed the border between Spain and Gibraltar. Britain had made Gibraltar a Crown colony in 1964. Its status was conflated with the issue of Spanish entry into the **European Union (EU)**, when, in 1982, some border traffic was allowed in exchange for British support for Spain's EU application. Full communications were restored in 1985.

By then, Spain itself was a very different country. Franco had died in 1975, and his successor, King Juan Carlos, veered sharply away from the authoritarianism and clericalism of the Franco period. Mass tourism had opened Spain to outside influences, and, from 1982–1996, it was ruled by the Socialist Felipe González. He took Spain into both the EU and the **North Atlantic Treaty Organization (NATO)** in 1986. The NATO entry was narrowly approved in a plebiscite. González was succeeded by the rather colorless Conservative José Maria Aznar (1996–2004). There were more talks about Gibraltar in 2001, when the government of Gibraltar seemed to genuinely fear a British handover to Spain, but this was never likely. In 2006, travel restrictions were removed and direct flights between Spain and Gibraltar instituted.

Aznar had taken Spain into war in **Iraq**, but he lost power in 2004, just as a murderous attack was made on Madrid by Islamic jihadists. He tried to blame Basque **terrorists** who had long wanted to separate from Spain. The attempt to link the Basques with the war on terrorism was misleading. A long-standing liberation struggle had been taken over by extremists. Another socialist government, under José Zapatero (2004–2011), reversed Spanish policy on Iraq. Aznar had sent 1,000 Spanish troops to support the Anglo–American effort there. Zapatero pulled them out. Like other governments in Europe, his was hamstrung by the credit crunch of 2007–2008, especially as there had been wild speculation in the Spanish property market. This involved thousands of British pensioners who lost out financially. The government of **David Cameron** was concerned about the possibility that Spain might be forced out of the **Eurozone** in 2011–2012, a result feared because of the euro "contagion" from **Greece**.

Gibraltar remained a bone of contention between Britain and Spain. In July 2009, Spain's minister of foreign affairs visited Gibraltar for talks with British **foreign secretary David Miliband** (2007–2010). Gibraltar's chief minister, Peter Caruana, was also present, but the sovereignty issue was not discussed given its controversial nature. Instead, talks were limited to maritime and environmental matters. An incident took place in December 2009, when a Civil Guard launch from Spain illegally entered Gibraltar's harbor. Four officers were arrested by the Gibraltar authorities. There have also been a number of fishing disputes between Britain and Spain since Spain entered the EU in 1986. The Spanish trawler fleet does much of its fishing off the coasts of Britain and **Ireland**. At a time when British fishing stocks have been depleted, this has caused some resentment. It is a paradox of the sometimes tense Anglo–Spanish relationship that an estimated 990,000 British people, mostly retirees, live in Spain. This is far more than the number of Spaniards in Britain (54,482 according to the 2001 census). British policy on the EU and the Eurozone sometimes seems oblivious of such facts.

SPEAIGHT, R. (1906–1976). A British diplomat who entered the Diplomatic Service in 1929, R. Speaight served in the Budapest legation (1931–1933), the Warsaw embassy (1935–1938), and the **Foreign Office** Central Department during **World War II**. Thereafter, he was posted to Cairo (1945–1948) and then became ambassador to Burma (1950–1953). Speaight was assistant undersecretary of state at the Foreign Office (1953–1956) and finished his career as minister to Bulgaria (1956–1958).

SPEARS, GENERAL SIR EDWARD (1886–1974). Edward Spears was a British liaison officer with the French Army in both **World War I** and **World War II** who played a crucial role in Anglo–French relations. When he resigned as head of the British Military Mission in Paris in 1920, Spears went into business with the highly colorful British master spy **Sidney Reilly**, whose activities he frequently found alarming. During the 1930s, Spears became close to **Winston Churchill**, and he advised him on matters relating to the French Army. As a Conservative member of Parliament, he was also joint chairman of the Anglo–French parliamentary group. Spears was a Francophile who campaigned hard to improve Anglo–French relations during the so-called "Phoney War" of 1939–1940. He wrote a vivid account of his liaison role with the French Army during World War II entitled *Assignment to Catastrophe* (1955), which describes the events behind the Fall of **France** in 1940.

SPECIAL OPERATIONS EXECUTIVE (SOE). On 16 June 1940, **Winston Churchill** invited **Hugh Dalton,** who was serving as minister of economic warfare at the time, to also take charge of a new organization called the Special Operations Executive (SOE). Its task was to liaise with resistance movements inside Occupied Europe. SOE agents were dropped by aircraft or from submarines into German-occupied Europe, while SOE headquarters in Baker Street, London, kept in touch with agents, both male and female, by radio. It was a feature of SOE that it had daring female agents like Odette Churchill and Violette Szabo. Such agents were thoroughly trained in sabotage and assassination techniques. Much valuable work was done by the SOE in **France, Belgium,** and **Yugoslavia**. There were also a few spectacular disasters. German military intelligence wrecked SOE's Dutch operation by capturing its agents, hiding this fact from Baker Street and luring dozens more agents into captivity by radio.

"SPECIAL RELATIONSHIP." The concept of the "special relationship" has come to be used regarding Anglo–American relations since **World War II**. It emerged from the emergency of 1940, when Great Britain was in need of U.S. support, and **Winston Churchill** tried to secure this by developing an especially close relationship between himself and President **Franklin D. Roosevelt**. Churchill believed that common cultural and legal ties made a special relationship possible, even though since 1945 the term has had greater meaning for Great Britain than the **United States**.

STANLEY, OLIVER (1896–1950). Elected Conservative member of Parliament for Westmoreland in 1924, Oliver Stanley held a variety of government posts in the 1931–1940 National Government in Great Britain. He was variously minister of transport (1933–1934), minister of labour (1934–1935), and president of the Board of Trade (1937–1940). In the wartime government of **Neville Chamberlain**, Stanley was briefly secretary of state for war, but he left office in May 1940, when **Winston Churchill** would not offer him a job with significant seniority. Stanley returned to government in 1942, as secretary of state for the colonies, a post he retained until **World War II** ended in 1945. *See also* BALDWIN, STANLEY; MACDONALD, RAMSAY.

STEVENSON, FRANCES (1888–1972). Private secretary and companion to **David Lloyd George**, a euphemism for mistress, Frances Stevenson married the former British prime minister in 1943. She became Countess Lloyd George, although her husband, then in great old age, died in 1945. Stevenson wielded considerable influence over him and was fiercely protective of his reputation.

STEWART, MICHAEL (1906–1990). Michael Stewart had two stints as British **foreign secretary** (1965–1966, 1968–1970) in the first and second Labour administrations of **Harold Wilson**. He also served as secretary of state for education (1964–1965), a rare example of a politician who actually had firsthand experience in the sector, as he had been a headmaster. Although rather reticent in manner, Stewart could be tough with Great Britain's U.S. allies, criticizing their use of gas in Vietnam in 1965. Wilson was also glad to have a safe pair of hands when Stewart replaced **George Brown** at the **Foreign and Commonwealth Office** in 1968. Stewart was in a strong enough position to insist on security of tenure in his case until the general election of June 1970.

STRANG, SIR WILLIAM (1893–1978). In 1949, William Strang succeeded **Orme Sargent** as permanent undersecretary at the **Foreign Office**, a post he held until 1953. Unusual for his time, Strang was a graduate of London University, rather than Oxbridge, who entered the Diplomatic Service in 1919, after military service in **World War I**. He served in Belgrade

(1919–1922) before returning to the Foreign Office, where he remained until 1930, when a further posting sent him to Moscow, a notoriously difficult and remote embassy. In Moscow, he was involved in the notorious Metropolitan-Vickers case, when British engineers were accused of spying on the Soviet Union (1933). Strang was then appointed head of the Central Department in 1937, in which role he flew to **Germany** with Prime Minister **Neville Chamberlain** in September 1938. Strang later wrote that the **Munich Agreement** was a tragic necessity, although he was critical of the **appeasement** policy. In 1939, Strang had the onerous task of acting as the head of a mission to the Soviet Union when Great Britain and **France** tried unsuccessfully to secure a military agreement with the Soviet dictator Joseph Stalin. Strang was then assistant undersecretary of state in the Foreign Office from 1939–1943, a United Kingdom representative to the European Advisory Commission from 1943–1945, and political advisor to the commander in chief of the British occupation forces in Germany from 1945–1947. This experience was useful when Strang was appointed permanent undersecretary (German section) from 1947–1949, before the culmination of his career, when he was made permanent undersecretary at the Foreign Office in 1949.

Strang had the task of running the new Permanent Undersecretary's Committee, which focused on long-term foreign policy issues and made recommendations to the **foreign secretary**, then **Ernest Bevin**. As chairman of the committee, Strang toured Southeast Asia in December 1949, along with the Far East and the Middle East, to examine areas of British influence that might be subject to Russian penetration. He published a career memoir entitled *Home and Abroad* in 1956. Strang was created Baron Strang of Stonesfield. *See also* VANSITTART, SIR ROBERT.

STRAW, JACK (1945–). A product of Labour student politics, Jack Straw worked his way up the party hierarchy to become Prime Minister **Tony Blair's foreign secretary** from 2001–2006. He supported Blair throughout the crisis over **Iraq** from 2001–2003 and helped to draft the **United Nations** Security Council resolutions. Where **Foreign and Commonwealth Office (FCO)** legal officers had grave doubts about the legality of Anglo–American action in Iraq, Straw had none that were demonstrated in public. In contrast, his predecessor as foreign secretary, **Robin Cook**, resigned over the Iraq invasion in March 2003. Straw developed a close relationship with his U.S. counterparts Colin Powell and **Condoleezza Rice** during the **Iraq War**. Rice was taken to Straw's Blackburn constituency in Lancashire, and she went with him to watch the local football team. In 2006, despite this apparent cordiality, there were rumors that Straw was removed from the FCO at the request of the **George W. Bush** administration because he would not sanction an attack on **Iran**. Straw also served as home secretary and justice secretary in the Tony Blair and **Gordon Brown** administrations until Labour's electoral defeat in May 2010.

SUDAN. The history of Sudan was closely linked to that of Great Britain and **Egypt** following a long period under Ottoman Turkish authority. In 1880, Britain had taken over effective control of Egypt, but its involvement in the Sudan was limited to the Red Sea ports and Khartoum. British prime minister **William Gladstone** did not wish to extend British control, but, in 1881, he was faced with a serious revolt against the Egyptian administration in Sudan. This was led by a charismatic Sudanese Muslim cleric, the Mahdi, or "Chosen One." In January 1884, Gladstone sent General Charles Gordon to the Sudan to evacuate Khartoum and hand Sudan back to the native population. Instead, Gordon posed as a champion of Christianity, tried to negotiate with the Mahdi, and was besieged by his forces. In 1885, the city was stormed and Gordon killed, in the process becoming a Victorian martyr. Gladstone was vilified as a murderer. Sudan was subsequently ruled (1885–1896) by the Mahdi and his successor, the Khalifa. Revenge for Gordon forced the British government to conquer Sudan, and this process was completed at the Battle of Omdurman in 1898. This battle, in which a young **Winston Churchill** fought as a cavalryman, was a massacre. Machine guns and artillery mowed down 11,000 of the Khalifa's followers. In 1899, the British created an Anglo–Egyptian condominium in Sudan, and it retained this status until just before independence. Unhealthy symptoms appeared quickly in Sudanese society, because the British tended to favor Muslim Northerners over Christian Southerners (about one-third of the population). A small cadre of British imperial officials gave Sudan an efficient administration. Sudanese troops contributed to the imperial war effort in both **World War I** and **World War II**.

After World War II, Britain was committed to granting independence to Sudan. This was made clear by British **foreign secretary Anthony Eden** in a statement in the House of Commons in 1951. Problems arose because Egypt tried to impose the rule of its king, Farouk, on Sudan, with U.S. support. Eden rejected the idea that Farouk should also become king of Sudan out of hand, unless the Sudanese people agreed. They did not approve this solution, and, after some delay, Britain granted full independence to Sudan on 1 January 1956, anxious that it should not fall under Egyptian influence. Its subsequent history was not a good advertisement for the benefits of British rule. In fact, they were also in too much of a hurry and did not insist on safeguards for Southerners in 1956. The new state was dominated by the Muslim North, and most of all by the army. There were military coups in 1958, 1969, and 1989. During most of the period since independence, Sudan has been in a state of civil war, brought on by Northern attempts to impose Islamic practices on the black African Christian South. The 1983 attempt to impose Sharia law triggered a civil war between the Khartoum government and the Sudanese People's Liberation Army. Between 1983–2000, an estimated 2 million Sudanese died, and another 4 million were made refugees. Britain's influence over such obscurantist Muslim regimes was strictly limited. As the former colonial power, Britain's involvement was unwelcome throughout the African continent. The military coup of 20 July 1989 led to the appointment in 1993 of an extreme Islamist, Omar Hassan Bashir, as president. The civil war continued until 2002, when U.S. pressure on the Bashir government secured a peace deal. It was agreed that the South would be given independence, but only in 2011. In the interim, another catastrophe emerged in the province of Darfur, where the ethnic black African population revolted against Bashir. The resulting genocide by the Sudanese army and Muslim paramilitaries was organized by Bashir, who was indicted as a war criminal by the International Criminal Court at The Hague. A Chinese veto at the **United Nations (UN)** Security Council prevented any intervention. The presence of an African Union peacekeeping force beginning in 2006 did little to improve the situation. Under **Tony Blair**, Britain supported UN action, but the international community failed to prevent the killing of 300,000 people by 2007, and the expulsion of a further 2 million.

When independence for South Sudan did come in 2011, it also left the problem of Nubaland inside the old Sudanese state. Another ethnic black revolt against the Arab Muslim regime of Bashir was responded to in the most brutal fashion. The extent of such massacres was plain in British television footage in March 2012. Britain, under Prime Minister **David Cameron**, strongly supported the emergence of South Sudan as a separate state.

SUDETENLAND. *See* CZECHOSLOVAKIA.

SUEZ CRISIS (1956). The 1956 Suez Crisis, which resulted from **Egypt's** nationalization of the Suez Canal in July of that year, was one of the most divisive in the modern history of Great Britain. It led to the resignation of Prime Minister **Anthony Eden** in January 1957. Yet, its genesis went back earlier, to the mutual suspicion between Eden and Egypt's president, **Jamal Abd al Nasser**, even though the two men had agreed to the 1954 Anglo–Egyptian Treaty, whereby Britain evacuated the Suez Canal Zone. In March 1956, King Hussein of **Jordan**, an ally of Britain in the Middle East, sacked the head of the Arab Legion, Sir John Glubb, and Eden persuaded himself that Nasser was behind the dismissal. In fact, Glubb's dismissal owed more to the impatience of the young 21-year-old king, a British-trained officer himself with a domineering, aging British general. Eden, whose behavior may have been influenced by health problems, became convinced that Nasser was a reincarnation of the Italian dictator Benito Mussolini, whom he had detested as a young **foreign secretary** in the 1930s. It was true that Nasser had authorized Cairo Radio to launch an anti-British propaganda campaign.

Nasser's nationalization of the Suez Canal was itself provoked by Anglo–American refusal to fund his favorite **Aswan Dam** project, based on a perception in London and Washington that Nasser, who obtained arms from **Czechoslovakia**, was flirting with the Communist Bloc. Eden had a double motive where Nasser and Egypt were concerned. The loss of the canal, even though Nasser was prepared to compensate the Anglo–French Suez Canal Company, which operated it, was deemed a threat to Britain's trade and supply routes. Oil was a chief concern. The Suez Canal was also traditionally perceived as the gateway to the Indian Ocean, which was why Prime Minister **Benjamin Disraeli** had bought a majority holding in the Suez Canal Company in 1876. Between August and October 1956, Eden, through his **foreign secretary**, **Selwyn Lloyd**, and the **Foreign Office**, tried to reach a diplomatic solution to the canal problem. Eden, a man who had been foreign secretary himself, almost continuously for 20 years, dominated policy and convinced himself that the **United States** would not object to the use of force to coerce Egypt. This was not an accurate analysis of the American position, much as they disliked Nasser, but the situation was not improved by Eden's notoriously poor relationship with U.S. secretary of state **John Foster Dulles**.

Eden was determined to bring Nasser down, and, on 22 October, he sent Selwyn Lloyd to Sèvres, on the outskirts of Paris, for a secret meeting with the French and Israelis, both anxious to destroy Nasser for their own reasons. The plan was for **Israel** to attack Egypt from east of the Suez Canal, allowing the Anglo–French the opportunity to issue an ultimatum demanding that both sides withdraw on either side of the canal. This was designed to be unacceptable to Nasser. British secrecy about the plan was underlined by the fact that it was only signed by Patrick Dean, deputy undersecretary at the Foreign Office, not by Lloyd or Eden. The Cabinet was not told about the Sèvres Protocol, and neither was the British ambassador in Cairo. Eden subsequently lied to the House of Commons about the collusion with **France** and Israel. As agreed, Israeli forces invaded Egyptian territory on 29 October 1956 and occupied the Sinai Desert. Nasser rejected the Anglo–French ultimatum, and, on 5 November, Anglo–French forces landed around Port Said at the mouth of the Suez Canal. This action was taken without U.S. approval, and it infuriated President **Dwight D. Eisenhower**, who was coming up for reelection that month. To make matters worse, the Suez operation coincided with the invasion of Hungary by the Soviet Union following the revolution there.

Anglo–French action seemed to negate any attempt by the West to claim the moral high ground over Hungary.

In Britain, Labour Party leader **Hugh Gaitskell**, who had attacked Nasser's forced nationalization of the canal, abandoned the previous bipartisan policy and savagely attacked Eden's behavior in the House of Commons and on television. The United States joined the Soviet Union in condemning the Suez operation at the **United Nations** Security Council in New York. Eisenhower demanded an Anglo–French withdrawal, and U.S. pressure on the pound sterling gave Eden little option but to withdraw, when France would have liked to continue. On 6 November, Britain was forced to accept a cease-fire and subsequent evacuation of the canal area. Suez demonstrated Britain's inability to act independently of the United States and, in the short run, did serious damage to its reputation in the Middle East and worldwide. *See also* KIRKPATRICK, SIR IVONE; TREVELYAN, SIR HUMPHREY; WATER-HOUSE, CAPTAIN CHARLES.

SYNNOTT, SIR HILARY (1945–2011). As regional representative for the Coalition Provisional Authority in Basra, Hilary Synnott had the unusual experience of being called back from retirement as a **Foreign and Commonwealth Office (FCO)** diplomat in July 2003. He subsequently gave testimony to the Chilcot Commission on the **Iraq War**. This, along with his 2008 memoir about his time in **Iraq**, gave graphic detail about his problems in Basra, then supposedly under British control. Upon arrival in Iraq, he lacked even a phone and a computer and had to beg the Americans for assistance. Synnott was scathing about FCO shortcomings in Iraq, especially the lack of any real postwar planning. He was equally critical of Prime Minister **Tony Blair** and President **George W. Bush** for their failure to see ahead of the military campaign.

Earlier in his life, Synnott had spent five years in submarines in the Royal Navy before joining the FCO in 1973. He served in Paris, Bonn, and Amman, before being made head of department at the FCO Western European Department in London. In 1991, as head of the FCO Security Coordination Department, Synnott was instrumental in securing the release of British hostages (one of whom was the Archbishop of Canterbury's aide, Terry Waite) in Lebanon. His last 10 years (1993–2003) at the FCO were spent as high commissioner in the **Pakistan** capital of Islamabad, and deputy high commissioner in New Delhi. Synnott was knighted in 2002.

T

TAVERNE, DICK (1928–). Labour member of Parliament for Lincoln and a treasury minister in the 1966–1970 **Harold Wilson** government, Dick Taverne was a strong pro-European. Taverne's pro-**European Economic Community** stance caused him to stand as an independent in a 1973 by-election in his constituency, which had become hostile toward Great Britain's membership on 1 January 1973. He won the election. Taverne lost the seat in October 1974, to the official Labour candidate **Margaret Beckett**, a future Labour **foreign secretary**. Taverne subsequently became a member of the pro-European Social Democratic Party, formed in 1981. He was created Baron Taverne.

TEDDER, AIR CHIEF MARSHALL, SIR ARTHUR (1890–1967). In 1944, ahead of the **D-Day Landings** in Normandy, Air Chief Marshall Sir Arthur Tedder was brought in to concert the operations of the Royal Air Force's strategic bomber force with those of its tactical air forces. Tedder was also given the post of deputy supreme commander of the Allied Forces under **Dwight D. Eisenhower.** He got along with Eisenhower much better than Bernard Montgomery, the commander in chief of the British land forces. At one point during the Normandy campaign, Tedder even suggested that Montgomery be relieved of his command.

TEHERAN CONFERENCE (1943). The so-called "Big Three," **Winston Churchill**, Joseph Stalin, and **Franklin D. Roosevelt**, met for the first time at Teheran, in **Iran**, in November 1943. A central issue between the leaders was when and where a second front in Europe would be opened. Stalin pressed the Anglo–Americans about this, and, whereas Churchill prevaricated, the American generals wanted **France** to be invaded in 1944. The British prime minister was still haunted by the Gallipoli disaster during **World War I**, when the amphibious operation had gone so horribly wrong. There was a distinct shift in the balance of power at Teheran. Roosevelt was impressed by the Red Army's heroic resistance on the Eastern Front and sought to get closer to Stalin, deliberately leaving Churchill out of conversations. He thought that "Operation Overlord," the invasion of Normandy set for June 1944, had been foisted on Great Britain by the Americans and the Russians. Churchill remained skeptical about the operation. Even his own Chiefs of Staff, however, were unenthusiastic about Churchill's own preferred option, an invasion of Europe from the southeast. A Balkan strategy was rejected.

Churchill also had to accept the appointment of an American supreme Allied commander, a decision that reflected the growing size of the U.S. contribution to the Allied war effort. Teheran was a defeat for Churchill, who could no longer fob off his allies' demands for a second front in France by demanding that conditions for invasion were right. *See also* D-DAY LANDINGS.

TEMPLER, SIR GERALD (1898–1979). In 1952, General Sir Gerald Templer was appointed to the combined post of high commissioner and director of operations for British Intelligence in Malaya. At the time, the country was facing a Communist insurgency. Templer brought in senior MI5 officers to overhaul the Special Branch intelligence organization. His leadership and the close liaison between the British security forces and the Special Branch created the most effective counterinsurgency operation in modern history. Templer was later made a field marshal in the British Army, a reward for the victory in Malaya, which was achieved by 1955.

TEN-YEAR RULE. On 15 August 1919, the British War Cabinet instructed its armed services to operate on the assumption that the **British Empire** would not be engaged in any great conflict for the next 10 years. No expeditionary force would be needed for this purpose. The treasury used this guideline to restrict expenditure on armaments. In 1925–1926, when **Winston Churchill** was chancellor of the exchequer, the Cabinet gave the treasury control of all armed service expenditure estimates. In July 1928, the Cabinet made a further statement that the presumption would be that there would be no major war for 10 years. This presumption rolled over from one year to the next. The Ten-Year Rule was supported by the **Foreign Office**, which was convinced that the world was at peace, and it surprisingly aroused little opposition from the Chiefs of Staff. Only in March 1932, after the Japanese attack on Manchuria, was the Ten-Year Rule abandoned. A further year passed before the **Defense Requirements Committee** was established to examine the shortcomings in the armed services that had accumulated in previous years.

TERRORISM. Great Britain has had a long history of dealing with both domestic and international terrorism. It started with bomb outrages by the Fenians, an Irish republican movement, in the 1860s. One result of these episodes was the establishment of Scotland Yard's Special Branch to deal with political extremists. The big Irish republican challenge came after Irish independence, when part of the **Irish Republican Army (IRA)** did not accept the 1921 settlement. It regarded attacks on the six counties of Northern **Ireland** and the mainland of Britain as legitimate. Serious campaigns of bombings and shootings were mounted in 1939–1940, from 1956–1962 (only in Northern Ireland), and continuously from 1969–1998. The IRA campaign reached its peak in the 1970s and 1980s, with a successful attempt on the life of **Lord Louis Mountbatten** in 1979, and an unsuccessful one on **Margaret Thatcher** in 1984. Massive bombs were exploded in London and Birmingham in 1974, and in Manchester and London in the 1990s. In Northern Ireland, there were persistent attacks on British troops and the Royal Ulster Constabulary. More than 3,000 people died in 30 years of urban republican terrorism, many of them civilians. Successive British governments adopted a carrot and stick policy. Although a severe Prevention of Terrorism Act (1974) increased police powers, even in the 1970s, the government of **Edward Heath** had secret back channel contacts with the leadership of the Provisional IRA (PIRA).

When Thatcher became prime minister in 1979, a more draconian policy was adopted. In 1980–1981, her government refused to accord political status to IRA prisoners who went on hunger strike. Thatcher also prevented the voices of republican speakers from being broadcast in Britain. This, she claimed, denied republican terrorism the "oxygen of publicity." Conversely, the PIRA leadership regarded itself as waging a war against British colonialism, in which any methods were justified. It ultimately came to realize that force alone would not attain republican ends. The Good Friday Agreement (1998) showed that this fact had been recognized. A slow, complex process of disarmament was begun by the IRA. Constitutional reform replaced terrorism, partly because, unlike many terrorist groups, it regarded itself as a liberation movement, while the PIRA had clearly discernible nationalist ends. The IRA did, however, have international assistance and a limited amount of money from Irish–American sympathizers in the 1960s and 1970s. A serious amount of explosive and other weaponry came from **Libya**. After the fall of Communism in Eastern Europe in 1989–1990, the Provisionals also obtained cheap weapons there. This made the presence of a former PIRA commander, Martin MacGuiness, as Northern Ireland's deputy first minister in 2012, all the more remarkable.

The process of decolonization in the 1950s and 1960s ran alongside emergencies, which the British characterized as terrorist episodes. The native populations sometimes tended to have a different view. In **Cyprus**, the National Organization of Cypriot Fighters (EOKA) demanded union with **Greece**. There was considerable support for EOKA amongst the 80-percent Greek population. British troops were killed in a campaign of terrorism that lasted from 1954–1959. Independence was conceded in 1960. In the **Malayan Emergency** (1948–1960), British security forces defeated an ethnic Chinese uprising, which had a Marxist orientation. Most important, the British had the support of the majority Malay population, and probably up to 80 percent of the Chinese population as well. In this sense, Malaya cannot be denoted as a real nationalist rising. Sophisticated intelligence gathering was a feature of the work by British counterintelligence officers, although 250,000 troops and police had to be used. Kenya provided another case. Here the issue was land ownership. The majority Kikuyu tribe believed that they had been robbed of their land by European settlers. The response was **Mau Mau**, a secret organization that attacked British farmers, police, and soldiers (1952–1959). The British introduced a state of emergency in October 1952. There were accusations of British misbehavior during the Mau Mau emergency, which resurfaced in 2010–2011. In reality, Mau Mau had little to do with European Middle Eastern-style terrorism.

The Middle East was a major area of concern for the British. From 1946–1948, the occupying British troops in **Palestine** were victims of Jewish terrorism, most notoriously with the blowing up of the King David Hotel in Jerusalem in July 1946. This experience hastened the British withdrawal from Palestine in 1948. At times, there were unpleasant anti-British episodes in Palestine, when British soldiers were kidnapped and murdered by Jewish terrorists. They also suffered at the hands of Arab extremists. From 1952–1954, there were similar episodes in the Canal Zone in **Egypt,** where the British presence was resented. Those whom the British regarded as terrorists saw themselves as freedom fighters. In the 1960s, an emergency in Aden provoked severe British military responses before ultimate withdrawal in 1968. The context widened because of the ongoing feud between **Israel** and its neighboring states. The catastrophic Arab defeat at the hands of the Israelis in June 1967 meant that orthodox military force was replaced by terrorist methods on the part of the Palestine Liberation Organization (PLO) and the Popular Front for the Liberation of Palestine (PFLP).

In 1970, Britain had its own experience of this new breed of terrorism. On 9 September, elements of the PFLP hijacked a British VC-10 aircraft to Dawson's Field in **Jordan**. Other aircraft, including one from the **United States,** were also involved. The British government refused to negotiate, and the VC-10 was blown up, although passengers were released in exchange for Palestinian prisoners. In September 1970, Britain sided with King Hussein in his struggle with the PLO, which ended with the ejection of its units from Jordan. As a reprisal, the PFLP made an attempt on the life of the Jordanian ambassador on a London street on 14 July 1971. This was not a direct attack on British interests, and the Heath government became more concerned with industrial turbulence. There was small-scale terrorism from the so-called "Angry Brigade," which bombed the home secretary's house in January 1971. There were also other bombings, including one on the house of the managing director of the Ford Motor Company. Four people were subsequently jailed, and the Angry Brigade, a small ineffective cousin of continental terrorist groups like the Baader-Meinhof group in West Germany, disappeared. Britain's intelligence services admitted to being too dilatory in dealing with the Angry Brigade.

In the 1970s and 1980s, the major terrorist threat still came from the PIRA. Other terrorist activity involved opponents of foreign regimes attacking their representatives or embassies. On 30 April 1980, for example, six terrorists broke into the Iranian embassy in London. They demanded the release of opponents of the Ayatollah Khomeini. Failing in this, they threatened to blow up the embassy, and a siege followed. When a hostage was shot, Margaret Thatcher authorized the sending in of a Special Air Services unit (for the first time on home soil). The remaining hostages were released and five terrorists killed. This success might have deterred other terrorist attacks in London, but it could not prevent the rogue and fatal attack on police constable Yvonne Fletcher outside the Libyan embassy in 1984.

In the 1980s, Scotland Yard's antiterrorist unit was preoccupied with trying to stop the Libyan regime from killing its political opponents on British soil, or indeed over it. The terrible Lockerbie bombing of December 1988 was attributed to Libyan secret service agents. The **Secret Intelligence Service** knew about Libyan attempts to arm PIRA. A new dangerous intervention took place on 3 June 1982, when the Israeli ambassador was shot while leaving London's Dorchester Hotel. Three men were arrested and found to belong to the Abu Nidal Organization (ANO), which was sponsored by **Iraq** and then by Libya. Born in Palestine, Abu Nidal was a dangerous criminal mastermind who had selected his assassins from a London language school. Two were Palestinian Arabs.

As late as 1994, MI5, in charge of gathering British intelligence at home, thought that the biggest terrorist threat came from Middle Eastern state-sponsored terrorism. This assessment excluded the long-lasting struggle against PIRA. The majority of state-sponsored activity in the 1990s was thought to originate with ANO. It had planned the assassination of a former Iranian premier in Paris in 1991. British security had been tightened to protect the writer Salman Rushdie against an assassination attempt encouraged by Khomeini in 1989. In fact, the MI5 assessment was wrong. The greatest threat to Britain's security proved to be transnational terrorism, which would in turn spawn a domestic British surrogate. MI5 and MI6 were subsequently criticized for allowing London to become a home for Islamic terrorist organizations. MI5 also initially saw Osama bin Laden as a paymaster of terrorists, rather than a mastermind. They opened a file on him as early as 1995, when there was a false report that bin Laden was planning a suicide attack in Britain. The first big terrorist attacks by bin Laden's al-Qaeda terrorist group took place in Kenya, in August 1998, the U.S. embassy being one target. This event caused MI5 to alter its 1994 assessment about state-sponsored terrorism. On 23 September 1998, it was able to arrest members of Egyptian Islamic Jihad (EIJ). They had planned a bomb attack against the U.S. embassy in Tirana, Albania, but it was circumvented. It was an example of cooperation between different Western intelligence agencies. EIJ operatives were also arrested in **Italy**.

The entire security landscape changed on 11 September 2001, when a jihadist attack on the World Trade Center, in New York City, and the Pentagon, in Arlington, Virginia, killed more than 3,000 people. Al-Qaeda claimed responsibility. British prime minister **Tony Blair** was quick to pledge support for the United States. Blair supported the subsequent invasion of **Afghanistan** after initial air strikes against al-Qaeda bases there. British SIS units assisted in trying to track down bin Laden, but without success. There was a massive increase in security at British airports to prevent a similar attack. In 2003, Britain supported the U.S. invasion of Iraq, although the thesis that Saddam Hussein supported al-Qaeda was doubted by many. Afghanistan and Iraq generated homegrown Islamic terrorism in Britain. Its adherents, usually of Pakistani origin, but not exclusively so, believed that as British Muslims, they had the right to protect the worldwide Muslim community. On 7 July 2005, four bombs were exploded by a terrorist cell, three on the London Underground system and one on a London bus. MI5 had information on the suspects but did not then consider them a primary risk. A second attack on the Underground on 20 July failed, but only because the bombs did not explode. A number of other jihadist plots were subsequently discovered and suspects arrested.

Judicial issues arose from Britain's role in the "war on terrorism" after 2001. One concerned the incarceration of British nationals in Guantanamo Bay, Cuba, after being subjected to the rendition process. Some were released, but others were kept imprisoned without trial and claim to have been tortured. The involvement of MI6 was alleged in questioning jihadist suspects. Torture was central to the British role. A notable case concerned the Jordanian national Abu Qatada, who was resident in Britain but wanted by the Jordanian authorities on terrorism-related charges. In this instance, there were concerns that evidence against Qatada had been obtained in Jordan via the use of torture. Qatada spent time in prison in Britain, but also, after court verdicts, under house arrest. Qatada appealed to the European Court of Human Rights in Strasburg. On 10 May 2012, the court rejected Qatada's appeal, seemingly freeing the way for his extradition to Jordan. Counterterrorism issues from the deep past could also arise. In May 2012, Malaysian litigants against the British Crown arrived in London. They claimed to be victims of an alleged outrage committed by Scots Guards units in colonial Malaya in the 1950s.

THATCHER, MARGARET (1925–). The first and only female British prime minister, Margaret Thatcher was elected on 4 May 1979. She was re-elected by the British people in 1983 and 1987, before being rejected by her own Conservative colleagues in 1990. Thatcher regarded herself as a conviction politician who rejected the Keynesian consensus of the period after 1945 in British politics in favor of free market economics, individualism, and more competition. In foreign policy, she was a robust nationalist, pro-American and generally hostile to the **European Union (EU)**. Thatcher was fond of referring to "Winston," claiming the legacy of **Winston Churchill**, even though he had been a very old man when Thatcher first entered the House of Commons in 1959 (after several previously unsuccessful attempts to do so), and she never held office under him.

At the core of Thatcher's foreign policy was a close relationship with President **Ronald Reagan**. The two were ideological soul mates who clearly admired one another. They had the closest personal relationship of any British and U.S. leaders since Winston Churchill and **Franklin D. Roosevelt** in **World War II**. But there were some blips. At the time of the **Falklands War** in 1982, Regan's support for Great Britain was not initially wholehearted because of U.S. interests in a Latin America, which sided with **Argentina**. He came around in the end, but Thatcher was furious in 1983, when Reagan sanctioned the U.S. invasion of the **British Commonwealth** island of **Grenada**. By 1986, relations between the two leaders were back on a cordial basis, and Thatcher gave U.S. aircraft en route to **Libya** access to British airfields.

Thatcher's pro-Americanism got her into some domestic trouble, most notably in 1985, when her preference for a takeover of the Westland Helicopter Company by the U.S.-based Sikorsky Corporation was strongly opposed by the British secretary of state for defense, Michael Heseltine, who favored a European consortium. Heseltine resigned over the issue in dramatic fashion, and Thatcher also lost her trade and industry minister, Leon Brittan, who was accused of leaking a letter that showed Heseltine in a poor light. There was more than a suspicion at the time that Thatcher had authorized the leak. In contrast, she deserved credit for her recognition that the 1985 Anglo–Irish Agreement was in Britain's best interests, when all her natural instincts favored the unionist position on Northern **Ireland**. This showed the sort of personal courage that Thatcher had displayed in 1984, when she survived an assassination attempt by the Provisional Irish Republican Army in a Brighton Hotel.

Thatcher was also perceptive enough to see that Mikhail Gorbachev, soon to become general secretary of the Soviet Communist Party, was a different kind of Soviet leader when he visited Britain in 1985. She also advised Reagan that his Star Wars plan would not work, although in public she loyally supported it.

Europe was another matter. Thatcher vigorously complained about the level of Britain's contribution to the EU budget, driving one German chancellor to feign sleep, and French representatives to rev up car engines ready for an early escape from one of Thatcher's tirades; therefore, it was a surprise in 1988, when she allowed the French and Germans to persuade her to sign the Single European Act, which committed Britain to closer integration with Europe and a loss of sovereignty, something Thatcher had always opposed. Both her **foreign secretary, Sir Geoffrey Howe,** and her chancellor, **Nigel Lawson,** pressed her to join the European Monetary System, but she held out until **John Major** replaced Lawson as chancellor. Against his wishes, Thatcher moved Howe out of the **Foreign and Commonwealth Office (FCO)** in July 1989, largely because since his appointment in 1983, he had failed to reform the FCO along Thatcherite lines. Instead, Howe had imbibed FCO ways and found globetrotting diplomacy too congenial. Like other prime ministers, including **David Lloyd George** and **Tony Blair,** Thatcher regarded the FCO with suspicion and wanted to run her own foreign policy without due reference to King Charles Street. Lawson followed Howe out of his post as chancellor, but the former foreign secretary had his revenge by resigning from the government in November 1990 and making a devastating attack on Thatcher's anti-Europeanism and style of diplomacy in his House of Commons resignation speech. By then, Thatcher had lost her colleagues' confidence. A final folly was an attempt to impose a highly unpopular poll tax, or community charge, after an experimental run in Scotland had been a disaster. Her leadership was challenged by Heseltine on a ballot, and Cabinet members warned her that she would not win a second ballot. Thatcher remained one of the most controversial premiers of modern British history, responsible for privatizing many of Britain's state-owned industries, including gas, water, and electricity. She believed that she had restored British greatness.

THOMPSON, SIR ROBERT (1916–1992). An important figure in the security regime during the Communist insurgency in British Malaya was Robert Thompson. His expertise was sought by the Americans in Vietnam in the 1960s, when Thompson led the British Advisory Mission. Thompson's ideas, based on his experience in Malaya under **Sir Gerald Templer,** had an influence on the "strategic hamlets" concept, whereby villages were supposed to be made immune to Communist Viet Cong influence in South Vietnam.

Thompson became disillusioned with U.S. leadership in Vietnam and thought that the bombing campaign, code-named "Rolling Thunder," was a serious tactical error. *See also* VIETNAM WAR.

THOMSON, GEORGE (1921–2008). As a minister of state at the **Foreign and Commonwealth Office (FCO)**, George Thomson played a significant role in the attempts during the second Labour administration of **Harold Wilson** (1966–1970) to enter the **European Economic Community (EEC)**. This failed following General Charles de Gaulle's second veto in 1967. In 1966, Wilson made Thomson chancellor of the Duchy of Lancaster outside the Cabinet in charge of the unsuccessful EEC talks, but he was returned to his post as minister of state at the FCO at the start of 1967. In 1972, Thomson, always associated with the pro-EEC faction of the Labour Party led by Roy Jenkins, resigned from the Shadow Cabinet when the party came out in opposition to EEC membership in a confusing turnabout. In 1968, Wilson had placed Thomson in the Cabinet as minister in charge of **Commonwealth** Relations, a post he held until Labour's election defeat of June 1970. He was created Lord Thomson of Monifieth.

THOR MISSILE. While Great Britain tried to evolve its own **Blue Streak** missile, a stopgap role was played by the U.S. intermediate-range **Thor missile**, with dual British–American control. This role was agreed during a meeting between Conservative prime minister **Harold Macmillan** and his old wartime colleague and friend, President **Dwight D. Eisenhower**, on 24 March 1957. The meeting was held in Bermuda, and 60 Thor missiles were to be stationed in the British Isles, as they had nuclear warheads. The final decision about launching the missiles rested with the **United States**. *See also* AMERICAN BASES IN BRITAIN.

THORNEYCROFT, PETER (1909–1994). A Conservative member of Parliament and party chairman, Peter Thorneycroft was Britain's defense secretary (1962–1964) during the **Skybolt Crisis**. He was much angered by the U.S. decision to cancel Skybolt, news he received on 11 December 1963. Thorneycroft was involved in one other serious crisis earlier in his career, in 1958. As chancellor of the exchequer (1957–1958) in the **Harold Macmillan** government, he insisted on resigning his position when the Cabinet refused to agree to £153 million expenditure cuts. This was only 1 percent of existing expenditure, but Thorneycroft and two other treasury colleagues made it a matter of principle, and they, too, resigned. It was this episode that Macmillan, about to go off on a **Commonwealth** tour, described as "a little local difficulty." Thorneycroft's financial policies had more in common with the monetarists of the 1980s than with the Keynesian Macmillan. It was remarkable that two years later, in 1960, Macmillan brought Thorneycroft back into government as secretary of state for defense, despite their earlier major difference of opinion.

THREE CIRCLES DOCTRINE. During the postwar era, British foreign policy makers evolved a doctrine based on the intersection of three circles to provide parameters for Great Britain's position in the world. This was designed to provide access through the "**special relationship**" to the leadership in the **United States**, while at the same time allowing Britain a leadership role in both the **Commonwealth** and Europe. In theory, this would allow Britain a unique status as a mediator between the West and the Soviet Union, and within the Western power framework. The danger was that Britain might become overabsorbed in one circle and lose its influence in the other two. The success of the **European Economic Community (EEC)** after 1958 caused the British government to make a wholesale review of its position, so that an application for full membership in the EEC was made as early as 1961. This was done because a feeling had arisen in the **Foreign and Commonwealth Office** that Britain would be sidetracked outside the EEC. The previous assumption that the three circles policy would be effective outside the process of European integration, which caused Britain to reject EEC membership from 1955–1957, was abandoned.

TIMES **NEWSPAPER.** The *Times* has been the best-known newspaper in Great Britain since the 18th century, with its headquarters in Printing House Square, London. It has produced many famous correspondents, including William Howard Russell, who highlighted British military incompetence at the time of the Crimean War. In the 1920s and 1930s, the *Times* was regarded by foreigners as the effective mouthpiece of the British government. This was an exaggeration, but editors like Geoffrey Dawson were close to both **Stanley Baldwin** and **Neville Chamberlain** when they were in **No. 10 Downing Street**. Its association with **appeasement** damaged the *Times*, and its postwar influence declined. It became part of the News International newspaper empire of Australian magnate Rupert Murdoch.

TREATY OF LOCARNO. *See* LOCARNO, TREATY OF.

TREATY OF MAASTRICHT. *See* MAASTRICHT, TREATY OF.

TREATY OF ROME. *See* ROME, TREATY OF.

TREATY OF VERSAILLES. *See* VERSAILLES, TREATY OF.

TREVELYAN, SIR HUMPHREY (1905–1985). Most notable for being the British ambassador in Cairo at the time of the 1956 **Suez Crisis,** Humphrey Trevelyan was shabbily treated by his prime minister, **Anthony Eden,** and kept ill-informed of the direction of government policy. He was deeply shocked by the terms of the Anglo–French ultimatum he was obliged to serve on the Egyptian government on 30 October 1956. He awoke the next day to find his embassy surrounded by Egyptian troops. Trevelyan made plain his disillusionment with British policy in a memoir entitled *The Middle East in Revolution* (1970). He was created Baron Trevelyan.

TRIDENT MISSILE. Great Britain negotiated with President Jimmy Carter to secure the Trident C-4 missile in 1980, but it was faced with the possibility of having no nuclear weapon at all when the **United States** decided to upgrade the C-4 to the D-5, a much more powerful, but much more expensive, weapon. Fortunately for Prime Minister **Margaret Thatcher,** who was desperate to acquire the D-5 when the United States announced the upgrade in 1981, President **Ronald Reagan** agreed to let the British have the D-5 at cost price, with a minimal charge for research and development. Thatcher, unlike her secretary of state for defense, **John Nott,** was prepared to pay almost any price to ensure that Britain had an independent deterrent. The Trident deal included a caveat whereby Britain had to make the missiles available to the **North Atlantic Treaty Organization,** unless its national interests were under threat.

TRIPARTITE DECLARATION (1950). On 25 May 1950, Great Britain, along with **France** and the **United States,** signed the Tripartite Declaration in an effort to control the sale of arms in a highly unstable Middle East. Britain was selling arms to **Egypt** under the terms of the 1936 Anglo–Egyptian Treaty. France was selling fighter jets to **Israel** and was seen to be helping it with its covert atomic program. The declaration did not solve the problem of arms sales in the long run, although, in theory, arms sales from the three states were supposed to be considered under the principles established by the agreement.

TRUMAN, HARRY S. (1894–1972). A failed haberdasher from Missouri, Harry S. Truman proved to be one of the most effective presidents in U.S. history. He became president in April 1945, when **Franklin D. Roosevelt** died amid doubts about his abilities, which proved groundless. Not least of Truman's attributes was a remarkable knowledge of modern history. There were some differences between his administration and Great Britain, notably regarding the issue of whether the People's Republic of China should be recognized in 1949. Under heavy pressure from a **China** lobby in Congress,

Truman did not recognize the new government, whereas the British did. They had to be concerned about China's potentially hostile attitude to **Hong Kong** if diplomatic recognition was withheld. They were also alarmed by some wild talk by Truman about possible use of the atomic bomb when the Chinese invaded Korea in 1950, driving back **United Nations** forces commanded by General Douglas MacArthur. The Labour prime minister **Clement R. Attlee** hurriedly flew to Washington in December 1950, to restrain the U.S. president. Attlee was reassured, but Truman was able to insist that Britain increase its level of defense spending from 8 percent to 14 percent of the gross national product between 1951–1953. *See also* TRUMAN DOCTRINE.

TRUMAN DOCTRINE (1947). At a time of growing **Cold War** tension, the British **Foreign Office** sent a historic note to the U.S. Department of State on 21 February 1947. It informed the **United States** that Great Britain was no longer in a position to sustain British aid to **Greece** and **Turkey** as of 31 March. At the time, Britain had 40,000 troops aiding the Greek government in fighting a Communist insurgency in the **Greek Civil War** (1944–1949), which would be withdrawn. Turkey was under pressure from the Soviet Union about control of the Dardanelles, which linked the Black Sea to the Mediterranean Sea. The U.S. undersecretary of state, **Dean Acheson**, persuaded President **Harry S. Truman** that it was crucial that the United States fill the vacuum created by the British withdrawal in the Eastern Mediterranean. On 12 March, Truman asked U.S. Congress for $400 million to assist Greece and Turkey and put forth what came to be known as the Truman Doctrine. Truman announced that the United States would "support free peoples" who were subject to external threats or internal subversion. The coded reference to Soviet Communism was well understood at the time.

In Britain, the **foreign secretary**, **Ernest Bevin,** had initially been skeptical about withdrawal, as had the Chiefs of Staff. It was Prime Minister **Clement R. Attlee** and the chancellor of the exchequer, **Hugh Dalton**, who had driven the decision through the Cabinet. It was one of a series of fateful decisions. During the same week, Britain decided to refer the **Palestine** problem back to the **United Nations** and announced the decision to leave **India** by June 1948, at the latest.

TUGENDHAT, CHRISTOPHER (1937–). A Conservative member of Parliament who became a European commissioner in Brussels for eight years (1977–1985), the last four as vice president, Christopher Tugendhat was critical of **Margaret Thatcher's** narrow approach to **European Union (EU)** issues. He claimed that she was obsessed with budgetary matters to the exclusion of everything else. In Tugendhat's view, this lessened Great Britain's chances of joining **France** and **Germany** as natural leaders of the EU.

TURKEY. The modern Turkish state was founded by Mustafa Kemal (Atatürk) on 29 October 1923. It succeeded the Ottoman Turkish Empire, founded in 1299, which was a dynamic, thrusting military machine in the 13th, 14th, and 15th centuries. The Turks overran the Middle East and captured the capital of the old Byzantine Empire, Constantinople, in 1453. They went on to conquer **Greece, Bulgaria, Yugoslavia,** and Romania. As late as 1683, the Ottoman Turks reached the gates of Vienna before being driven back. They imposed Islam in the Balkans, but, by the 18th century, the Ottoman Empire was in steep decline and increasingly relied upon Great Britain to ward off disaster. At odds with Turkey's main enemy, **Russia,** beginning in the 1790s, the British wanted the Turks to survive as a bulwark against Tsarist expansion. Britain temporarily abandoned this policy to assist the Greeks in their war of independence against Turkey (1821–1829).

The **Foreign Office,** which tried in the 1840s to persuade the Turkish sultan to reform his ramshackle empire, preferred a corrupt Turkey to Russian control of the Straits. Britain sided with Turkey in the Crimean War (1854–1856) to prevent this. Russia's defeat in the **Crimea** could not halt the process of Ottoman Turkish decline. In 1878, Turkey lost control of Bulgaria, **Bosnia,** and **Montenegro.** Britain's intervention prevented its defeat at the hands of Russia in 1877 from being even more serious. In Britain itself, elements in the Liberal Party, led by **William Gladstone,** regarded Turkey as being an alien Muslim influence. Gladstone demanded that the Turks be thrown out of Europe "bag and baggage." Official British policy was that the Ottoman Empire had to be preserved, but this later changed.

In the 1890s, imperial **Germany** adopted an aggressive global policy that involved cultivating Turkey, posing as the protector of Muslims, and building the Berlin–Baghdad Railway. Conversely, the British settled their long-standing issues with Russia in 1907. Constantinople and the Straits were a Russian objective that successive British governments no longer thought to be a major danger. The revolution of 1908 in Turkey, which brought in the so-called "Young Turk" government, made ties with Germany even closer. Turkey's hold in Europe weakened further in the Balkan Wars of 1912–1913. A thin strip of European Turkey remained. When **World War I** began in 1914, Turkey opted to align itself with Germany and Austria-Hungary. In 1915–1916, the Turks fought well at Gallipoli and repulsed the Anglo–French landing. British troops also suffered a humiliating surrender at Kut, in Mesopotamia (later **Iraq**), in 1916. The British also indulged in unwise pledges. In October 1916, the McMahon Pledge promised an Arab kingdom in **Palestine** and Arabia. The Anglo–French Sykes–Picot Agreement of April 1916 had already divided most of the Middle East between the two colonial powers.

The British found a winning general in Sir Edmund Allenby. In December 1916, Allenby captured Jerusalem. Palestine and Syria were conquered by

September 1917. In 1918, Ottoman Turkey and its allies were defeated. The Treaty of Sèvres (1920) imposed a humiliating peace on the Ottomans. Their great empire in the Middle East was lost forever. Even worse, British prime minister **David Lloyd George**, often ignoring Foreign Office advice, favored a partition of the core Turkish territory. Lloyd George encouraged Greek aspirations in Turkey, while Cabinet colleagues like **Winston Churchill** and **Arthur Balfour** did not. The Turks were underestimated. They had found an effective new leader in Mustafa Kemal (Atatürk), whom the British wrote off as a bandit. The Greeks invaded Turkey in 1921, but, in August, Kemal launched a brilliant offensive and drove the Greeks out of his country. British troops were stationed at Chanak, near Constantinople, and a confrontation threatened. Britain was deserted by its allies, **France** and **Italy**. No fighting ensued. In November 1922, as a direct result of the Chanak Crisis, Lloyd George's coalition government was brought down by a revolt by Conservative members of Parliament. He never held public office again.

In what was a triumph for Kemal, Turkey got a new settlement, the Treaty of Lausanne (1923), which restored territories lost to Greece. Unusually, the treaty involved exchanges of population. Ankara became Turkey's new capital, and, on 29 October 1923, the Turkish Republic was proclaimed, with Kemal as its first president. Atatürk (the Father of the Turks), as he became known, carried out a rapid secularization program and exiled surviving members of the Ottoman dynasty. The fez, a traditional headgear, was abolished, along with veiling of women. Relations with Britain were generally cordial. On 5 June 1926, the Anglo–Turkish Treaty established Turkey's southeastern border. Mosul was ceded to Iraq, given to the British under a **League of Nations** mandate. Turkey wanted the Straits settlement modified and was fully supported by British **foreign secretary Anthony Eden**. On 20 July 1936, the Montreux Convention allowed Turkish troops back into the Straits zone and made Turkey responsible for free navigation into the Black Sea. The sympathetic British policy paid dividends in **World War II**. Turkey kept a solidly pro-Allied neutrality before declaring war on Germany and **Japan** in January 1945. This ensured Turkey's membership in the **United Nations**.

In the postwar world, Turkey became a key **Cold War** player. Its vulnerability to Soviet pressure made Britain seek the U.S. commitment in the Eastern Mediterranean enshrined in the **Truman Doctrine** (1947). In 1952, Turkey became the most easterly member of the **North Atlantic Treaty Organization**. Turkey sent troops to Korea. It signed the Baghdad Pact in 1955, along with Britain. At home, Turkey showed the typical tensions between democracy and militarism in Islamic states. The army regarded itself as the guarantor of Atatürk's secularization. It staged coups in 1960, 1970, and 1980. The first coup resulted in the hanging of Prime Minister Adrian Menderes in 1960.

Britain, with a substantial Turkish Cypriot population, tended to favor Turks in its colony **Cyprus**, but it fell out with the Ankara government in 1974. This was a result of the Turkish invasion of northern Cyprus, when a Greek Cypriot coup threatened a takeover of the entire island. Turkish prime minister Bulent Ecevit (prime minister, 1974, 1977, 1978–1979, 1991–1993) ordered the army to occupy the Turkish area on 20 July 1974. It became the Republic of Northern Cyprus, but Britain, like the rest of the international community, except Turkey, refused to extend diplomatic recognition to the enclave. Greeks made up 80 percent of the island, and they established the Republic of Cyprus. Turkey refused to recognize the Republic of Cyprus. British efforts to secure Turkey's removal from its surrogate territory after 1974 failed.

In mainland Turkey, Islamism came to the fore. Alongside Ecevit, Süleyman Demirel (prime minister, 1965–1971, 1975–1977, 1979–1980; president, 1993–2000) dominated Turkey during the 1970s. He was banned by the military for 10 years, from 1980–1990. In the meantime, Turkey dreamed of membership of the **European Union (EU)**, an aspiration that Britain supported. Turkey had problems with human rights, Kurdish separatism, and a lingering issue about the Armenian genocide during World War I. Unlike France, Britain would not insist on Turkey's guilt, which Turkey bitterly refuted. The emergence of a moderate Islamic party saw two election victories for the Justice and Development Party, led by Recep Erdogan, in 2002 and 2007. Erdogan's party became frustrated with the EU attitude toward the Turkish application, to which France strongly objected.

In May 2008, **Queen Elizabeth II** visited Turkey on an official visit and, in a speech, referred to the country as a bridge between east and west. Britain is a signatory to the treaty, which guarantees the independence of Cyprus. Turkey and Greece are the other signatories. Cyprus remains the main bone of contention between Turkey and Greece, although Britain retains sovereign bases on the island.

U

UGANDA. In October 1962, the British colony of Uganda received its independence from Great Britain. Its early history was troubled. In 1971, the left-inclined President Milton Obote was overthrown in a military coup by Idi Amin. A former sergeant in the British Army, Amin was often regarded as a comic figure in Britain, but he developed into a bloodthirsty tyrant. His government was responsible for the wholesale expulsion of Ugandan Asians in 1972, and the confiscation of their property. As the Asians had British citizenship, many of them fled to Britain. Amin was overthrown by invading Tanzanian troops in 1978, after his rule had become an embarrassment to the international community.

ULSTER. One of four historic Irish provinces, Ulster actually consists of nine Irish counties, rather than the six normally associated with Ulster or Northern **Ireland**. Three counties, Donegal, Cavan, and Monaghan, are in the Irish Republic, and the remaining six, Londonderry, Antrim, Down, Armagh, Tyrone, and Fermanagh, are in Northern Ireland, which is part of the United Kingdom, thus keeping the British link. The Government of Ireland Act of 1920 created the Northern Ireland statelet, with its own separate parliament at Stormont, in Belfast. This arrangement ended in 1971, when, as a result of sectarian troubles, Prime Minister **Edward Heath** imposed direct rule by the Westminster parliament. After decades of violence, devolved government, properly representing Catholics and Protestants, was restored in 2007, with the new Northern Ireland Assembly. Northern Ireland continued to send representatives to the House of Commons as well.

UNILATERAL DISARMAMENT. A topic for vigorous debate in the British Labour Party from the 1950s to the 1980s, unilateral disarmament involved Great Britain giving up its nuclear bomb regardless of policy in the **North Atlantic Treaty Organization.** In 1960, it took a powerful speech at the Labour Conference by the shadow **foreign secretary, Aneurin Bevan,** to defeat the unilateralists on the left. The issue arose again 20 years later, and Labour's unilateralist platform contributed to its heavy defeat in the 1983 general election. Thereafter, the party reverted to its pronuclear stance.

UNITED NATIONS (UN). The tragic failure of the old **League of Nations** during the interwar period meant that lessons had to be learned about the safeguarding of international peace in the postwar world. The structure of its successor organization, the United Nations (UN), was worked out by the Allied leaders **Winston Churchill, Franklin D. Roosevelt,** and Joseph Stalin in 1944, and confirmed when they met at **Yalta** in the penultimate wartime conference in February 1945. There were significant differences between the League of Nations and the UN. The former had no provision for an armed force, whereas the UN was to have peacekeeping forces recruited from the member states. The UN was effectively dominated by the five Great Powers, Great Britain, **China,** the Soviet Union, **United States,** and **France.** They were permanent members of the UN Security Council, with a veto power on any issue, while other powers only had temporary membership and lacked a veto. The UN General Assembly, of which Britain is also a member, needs a simple majority to pass resolutions. They are binding when on matters of international security, but only recommendations when referring to the internal affairs of member states. Britain supported the "Uniting for Peace" resolution in 1950, which sanctioned military assistance to South Korea.

At the outset, the UN's foundation avoided some issues, including colonialism. President Roosevelt had been a stern critic of British, and especially French, colonialism, but faced with Winston Churchill's opposition, President **Harry S. Truman** avoided the colonial issue at the **San Francisco Conference** in June 1945. The UN officially came into existence on 24 October 1945.

On the whole, Britain has been a loyal supporter of the organization and its principles. Prime Minister **Clement R. Attlee** supported the UN intervention in Korea in 1950, just as **John Major** supported the UN action against Saddam Hussein in **Iraq** in 1991. It was the British UN representative Lord Caradon who steered through UN Resolution 242 in 1967, which called on Israel to withdraw its forces from the Occupied Territories, and this has been at the core of Britain's Middle Eastern policy since then. The major catastrophe in Britain's relationship with the UN happened a decade earlier over the **Suez Crisis,** when not only the United States and the Soviet Union (a unique combination), but also **Commonwealth** states like **India,** opposed British policy over **Egypt.** In 2003, it was Britain, rather than the United States, that wanted a second UN resolution to back up UN Resolution 1441 over Iraq, although, in the end, Britain supported the United States without such a resolution. Lessons were learned after the controversy that ensued. Britain was careful to obtain UN sanction for its action against **Libya** in 2011, while taking the lead in such action, along with France.

Britain has gained credit for accepting the United Nations Conference on Trade and Development figure of 0.7 percent of the gross national product as a target for its allocation of international aid. It has also contributed a large number of distinguished international civil servants to the UN throughout its history and, unlike some member states, has been prompt with its financial contributions. Britain has also been a key member of such important UN agencies as the World Health Organization, the United Nations Educational, Scientific, and Cultural Organization, the Food and Agricultural Organization, and the International Monetary Fund. The range of UN activities continues to develop. In June 2012, a UN report written by leading British lawyer Ben Emmerson, the UN's special rapporteur on counterterrorism and human rights, recommended the automatic right of compensation for victims of **terrorism** and rehabilitation. *See also* GULF WAR; KOREAN WAR; KOSOVO; YUGOSLAVIA.

UNITED STATES. On 3 September 1783, a year after the British **Foreign Office** had come into existence as a separate department of state, Great Britain and the United States signed the Treaty of Paris. This ended the War of Independence (1775–1783), whereby Britain acknowledged the independence of the 13 colonies in the teeth of King George III's objections. The treaty fixed the boundaries of the new United States. The treaty also marked a major defeat for Britain as a great power, especially as the United States had been assisted in its war of independence by Britain's hereditary enemy, **France**. Its representative in the peace talks, David Harley, secured modest consolation by getting access to the Mississippi River. The House of Commons ratified the Paris treaty on 9 April 1784, the American Continental Congress having already done so on 14 January 1784.

Relations between the new republic and Britain affected the political divide in the United States. Alexander Hamilton, the secretary for the treasury, and his Federalist Party saw Britain as the repository of order, property, and religious freedom, whereas his political rival, Thomas Jefferson, continued to see Britain as the enemy of freedom. The key event of the first decade of U.S. independence was the French Revolution of 1789, which alarmed European governments and resulted in war between Britain and France in 1793, when the government of **William Pitt the Younger** tired of French provocations. In the United States, Hamilton sympathized with Britain, whereas Jefferson was attracted by the principles of the French Revolution. In theory, the 1778 Treaty of Alliance between the United States and France obligated the Americans to assist France in its revolutionary war. Hamilton argued in the Cabinet that the downfall of King Louis XVI (he was executed in 1793) removed any obligation to assist the French. Hamilton won the argument. President George Washington issued a declaration of American neutrality in April 1793.

This declaration did not remove the potential for Anglo–American tensions. They focused on two issues, the North-West Frontier area with British **Canada**, and the high seas. In the first instance, Britain had not followed the promise made in the settlement of 1783 to evacuate its forts south of the Great Lakes. Even worse from a U.S. standpoint were the British Orders in Council of November 1793, which stated that practices that Britain deemed illegal in peacetime (such as U.S. trade with the British West Indian islands) would remain illegal in wartime. As a result of the Orders in Council, 250 U.S. vessels were seized by the Royal Navy. Britain and the United States were close to war by the spring of 1794, and it took the mission of U.S. chief justice John Jay to prevent hostilities. The British promised to withdraw from their northwestern forts by 1796. A principle in Anglo–American relations was established when the United States agreed to submit cases of ship seizures and the issue of trade with the British West Indian islands to arbitration. Britain had still won the contentious debate about neutral rights at sea. The Jay Treaty was unpopular in the United States and barely made it through the Senate for ratification. The British still regarded the United States as a bumptious young upstart. They were heavily concentrated on the life-and-death struggle with Revolutionary and Napoleonic France, which lasted, with one short interval (1801– 1803), continuously from 1793–1814.

British naval power and French military power had effectively cancelled one another out by 1807, although **Napoleon Bonaparte** had seized the opportunity to sell the vast territory of Louisiana to the United States on 30 April 1803, for $15 million dollars (it worked out to three cents per acre). Bonaparte had obtained Louisiana from **Spain** in 1800, and U.S. president Thomas Jefferson (1801–1809) had feared the prospect of a strong expansionist France on his southern borders when British Canada already flanked the United States in the north. The French response to the difficulty of defeating Britain was the Continental System of 1806, which closed European ports to British trade and was designed to starve out the islanders. Once again, the British resorted to the Orders in Council mechanism, claiming the right to intercept vessels from neutral states heading for European ports, which obviously affected the United States. The constant harassment of American shipping by the British had reached a crisis point by 1812. On 1 June, President James Madison (1809–1817) sent a war message to the U.S. Congress setting out British offenses linked to the British Orders in Council, while also accusing Britain of inciting Indian border tribes to revolt. Congress declared war on Britain on 18 June. There was an irony in the situation, because two days earlier, on 16 June, the British **foreign secretary**, Lord Castlereagh, had announced that Britain intended to revoke the Orders in Council to help reopen trade with the United States and thus alleviate the impact of Bonaparte's

Continental System on Britain's trade, which was starting to suffer badly. Castlereagh's action had, in fact, been delayed by the assassination of British prime minister Spencer Percival in the House of Commons on 11 May. The news did not reach the United States until after war had been declared.

The United States then invaded Canada, which was garrisoned by only 4,500 British troops, as Great Britain was fighting a campaign against France in Spain and Portugal and could not send more troops. British Canada itself had a population of only 500,000 people, against the U.S. population of 7.5 million. Two successive U.S. invasions achieved little, although the Americans briefly occupied the Canadian capital of Toronto and burned down public buildings. A reversal of fortune in 1813 mean that Britain, victorious in Spain, was able to send 20,000 reinforcements to Canada, thus ending any U.S. hopes there. American privateers at sea caused some havoc and took 1,300 prizes, but this had little overall impact on the course of the war.

In 1814, a rigorous Royal Navy blockade was enforced on the U.S. coast, which crippled trade. A British force landed on Chesapeake Bay, seized Washington, and exacted revenge for the burning of Toronto by burning down the White House and the Capitol. Britain did not launch its own offensive against the United States, instead choosing to send a force against New Orleans under Sir Edward Pakenham, the brother-in-law of its great contemporary general, Arthur Wellesley, Duke of Wellington, who proved to be incompetent. Surprisingly, this seasoned force was defeated by the future U.S. president Andrew Jackson on 8 January 1815, at a time when Napoleon Bonaparte had been defeated and exiled to the Mediterranean island of Elba. In another historical irony, the participants in the battle did not know that the Anglo–American war had been brought to a conclusion, after lengthy talks, by the Treaty of Ghent (modern **Belgium**) on 24 December 1814, the news again being slow to reach the United States across the Atlantic. The British regarded the treaty as marking the end of a tiresome sideshow on the other side of the world. It had much more significance for the United States, now making its predominance on the North American continent clear to all. Another result of the war was that its experience inculcated the U.S. establishment with Anglophobia for generations to come, even though President James Madison was, if anything, pro-British. The commercial classes in New England had strongly opposed any war with Britain. In Britain, the Duke of Wellington had been invited to take over the unsuccessful Crown forces in Canada in November 1814, but he wisely declined, believing that the British should not try to revise their boundaries with the United States. Had he not done so, Wellington and his men might have been fighting the United States at the time when his services were required against the escaped Bonaparte at Waterloo in June 1815.

Remaining issues in Anglo–American relations between the governments of Lord Castlereagh (1812–1822) and secretary of state John Quincy Adams (1817–1825) were dealt with in 1817–1818. The Rush–Bagot Agreement of 1817 placed limitations on those British and U.S. vessels involved in customs and excise work on the Great Lakes, while the Anglo–American Convention of 1818 recognized American fishing rights off Newfoundland and Labrador in Canada. The 49th parallel was accepted as the boundary of the Louisiana Purchase, while Oregon was to be jointly occupied by the United States and Britain for 10 years. Such agreements allowed Castlereagh to fix his attention on the arrangements of post-Napoleonic Europe in the years from 1815–1818, during which Britain played a prominent role.

Castlereagh did not live to see the crisis of 1823, created by the so-called "Holy Alliance" of Austria, Prussia, **Russia**, and France, which Britain had refused to join. The Holy Alliance was a reactionary concept, with monarchical regimes uniting to crush any movements against the 1815 Vienna Settlement. It did so in **Italy** and Spain in 1820–1821, and French troops reentered Spain in April 1823 to crush a new antimonarchist revolt. There were rumors that the authoritarian European powers were even prepared to intervene in Latin America to restore Spanish colonial rule. Such a prospect united both Britain and the United States. The new British foreign secretary, George Canning, warned off France and the other European powers in a speech in October 1823. On 2 December, President James Monroe laid down the crucial **Monroe Doctrine**, which stipulated that the United States would regard any European interference in Latin America as a hostile act. The United States rejected Britain's offer of an alliance because its government knew that the British did not want continental European interference with its lucrative Latin American trade. A return of Spanish colonial rule would certainly sabotage this. The Americans therefore knew that they could rely on British naval intervention to preserve Latin America's newly won independence. The Monroe Doctrine rested on British naval power, but, in London, the press reacted favorably to Monroe's speech.

In North America, issues remained between the British and the United States. One was the Oregon Territory, a vast area stretching from California to Alaska (then in Russian hands). The Anglo–American Convention of 1818 had placed Oregon under "joint occupation." The British continued to dominate the fur trade, but, by the 1840s, there was a campaign in the United States to end joint occupation. In 1845, President James K. Polk surprisingly offered to divide Oregon along the 19th Parallel. The British refused his offer, and, in December 1845, Polk demanded an end to joint occupation. Polk invoked the Monroe Doctrine to state that no new European colony could be established in North America. Britain responded in 1846 by reusing the 49th

Parallel offer itself. As the United States was then at war with Mexico, Polk agreed. The 1846 Oregon Treaty established the 49th Parallel as the boundary between British Canada and the United States. Britain also acquired Vancouver Island.

There were other Anglo–American issues about alleged ambitions. The state of Texas had become independent of Mexico in 1836, and it ideally wanted incorporation into the United States. Britain wanted an independent Texas as a means of obstructing U.S. expansion. Texas would also relieve the dependence of Lancashire textile mills on U.S. cotton. While there were American reservations about annexing Texas to the Union, British interest in its independence aroused alarm in Washington. The result was that the U.S. government agreed to annexation in 1845. It also had suspicions about British designs on California in the 1840s. These were unwarranted, but their existence demonstrated the degree to which the U.S. political establishment remained wary of the former colonial power. The next great event in 19th-century Anglo–American relations was the outbreak of the U.S. Civil War in 1861. There was considerable sympathy for the Confederacy in Britain, which its prime minister, Lord **Palmerston**, was thought to share. His foreign secretary, Lord John Russell, and chancellor of the exchequer, **William Gladstone**, favored British mediation between the North and the South in 1862, but Palmerston refused to become involved. Palmerston's government was not, as has been suggested, swayed by antislavery sentiment among the British working class. The leaders of the Confederacy assumed that dependence on Southern cotton would make British intervention inevitable, but this was not the case. Britain's manufacturers had large stocks of U.S. cotton when the war broke out, and, by the time there were shortages in 1863, alternative options were available in **India** and **Egypt**. As in the earlier part of the century, there were problems on the high seas, but Britain, as the leading maritime power, did not challenge the North's right to blockade the Confederacy. It also did well out of the war. Northern troops wore British boots, and President Abraham Lincoln's government also bought British munitions, steel, and ships. There was no need to hazard relations by intervention, and Britain was not prepared to do so unless the South was clearly seen to be winning. Any such prospect disappeared in 1863. The South also had hopes of French intervention, but they followed Britain's lead and stayed neutral.

British neutrality did not prevent tensions over maritime rights. The most famous concerned the Confederate commerce raider the *Alabama*, which was built in Merseyside. Under the terms of the 1819 British Foreign Enlistment Act, the construction of warships for belligerents was banned. Confederate agents only circumvented this by arming the *Alabama* (and other commerce raiders) after they had left British waters. The *Alabama* slipped away from Liverpool in July 1862, and its activities made it a subject of controversy for the next decade. In 1865, the North won the Civil War and demanded compensation for damage done by the *Alabama*. The dispute lasted for seven years. Only in 1871, largely thanks to the pragmatism of Gladstone, who was now prime minister, did the Treaty of Washington partially settle the problem. Britain expressed regret in the treaty for the *Alabama* episode, but it was only on 14 September 1872 that an arbitration tribunal settled the matter. Britain agreed to pay the United States $15,500,000 in compensation.

In the 1890s, a more aggressive stance was taken toward the British by elements in the U.S. Government. There had already been a U.S.–Canadian dispute over fisheries in 1887. Now the point of dispute had shifted southward, to Venezuela, well away from the American heartland. On 20 July 1895, U.S. secretary of state Richard Olney challenged Britain's right to hold its colony of British Guiana, which had a disputed border with Venezuela. Olney further accused the British of infringing on the Monroe Doctrine and demanded arbitration. The response of the British prime minister (and foreign secretary), Lord Salisbury, was tart. He rejected arbitration out of hand and even queried Olney's interpretation of the Monroe Doctrine. This infuriated President Grover Cleveland, who threatened to use force unless Britain went to arbitration. British possession of Guiana was described as "unnatural." Their diplomats in Washington told the Foreign Office about a wave of Anglophobia in the United States. The key point was, in fact, Britain's unwillingness to get involved in a serious dispute with the Americans. Britain already faced serious problems in **South Africa** and was dealing with the threat of **Germany**, with its massive naval expansion program. Salisbury agreed to go to arbitration after signing a treaty with the Venezuelans. In October 1899, Britain was awarded virtually all the land disputed by Venezuela and its U.S. backer.

Afterward, there was actually an improvement in Anglo–American relations. The British had to face the new, irrefutable facts in their diplomacy. In 1900, the United States had more than 23 percent of the share of global manufacturing, first in the world. Britain, with 18 percent, now ranked second. The United States had not yet translated industrial power into military power, but its navy was now the third largest in the world. Britain's naval predominance, which gave weight to its diplomacy, was under threat.

Less than 20 years after the Venezuelan dispute, Britain and the United States were allies in war. The outbreak of **World War I** in the autumn of 1914 caught Americans by surprise. The diverse nature of their society made it far from a certainty that the United States would back Britain and its allies. The biggest migrant minority in the United States was German, and the large Irish American community was outraged by Britain's handling of the Easter

Rising in Dublin in 1916. As it turned out, Britain had clout where it mattered. President **Woodrow Wilson** (1913–1921) was a strong Anglophile, and his entire administration, save his secretary of state, William Jennings Byran, was pro-Allied. The links cut two ways. Britain's first lord of the **Admiralty, Winston Churchill,** was half American. Cultural links between Britain and the East Coast of the United States were strong; however, maritime issues still loomed, much as they had in 1812 and 1861. The British classified almost all neutral goods bound for Germany as contraband. U.S. ships going to Germany and neutral Europe had to put into British ports for sailing directions first. Even Wilson's administration complained about the British blockade of Germany and its effects. Those complaints were rendered ineffective by the notoriously pro-British U.S. ambassador in London, who even advised Britain's foreign secretary, **Sir Edward Grey,** on how to answer them.

The British were lucky that their German foe was so inept. In February 1915, Imperial Germany announced that all enemy merchant shipping entering a stipulated war zone around Britain would be sunk. The Americans were angered by an additional statement that neutral ships avoid the war zone lest they, too, be sunk. This was a dangerous strategy, and, on 7 May, the huge Cunard liner RMS *Lusitania*, sailing from New York to Liverpool, was sunk by a submarine off the Irish coast. Among the 1,198 victims were 128 Americans. The U.S. public was infuriated, but Wilson refused to allow the provocation to lead to war. Additional sinkings brought the possibility of severing diplomatic relations with Germany. Under such pressure, Germany promised not to sink ships without warning or search. Attention then switched to Britain. The Americans were irritated by British interference with transatlantic mail and angered by a July 1916 blacklist of U.S. citizens deemed to have been traded with Germany or its allies. The Americans were also antagonized by Britain's decision to cut the transatlantic cable, which allowed it to effectively censor any war news from Germany. The British, with the advantage of a common language, flooded the United Sttaes with pro-Allied propaganda. It was a well-executed campaign. Most effective was the Bryce Report, a catalogue of German atrocities in Belgium long thought to be overstated but now known to be true. James Bryce was a well-respected former British ambassador to Washington.

President Wilson was reelected in November 1916, on a peace platform, but within months, the United States found itself at war. British naval intelligence played an important role in the U.S. decision to go to war, since it decoded the notorious Zimmermann Telegram and handed it over to the Americans. The telegram contained evidence that Germany was encouraging Mexico to enter the war on its side. In exchange, Mexico would receive its "lost territories," Texas, Arizona, and New Mexico. Germany compounded its folly by reverting to unrestricted submarine warfare on 31 January 1917. The sinking of three unarmed U.S. ships in March gave Wilson little choice but to declare war, which came with congressional agreement on 4 April. The entry of the United States into war was crucial for Britain, whose Russian ally was in a state of instability, while France was exhausted by the attritional struggle on the Western Front. When the United States came into the war, Britain had only six weeks food supply left, thanks to German submarines. It still took nearly a year to get 300,000 American troops into France by March 1918, although there were 2 million there by the time the war ended in November.

On 8 January 1918, Wilson spearheaded a diplomatic initiative with his **Fourteen Points**. Britain had reservations about two of them: Wilson's demand for freedom on the high seas and adjustment of colonial claims. The president wanted open diplomacy, but Britain was already involved in secret diplomacy with France regarding the Middle East with the 1916 Sykes–Picot Agreement. There was also skepticism in the British government, led by **David Lloyd George**, about Wilson's 14th point, a plan for a **League of Nations**. Yet, its position was altered forever. While the British had been concentrating on war since 1914, the United States had seized its markets in Latin America. The war made the United States a net creditor nation rather than a net debtor in the global economy. The world monetary system now had two centers, London and New York. This had its impact on America's diplomatic clout, as well as Britain's.

When Wilson attended the **Paris Peace Conference** in January 1919, he was greeted by many as a hero. Lloyd George regarded Wilson as a utopian idealist, and he was determined to achieve Britain's war aims. This meant crippling German naval power and destroying its colonial empire. Both aims were achieved, but Wilson was less successful. His beloved League of Nations Covenant was rejected by the U.S. Senate in 1920, but it was signed by other powers in June 1919. The United States signed a separate peace with Germany in 1921, and it refused to honor Wilson's pledge to guarantee French security if they accepted the League of Nations Covenant. From 1921–1933, U.S. policy reverted to one of isolation under a succession of republican presidents. Money remained a serious matter, and the United States was zealous in insisting that Britain repay wartime loans. The United States played a prominent role in setting up the **Dawes Plan** in 1924 and the **Young Plan** in 1929, to enable a shattered Germany to recover their economic health. Britain supported these initiatives and resisted what were seen as French attempts to bully Germany, most notably in January 1923, when French troops occupied the industrial Ruhr. The United States supported Britain in its opposition, yet remained outside the League of Nations.

The United States was interested in reducing Japanese naval power in the Pacific, and it secured its objective at the 1921–1922 **Washington Naval Conference**. The fact that Britain was prepared to abandon its 1902 treaty with **Japan** in the interest of getting American goodwill was a sign of the new powerful position of the United States. Britain also had to agree due to the fact that crippled as it was by postwar debt, it could not sustain an arms race with a more powerful America. Both powers were to have the same number of capital ships in the Pacific. In the 1920s and 1930s, the British hoped that the United States would join it in the role of global policeman, but they were to be disappointed. The only thing that the United States would commit to was the rather meaningless **Kellogg–Briand Pact** (1928), which outlawed war as an instrument of national policy. Frank B. Kellogg was the U.S. secretary of state. Britain's foreign secretary at the time, **Austen Chamberlain**, signed more in hope than expectation. Expectations that the United States might act decisively over Japan's invasion of Manchuria in 1931 also proved illusory. Britain could not act without the United States. Washington made the right anti-Japanese noises but also would not act. Neither was there any real coordination of Anglo–American policy when both countries were smitten after the Great Depression in 1929. Economic protectionism ruled the day in both states.

Beginning in 1931, Britain was increasingly perplexed about how to deal with authoritarian Japan, Fascist Italy, and Nazi Germany. Each of these powers flouted international law. The new U.S. president, **Franklin D. Roosevelt** (1933–1945), might have sympathized, but he had no intention of using military force to support Britain. Domestic opinion in the United States was strongly opposed to the prospect of another European war, as it was in Britain. Hopes of any joint Anglo–American action against Japan was sabotaged by a U.S. statement in July 1934 that, short of a Japanese attack on Hawaii or Honolulu, the Americans would not respond by force to any Japanese action. Japan attacked mainland **China** in 1937, and it bombed British and U.S. vessels on the River Yangste. Britain, which had substantial interests in China, felt unable to impose sanctions without U.S. support. Unlike the United States, Britain also faced real threats from Italy and Germany. Roosevelt's attitude toward the British policy of **appeasement** was ambivalent at best. In January 1938, he put forth an initiative demanding an international peace conference. This was flatly rejected by British prime minister **Neville Chamberlain**, although his foreign secretary, **Anthony Eden**, wanted to respond. In September 1938, Roosevelt, whose ambassador in London, **Joseph P. Kennedy,** strongly supported appeasement, appeared to favor Chamberlain's policy over **Czechoslovakia**. When substantial Czech territory was given to Germany via the **Munich Agreement** (1938), Roosevelt sent the two-word telegram "Good man" to Chamberlain. **World War II** broke out in September 1939, without U.S. involvement. Winston Churchill worked hard to make Anglo–American relations closer when he became prime minister on 10 May 1940.

Nonetheless, there seemed little chance of U.S. entry into the war. Roosevelt was reelected on a peace platform in November 1940. There was U.S. assistance in guarding merchant convoys in the Atlantic, but it was only in December 1941 that the United States entered the war, when Japan executed an attack on **Pearl Harbor**. Adolf Hitler declared war on the United States on 11 December. Britain and the United States were allies once again. The two countries fought together in North Africa, in 1942, in the Battle of the Atlantic, and in the growing aerial bombardment of Germany in 1942–1943. The Pacific War was largely a U.S. operation, although Roosevelt promised to give the German war priority. There was close coordination between the military staffs of the two allies. The biggest problem was their reliance on a third ally, the Soviet Union.

As the war raged on, and certainly by the time of the conferences at **Yalta** and **Potsdam** in 1945, Churchill felt himself being increasingly sidelined. He also had fears about a premature invasion of France, the so-called "second front" that Soviet leader Joseph Stalin was demanding. Roosevelt and the U.S. generals reluctantly agreed that the invasion would not be launched in 1942–1943. There was also disagreement about the legitimate French government. While Churchill and the British supported Charles de Gaulle and the Free French, the Americans were more inclined to support Vichy and other alternatives. The United States increasingly dominated. It supplied the supreme allied commander, **Dwight D. Eisenhower**, when France was eventually invaded in June 1944. In Asia, the United States felt disinclined to prop up Britain's empire, christening **Lord Louis Mountbatten's** South-East Asia Command (SEAC) "Save England's Asian Colonies." Only in Burma was there a substantive British military effort in Asia.

Britain was the only Allied Power to fight right through World War II. By the time the war ended in 1945, Britain was undisputedly the weakest of the three Great Powers, albeit still with a great empire. By the time of the Potsdam Conference in July 1945, the United States had an atomic bomb, and its industrial and military power was vastly greater than that of Britain. Churchill realized this, as did his successor, Labour prime minister **Clement R. Attlee**. Britain had overwhelmingly depended on U.S. materials and financial assistance to win the war. This included the **Lend–Lease** system, which allowed Britain to run up $21 billion in debts. The United States agreed to write off those debts in exchange for a $3.75 billion loan at 2 percent interest. Britain was further obliged to ratify the 1944 **Bretton Woods Agreement**, whereby the pound was made convertible into dollars. These terms were actually more generous than the post–World War I terms, but an embattled and impoverished Britain was resentful. It was still going to need millions of U.S. dollars (and goods) under the 1947 **Marshall Plan** to recover.

On the foreign policy front, there was broad consensus about how to deal with the Soviet Union, once the Attlee government realized that being left wing would not ease relations with Stalin. Churchill's 1946 "**Iron Curtain**" speech, delivered in the United States, reflected a new reality. Soviet Communism and Western democracy were not compatible. Britain and the United States helped create a unified West Germany, and they saw off Stalin's attempt to force the Western powers out of Berlin in 1948–1949. Both states kept large occupying forces in West Germany to protect it from possible Soviet invasion. Britain's foreign secretary, **Ernest Bevin**, played a leading role in setting up the U.S.-led **North Atlantic Treaty Organization (NATO)** in 1949.

Consensus in Europe was not reflected in the Far East. Britain, always inclined to be more pragmatic, recognized the Chinese Communist government of Mao Zedong in 1950. The United States, more focused on an ideological threat, would not. In June 1950, Britain supported the U.S. decision to lead a **United Nations (UN)** force to aid South Korea when it was invaded by its northern neighbor. The Foreign Office was sure that the attack was instigated by the Soviet Union. The British government was alarmed by President **Harry S. Truman's** rather wild talk about using an atomic bomb when the People's Republic of China intervened in the war in November 1950. Prime Minister Attlee went to Washington in December to voice British concerns. There were to be other differences over **Indochina**. The British government did not support U.S. pleas for an air strike against Communist positions at **Dien Bien Phu** in 1954, nor would it have objected to a victory by Ho Chi Minh in national Vietnamese elections. The United States was fiercely opposed to Vietnamese Communism, which it viewed as part of a global conspiracy. Washington also objected to Churchill, restored to power in 1951, going to Moscow for a summit with Stalin's successors.

Both the Labour and Conservative parties in Britain agreed on the need for an atomic bomb. The first British one was duly exploded in October 1952. This test was almost certainly delayed by the 1946 U.S. **McMahon Act**, which ended wartime cooperation over nuclear development. This caused much annoyance in Britain at the time, but did not prevent its Labour government from allowing American B-29 bombers into Britain and siting U.S. bases there in 1949. Soon the B-29s could operate with atomic bombs. Parliament was not consulted over these moves, which were deemed essential at a time of **Cold War**. In 1957, Britain exploded a hydrogen bomb, but its nuclear deterrent had one fatal flaw. The British proved unable to evolve their own delivery system. This increased Britain's defense dependence on the United States, so that it ultimately had to rely on the U.S. submarine-based **Polaris missile** system, centered in Scotland. If there was a "**special relationship**," there was no doubt who was in charge. Britain demonstrated its loyalty to the U.S. alliance at the time of the **Cuban Missile Crisis** in October 1962.

Elsewhere, Britain's relationship with the United States made it slow-moving and confused in its attitude toward an integrated Europe. President **John F. Kennedy** certainly encouraged Premier **Harold Macmillan's** belated application to join the **European Economic Community (EEC)** in 1961. It took Britain another 11 years to secure membership, but successive U.S. administrations thought British EEC membership a positive development. In the Middle East, there was U.S. animosity toward Britain over its policy in **Palestine** until **Israel** was created in 1948. Then came the most serious problem in postwar Anglo–American relations: with the 1956 **Suez Crisis**. The United States uniquely voted against Britain on the UN Security Council when Anthony Eden's government invaded Egypt. Britain's economic vulnerability was underlined by U.S. pressure on the pound, which forced a premature withdrawal. The period following the Suez Crisis saw increasing U.S. influence in the Middle East, while Britain surprisingly retained influence in **Jordan** and the Persian Gulf. Britain was much more critical of Israel's refusal after the 1967 Six-Day War to implement UN Resolution 242 and evacuate the Occupied Territories in Egypt, Jordan, and Syria. Loyalty to Israel became an axiom of U.S. foreign policy.

In the 1960s and 1970s, Vietnam was a bone of contention between London and Washington. This was especially true when **Harold Wilson** was prime minister (1964–1970) and **Lyndon B. Johnson** was president. Wilson, leader of a Labour Party that was partly hostile toward Johnson's policy, refused to send even a token British force to Vietnam, even though **Australia** and **New Zealand** did so. There were widespread public demonstrations against U.S. policy in Britain in 1968–1969. Matters did not improve when **Edward Heath** became prime minister in June 1970. He regarded Britain's entry into the EEC, achieved in 1973, as crucial. Relations with Washington were accordingly cool. The succeeding Labour government of 1974–1979 was beset with economic problems. It needed an International Monetary Fund loan in 1976, with U.S. support to halt galloping inflation.

Anglo–American relations changed dramatically in May 1979, when **Margaret Thatcher** became Britain's prime minister. Thatcher admired her U.S. counterpart, President **Ronald Reagan,** and they were ideological bedfellows. She supported the U.S. stance on **Afghanistan** when the Soviet Union invaded it in December 1979, and this bore fruit in 1982. When **Argentina** invaded the Falkland Islands, Reagan strongly supported Britain, although other members of his administration were disinclined to do so. In 1984–1985, Thatcher also pointed out that Mikhail Gorbachev was a new style of Soviet leader, one that the West could do business with. In her robust manner, she did not hold back from castigating Reagan when he launched an invasion of the **British Commonwealth** island of **Grenada** in 1983. This was to overthrow a far-left regime, but Reagan had not cleared it with Thatcher first. The episode did not prevent her from supporting U.S. air strikes against **Libya** in 1986. The two states were united in their belief that the Libyan regime was responsible for the bombing of Pan Am Flight 103 over Lockerbie, in Scotland, in December 1988. The **"special relationship"** probably meant more to Thatcher than any other postwar British prime minister, including her great hero, Winston Churchill.

Britain and the United States were again united in a common approach when the Iraqi dictator Saddam Hussein invaded Kuwait in 1990. Prime Minister **John Major** had succeeded Thatcher as leader in December 1990, before the U.S.-led, UN-sanctioned force invaded **Iraq** in 1991. Britain provided the deputy commander of the force. A rare degree of disunity during a 20-year period occurred over the civil war in **Yugoslavia**. The West was generally unwilling to intervene in the struggle between **Croatia, Serbia,** and **Bosnia** from 1992–1995. The 1995 Dayton Agreement, sponsored by the United States, ended the war and established the Implementation Force to enforce this. Both British and U.S. forces were part of the force. The problem of the largely Muslim Serbian province of **Kosovo** remained. In 1999, there was evidence of Serbian genocide, but President **Bill Clinton** did not want to commit U.S. ground forces. U.S. aircraft were part of an intensive bombing campaign on Serbia from March through June 1999, which forced its surrender. British-led NATO forces entered Kosovo. As the initiator of this action in Kosovo, Britain's new prime minister, **Tony Blair**, gained much prestige. Kosovo demonstrated that America's Vietnam syndrome still existed.

On another front, the United States made a distinctive contribution. President Clinton was more involved in trying to solve the Northern **Ireland** problem than any U.S. president then or since. He sent Senator **George Mitchell** to Ireland as an envoy, and, 10 April 1998, the Good Friday Agreement was signed in Belfast, creating devolved government in Northern Ireland. Blair's British government was duly grateful. The closeness of the Blair–Clinton relationship was fully demonstrated as both Bill and Hillary Clinton visited Belfast.

Doubts were expressed about whether Blair could have such a close relationship with Clinton's Republican successor, **George W. Bush**, who became president in January 2001. Bush was a right-winger who initially showed little interest in foreign affairs. The events of 11 September 2001, "9/11," changed all that. Blair immediately showed a willingness to align Britain's policy against **terrorism** with that of the United States. He supported the U.S. decision to invade Afghanistan in 2001 and Iraq in 2003, despite the overwhelming opposition to the Iraq War in Britain. Blair's former foreign secretary, **Robin Cook,** resigned from the government over the issue, and even Bush was prepared to act without Britain because he knew of Blair's domestic difficulties. Blair accepted the U.S. claim there were weapons of mass destruction in Iraq, despite the widespread opposition to the war in the **European Union.** The mutual admiration between Blair and Bush remained until Blair resigned as prime minister on 27 June 2007. Relations were cooler between Bush and Blair's successor, **Gordon Brown,** but this was not because Brown lacked sympathy for the United States, which he knew well, and where he frequently went on holiday.

The election of **Barack Obama** in November 2008 led to a change in Anglo–American relations. Obama did not have any great interest in Britain, and stories circulated about Brown being fobbed off with a present of DVDs when he visited Washington in 2009. When **David Cameron** became prime minister in May 2010, there seemed to be a change of atmosphere. There was Anglo–American agreement on action against Libya in 2011, although Obama was content to allow Britain and France to take the lead with air strikes. Both states deplored the bloodthirsty behavior of the regime in Syria in 2011–2012. Historic differences of nuance about relations with Israel remained. Consensus on the dangers of an Iranian nuclear weapon prevailed in London and Washington. This produced results for Britain when Cameron visited the United States in February 2012. There was lavish praise of the British prime minister, and the Obama administration treated Cameron with considerable deference. British relations with the United States have generally remained good. There was a niggle in 2012 about the British extradition treaty with the United States, which was seen in Britain to disadvantage its citizens. Otherwise, Britain remains what it has been for more than 70 years, America's main ally. *See also* ACHESON, DEAN; DULLES, JOHN FOSTER; KISSINGER, HENRY; RICE, CONDOLEEZZA; RUSK, DEAN; VANCE, CYRUS; WEINBERGER, CASPAR.

VANCE, CYRUS (1917–2002). The problem of **Bosnia**, a component of the former **Yugoslavia**, exercised former U.S. secretary of state Cyrus Vance and former British **foreign secretary Lord David Owen** in 1992. They had previously worked together on the problem of **Southern Rhodesia**. The two men produced the Vance–Owen Plan, but President **Bill Clinton** was more interested in the lead-up to the 1992 U.S. presidential election, and the plan was reduced to nothing of substance.

VANSITTART, SIR ROBERT (1881–1957). As permanent undersecretary at the **Foreign Office** from 1930–1937, Robert Vansittart, or "Van" as he was commonly known, was a key figure in the formulation of interwar British foreign policy. He was critical of **Neville Chamberlain's appeasement** policy but was not the professional anti-German he has sometimes been made out to be. It was this perception, however, that led to Vansittart's sacking at the end of 1937, and his translation to the meaningless sinecure of chief diplomatic advisor to the government. In this position, Vansittart was kept out of the policy loop. Embittered by loss of influence, he wrote a vehemently anti-German book entitled *Black Record* (1941), which did little for his reputation at a time when the British government was thinking about a postwar settlement with a rehabilitated **Germany**. Vansittart was made a peer in 1941, upon giving up his post at the Foreign Office. He was then made chief advisor to **Hugh Dalton**, the head of the **Special Operations Executive**, with whom he had worked during the second Labour government (1929–1931).

Vansittart was a controversial figure after 1945, being accused of allowing excessive treasury influence on appointments when he was permanent undersecretary, a charge he strongly denied. He opposed German rearmament in the 1950s and criticized Prime Minister **Anthony Eden** because of his Suez policy. Vansittart believed that Eden should have gone ahead with the military operation regardless of U.S. opposition. He had never been an admirer of Eden, believing (rightly) that he had been responsible for his sacking in 1937. Vansittart was an unusual Foreign Office mandarin who wrote poetry; plays, which were put on in the West End of London; and film scripts under a pseudonym. The best-known of these is the original version of *The Four*

Feathers (1939).Vansittart was the brother-in-law of **Eric Phipps**. *See also* BALDWIN, STANLEY; HENDERSON, SIR NEVILE; MACDONALD, RAMSAY; SARGENT, SIR ORME.

VASSALL, WILLIAM (1924–1996). One of several security scandals in Great Britain during the 1960s, the Vassall case involved a homosexual British cipher clerk in the Moscow Embassy. William Vassall lived beyond his means and was entrapped by the KGB into handing over secret documents. The case came to light in September 1962, and, on 22 October, Vassall was sentenced to 18 years imprisonment. Prime Minister **Harold Macmillan** blamed the British ambassador in Moscow for the embarrassment, saying that he had not kept track of what Vassall was up to. Vassall had actually been seconded to the **Foreign Office** from the **Admiralty**, and the scandal widened when letters between Vassall and the former junior minister at the Admiralty, Thomas Galbraith, were found. They were relatively innocuous, but the press hounded Galbraith, who was forced to resign. Macmillan set up the Ratcliffe Tribunal to examine security issues.

VENLO INCIDENT (1939). The Venlo Incident of 9 November 1939 was one of the most embarrassing episodes in the history of the **Secret Intelligence Service (SIS)**. As a result of a disastrously bungled intelligence operation arranged from the passport control office in The Hague, the Dutch capital, two SIS operatives, Major Richard Stevens and Sigismund Payne Best, were kidnapped by the Germans on the Dutch–German border and imprisoned for the duration of **World War II**. The episode was made even worse by the fatal wounding of a Dutch agent who was working with the British. They had naively swallowed a German intelligence ruse about a conspiracy against Adolf Hitler and allowed Stevens and Best to be lured into a bogus meeting with German security agents.

VERSAILLES, TREATY OF (1919). The core component of the 1919 **Paris Peace Conference**, the Treaty of Versailles, was signed on 28 June. It dealt with defeated **Germany** and deprived it of its former colonies and navy. The treaty also contained territorial clauses, which gave **Poland** a corridor to the Baltic Sea through eastern Germany and returned **Alsace-Lorraine** to **France**. A special demilitarized zone was created on the east bank of the Rhine River, where Germany was not allowed to station troops. Article 231 imposed massive reparations payments on Germany to compensate France and **Belgium** for damage done to their territory by occupying German forces during **World War I**.

Great Britain fared well under the terms of Versailles, securing the surrender of the German High Seas Fleet, which removed a threat to the Royal

Navy, and making Germany responsible for its military pensions. Yet, its prime minister, **David Lloyd George**, was critical of aspects of the treaty, notably the Polish settlement. He supported the concept of the **League of Nations**, the brainchild of U.S. president **Woodrow Wilson**, which was included in the Versailles Treaty through a covenant, but warned against treating Germany too harshly. Critics argued that Great Britain was happy to take its share of reparations, while criticizing devastated France for insisting on its share. Versailles was unpopular with British intellectuals and politicians during the interwar period and often blamed for the outbreak of **World War II**. *See also* KEYNES, JOHN MAYNARD; LOCARNO, TREATY OF; LOTHIAN, LORD.

VICTORIA, HM, QUEEN (1819–1901). As the longest-reigning monarch in British history (64 years), Queen Victoria had more influence than her constitutional position strictly entitled her to. She was strongly swayed by her personal likes and dislikes, loathing such prime ministers as **Lord Henry John Palmerston** and **William Gladstone**, as much as she admired **Benjamin Disraeli**, who made her empress of India in 1876. The sheer longevity of Victoria's reign made her an influence on policy, as did the fact that she was united by marriage to almost every crowned head of Europe, including the German emperor and the Russian tsar. Her golden jubilee in 1897 was made the occasion for a massive display of British imperial power, albeit one that was in sunset.

VIENNA CONGRESS (1814–1815). The Vienna Congress of 1814–1815 was interrupted by **Napoleon Bonaparte's** escape from Elba and his unsuccessful attempt to regain the throne of **France**. The principle behind it was that the balance of power, disrupted by France, should be restored, although the Vienna Settlement ignored national aspirations in **Italy**, **Poland**, and **Belgium**. The Vienna congresses are frequently compared by historians with the **Treaty of Versailles**, which did acknowledge the ethnic principle. *See also* NAPOLEONIC WARS.

VIETNAM WAR (1954–1975). Great Britain's involvement in Vietnam goes back a good deal longer than is generally realized, in fact, to 1945–1946. A British division under General Douglas Gracey played a pivotal role in reestablishing French colonial rule in Vietnam. This was followed by an eight-year war, which ended with the decisive French defeat at **Dien Bien Phu** in 1954. Britain's **foreign secretary, Anthony Eden**, was then a major player at the **Geneva Conference**, while his U.S. equivalent, **John Foster Dulles**, refused to play any part in the proceedings. The British supported the concept of All-Vietnam elections in 1956, whereas the Americans sabotaged them and imposed their own candidate, the corrupt Ngo Dinh Diem, as president of South Vietnam (1955–1963).

Considerable differences subsequently arose between U.S. and British policy on Vietnam. In 1954, Eden and his prime minister, **Winston Churchill**, had refused to be involved in air strikes against the Communists at Dien Bien Phu. His successors, **Harold Macmillan** and **Harold Wilson**, also refused to send any military assistance to the Americans in Vietnam. The vehement opposition to U.S. policy in Vietnam on the Labour left made it impossible for Wilson to risk involvement, even if he wanted to. Student demonstrations against the war were a feature of 1968–1969, which resulted in the closure of the London School of Economics for an entire term.

Wilson resisted pressure from President **Lyndon B. Johnson**, but also from the **Foreign Office** and the treasury, to get British troops sent to Vietnam. Instead, he tried to act as a mediator, along with his pro-American foreign secretary, **Michael Stewart**. In June 1965, for example, Wilson tried to use the occasion of the **Commonwealth** Conference in London to put forward a plan to send a Commonwealth prime minister's delegation to tour key capitals in search of a peace settlement. The scheme failed, as did Wilson's other attempts to bring peace to Vietnam. He publicly disassociated Britain from the U.S. bombing of Hanoi, the capital of North Vietnam, and its port, Haiphong, on 28 June 1966. Many people in Britain were shocked by the use of napalm in Vietnam, and many others deemed the war immoral. There was criticism of the fact that the Wilson government, although critical of aspects of U.S. policy in Vietnam, did not completely disassociate itself from America's war. A Conservative government might have been more prepared to help the **United States** with ground troops.

VIVIAN, MAJOR VALENTINE (1886–1969). As head of counterespionage in the **Secret Intelligence Service (SIS)**, Major Valentine Vivian discovered that the Italian secret service was pilfering the safe of the British ambassador in Rome, Sir Eric Drummond, in February 1937. This meant that the Italian government had direct access, thanks to the presence of an agent in the embassy staff, to British diplomatic secrets. Vivian visited the British embassy five months later, in July 1937, where embassy security was little better, and issued a damning report for the **Foreign Office**. In September 1939, he was involved in the unmasking of a Soviet spy, Captain John King, in the Communications Department of the Foreign Office. King was subsequently sentenced to 20 years imprisonment. Vivian served as deputy chief of SIS during **World War II**. It was a major misfortune for him that through a meeting in **India** with the father of the notorious Soviet agent "Kim" Philby, he became Philby's mentor in the SIS, and thus inadvertently undermined Britain's intelligence system.

WARNER, SIR CHRISTOPHER (1890–1970). As undersecretary of the **Foreign Office** Northern Department from 1941–1946, Christopher Warner played a key role in the evolution of British foreign policy toward the **Soviet Union**. On 2 April 1946, Warner produced a key memorandum under the title "The Soviet Campaign against This Country and Our Response to It." By coincidence, it was the same date as the first meeting of the important Foreign Office **Russia Committee**, of which Warner was a leading member. In his memorandum, Warner said that the Soviet Union had adopted an aggressive policy toward the West that was based on a mixture of Communism and nationalism. He argued that Great Britain was singled out for hostility because it was perceived to be the more vulnerable of the two Western Great Powers. Warner believed that the campaign had to be counteracted by vigorous British propaganda. His view had altered from the one he had held from 1942–1944, which was that for the first five years after **World War II**, the Soviet Union would cooperate with the British and the Americans because it needed to recover from the war. His memorandum of 2 April was a recognition that this was an overoptimistic analysis, and it has been identified as the start date for British **Cold War** policy. Warner had previously been British ambassador to the Belgian government in exile (1940–1941).

WASHINGTON NAVAL CONFERENCE (1921–1922). A turning point in Great Britain's relationship with both the **United States** and **Japan** was marked by the Washington Naval Conference of 1921–1922. The British accepted the principle of naval parity with the United States because they could not afford a naval arms race with the Americans. They also rejected the 1902 alliance with Japan in favor of a Pacific partnership with the United States. Japan was forced to keep its navy at 60 percent of British or American strength in respect to capital ships (battleships and battle cruisers). The Washington Naval Treaty was signed on 6 February 1922. Former prime minister and current **foreign secretary Arthur Balfour** signed on behalf of Britain.

WATERHOUSE, CAPTAIN CHARLES (1893–1975). A leading member of the so-called "Suez Group" in the Conservative Party in 1956, Charles

Waterhouse was critical of **Anthony Eden's** earlier involvement in the British withdrawal from the Suez Canal Zone in 1954. Waterhouse represented the extreme right-wing fringe of the party, which put pressure on Eden as prime minister to act in a hawkish manner toward **Egypt**.

WAVELL, ARCHIBALD (1883–1950). One of Great Britain's leading generals in **World War II**, Archibald Wavell was, in many respects, an unlucky leader. He achieved a brilliant success with Operation Compass in December 1940, against the Italians in the Libyan desert, but Prime Minister **Winston Churchill** was impatient for greater success. Wavell was removed from his command in the North African desert and replaced by General Claude Auchinleck on 21 June 1942. He was then made commander in chief of British Forces in **India**, before becoming the next to last viceroy of India in 1943. Wavell dealt with the complex, internecine politics of India as best he could before the Labour Government, anxious to resolve the issue of independence, replaced him with **Lord Louis Mountbatten** in 1947. He was created Viscount Wavell.

WEINBERGER, CASPAR (1917–2006). An Anglophile who served as U.S. secretary of defense from 1981–1987, Caspar Weinberger's period of office coincided with the premiership of **Margaret Thatcher**. He supervised the transfer of **Trident (D-5) missiles** to Great Britain on favorable terms. Weinberger was a **Cold War** warrior, but a staunch friend of Britain who took its side in the 1982 **Falklands War** at the start of the crisis, unlike some other members of President **Ronald Reagan's** administration. This was one reason why Weinberger received the unusual award of an honorary knighthood from the British government in 1988. *See also* LEACH, SIR HENRY; NOTT, SIR JOHN.

WESTERN EUROPEAN UNION (WEU). The Western European Union (WEU) emerged from the first attempt at postwar Anglo–French cooperation in the **Brussels Treaty**, signed in 1948. The WEU founding treaty was signed on 23 October 1954. It was really a vehicle for including the Federal Republic of Germany in a supranational defense organization (it was allowed to join the **North Atlantic Treaty Organization** in 1955), while setting limits on the size of its defense forces to allay French fears. The WEU effectively recognized the right to full sovereignty of the Federal Republic. The more ambitious **European Defense Community (EDC)** project had failed to secure ratification by the French parliament earlier in the year, and Great Britain rejected the supranational principle of the EDC, just as it had refused to join the **European Coal and Steel Community** in 1950.

WESTLAND AFFAIR (1985). A notable crisis during Prime Minister **Margaret Thatcher's** period of government was created by her desire to bring in the American Sikorsky Corporation to rescue the Westland Helicopter Company rather than a European consortium. This was the preferred option of her defense secretary, Michael Heseltine, who resigned over the issue in 1986. It was a classic example of Thatcher's instinctive pro-American bias.

"WHITE MAN'S BURDEN." In 1899, the great British poet Rudyard Kipling wrote his poem "The White Man's Burden" to express the ethos of empire in which the British ruling class believed. It was also Kipling who used the phrase "the empire on which the sun never sets" about Britain's vast possessions. In fact, by 1900, this empire was already in decline, threatened by growing U.S. and German industrial power.

WILSON, HAROLD (1916–1995). The Labour Party's third prime minister, Harold Wilson, won four general elections before retiring early from the political scene in 1976. An Oxford-trained economist, Wilson resigned from the 1945–1951 Labour government in support of **Aneurin Bevan** over health cuts in the 1951 budget. Underlying these cuts was a drastic increase in British defense expenditure because of the **Korean War.** After 13 years in opposition, Wilson came to power as Labour's prime minister in October 1964, when Great Britain had an £800 million deficit on its balance of payments, then accorded much importance by financial pundits. A struggling economy that forced a devaluation of the pound sterling in 1967 was one of the factors that undermined Wilson's attempt to secure entry into the **European Economic Community (EEC).** The left wing of the Labour Party was fiercely against the EEC and the **Vietnam War** throughout Wilson's first government, from 1964–1970. Wilson always saw it as his paramount role to hold the party together and was prepared to make turnabouts in policy to do so. These sometimes opened him to accusations of opportunism.

He showed some mettle in resisting strong pressure from President **Lyndon B. Johnson** to involve Britain in the Vietnam War. The decision to withdraw British troops East of Suez, the **East of Suez Decision,** in 1968, also upset Johnson, but Wilson claimed (not unreasonably) that Britain lacked the financial resources to maintain its presence there. As a young Labour minister, Wilson had been a strong **Commonwealth** man, and it was painful for him to have to deal with Ian Smith's Declaration of Unilateral Independence in 1965. Wilson undoubtedly made an error by stating that Britain would not use force against the illegal white separatist regime in **Southern Rhodesia.** The pretense that economic sanctions would bring down the Smith regime fooled no one.

After a shocking defeat in the election in 1970, Wilson returned to office as prime minister in February 1974, but he presided over a minority government, which forced him to hold a second election in October, and this gave Labour a working majority in the House of Commons. This last phase (1974–1976) saw a classic exposition of Wilson's skill as a party leader. Europe was the key issue, and he devised a devious strategy, whereby a referendum would be held in 1975 on a supposed renegotiation of the terms of EEC entry obtained by the Conservative government in 1971–1972. In reality, no such renegotiation had been achieved, but Wilson used the big guns in the Labour leadership to secure a "yes" vote in the referendum. Withdrawal from the EEC, which Britain had only entered in 1973, was, as Wilson well knew, never going to be practical politics. The referendum verdict was grudgingly accepted by the Labour Party, and Wilson saved party unity, something his successors failed to do. Wilson's sudden retirement in 1976 sparked all sorts of speculation, as he was only 60 years of age, but it was, in fact, a result of the onset of Alzheimer's, which dogged his last years. In 1983, he was created Baron Wilson of Rievaulx.

WILSON, WOODROW (1856–1924). Elected president as a Democrat in 1912, Woodrow Wilson was a former academic who came to power as a result of a split in the Republican Party. He was reelected in 1916. Wilson was reluctant to take the **United States** into **World War I** until German provocations gave him little choice in April 1917. When the war ended in 1918, he briefly seemed to be the dominant figure in the Allied leadership. Wilson suspected Great Britain of harboring imperialist ambitions, but his idealism provoked scorn from the much more pragmatic British prime minister, **David Lloyd George**. Wilson's **Fourteen Points** laid down principles that included self-determination for all nations, freedom of the seas (which the British especially disliked), and free trade. Above all else, Wilson hoped that the **League of Nations**, his 14th point would preserve international peace. It was included in the 1919 **Treaty of Versailles** as a covenant, but Wilson was disturbed by the Anglo–French insistence on Article 231, which made **Germany** accept its war guilt and the huge level of war reparations imposed on it. His worst disappointment was the refusal of the U.S. Senate to ratify the treaty, thus ruling out American involvement in the league. A serious stroke prevented Wilson from standing for reelection in the 1920 presidential election.

WILTON PARK. Wilton Park is a well-known **Foreign and Commonwealth Office (FCO)** discussion forum, now located in a country house in Sussex, England. The original Wilton Park, in Buckinghamshire, became a place where courses were run for German prisoners of war in 1945. In July

1947, it was bought by the FCO as a venue for international discussions, although its future was troubled by constant threats of closure due to budget cuts. **Anthony Eden,** who was **foreign secretary** at the time, saved it from a serious threat of closure in 1952, prior to the purchase of the Sussex house, which kept the original name. It had previously been the home of the Goring family.

WORLD WAR I (1914–1918). Great Britain entered World War I on 4 August 1914, as a result of **Germany's** invasion of neutral **Belgium,** which breached the 1839 treaty of which Britain was a guarantor. Britain was part of the Triple Entente, along with **France** and **Russia,** which faced the Central Powers of Germany, Austria-Hungary, and **Turkey.** The war on the Western Front, which was confidently expected to be over by Christmas, soon degenerated into a war of attrition along lines of trenches that stretched from the Swiss border with France to the English Channel. It was a type of warfare for which Britain, with its small, largely colonial army, was ill-equipped. A huge volunteer army had to be raised between 1914–1916. Nevertheless, it is recognized that the small British Expeditionary Force played an important role in the Battle of the Marne in 1914, which prevented the German army from reaching Paris.

By the end of 1914, dreadful losses had been suffered by both the British and the French, so it was deemed necessary to open a new front against Turkey in the east. This was designed to seize the Dardanelles, which linked Russia to the Mediterranean Sea, and capture the Turkish capital of Constantinople. The main backer of this strategy in 1915–1916 was **Winston Churchill,** the first lord of the **Admiralty** in the British War Cabinet. He believed that the Royal Navy could knock out the Dardanelles forts, but this proved to be an illusion. A fatal delay before the Anglo–French landings gave the Turks extra time to prepare. The campaign was a catastrophic failure and brought about Churchill's dismissal from the British government. The loss of a large number of Australian and New Zealand Army Corps troops caused great bitterness in those countries.

Thereafter, the emphasis was on trying to defeat Germany in the west. The effort was immensely costly, most notoriously in the Battle of the Somme in 1916, when 20,000 British soldiers died on the first day, and 250,000 died in total as the battle dragged on. France was suffering even worse losses at Verdun, and Russia was on the verge of revolution by the end of 1916. Two key factors changed the outlook for Britain and its allies in 1916–1917. In December 1916, **David Lloyd George** became prime minister and offered a new, dynamic style of leadership. Then, in April 1917, the **United States,** antagonized by unrestricted German U-boat attacks and the notorious

Zimmermann Telegram, which disclosed German attempts to pit Mexico against the United States, came into the war on the Anglo–French side. Although Russia withdrew from the war in March 1918, this loss was balanced by the increasing number of U.S. troops crossing the Atlantic. The last desperate German attacks in France were defeated between March and July 1918. Led by Field Marshal Haig, the British Army, which had not suffered from the mutinies that threatened to undermine the French in 1917, was at the heart of the victorious Allied counteroffensive.

Lessons had been learned since the bloody battles of 1915–1917, and the British pioneered the use of tanks, a key resource in the final offensives. Subsidiary British attacks in the Middle East brought down Germany's ally, Turkey, and the ramshackle **Austro-Hungarian** monarchy sued for peace in October. On 11 November 1918, even the German army had reached the end of its resistance. Its emperor was obliged to abdicate, and an armistice was signed. Britain had emerged as a victor power, but the human and financial cost involved in winning World War I was immense. Lloyd George claimed that he would make Britain a land "fit for heroes." In reality, Britain had forever surrendered its global financial dominance to the Americans. *See also* VERSAILLES, TREATY OF.

WORLD WAR II (1939–1945). Great Britain's involvement in World War II began on 3 September 1939, two days after **Germany** had invaded **Poland**. In March, Britain had already pledged to defend Polish sovereignty against external attack, although it and its French ally could do little to assist the Poles in their gallant but hopeless resistance. This followed the strange period that the American media nicknamed the "Phoney War," when hostilities were restricted to the air and the oceans. In Britain, there was unhappiness with **Neville Chamberlain's** wartime leadership, and on the day Germany invaded **France, Belgium**, and Holland, he was replaced as prime minister by **Winston Churchill**. It was an irony of the situation that Churchill, in his old job of first lord of the **Admiralty**, had been responsible for planning a failed campaign in Norway in April. He became prime minister on 10 May 1940 and had to deal with a rapidly worsening situation. The British Expeditionary Force had to be evacuated from the continent, and France was forced to surrender. Some ministers in the coalition government, which included Labour, were prepared to consider peace talks with Adolf Hitler, notably **Lord Halifax**, the **foreign secretary**; however, Winston Churchill was not, rightly believing that Hitler and the Nazis could not be trusted. He kept British morale high with inspiring radio broadcasts, while between July and September 1940, the Royal Air Force won the Battle of Britain.

In 1940–1941, Britain's resistance to Germany and Fascist **Italy** was heroic, but Britain alone could not win the war. Churchill spent much time and energy trying to bring the **United States** into the conflict. He developed a friendly personal relationship with President **Franklin D. Roosevelt**, and the two men signed the Destroyers for Bases Agreement in August 1940. A year later, the two men met in Newfoundland. The result was the **Atlantic Charter**. In December 1941, the United States entered the war, months after Hitler had predictably attacked the Soviet Union in June. Churchill now knew that the war against Germany would be won. Roosevelt had agreed that the German war, rather than the one against **Japan** in the Pacific, should get priority. The Pacific War was largely an American-led and resourced operation, and this increasingly proved to be the case in Western Europe. The ferocious war in the east (in which 27 million Soviet citizens died) broke German strength there. Britain tried to help by sending convoys on the perilous Arctic route. Eventual victory was signposted by the desert victory at El Alamein in November 1942. The Americans were also involved in North Africa, and, in 1942–1943, the air forces of the two countries relentlessly pounded German cities by day and night.

Postwar planning became increasingly important from 1943 onward, and it also involved the Soviet dictator Joseph Stalin. In November 1943, Churchill, Roosevelt, and Stalin met in the Iranian capital of Teheran. The **Teheran Conference** acknowledged Churchill's anxieties about a sea invasion of France, and it was put off until June 1944. The Mediterranean strategy preferred by Churchill did not lead to easy victories in 1943. Italy was a tough nut for Anglo–American forces to crack. In the Far East, **Lord Louis Mountbatten's** South-East Asia Command supervised the reconquest of Burma from the Japanese, while the Americans took countless Japanese-occupied Pacific islands.

There were setbacks in Europe, especially at Arnhem in September 1944, when an attempt to shorten the war by seizing Rhine River bridges failed badly. This failure might have lengthened the western campaign by several months, but, by early 1945, the Red Army was threatening eastern Germany, and Anglo–American forces crossed the Rhine. Further Anglo–U.S. cooperation was evident in "Operation Manhattan," which produced an atomic bomb. Germany surrendered on 8 May, and the atomic bomb was used on Hiroshima and Nagasaki to speed the Japanese surrender in September. The three Allied leaders had further conferences at **Yalta** (February 1945) and **Potsdam** (July 1945) to determine the shape of the postwar world. Churchill had become increasingly aware that Britain was now the junior partner in the alliance. Franklin Roosevelt had died in April, but he had made it clear that his relationship with Stalin was more important than the one with Churchill.

Churchill lost political power in the middle of the Potsdam Conference as a result of the general election of July 1945. This was not a vote by the British people against Churchill's wartime leadership, but a verdict on Conservative governments in the 1930s. *See also* D-DAY LANDINGS; DUNKIRK; MORGENTHAU PLAN; NARVIK EXPEDITION; *PRINCE OF WALES*, HMS; QUEBEC CONFERENCE; SAN FRANCISCO CONFERENCE; SPECIAL OPERATIONS EXECUTIVE.

WRIGHT, PETER (1916–1995). The author of the notorious book *Spycatcher* (1986), Peter Wright was a longtime MI5 service agent who seemed obsessed with the idea that the government of **Harold Wilson** had been penetrated by Soviet intelligence, and that Wilson himself was a Soviet mole. From 1985–1988, the British government, under **Margaret Thatcher**, wasted much time trying to prevent Wright's book from being published, but it could not prevent its publication outside Britain. Wright had retired to **Australia**, and the government failed in an embarrassing attempt to prevent its publication there.

WRIGHT, SIR OLIVER (1921–2009). Few diplomats retire from the **Foreign and Commonwealth Office (FCO)** and are then called back to serve in the Washington embassy, the plum post in the British Diplomatic Service. This was Oliver Wright's experience in 1982, and he remained in the **United States** until 1986. He had joined the Diplomatic Service in 1945, after war service in the Royal Navy (1941–1945), and was posted variously to New York, Bucharest, Singapore, Berlin, and Pretoria, before coming back to the **Foreign Office** in London in 1959. From 1960–1963, Wright was closely associated with **Sir Alec Douglas-Home**, who was **foreign secretary** at the time, as a speechwriter and assistant private secretary. In 1966, he was sent as ambassador to Denmark, returning in 1973 to become deputy undersecretary at the FCO in charge of the European departments. Wright's appointment to the West German capital of Bonn as ambassador in 1976, where he stayed in post until 1981, seemed to mark a highly creditable end to a successful career. His surprise appointment to Washington in 1982 allowed him to spend four years acting as a diplomatic link with President **Ronald Reagan**, with whom he got along well. He was knighted in 1974.

Y

YALTA CONFERENCE (1945). Yalta was a Black Sea coastal resort where Prime Minister **Winston Churchill**, President **Franklin D. Roosevelt**, and General Secretary Joseph Stalin met for the penultimate conference of **World War II**. The conference lasted from 4 February–11 February 1945, and it continued the postwar planning process, which had begun at the **Teheran Conference** in 1943. Great Britain's **foreign secretary, Anthony Eden**, also attended the meeting, together with the permanent undersecretary at the **Foreign Office, Alexander Cadogan**. The members of the British delegation, from Churchill downward, all believed that their living quarters at Yalta were being bugged by the Russians. Churchill used this knowledge to make his displeasure with Stalin's tactics known in conversations with Eden and others. He was equally disappointed by Roosevelt's obvious preference for intimate conversations with Stalin, from which he, the British prime minister, was excluded.

Stalin was persuaded to enter the war in the Far East 90 days after the war in Europe ended, and he also accepted the plans to establish the **United Nations** as a successor to the defunct **League of Nations. Poland** was at the center of conversations between the "Big Three." Britain had gone to war to preserve Polish independence in September 1939, and by now, Churchill was suspicious of Soviet intentions. A puppet Polish Communist regime in waiting, the so-called "Lublin Committee," already existed in Russian occupied Poland. It was agreed upon at Yalta that to accommodate Russian retention of the territory in eastern Poland, acquired in the notorious Nazi–Soviet pact of August 1939, the Polish frontier would be moved many miles westward to the line of the rivers Oder and Neisse. Territory annexed elsewhere by the Soviet Union, which included the Baltic states of Lithuania, Latvia, and Estonia, would remain under its control (putting an end to the brief experience of independence by those small states). Free elections were supposed to be held in Poland under the terms of Yalta. Both Churchill and Roosevelt were subsequently criticized for allegedly conceding too much to the Soviet Union at Yalta, with comparisons being made to the 1938 **Munich Agreement**. In practice, Churchill and Roosevelt had little option but to do as they did.

Soviet help was needed against the Japanese, and the Anglo–Americans were in no position to contest the Soviet occupation of Poland and Eastern Europe.

YOUNG PLAN (1929). Chaired by the American banker Owen D. Young, a committee of financial experts produced a report in 1929 that considerably reduced the annual reparations payments that **Germany** was obliged to pay by the 1919 **Treaty of Versailles**. The original amount had already been reduced by the 1924 **Dawes Plan**. The Young Plan fixed the date for a final payment as 1988. The new settlement was supported by Great Britain, but only after the British chancellor of the exchequer, Philip Snowden, secured a reallocation of reparations receipts to Britain's advantage.

YUGOSLAVIA. The origins of the Yugoslav state date back to 1878, when **Serbia** secured its independence from the Ottoman Turkish Empire, a development that Great Britain, anxious about Russian influence in the Balkans, had concerns about. Independent Serbia acted as a beacon of hope for other Slav peoples. There was an important fault line in what was to make up Yugoslavia. Catholic **Slovenia** and **Croatia** were in the Habsburg Empire, and **Bosnia-Herzegovina** and Serbia and **Montenegro** were in the Ottoman Empire. They were Orthodox in the case of Serbia and Montenegro, and Muslim and Orthodox in Bosnia. One result of the 1878 Congress of Berlin was a historical oddity. Bosnia-Herzegovina was ruled by Austria-Hungary, although still technically part of the Ottoman Empire. This situation went on until 1908, when subtle diplomacy by Austria-Hungary secured its annexation. Britain refused to risk a war to support Russian objections to the annexation. The war between **Turkey** and the small Slav powers of Serbia, **Bulgaria**, and Montenegro in 1912 (with **Greece** also an anti-Turkish ally) significantly lessened Ottoman territory in Europe. Serbia was regarded with great suspicion by Austria-Hungary. It accused Serbia of complicity in the assassination of the heir to the **Austro-Hungarian** throne, Franz Ferdinand, in the Bosnian capital of Sarajevo on 28 June 1914. **Russia** and **Germany** came into the equation, but Britain was reluctant to do so. Its attitude was summed up by Queen Mary's remark, "and all for tiresome Serbia."

Britain, with a divided Cabinet, ultimately entered **World War I** not to defend Serbia, but **Belgium**. Serbia was simultaneously attacked by Austria-Hungary and its ally, Germany. Most of its territory was overrun and its army forced to carry out a heroic retreat into Albania in 1915. These privations on behalf of the Allied cause were rewarded when World War I ended. On 1 December 1918, the Kingdom of Serbs, Croats, and Slovenes was created. This became Yugoslavia, the Kingdom of the Southern Slavs, in 1928. Despite its name, Yugoslavia was dominated by a Serbian monarchy. Slovenes and Croats had entered the monarchy to ensure their security against Austrian and Italian attempts to reconquer them. As time passed, resentment against the Serbian royal family increased, especially in Croatia. Croatian **terrorism** against Serbia was encouraged by the Italian dictator Benito Mussolini. In 1934, King Alexander I, who had abolished democracy in Yugoslavia in 1928, was assassinated by Croat terrorists while on a visit to **France**. Religious and ethnic fault lines still dominated Yugoslavia.

This became more evident as Yugoslavia became involved in **World War II** in 1941, on Britain's side. Its young King Peter was persuaded by the British to abandon the pro-Axis position of his uncle, Paul, who had been acting as regent. Yugoslavia suffered greatly as a result of this decision. Italian and German forces occupied the country. There was fierce resistance, on the one hand from multiethnic Communist partisans, and on the other from royalist Serbs known as Chetniks. There was also collaboration. A right-wing fascist dictatorship in Croatia supported the Axis powers. It carried out ethnic cleansing against the Serb minority in Croatia. At least 600,000 Serbs were murdered or expelled. Britain was a key player in the story of Yugoslav resistance. The **Special Operations Executive** provided material and human assistance to Yugoslav resisters. A crucial decision by **Winston Churchill** in 1943 meant that the Communist partisans under the Croat Joseph Broz, known as Tito, were earmarked for aid. The Chetniks were thought to have thrown in their lot with the Axis powers, but this was not entirely true.

Tito proved to be the man who would dominate postwar Yugoslav politics (1945–1980). His partisans defeated the Axis powers without Soviet assistance. This was a unique achievement in Eastern Europe, one that created the basis for Communist rule in Yugoslavia, but rule with clearly Yugoslav characteristics. On 31 January 1946, Tito created the Federal Yugoslav Republic. It consisted of six republics, Serbia, Croatia, Slovenia, Bosnia-Herzegovina, Macedonia, and Montenegro. In addition, there were two autonomous provinces, **Kosovo** and Vojvodina. Tito's personality cult overlaid Yugoslav life. He survived an attempt by the Soviet leader Joseph Stalin to unseat him in 1948, because he was seen as the man who defeated wartime fascism. Even in the British Conservative Party, Tito had many admirers, one of whom, Fitzroy Maclean, a wartime British agent, wrote a biography. But there were cracks in Communist Yugoslavia. They were evident in the so-called "Croatian Spring" (1967–1972), a cultural and nationalist revival that was crushed by Tito. This was a warning of what was to come. When Tito died in 1980, an experiment was carried out with a rotating presidency, with a different republic holding the post each year. It only survived for a decade.

Z

ZIMBABWE. *See* SOUTHERN RHODESIA.

Appendix A
List of British Prime
Ministers and Foreign Secretaries

Note: (W) = Whig; (T) = Tory; (C) = Conservative; (Lib) Liberal; (L) = Labour; (NG) = National Government; (LC) = Liberal Conservative Coalition

PRIME MINISTERS

Prime Minister	Term in Office
George Grenville (W)	1763–1765
The Marquis of Rockingham (W)	1765–1766
William Pitt the Elder (W)	1766–1768
The Duke of Grafton (W)	1968–1770
Lord North (W)	1770–1782
The Marquess of Rockingham (W)	March–July 1782
The Earl of Shelburne (W)	1782–1783
The Duke of Portland (W)	April–December 1783
William Pitt the Younger (T)	1783–1801
Henry Addington (T)	1801–1804
William Pitt the Younger (T)	1804–1806
The Lord Granville (W)	1806–1807
The Duke of Portland (T)	1807–1809
Spencer Percival (T)	1809–1812
The Earl of Liverpool (T)	1812–1827
George Canning (T)	April–August 1827
Viscount Goderich	1827–1828
The Duke of Wellington (T)	1828–1830
The Earl Grey (W)	1830–1834
Viscount Melbourne (W)	July–November 1834
The Duke of Wellington (T)	November–December 1834
Sir Robert Peel (T)	1834–1835
Viscount Melbourne (W)	1835–1841
Sir Robert Peel (T)	1841–1846
Lord John Russell (W)	1846–1852
The Earl of Derby (C)	February–December 1852
The Earl of Aberdeen	1852–1855

Prime Minister	Term in Office
Viscount Palmerston (Lib)	1855–1858
The Earl of Derby (C)	1858–1859
Viscount Palmerston (Lib)	1859–1865
The Earl Russell (Lib)	1865–1866
The Earl of Derby (C)	1866–1868
Benjamin Disraeli (C)	February–December 1868
William Gladstone (Lib)	1868–1874
Benjamin Disraeli (C)	1874–1880
William Gladstone (Lib)	1880–1885
The Marquess of Salisbury (C)	1885–1886
William Gladstone (Lib)	February–July 1886
The Marquess of Salisbury (C)	1886–1892
William Gladstone (Lib)	1892–1894
The Earl of Roseberry (Lib)	1894–1895
The Marquess of Salisbury (C)	1895–1902
Arthur Balfour (C)	1902–1905
Sir Henry Campbell Bannerman (Lib)	1905–1908
Herbert H. Asquith (Lib)	1908–1916
David Lloyd George (Lib–Con)	1916–1922
Andrew Bonar Law (C)	1922–1923
Stanley Baldwin (C)	1923–1924
Ramsay MacDonald (Lab)	January–November 1924
Stanley Baldwin (C)	1924–1929
Ramsay MacDonald (L)	1929–1931
Ramsay MacDonald (NG)	1931–1935
Stanley Baldwin (C)	1935–1937
Neville Chamberlain (C/NG)	1937–1940
Winston Churchill (C/Lab/Lib)	1940–1945
Clement Attlee (Lab)	1945–1951
Winston Churchill (C)	1951–1955
Anthony Eden (C)	1955–1957
Harold Macmillan (C)	1957–1963
Alec Douglas-Home (C)	1963–1964
Harold Wilson (Lab)	1964–1970
Edward Heath (C)	1970–1974
Harold Wilson (Lab)	1974–1976
James Callaghan (Lab)	1976–1979
Margaret Thatcher (C)	1979–1990
John Major (C)	1990–1997
Tony Blair (Lab)	1997–2007
Gordon Brown (Lab)	2007–2010
David Cameron (C)	2010–present

FOREIGN SECRETARIES

Foreign Secretary	Term in Office
Charles James Fox	March–July 1782
The Lord Grantham	1782–1783
Charles James Fox	April–December 1783
The Earl Temple	December 1783
The Duke of Leeds	1783–1791
The Lord Granville	1791–1801
The Lord Hawkesbury	1801–1804
The Lord Harrowby	1804–1805
The Lord Mulgrave	1805–1806
Charles James Fox	February–September 1806
Viscount Howick	1806–1807
George Canning	1807–1809
The Earl Bathurst	October–December 1809
The Marquess Wellesley	1809–1812
The Viscount Castlereagh	1812–1822
George Canning	1822–1827
The Earl of Dudley	April–August 1827
The Earl of Dudley	1827–1828
The Earl of Aberdeen	1828–1830
The Viscount Palmerston	1830–1834
The Viscount Palmerston	July–November 1834
The Viscount Palmerston	November–December 1834
The Duke of Wellington	1834–1835
The Viscount Palmerston	1836–1841
The Earl of Aberdeen	1841–1846
The Earl of Granville	1846–1852
The Earl of Malmesbury	February–December 1852
Lord John Russell	1852–1853
The Earl of Clarendon	1853–1855
The Earl of Clarendon	1855–1858
The Earl of Malmesbury	1858–1859
The Earl Russell	1859–1865
The Earl of Clarendon	1865–1866
The Lord Stanley	1866–1868
The Lord Stanley	February–December 1868
The Earl of Clarendon	1868–1870
The Earl Granville	1870–1874
The Earl of Derby	1874–1878
The Marquess of Salisbury	1878–1880
The Earl Granville	1880–1885

Foreign Secretary	Term in Office
The Marquess of Salisbury	1885–1886
The Earl of Roseberry	February–July 1886
The Earl of Iddesleigh	1886–1887
The Marquess of Salisbury	1887–1892
The Earl of Roseberry	1892–1894
The Earl of Kimberley	1894–1895
The Marquess of Salisbury	1895–1900
The Marquess of Landsdowne	1900–1902
The Marquess of Landsdowne	1902–1905
Sir Edward Grey	1905–1908
Sir Edward Grey	1908–1916
Arthur Balfour	1916–1919
The Marquess Curzon of Kedleston	1919–1922
The Marquess Curzon of Kedleston	1922–1923
The Marquess Curzon of Kedleston	1923–1924
Ramsay MacDonald	January–November 1924
Sir Austen Chamberlain	1924–1929
Arthur Henderson	1929–1931
The Marquis of Reading	August–November 1931
Sir John Simon	1931–1935
Anthony Eden	1935–1937
Anthony Eden	1937–1938
Viscount Halifax	1938–1940
Anthony Eden	1940–1945
Ernest Bevin	1945–1951
Herbert Morrison	March–October 1951
Anthony Eden	1951–1955
Harold Macmillan	April–December 1955
Selwyn Lloyd	1955–1957
Selwyn Lloyd	1957–1960
The Earl of Home	1960–1963
R. A. Butler	1963–1964
Patrick Gordon-Walker	1964–1965
Michael Stewart	1965–1966
George Brown	1966–1968
Michael Stewart	1968–1970
Sir Alec Douglas-Home	1970–1974
James Callaghan	1974–1976
Anthony Crosland	1976–1977
David Owen	1977–1979
Lord Carrington	1979–1982
Francis Pym	1982–1983

Foreign Secretary	Term in Office
Sir Geoffrey Howe	1983–1989
John Major	1989–1989
Douglas Hurd	1989–1990
Douglas Hurd	1990–1995
Malcolm Rifkind	1995–1997
Robin Cook	1997–2001
Jack Straw	2001–2006
Margaret Beckett	2006–2007
David Miliband	2007–2010
William Hague	2010–present

Appendix B
List of Permanent Undersecretaries at the Foreign Office

Permanent Undersecretaries at the Foreign Office	Term in Office
George Aust	1790–1795
George Hammond	1795–1807
George Hammond	1807–1809
William Richard Hamilton	1809–1817
Joseph Planta	1817–1827
John Backhouse	1827–1842
Henry Unwin Addington	1842–1854
Edmund Hammond	1854–1873
Lord Tenterden	1873–1882
Sir Julian Pauncefote	1882–1889
Sir Philip Currie	1889–1894
Sir Thomas Sanderson	1894–1906
Sir Charles Hardinge	1906–1910
Sir Arthur Nicolson	1910–1916
Lord Hardinge of Penshurst	1916–1920
Sir Eyre Crowe	1920–1925
Sir William Tyrrell	1925–1928
Sir Ronald Lindsay	1928–1930
Sir Robert Vansittart	1930–1938
Sir Alexander Cadogan	1938–1946
Sir Orme Sargent	1946–1949
Sir William Strang	1949–1953
Sir Ivone Kirkpatrick	1953–1957
Sir Frederick Hoyer Millar	1957–1962
Sir Harold Caccia	1962–1965
Sir Paul Gore-Booth (also head of diplomatic service, 1968)	1965–1969
Sir Denis Greenhill	1969–1973
Sir Thomas Brimelow	1973–1975
Sir Michael Palliser	1975–1982
Sir Anthony Acland	1982–1986
Sir Patrick Wright	1986–1991
Sir David Gillmore	1991–1994

Permanent Undersecretaries at the Foreign Office	Term in Office
Sir John Coles	1994–1997
Sir John Kerr	1997–2002
Sir Michael Jay	2002–2006
Sir Peter Ricketts	2006–2010
Simon Fraser	2010–present

Bibliography

CONTENTS

I. INTRODUCTION

There is a tremendous amount of material on British foreign policy that must, by its very nature, cross-reference with imperial and colonial policy. Some studies provide overviews of the role of the Foreign Office since its inception at the end of the 18th century; others offer specialist insights, for example, into Britain's "special relationship" with the United States, Anglo–Russian relations, and, more recently, Britain's close relations with the European Union. Most try to define Great Britain's national interest and foreign policy objectives in relation to international events, with the defense aspect also receiving a good deal of attention. An increasing number of diplomatic memoirs reflect the experience of individual foreign secretaries, permanent undersecretaries at the Foreign Office and Commonwealth Office (as it now is), and diplomats in the field.

The second section of this bibliography contains general reference works that provide an overview of the role and influence of the Foreign Office, as well as its day-to-day workings. Classic works by Roger Bullen (*The Foreign Office, 1782–1982*) and Raymond A. Jones (*The British Diplomatic Service, 1815–1914*) set traditional British foreign policy in a historical and functional context. This is also done by Christopher Baxter and Keith Hamilton's *The Permanent Under-Secretary of State: A Brief History of the Office and Its Holders*, with its focus on the most important official in Britain's policymaking apparatus, apart from the foreign secretary.

Not included in this bibliography, but of great value to readers and researchers, are the other volumes in the Historical Dictionaries of U.S. Diplomacy series, in which the material dovetails with what can be found in this volume. Among them are installments on Anglo–American relations, World War I, World War II, the Cold War, the Korean War, and the Vietnam War. These books are published by Scarecrow Press and can be accessed on the website at www.scarecrowpress.com.

The third section of the bibliography contains a selection of books on the 19th century. Such works as Paul Kennedy's *The Realities behind Diplomacy: Background Influences on British External Policy, 1865–1980* and John Charmley's *Splendid Isolation? Britain and the Balance of Power, 1874–1914* are key to forming an understanding of this period, as is David Reynolds's *Britannia Overruled: British Policy and World Power in the 20th Century*, in its introductory three chapters. Britain's 19th-century imperial dynamic is thoroughly covered in Bernard Porter's *The Lion's Share: A Short History of British Imperialism, 1850–1983*, and there are valuable insights into the conduct of early 19th-century British policy in former foreign secretary Douglas Hurd's *Choose Your Weapons: The British Foreign Secretary, 200 Years of Argument, Success, and Failure*. A newer biography that sheds light on post–Napoleonic British diplomacy is John Bew's *Castlereagh: Enlightenment, War, and Tyranny*. On the late Victorian Foreign Office, Zara S. Steiner's *The Foreign Office and Foreign Policy, 1895–1914* is an important contribution. A subsection is devoted to Britain and the origins of World War I, and, here again, Steiner's *Britain and the Origins of the First World War* is invaluable, along with Paul Kennedy's *The Rise of Anglo–German Antagonism, 1860–1914*.

In the section on World War I, John Terraine's *The First World War* provides an excellent military overview, while John Grigg's *Lloyd George: War Leader* is a key study. There is also Niall Ferguson's *The Pity of War*. A good picture of the Foreign Office experience during World War I is provided in Robert Vansittart's *The Mist Procession*.

In relation to World War II, there is a mass of material, and intelligence is an important area well surveyed by Richard J. Aldrich in *Intelligence and the War against Japan: Britain, America, and the Politics of Secret Service*. Richard Breitman's *Official Secrets: What the Nazis Planned, What the British and Americans Knew* is seminal, as is Sir E. Llewellyn Woodward's *British Foreign Policy in the Second World War* (4 volumes). Charles Cruickshank's *SOE in the Far East: The Official History* offers challenging insights, while Martin Kitchen's *British Policy towards the Soviet Union during the Second World War* is essential for understanding Anglo–Soviet relations. Herbert Feis's *Churchill, Roosevelt, and Stalin* is still worthwhile, along with Christopher Thorne's *Allies of a Kind: The United States, Britain, and the War against Japan 1941–1945*, and Keith Sainsbury's *Churchill and Roosevelt at War: The U.S.–U.K. Alliance and the Emerging Cold War, 1943–1946*. Robert A. C. Parker's *The Second World War* is an admirable overall survey, and, in *The Foreign Office and the Kremlin*, Graham Ross provides useful information.

There is also an immense amount of literature on the diplomatic history of the period between the world wars. Margaret Macmillan's *Peacemakers: The Paris Confer-*

ence of 1919 and Its Attempt to End War covers the Paris Peace Conference of 1919, as does Antony Lentin's *Lloyd George, Woodrow Wilson, and the Guilt of Germany: An Essay in the Pre-History of Appeasement*. A prime minister's perspective is given in David Lloyd George's *The Truth about the Peace Treaties* (2 volumes), and the important subject of the League of Nations is dealt with in Frederick S. Northedge's *The League of Nations: 1920–1946*. There are a multitude of studies about British appeasement policy, and among the best are Parker's *Chamberlain and Appeasement: British Policy and the Coming of the Second World War*, as well as his *Churchill and Appeasement*, and Charmley's *Chamberlain and the Lost Peace*. Parker's works are critical of appeasement, while Charmley takes on a revisionist proappeasement line. Steiner's *The Triumph of the Dark: European International History, 1933–1939* provides the essential European context. And an important study on Anglo–American relations during the period is Callum MacDonald's *The United States, Britain, and Appeasement*.

The largest single section of the bibliography is on the Cold War, a subject of immense complexity that subsumes the issue of Britain's membership of, and relations with, the European Union. This section includes such classic studies as Lewis Gaddis's *The Cold War*, Callum MacDonald's *Britain and the Korean War*, and Henry Pelling's *Britain and the Marshall Plan*. A neglected area of British Cold War policy can be found in Peter Neville's *Britain in Vietnam: Prelude to Disaster, 1945–1946*. The later period in Vietnam is dealt with by Sylvia Ellis in *Britain, America, and the Vietnam War*. General studies of the postwar period are provided by Corelli Barnett in *The Collapse of British Power* and Frederick S. Northedge in *Descent from Power: British Foreign Policy, 1945–1973*, and the important area of nuclear policy is examined by Ian Clark in *Nuclear Diplomacy and the Special Relationship: Britain's Deterrent and America, 1957–1962*. Outside of Europe, the Suez Crisis has found critical analysts of British policy in Scott Lucas's *Divided We Stand: Britain, the United States, and the Suez Crisis*, along with Keith Kyle's *Suez: Britain's End of Empire in the Middle East*. The problems related to dealing with the Soviet Union are addressed in Sir Curtis Keeble's *Britain and the Soviet Union, 1917–1989* and Bill Jones's *The Russia Complex: The British Labour Party and the Soviet Union*. These books should be read in parallel with Alan Bullock's *The Life and Times of Ernest Bevin, Volume II Ernest Bevin, Foreign Secretary, 1945–1951*. And Bevin's successor, Anthony Eden, has found a biographer in David Dutton, who wrote *Anthony Eden: A Life and Reputation*.

The literature on Britain's relationship with Europe since 1945 continues to mushroom. Important studies include Alan Milward's *The UK and the European Community, Volume I: The Rise and Fall of a National Strategy, 1945–1963*, Sean Greenwood's *Britain and European Integration since the Second World War*, and James Ellison's *Threatening Europe: Britain and the Creation of the European Community, 1955–1958*. The nuances of the British–European relationship are also traced in Hugo Young's *This Blessed Plot: Britain and Europe from Churchill to Blair* in a manner that is both interesting and entertaining. The memoirs of political leaders should be treated with caution, but Anthony Eden's *Full Circle* and Harold Macmillan's *Riding the Storm, 1956–1959* are worth a look. The key area of defense forms the subject of

Phillip Darby's *British Defence Policy: East of Suez, 1947–1968.* Those who wish to study the impact of the betrayal of British defense secrets should read Robert Cecil's *A Divided Life: A Biography of Donald Maclean.*

There are an increasing number of good biographies of diplomats. Donald Gillies's *Radical Diplomat: The Life of Archibald Clark Kerr, Lord Inverchapel, 1882–1951* is a superior example of the genre. Many British diplomats have produced their own memoirs and published diaries. Among the best are Lord Gladwyn's *The Memoirs of Lord Gladwyn* and Sir Nicholas Henderson's *Mandarin: The Diaries of an Ambassador, 1969–1982.*

The fifth section of the bibliography deals with the events and historical debates that took place during the period after the Cold War. A key area of debate has focused on Tony Blair's support for the U.S. invasion of Iraq, and Peter Riddell's *Hug Them Close: Blair, Clinton, Bush, and the "Special Relationship"* is essential reading for gaining an understanding of the Blair–Bush relationship. In *Blair's War*, John Kampfner addresses the issues surrounding liberal interventionism, while Brendan Simms's *Unfinest Hour: Britain and the Destruction of Bosnia* offers a critique of British policy during the wars in Yugoslavia in the 1990s.

The National Archives (formerly the Public Record Office) in Kew, London, holds the papers of British foreign secretaries, foreign official officials, and diplomats. Churchill College, Cambridge, is also an important archive for the papers of many important 20th-century figures, including Winston Churchill, Lord Halifax, Alfred Duff Cooper, and Sir Robert Vansittart. It contains some 5,000 files. Another useful source of information is the British Broadcasting Company (www.news.bbc.co.uk/1/hi/world/americas/1913522.stm), through both its websites and its written archive at Caversham Park, Reading. Additional information can be obtained on the British Embassy website in Washington, D.C. (www.britain-info.org). Likewise, the Foreign and Commonwealth Office has its own website (www.fco.gov.uk), as does the Royal Institution for International Affairs (Chatham House at www.chathamhouse.org), both in London.

II. GENERAL WORKS AND REFERENCE WORKS

Allen, Harry C. *Conflict and Concord: The Anglo–American Relationship since 1783.* New York: St. Martin's Press, 1960.

Anon. *Foreign Office, Diplomatic and Consular Sketches.* London: Allen, 1883.

Aster, Sidney. *The Making of the Second World War.* London: Andre Deutsch, 1972.

Barnett, Corelli. *The Collapse of British Power.* London: Eyre Methuen, 1964.

Bartlett, C. J. *British Foreign Policy in the Twentieth Century.* Basingstoke, England: Macmillan, 1989.

Baxter, Christopher, and Keith Hamilton. *The Permanent Under-Secretary of State: A Brief History of the Office and Its Holders.* History Notes, No. 15. London: FCO Historians, 2002.

Bell, Coral. *The Debatable Alliance. An Essay in Anglo–American Relations.* Oxford, U.K.: Oxford University Press, 1964.

Bullen, Roger, ed. *The Foreign Office, 1782–1982.* New York: University of America Press, 1984.

Charmley, John. *Splendid Isolation? Britain and the Balance of Power, 1874–1914.* London: Hodder & Stoughton, 1999.

Connell, John *"The Office": A Study of British Foreign Policy and Its Makers, 1919–1951.* London: Allan Wingate, 1958.

Cromwell, Valerie, and Zara Steiner. "The Foreign Office before 1914: A Study in Resistance." In Gillian Sutherland, ed., *Studies in the Growth of Nineteenth-Century Government.* London: Routledge, 1972.

Dockrill, Michael, and Brian McKercher. *Diplomacy and World Power: Studies in British Foreign Policy, 1890–1950.* Cambridge, U.K.: Cambridge University Press, 1996.

Edwards, Ruth Dudley. *True Brits: Inside the Foreign Office.* London: BBC Books, 1994.

Ellis, Sylvia. *Anglo–American Relations.* Lanham, Md.: Scarecrow Press, 2009.

Englander, David, ed. *Britain and America: Studies in Comparative History, 1760–1970.* New Haven, Conn.: Yale University Press, 1997.

Foreman, Susan. *From Palace to Power: An Illustrated History of Whitehall.* London: Sussex Academic Press, 1995.

Goldstein, Eric. *Winning the Peace: British Diplomatic Strategy, Peace Planning, and the Paris Peace Conference, 1916–1920.* Oxford, U.K.: Clarendon Press, 1991.

Hennessey, Peter. *The Prime Minister: The Office and Its Holders.* London: Allen Lane, 1995.

Hoare, James E. *Embassies in the East: The Story of the British and Their Embassies in China, Japan, and Korea from 1859 to the Present.* London: Curzon, 1999.

Hurd, Douglas. *Choose Your Weapons: The British Foreign Secretary, 200 Years of Argument, Success, and Failure.* London: Weidenfeld & Nicolson, 2010.

Jones, Raymond A. *The British Diplomatic Service, 1815–1914.* Gerrards Cross, England: Smythe, 1983.

Jordan, William M. *Great Britain, France, and the German Problem, 1919–1939.* Oxford, U.K.: Oxford University Press, 1943.

Kennedy, Paul. *The Realities behind Diplomacy: Background Influences on British External Policy, 1865–1980.* London: Fontana, 1981.

———. *The Rise and Fall of the Great Powers: Economic Change and Military Conflict from 1500 to 2000.* New York: Random House, 1987.

Louis, William Roger, and Hedley Bull, eds. *The Special Relationship: Anglo–American Relations since the Second World War.* New York: St. Martin's Press, 1974.

Maclean, Donald. *British Foreign Policy since Suez.* London: Hodder & Stoughton. 1970.

Maisel, M. E. *The Foreign Office and Foreign Policy.* Brighton, England: Sussex Academic Press, 1984.

Mayne, Richard. *In Victory Magnanimity, in Peace Goodwill: A History of Wilton Park.* London: Whitehall History, 2003.

Medlicott, William Norton. *British Foreign Policy since Versailles, 1919–1963.* London: Methuen, 1968.

Mihalkanin, Edward, ed. *American Statesmen: Secretaries of State from John Jay to Colin Powell*. Westport, Conn.: Greenwood Press, 2004.

Northedge, Frederick S. *The Troubled Giant: Great Britain among the Great Powers, 1919–1939*. London: G. Bell & Sons, 1966.

Platt, D. C. M. *Finance, Trade, and Politics: British Foreign Policy, 1815–1914*. Oxford, U.K.: Oxford University Press, 1968.

Porter, Bernard. *The Lion's Share: A Short History of British Imperialism, 1850–1983*. New York: Longman, 1983.

Renwick, Robin. *Fighting with Allies: Britain and America in Peace and War*. Basingstoke, England: Macmillan, 1996.

Reynolds, David. *Britannia Overruled: British Policy and World Power in the Twentieth Century*. London: Longman, 1991.

Saltzman, Stephanie. *Great Britain, Germany, and the Soviet Union: Rapallo and After, 1922–1934*. London: Royal Historical Society, 2003.

Seldon, Anthony. *The Foreign Office: An Illustrated History of the Place and Its People*. London: HarperCollins, 2000.

Smith, Michael, Steve Smith, and White, Brian, eds. *British Foreign Policy: Tradition, Change, and Transformation*. London: Unwin Hyman, 1988.

Strange, Susan. *Sterling and British Foreign Policy*. Oxford, U.K.: Oxford University Press, 1971.

Toplis, Ian. *The Foreign Office: An Architectural History*. London: Mansell, 1987.

Tsoukalis, Loukes, (ed.), *The European Community: Past, Present and Future*. Oxford: Blackwell, 1983.

Wallace, William. *The Foreign Policy Process in Britain*. London: Allen & Unwin/ Royal Institute of International Affairs, 1975.

Wallace, William, and Christopher Tugendhat. *Options for British Foreign Policy in the 1990s*. London: Routledge & Kegan Paul/Royal Institute of International Affairs, 1988.

Young, Hugo. *This Blessed Plot: Britain and Europe from Churchill to Blair*. London: Macmillan, 1998.

III. BRITISH FOREIGN POLICY IN THE 19TH CENTURY

Bew, John. *Castlereagh: Enlightenment, War, and Tyranny*. London: Quercus Publishing, 2011.

Blake, Robert. *Disraeli*. London: Eyre & Spottiswoode, 1966.

Brown, David, and Miles Taylor, eds. *Palmerston Studies*. Southhampton, U.K.: University of Southampton, Hartley Institute, 2007.

Cecil, Algernon. *British Foreign Secretaries, 1807–1916: Studies in Personality and Policy*. London: G. Bell & Sons, 1927.

Chamberlain, Muriel E. *Lord Aberdeen: A Political Biography*. New York: Longman, 1983.

Chambers, James. *Palmerston: "The People's Darling."* London: John Murray, 2004.

Charmley, John. *Splendid Isolation? Britain and the Balance of Power, 1874–1914.* London: Hodder & Stoughton, 1999.

Cook, Adrian. *The Alabama Claims: American Politics and Anglo–American Relations, 1865–1872.* Ithaca, N.Y: Cornell University Press, 1975.

Dixon, Peter. *Canning, Politician and Statesman.* London: Weidenfeld & Nicolson, 1976.

Hernon, Joseph. "British Sympathies in the American Civil War: A Reconsideration." *Journal of Southern History*, 33, no. 3 (1967): 357–67.

Hinde, Wendy. *Castlereagh.* London: Collins, 1981.

Hurd, Douglas. *The Arrow War: An Anglo–Chinese Confusion, 1856–1860.* London: Collins, 1967.

———. *Choose Your Weapons: The British Foreign Secretary, 200 Years of Argument, Success, and Failure.* London: Weidenfeld & Nicolson, 2010.

Jones, Wilbur D. "The British Conservatives and the American Civil War." *American Historical Review*, 58, no. 3 (1953): 527–43.

Kennedy, Paul. *The Realities behind Diplomacy: Background Influences on British External Policy, 1865–1980.* London: Fontana, 1981.

Kissinger, Henry. *A World Restored: Metternich, Castlereagh, and the Problems of Peace, 1812–1822.* Boston: Houghton Mifflin, 1957.

Longford, Elizabeth. *Victoria R.I.* London: Weidenfeld & Nicolson, 1964.

Lowe, Cedric J. *The Reluctant Imperialists: British Foreign Policy, 1878–1902.* London: Routledge and Kegan Paul, 1967.

Magnus, Philip. *Gladstone: A Biography.* London: John Murray, 1954.

Middleton, Charles R. *The Administration of British Foreign Policy, 1782–1846.* Durham, N.C.: Duke University Press, 1977.

Munch-Peterson, Thomas. *Defying Napoleon: How Britain Bombarded Copenhagen and Seized the Danish Fleet in 1807.* Stroud, England: Sutton Publishing, 2007.

Porter, Bernard. *The Lion's Share: A Short History of British Imperialism, 1850–1983.* London: Longman, 1975.

Ridley, Jasper. *Lord Palmerston.* London: Constable, 1970.

Roberts, Andrew. *Salisbury: A Political Biography.* London: Routledge, 2001.

Steiner, Zara. *The Foreign Office and Foreign Policy, 1898–1914.* Cambridge, U.K.: Cambridge University Press, 1969.

Taylor, Alan J. P. *The Struggle for Mastery in Europe, 1848–1918.* Oxford, U.K.: Oxford University Press, 1971.

Temperley, Harold. *The Foreign Policy of Canning, 1822–1827: England, the Neo-Holy Alliance, and the New World.* London: Cass, 1966.

Wilson, Keith. *British Foreign Secretaries and Foreign Policy from the Crimean War to the First World War.* London: Croom Helm, 1987.

A. Britain and the Origins of World War I

Conwell-Evans, Thomas P. *Foreign Policy from a Back Bench, 1904–1918.* Oxford, U.K.: Oxford University Press, 1932.

Corp, Edward T. "Sir William Tyrell: The Eminence Grise of the British Foreign Office." *Historical Journal*, 25, no. 4 (1982): 697–708.

Cromwell, Valerie, and Zara Steiner. "The Foreign Office before 1914: A Study in Resistance." In Gillian, Sutherland ed., *Studies in the Growth of Nineteenth-Century Government*. London: Routledge, 1972.

Crowe, Sibyl E., and Edward T. Corp. *Our Ablest Public Servant, Sir Eyre Crowe, 1864–1925*. Braunton, England: Merlin, 1993.

Ferguson, Niall. *The Pity of War*. London: Penguin, 1999.

Gooch, George P., and H. M. V. Temperley, eds. *British Documents on the Origins of the War, 1898–1914*. London: Her Majesty's Stationary Office, 1927–1938.

Halpern, Paul G. *The Mediterranean Naval Situation, 1908–1914*. Cambridge, Mass.: Harvard University Press, 1971.

Holger, Herwig, and Richard Hamilton, eds. *The Origins of World War I*. Cambridge, U.K.: Cambridge University Press, 2003.

Kennedy, Paul. *The Rise of Anglo–German Antagonism, 1860–1914*. London: Allen & Unwin, 1980.

McClean, David. *Britain and Her Buffer State: The Collapse of the Persian Empire, 1890–1914*. London: Royal Historical Society, 2002.

Monger, George W. *The End of Isolation: British Foreign Policy, 1900–1907*. London: Nelson, 1963.

Mulligan, William. "From Case to Narrative: The Marquis of Lansdowne, Sir E. Grey, and the Threat from Germany, 1900–1906." *International History Review*, 30, no. 2 (2008): 273–302.

Neilson, Keith. *Britain and the Last Tsar: British Policy and Russia, 1894–1914*. Oxford, U.K.: Clarendon Press, 1995.

Otte, Thomas G. "Almost a Law of Nature? Sir Edward Grey, the Foreign Office, and the Balance of Power in Europe, 1905–1912." In Erik Goldstein and Brian McKercher, eds., *Power and Stability: British Foreign Policy, 1865–1965*. London: Cass, 2003.

——. "The Winston of Germany: The British Foreign Policy Elite and the Last German Emperor." *Canadian Journal of History*, 36, no. 4 (2001): 471–504.

Robbins, Keith. "The Foreign Secretary, the Cabinet, Parliament, and the Parties." In Francis H. Hinsley, ed., *British Foreign Policy under Sir Edward Grey*. Cambridge, U.K.: Cambridge University Press, 1977.

——. *Sir Edward Grey: A Biography of Lord Grey of Fallodon*. London: Cassell, 1971.

Siegel, Jennifer. *Endgame: Britain, Russia, and the Final Struggle for Central Asia*. London: I. B. Taurus, 2002.

Steiner, Zara. *Britain and the Origins of the First World War*. London: Macmillan, 1977.

——. *The Foreign Office and Foreign Policy, 1898–1914*. Cambridge, U.K.: Cambridge University Press, 1969.

IV. BRITISH FOREIGN POLICY IN THE 20TH CENTURY

Adams, Leskyn. *Brothers across the Ocean: British Foreign Policy and the Origins of the Anglo–American "Special Relationship," 1900–1905*. London: I. B. Taurus, 2005.

Andrew, Christopher. *The Making of the British Intelligence Community*. London: Heinemann, 1985.

Aster, Sidney. *1939: The Making of the Second World War*. London: Andre Deutsch, 1973.

Bobbitt, Philip. *The Shield of Achilles: War, Peace, and the Course of History*. London: Penguin, 2003.

Burk, Kathleen. "The Lineaments of Foreign Policy: The United States and a 'New World Order,' 1919–1939." *Journal of American Studies*, 26, no. 3 (December 1992): 377–92.

Carley, Michael. *1939: The Alliance That Never Was and the Coming of World War II*. London: Stratus, 1999.

Charmley, John. *Chamberlain and the Lost Peace*. London: Hodder & Stoughton, 1989.

———. *Churchill: The End of Glory*. London: Hodder & Stoughton, 1996.

Dilks, David, ed. *The Diaries of Sir Alexander Cadogan, 1938–1945*. London: Cassell, 1971.

Dockrill, Michael. *British Establishment Perspectives on France, 1936–1940*. Basingstoke, England: Macmillan, 1999.

Dutton, David. *Anthony Eden: A Life and Reputation*. London: Hodder & Stoughton, 1997.

———. *Austen Chamberlain, Gentleman in Politics*. Bolton, England: Ross Anderson Publications, 1985.

———. *Neville Chamberlain*. London: Arnold, 2001.

Eden, Anthony. *Facing the Dictators*. London: Cassell, 1962.

Emmerson, James Thomas. *The Rhineland Crisis, 7 March 1936*. London: Temple Smith, 1977.

Feiling, Keith. *Neville Chamberlain*. London: Macmillan, 1946.

Gilbert, Martin. *The Roots of Appeasement*. London: Weidenfeld & Nicolson, 1966.

Gilbert, Martin, and Richard Gott. *The Appeasers*. London: Weidenfeld & Nicolson, 1963.

Gilmour, David. *Curzon*. London: John Murray, 1994.

Goldstein, Erik. "The Evolution of British Diplomacy and Strategy for the Washington Conference." *Diplomacy and Statecraft*, 4, no. 3 (November 1993): 35–39.

Johnson, Gaynor, ed. *Our Man in Berlin: The Diary of Sir Eric Phipps, 1933–1937*. Basingstoke, England: Palgrave, 2008.

Kennedy, Greg. "Neville Chamberlain and Strategic Relations with the United States during his Chancellorship." *Diplomacy and Statecraft*, 13, no. 1 (March 2002): 95–120.

Kennedy, Paul. "The Tradition of Appeasement in British Foreign Policy, 1865–1935." *British Journal of International Studies*, 2, no. 3 (October 1976): 195–215.

Kitching, Caroline. *Britain and the Problem of International Disarmament, 1919–1934*. London: Routledge, 1999.

Lee, Bradford A. *Britain and the Sino-Japanese War, 1937–1939: A Study in the Dilemmas of British Decline*. Palo Alto, Calif.: Stanford University Press, 1973.

Lentin, Anthony. *Lloyd George and the Lost Peace: From Versailles to Hitler, 1919–1940*. Basingstoke: Palgrave, 2001.

———. *Lloyd George, Woodrow Wilson, and the Guilt of Germany: An Essay in the Pre-History of Appeasement*. Baton Rouge: Louisiana State University, 1984.

Lloyd George, David. *The Truth about the Peace Treaties*. 2 vols. London: Gollanz, 1938.

MacDonald, Callum. *The United States, Britain, and Appeasement*. Basingstoke: Palgrave, 1981.

Macmillan, Margaret. *Peacemakers: The Paris Conference of 1919 and Its Attempt to End War*. London: John Murray, 2001.

Marquand, David. *Ramsey MacDonald*. London: Richard Cohen, 1997.

McKercher, Brian. *Anglo–American Relations in the 1920s: The Struggle for Supremacy*. Edmonton: University of Alberta Press, 1991.

Namier, Lewis. *Diplomatic Prelude*. London: Macmillan, 1948.

Neville, Peter. *Appeasing Hitler: The Diplomacy of Sir Nevile Henderson, 1937–1939*. Basingstoke, England: Palgrave, 2000.

———. "The Foreign Office and Britain's Ambassadors to Berlin, 1933–1939." *Contemporary British History*, 18, no. 3 (Autumn 2004): 110–29.

———. *Hitler and Appeasement: The British Attempt to Prevent the Second World War*. London: Continuum, 2005.

———. "Sir Alexander Cadogan and Lord Halifax's 'Damascus Road' Conversion over the Godesberg Terms, 1938." *Diplomacy and Statecraft*, 11, no. 3 (November 2000): 81–91.

Nicolson, Harold. *Peacemaking, 1919*. London: Methuen, 1964.

Northedge, Frederick S. *The League of Nations, 1920–1946*. Leicester, England: Leicester University Press, 1986.

———. *The Troubled Giant*. London: G. Bell & Sons, 1966.

Offner, Arnold. "Appeasement Revisited: The United States, Great Britain, and Germany, 1933–1940." *Journal of American History*, 62, no. 2 (September 1977): 384–93.

Parker, Robert A. C. *Chamberlain and Appeasement: British Policy and the Coming of the Second World War*. Basingstoke, England: Macmillan, 1996.

———. *Churchill and Appeasement: Could Churchill Have Prevented the Second World War?* Basingstoke, England: Macmillan, 2000.

———. "The Pound Sterling, the American Treasury, and British Preparations for War, 1938–1939." *English Historical Review*, 98, no. 387 (April 1983): 261–79.

Reynolds, David. *Britannia Overruled: British Policy and World Power in the 20th Century*. London: Longman, 1991.

Robbins, Keith. *Appeasement*. Oxford, U.K.: Blackwell, 1988.

———. *Munich, 1938*. London: Cassell, 1968.

Roberts, Andrew. *"The Holy Fox": A Life of Lord Halifax*. London: Weidenfeld & Nicolson, 1991.

Rose, Norman. *Churchill: An Unruly Life*. London: Simon & Schuster, 1994.

———. *Vansittart: Study of a Diplomat*. London: Heinemann, 1978.

Rostow, Nicholas. *Anglo–French Relations, 1934–1936*. London: Macmillan, 1984.

Schroeder, Paul W. "Munich and the British Tradition." *Historical Journal*, 19, no. 1 (1976): 223–43.

Smetana, Vit. *In the Shadow of Munich: British Policy towards Czechoslovakia from the Establishment to the Renunciation of the Munich Agreement (1938–1942)*. Prague, Czech Republic: Karolinum Press, 2008.

Steiner, Zara. *The Triumph of the Dark: European International History, 1933–1939*. Oxford, U.K.: Oxford University Press, 2011.

Strang, Lord. *Home and Abroad*. London: Andre Deutsch, 1956.

Taylor, Alan John Percivale. *The Origins of the Second World War*. London: Hamish Hamilton, 1961.

Thomas, Martin. *Britain, France, and Appeasement: Anglo–French Relations in the Popular Front Era*. New York: Berg, 1996.

Thorpe, D. R. (Richard). *Eden: The Life and Times of Anthony Eden, First Earl of Avon*. London: Chatto & Windus, 2003.

Templewood, Lord. *Nine Troubled Years*. London: Collins, 1954.

Vansittart, Robert. *The Mist Procession*. London: Hutchinson, 1958.

Vysny, Paul. *The Runciman Mission to Czechoslovakia, 1938: Prelude to Munich*. London: Palgrave, 2003.

Wark, Wesley. *The Ultimate Enemy: British Intelligence and Nazi Germany*. Oxford, U.K.: Oxford University Press, 1986.

Watt, Donald Cameron. *How War Came: The Immediate Origins of the Second World War, 1938–1939*. London: Heinemann, 1989.

———. *Personalities and Politics*. London: Longman, 1965.

———. *Succeeding John Bull: America in Britain's Place, 1900–1975*. Cambridge, U.K.: Cambridge University Press, 1984.

Williamson, Philip. *Stanley Baldwin*. Cambridge, U.K.: Cambridge University Press, 1989.

A. World War I, 1914–1918

Bunselmeyer, Robert. *The Cost of War, 1914–1919: British Economic War Aims and the Origins of Reparations*. London: Archon Books, 1975.

Burk, Kathleen. *Britain, America, and the Sinews of War, 1914–1918*. Boston: Allen & Unwin, 1985.

Ferguson, Niall. *The Pity of War*. London: Penguin, 1999.

Goldstein, Erik. *Winning the Peace: British Diplomatic Peace Planning and the Paris Peace Conference, 1916–1919*. Oxford, U.K.: Oxford University Press, 1991.

Grigg, John. *Lloyd George: War Leader*. London: Allen Lane, 2002.

Howard, Michael. *War and the Liberal Conscience*. Oxford, U.K.: Oxford University Press, 1981.

Nelson, Harold I. *Land and Power: British and Allied Policy on Germany's Frontiers, 1916–1919.* London: Routledge and Kegan Paul, 1963.

Stevenson, David. "Britain, France, and the Origins of German Disarmament, 1916–1919." *Journal of Strategic Studies,* 29, no. 2 (2006): 195–224.

Terraine, John. *The First Word War.* London: Secker & Warburg, 1983.

Vansittart, Robert. *The Mist Procession.* London: Hutchinson, 1958.

B. World War II, 1939–1945

Aldrich, Richard J. *Intelligence and the War against Japan: Britain, America, and the Politics of Secret Service.* Cambridge, U.K.: Cambridge University Press, 2000.

———. *The Key to the South: Britain, the United States, and Thailand during the Approach of the Pacific War, 1929–1942.* Kuala Lumpur, Malaysia: Oxford University Press, 1993.

Best, Anthony. *Britain, Japan, and Pearl Harbor: Avoiding War in East Asia, 1936–1941.* London: Routledge, 1995.

Bond, Brian. *France and Belgium, 1939–1940.* London: Poynter Davis, 1975.

Bower, Tom. *Blind Eye to Murder: Britain, America, and the Purging of Nazi Germany.* London: Andre Deutsch, 1991.

Breitman, Richard. *Official Secrets: What the Nazis Planned, What the British and Americans Knew.* London: Allen Lane/Penguin Press, 1999.

Charmley, John. *Churchill's Grand Alliance: The Anglo–American Special Relationship, 1940–1957.* London: Hodder & Stoughton, 1995.

Churchill, Winston. *The Hinge of Fate.* London: Cassell, 1951.

Clifford, Nicholas R. *Retreat from China: British Policy in the Far East, 1937–1941.* London: Longman, 1967.

Cruickshank, Charles. *SOE in the Far East: The Official History.* Oxford, U.K.: Oxford University Press, 1983.

Dalton, Hugh. *The Fateful Years, 1931–1945.* London: Muller, 1957.

Davies, John Paton. *Dragon by the Tail: American, British, Japanese, and Russian Encounters with China and One Another.* New York: W. W. Norton, 1972.

Dennis, Peter. *Troubled Days of Peace: Mountbatten and South East Asia, 1945–1946.* Manchester, U.K.: Manchester University Press, 1987.

Dixon, Piers. *Double Diplomat: The Life of Sir Pierson Dixon.* London: Hutchinson, 1968.

Elphick, Peter. *Singapore: The Pregnable Fortress.* London: Hodder & Stoughton, 1995.

Feis, Herbert. *Churchill, Roosevelt, and Stalin.* Princeton, N.J.: Princeton University Press, 1957.

Gilbert, Martin. *Finest Hour: Winston S. Churchill, 1939–1941.* London: Cassell, 1983.

Gillies, Donald. *Radical Diplomat: The Life of Archibald Clark Kerr, Lord Inverchapel, 1882–1951.* New York: I. B. Taurus, 1999.

Halifax, Lord. *Fullness of Days.* London: Collins, 1957.

Harriman, W. A., and E. Abel. *Special Envoy to Churchill and Stalin*. London: Hutchinson, 1976.

Harvey, John, ed. *The War Diaries of Oliver Harvey, 1941–1945*. London: Collins, 1978.

Hauner, Milan. *India in Axis Strategy: Germany, Japan, and Indian Nationalists in the Second World War*. Stuggart, Baden-Württemberg. Germany: Klett-Cotta, 1981.

Hayter, William. *A Double Life*. London: Hamish Hamilton, 1974.

Jackson, Julian. *The Fall of France: The Nazi Invasion of 1940*. Oxford, U.K.: Oxford University Press, 2003.

Kitchen, Martin. *British Policy towards the Soviet Union during the Second World War*. Basingstoke, England: Macmillan, 1986.

Lamb, Richard. *Churchill as War Leader: Right or Wrong?* London: Bloomsbury, 1991.

Lash, Joseph. P. *Roosevelt and Churchill, 1939–1941*. London: Andre Deutsch, 1977.

Lawler, Sheila. *Churchill and the Politics of War, 1940–1941*. Cambridge, U.K.: Cambridge University Press, 1994.

Liddell Hart, Basil. *Defense of the West*. London: Cassell, 1950.

Louis, William Roger. *Imperialism at Bay: The United States and the Decolonization of the British Empire, 1941–1945*. Oxford, U.K.: Clarendon Press, 1977.

———. *In the Name of God, Go! Leo Amery and the British Empire in the Age of Churchill*. New York: W. W. Norton, 1992.

Macmillan, Harold. *War Diaries: The Mediterranean, 1943–1945*. Basingstoke: Macmillan, 1984.

MacNeal, W. H. *America, Britain, and Russia, 1941–1946*. London: Oxford University Press, 1953.

Overy, Richard. *Russia's War*. London: Allen Lane/Penguin Press, 1999.

———. *Why the Allies Won*. New York: W. W. Norton, 1997.

Parker, Robert A. C. "Britain, France, and Scandinavia in the 'Phoney War.'" *Scandinavian Journal of History*, no. 2 (1977): 29–51.

———. *The Second World War*. Oxford, U.K.: Oxford University Press, 1989.

Reynolds, David. "Churchill and the British 'Decision' to Fight on in 1940: Right Policy, Wrong Reasons." In Richard Langhorne, ed., *Diplomacy and Intelligence in the Second World War*. Cambridge, U.K.: Cambridge University Press, 1985.

———. "Churchill: The Appeaser? Between Hitler, Roosevelt, and Stalin in World War II." In M. Dockrill and B. McKercher, eds., *Diplomacy and World Power: Studies in British Foreign Policy, 1890–1950*. Cambridge, U.K.: Cambridge University Press, 1996.

Ross, Graham. *The Foreign Office and the Kremlin*. Cambridge, U.K.: Cambridge University Press, 1984.

———. "Operation Bracelet: Churchill in Moscow, 1942." In D. Dilks, ed., *Retreat from Power, Vol. 2*. London: Macmillan, 1981.

Rothwell, Victor. *Britain and the Cold War, 1941–1947*. London: Jonathan Cape, 1982.

Sainsbury, Keith. *Churchill and Roosevelt at War: The U.S.–U.K. Alliance and the Emerging Cold War, 1943–1946*. Cambridge, U.K.: Cambridge University Press, 1987.

Skidelsky, Robert. *John Maynard Keynes. Vol 3: Fighting For Britain, 1937–1946*. London: Macmillan, 2000.

Spears, Edward Louis. *Assignment to Catastrophe*. London: Heinemann, 1954.

Stafford, David. *Roosevelt and Churchill: Men of Secrets*. London: Little Brown, 1999.

Tarling, Nicholas. *The Fall of British Imperialism in South East Asia*. Kuala Lumpur, Malaysia: Oxford University Press, 1992.

Thorne, Christopher. *Allies of a Kind: The United States, Britain, and the War against Japan, 1941–1945*. New York: Oxford University Press, 1979.

Watts, Franklin, ed. *Voices of History, 1943–1944: Speeches and Papers of Roosevelt, Churchill, Stalin, Chiang, and Other Leaders Delivered in 1943*. New York: Gramercy, 1944.

Woodward, Sir E. Llewellyn. *British Foreign Policy in the Second World War*. 4 vols. London: Her Majesty's Stationery Office, 1970–1976.

Ziegler, Philip. *Mountbatten*. London: Collins, 1985.

C. The Cold War, 1945–1991

Aldous, Richard, and Sabine Lee, eds. *Harold Macmillan and Britain's World Role*. Basingstoke, England: Macmillan, 1995.

Aldrich, Richard. "British Intelligence and the Anglo–American 'Special Relationship' during the Cold War." *Review of International Studies*, 24, no.1 (1998): 331–51.

Andrew, Christopher, and Oleg Gordievsky. *The KGB: The Inside Story*. London: Hodder & Stoughton, 1991.

Ashton, Nigel. *Eisenhower, Macmillan, and the Problem of Nasser: Anglo–American Relations and Arab Nationalism, 1955–1959*. Basingstoke, England: Macmillan, 1996.

———. *Kennedy, Macmillan, and the Cold War: The Irony of Interdependence*. Basingstoke, England: Palgrave Macmillan, 2002.

———. "A Rear Guard Action: Harold Macmillan and the Making of British Foreign Policy, 1957–1962." In T. G. Otte, ed., *From Pitt to Thatcher*. Basingstoke, England: Palgrave, 2002.

Ball, Simon. "Military Nuclear Relations between the United States and Great Britain under the Terms of the McMahon Act, 1946–1958." *Historical Journal*, 38, no. 2 (1995): 439–54.

Barker, Elizabeth. *Britain between the Superpowers, 1945–1950*. London: Macmillan, 1953.

Barnett, Corelli. *The Collapse of British Power*. London: Eyre Methuen, 1964.

———. *The Verdict of Peace: Britain between Her Yesterday and the Future*. London: Pan, 2002.

Baylis, George. *In My Way*. Harmondsworth, England: Penguin, 1971.

Beckett, Ian. "Robert Thompson and the British Advisory Mission to South Vietnam, 1961–1965." *Small Wars and Insurgencies*, 8, no. 3 (October 1997): 43–44.

Bullen, Roger, M. Pelly, and H. J. Yasamee, eds. *Documents on British Policy Overseas*. London: Her Majesty's Stationery Office, 1984–2011.

Bullock, Alan. *The Life and Times of Ernest Bevin, Volume II Ernest Bevin, Foreign Secretary, 1945–1951*. London: Heinemann, 1983.

Cable, James. *The Geneva Conference on Indochina*. Basingstoke, England: Macmillan, 1986.

Cain, Peter, and Anthony Hopkins. *British Imperialism: Crisis and Decolonization*. London: Longman, 1993.

Callahan, Raymond. *Churchill: Retreat from Empire*. Wilmington, Del.: Scholarly Resources, 1984.

Carrington, Lord Peter. *Reflect on Things Past*. London: Collins, 1988.

Catterall, Peter, ed. *The Macmillan Diaries, 1950–1957*. Basingstoke, England: Macmillan, 2003.

Cecil, Robert. *A Divided Life: A Biography of Donald Maclean*. London: Bodley Head, 1988.

Charmley, John. *Duff Cooper, the Authorized Biography*. London: Weidenfeld & Nicolson, 1986.

Clark, Ian. *Nuclear Diplomacy and the Special Relationship: Britain's Deterrent and America, 1957–1962*. Oxford, U.K.: Clarendon Press, 1994.

Cloak, John. *Templer: Tiger of Malaya*. London: Harrap, 1985.

Croft, Stuart. *The End of Superpower: British Foreign Office Conceptions of a Changing World, 1945–1951*. Aldershot, England: Dartmouth, 1994.

Darby, Phillip. *British Defense Policy: East of Suez, 1947–1968*. Oxford, U.K.: Oxford University Press, 1976.

Deighton, Ann, ed. *Britain and the First Cold War*. London: Macmillan, 1990.

Dockrill, Michael. "Restoring the Special Relationship: The Bermuda and Washington Conferences, 1957." In D. Richardson and G. Stone, eds., *Decisions and Diplomacy: Essays in Twentieth-Century International History*. London: Routledge, 1995.

Eden, Anthony. *Full Circle*. London: Cassell, 1960.

Ellis, Sylvia. *Britain, America, and the Vietnam War*. Westport, Conn.: Praeger, 2004.

Ellison, James. *Threatening Europe: Britain and the Creation of the European Community, 1955–1958*. New York: St. Martin's Press, 2000.

Fish, S. "After Stalin's Death: The Anglo–American Debate over a New Cold War." *Diplomatic History*, 10, no. 4 (Fall 1996): 333–56.

Foot, Michael. *Aneurin Bevan: A Biography, Vol. II, 1945–1960*. London: MacGibbon & Kee, 1962.

Frankel, Joseph. *British Foreign Policy, 1945–1973*. Oxford, U.K.: Oxford University Press, 1973.

Frazier, Robert. *Anglo–American Relations with Greece: The Coming of the Cold War*. New York: St. Martin's Press, 1991.

Gaddis, Lewis. *The Cold War*. London: Allen Lane, 2006.

George, Stephen. *An Awkward Partner: Britain and the European Communities*. London: Oxford University Press, 1990.

Gladwyn, Lord. *The Memoirs of Lord Gladwyn*. London: Weidenfeld & Nicolson, 1972.

Good, Robert. *The International Policies of the Rhodesian Rebellion*. London: Faber, 1973.

Gowland, David, and Arthur Turner. *Reluctant Europeans: Britain and European Integration, 1945–1998*. London: Longman, 2000.

Greenwood, Sean. *Britain and the Cold War, 1945–1991*. Basingstoke, England: Macmillan, 2000.

———. *Britain and European Integration since the Second World War*. Manchester, England: Manchester University Press, 1996.

———. "Ernest Bevin, France, and Western Union." *European History Quarterly*, 14 (1984): 319–37.

Hamilton, Keith. "Britain, France, and America's Year of Europe, 1973." *Diplomacy and Statecraft*, 17, no. 4 (December 2006): 1–17.

Harris, Kenneth. *Attlee*. London: Weidenfeld & Nicolson, 1962.

Hathaway, Robert M. *Great Britain and the United States: Special Relations since World War II*. Boston: Twayne, 1990.

Healey, Dennis. *The Times of My Life*. London: Michael Joseph, 1989.

Henderson, Sir Nicolas. *Mandarin: The Diaries of an Ambassador, 1969–1982*. London: Weidenfeld & Nicolson, 1994.

Hennessey, Peter. *Never Again: Britain, 1945–1951*. London: Vintage, 1993.

Hopkins, Michael. "Worlds Apart: The British Embassy in Moscow and the Search for East-West Understanding." *Contemporary British History*, 14, no. 3 (Autumn 2000): 131–48.

Horne, Alistair. *Macmillan, 1957–1986: Volume II of the Official Biography*. London: Macmillan, 1989.

Jones, Bill. *The Russia Complex: The British Labour Party and the Soviet Union*. Manchester, England: Manchester University Press, 1978.

Jones, Matthew. "Anglo–American Relations after Suez: The Rise and Decline of the Working Group Experiment and the French Challenge to NATO, 1957–1959." *Diplomacy and Statecraft*, 14, no. 1 (March 2003): 49–79.

Keeble, Sir Curtis. *Britain and the Soviet Union, 1917–1989*. London: Macmillan, 1990.

Kelly, Saul. *Cold War in the Desert: Britain, the United States, and the Italian Colonies, 1945–1952*. Basingstoke, England: Palgrave, 2002.

Kitzinger, Uwe W. *The Second Try: Labour and the EEC*. Oxford, U.K.: Pergamon Press, 1968.

Krug, Mark M. *Aneurin Bevan, Cautious Rebel*. New York: Yoseloff, 1961.

Kyle, Keith. *Suez: Britain's End of Empire in the Middle East*. London: I. B. Taurus, 2002.

Leeper, Sir Reginald. *When Greek Meets Greek*. London: Chatto & Windus, 1950.

Lord, Christopher. *British Entry into the European Community under the Heath Government*. Aldershot, England: Dartmouth, 1993.

Louis, William Roger. "The Dissolution of the British Empire in the Era of Vietnam." *American Historical Review*, 107, no. 1 (February 2002): 1–25.

Lucas, Scott. *Divided We Stand: Britain, the United States, and the Suez Crisis*. London: Sceptre, 1996.

MacDonald, Callum. *Britain and the Korean War*. Oxford, U.K.: Basil Blackwell, 1990.

Macmillan, Harold. *Pointing the Way, 1959–1961*. London: Macmillan, 1972.

———. *Riding the Storm, 1956–1959*. London: Macmillan, 1971.

Maeur, Victor. "Harold Macmillan and the Deadline Crisis over Berlin." *Twentieth Century British History*, 9, no. 1 (March 1998): 54–85.

Milward, Alan. *The UK and the European Community, Volume I: The Rise and Fall of a National Strategy, 1945–1963*. London: Frank Cass, 2002.

Moore, Robin James. *Escape from Empire: The Attlee Government and the Indian Problem*. Oxford, U.K.: Oxford University Press, 1983.

Moorhouse, Geoffrey. *The Diplomats*. London: Jonathan Cape, 1977.

Morgan, Kenneth. *Labour in Power, 1945–1951*. Oxford, U.K.: Pergamon, 1968.

Morrison, Herbert. *Autobiography*. London: Odhams, 1960.

Murray, Donette. *Kennedy, Macmillan, and Nuclear Weapons*. New York: St. Martin's Press, 2000.

Myers, Frank. "Conscription and the Politics of Military Strategy in the Attlee Government." *Journal of Strategic Studies*, 7 (1984): 55–73.

Neville, Peter. *Britain in Vietnam: Prelude to Disaster, 1945–1946*. London: Routledge, 2007.

Nicolson, Harold. *The Diaries and Letters of Harold Nicolson, 1945–1962*. London: Collins, 1968.

Northedge, Frederick S. *Descent from Power: British Foreign Policy, 1945–1973*. London: Allen & Unwin, 1974.

Nunnerly, David. *President Kennedy and Britain*. London: Bodley Head, 1972.

O'Malley, Sir Owen. *The Phantom Caravan*. London: John Murray, 1953.

Owen, David. *Balkan Odyssey*. London: Gollanez, 1995.

———. *Time to Declare*. London: John Murray, 1991.

Pelling, Henry. *Britain and the Marshall Plan*. Basingstoke, England: Macmillan, 1988.

Philby, Kim. *My Silent War*. London: MacGibbon & Kee, 1968.

Phillips, Horace. *Envoy Extraordinary: A Most Unlikely Ambassador*. London: Radcliffe, 1995.

Pimlott, Ben. *Harold Wilson*. London: HarperCollins, 1992.

———. *Hugh Dalton*. Basingstoke, England: Macmillan, 1985.

Pointing, Clive. *Breach of Promise: Labour in Power, 1964–1970*. London: Penguin, 1990.

Rendel, George. *The Sword and the Olive: Recollections of Diplomacy and the Foreign Office, 1913–1954*. London: John Murray, 1957.

Reynolds, David. "Eden the Diplomatist, 1931–1956: Suezide of a Statesman?" *History*, 74, no. 12 (1989): 64–84.

Rhodes, James R. *Anthony Eden*. London: Weidenfeld & Nicolson, 1986.

Roberts, Andrew. *Eminent Churchillians*. London: Weidenfeld & Nicolson, 1994.

Roberts, Sir Frank. *Dealing with Dictators: The Destruction and Revival of Europe*. London: Weidenfeld & Nicolson, 1994.

Ruane, Kevin. "Containing America: Aspects of British Foreign Policy and the Cold War in S.E. Asia." *Diplomacy and Statecraft*, 7, no. 1 (March 1996): 143–62.

——. *The Rise and Fall of the European Defence Community: Anglo–American Relations and the Crisis of European Defence, 1950–1955*. London: Macmillan, 2000.

Saville, John. *The Politics of Continuity: British Foreign Policy and the Labour Government, 1945–1946*. London: Verso, 1998.

Schrafstetter, Susanna, and Stephen Twigge. "Trick or Truth? The British ANF Proposal, West Germany, and U.S. Nonproliferation Policy." *Diplomacy and Statecraft*, 11, no. 2 (July 2000): 161–84.

Scott, David. *Three Years as British Ambassador in South Africa*. Braamfontein, South Africa: Institute of International Affairs, South Africa, 1980.

Smith, Geoffrey. *Reagan and Thatcher*. London: Bodley Head, 1990.

Smith, Tim O. "Britain and Cambodia, September 1945–November 1946: A Reappraisal." *Diplomacy and Statecraft*, 17, no. 1 (March 2006): 73–91.

Springall, John. "British Military Rule of Singapore, 1945–1946." *Journal of Contemporary History*, 36, no. 4 (October 2001): 636–52.

——. "Kicking Out the Viet Minh: How Britain Allowed France to Reoccupy South Vietnam, 1945–1946." *Journal of Contemporary History*, 40, no. 1 (January 2005): 115–30.

Taylor, Richard. *Against the Bomb: The British Peace Movement*. Cambridge, U.K.: Cambridge University Press, 1998.

Thorne, Christopher. "Indochina and Anglo–American Relations." *Pacific History Review*, 45, no. 1 (February 1976): 73–96.

Tratt, Jacqueline. *The Macmillan Government and Europe*. Basingstoke, England: Macmillan, 1996.

Trevelyan, Humphrey. *Worlds Apart*. London: Macmillan, 1971.

Truman, Harry S. *Memoirs Volume I: Year of Decision*. London: Hodder & Stoughton, 1995.

Walker, John W. *The Queen Has Been Pleased: The British Honours System at Work*. London: Secker & Warburg, 1986.

Young, Hugo. *One of Us*. London: Macmillan, 1989.

——. *This Blessed Plot: Britain and Europe from Churchill to Blair*. London: Macmillan, 1998.

Young, Kenneth. *Rhodesia and Independence. A Study in British Colonial Policy*. London: Eyre & Spottiswoode, 1967.

V. BRITISH FOREIGN POLICY SINCE THE END OF THE COLD WAR

Andrews, David. *The Atlantic Alliance under Stress: U.S.–European Relations after Iraq*. Cambridge, U.K.: Cambridge University Press, 2005.

Blix, Hans. *Disarming Iraq: The Search for Weapons of Mass Destruction*. London: Bloomsbury, 2004.

Bluth, Christopher. "The British Road to War: Bush, Blair, and the Decision to Invade Iraq." *International Affairs*, 80, no. 5 (2004): 871–92.

Bower, Tom. *Gordon Brown*. London: Simon & Schuster, 2003.

Cook, Robin. *The Point of Departure*. London: Simon & Schuster, 2003.

Coughlin, Con. *American Ally: Tony Blair and the War on Terror*. London: Politicos, 2006.

Danchev, Alex. "Tony Blair's Vietnam: The Iraq War and the 'Special Relationship' in Historical Perspective." *Review of International Studies*, 33, no. 2 (2007): 189–203.

De la Billière, Peter. *Storm Command: A Personal Account of the Gulf War*. London: HarperCollins, 1995.

Dyson, Stephen B. "Personality and Foreign Policy: Tony Blair's Iraq Decisions." *Foreign Policy Analysis*, 2, no. 2 (2006): 893–909.

Finlan, Alastair. *The Royal Navy in the Falklands Conflict and the Gulf War*. London: Routledge, 2004.

Freedman, Lawrence, and Efraim Karsh. *The Gulf War, 1990–1991: Diplomacy and War in the New World Order*. London: Faber and Faber, 1994.

Haggett, Paul. "Iraq: Blair's Mission Impossible." *British Journal of Politics and International Relations*, 7, no. 3 (2005): 418–28.

Kampfner, John. *Blair's War*. London: HarperCollins, 2003.

Little, Richard, and Mark Wickham-Jones, eds. *New Labour's Foreign Policy: A New Moral Crusade*. Manchester, England: Manchester University Press, 2000.

Lynch, Timothy J. "The Gerry Adams Visa in Anglo–American Relations." *Irish Studies in International Affairs*, 14, no. 1 (November 2003): 33–44.

Major, John. *The Autobiography*. London: HarperCollins, 1999.

Marsh, Steve. "Crude Diplomacy: Anglo–American Relations and Multinational Oil." *Journal of Contemporary History*, 21, no. 1 (2007): 25–34.

Riddell, Peter. *Hug Them Close: Blair, Clinton, Bush, and the "Special Relationship."* London: Politicos, 2003.

Seldon, Anthony. *Blair*. London: Free Press, 2004.

Simms, Brendan. *Unfinest Hour: Britain and the Destruction of Bosnia*. London: Allen Lane, 2001.

Stothard, Peter. *30 Days: A Month at the Heart of Blair's War*. London: HarperCollins, 2003.

Thatcher, Margaret. *Statecraft: Strategies for a Changing World*. London: HarperCollins, 2002.

Wither, James. "British Bulldog or Bush's Poodle? Anglo–American Relations and the Iraq War." *Parameters*, 33, no. 4 (Winter 2003–2004): 67–82.

About the Author

Peter Neville is a research associate at the University of Westminster, having been a research fellow at Kingston University (2006–2009) and having also taught history at the University of East Anglia (2002–2005). He was previously a senior lecturer at the University of Wolverhampton and University of Luton, and a visiting lecturer at Queen Mary, University of London. He received a master's degree from the London School of Economics and a doctorate from the Open University. Neville has published widely on 20th-century British foreign policy. His publications include "Nevile Henderson and Basil Newton: Two British Envoys in the Czech Crisis, 1938" in *The Munich Crisis* (1999), *Appeasing Hitler: The Diplomacy of Sir Nevile Henderson, 1937–1939* (2000), *Hitler and Appeasement: The British Attempt to Prevent the Second World War* (2005), and *Britain in Vietnam: Prelude to Disaster, 1945–1946* (2007). He is also the author of "British Appeasement Policy and the Military Disaster in 1940" (2009) in the U.S. academic journal *World War II Quarterly*. Additional titles include *Neville Chamberlain: A Study in Failure?*" (1992) and *Winston Churchill: Statesman or Opportunist?* (1996). Neville is also a contributor to the *New Oxford Dictionary of National Biography*. In addition, he writes on aspects of European history. Titles include *The Holocaust* (1999), *Russia, the USSR, the CIS, and the Independent States: A Complete History* (2000), *Mussolini* (2004), and *Makers of the Modern World: Benes and Masaryk* (2010). Peter Neville is a fellow of the Royal Historical Society.

Lightning Source UK Ltd.
Milton Keynes UK
UKOW051929300413

209998UK00006B/34/P